I0760126

Dear Shareholder and Friend of Fairfax,

You are holding in your hands our history and the secret to our future success. Actually, it's not much of a secret if you have been reading my annual letters and coming to Fairfax Financial's annual meetings over the past forty years! As you know, we have never courted media or public attention, and we'd rather keep our heads down and let our performance speak for itself. (Lately, it has been speaking rather loudly, as you may have noticed from your brokerage statement.)

As we approached our fortieth year, we decided to open up to author David Thomas so he could capture our story for our employees and shareholders, both present and future. There is a lot to tell. Some of us have worked together now for more than fifty years, and we are all actively setting a course for the company to outlive us for generations to come. Our long-term strategy, I will remind you, is very, *very* long term!

People often say that value investing is simple—but not easy. Our story is much the same: a simple one but, as you will learn, often anything but easy. Our ambition was always to build shareholder value over time. We are grateful to have been able to post a compound annual return of 19.2 percent from our start in 1985 to the end of 2024. Our performance speaks for itself—but we are even more grateful for *the way* we achieved that, which is a big part of Thomas's book. The secret to our real success, you might say.

We improvised a lot, and some things did not work out. But we also got a lot of things right, and after smoothing out some of the rougher spots, today we find ourselves in the best shape we have ever been. The future looks bright for insurance and investing.

Perhaps most importantly, we are committed to sustaining the culture that we decided was right for us. We always wanted to build a good company. We believe in business as a calling and for us that has always meant treating people right—both internally and among our partners. The key ingredient has always been to manage in a decentralized way that drives accountability and trust down to our leaders and employees. The "Fairfax Way" has always been the fair and friendly way. Acquiring as many companies as we did while building and sustaining our culture was a simple but not always easy idea. We humbly share our learnings and hope it inspires others. After forty years, there is much to celebrate and, I think, even more to look forward to!

Let me end by thanking my wife Nalini, to whom I've been married for fifty-two years; my children, Ben (and his wife Molly), Christine (and her husband Quinn), and Stephanie; and grandchildren, Chloe, Leo, Logan, Kiran, and Mira. I am truly blessed!

Prem Watsa

THE FAIRFAX WAY

THE FAIRFAX WAY

Inside Prem Watsa's Secret to Lasting Success

DAVID THOMAS

VIKING

VIKING
an imprint of Penguin Canada, a division of Penguin Random House Canada Limited

Canada • USA • UK • Ireland • Australia • New Zealand • India • South Africa • China

First published 2025

Viking, an imprint of Penguin Canada
A division of Penguin Random House Canada
320 Front Street West, Suite 1400
Toronto, Ontario, M5V 3B6, Canada
penguinrandomhouse.ca

The authorized representative in the EU for product safety and compliance is Penguin Random House Ireland, Morrison Chambers, 32 Nassau Street, Dublin D02 YH68, Ireland, https://eu-contact.penguin.ie

LIBRARY AND ARCHIVES CANADA CATALOGUING IN PUBLICATION

Title: The Fairfax way : inside Prem Watsa's secret to lasting success / David Thomas.
Names: Thomas, David (Business journalist), author.
Description: Special edition that includes a letter from the founder.
Simultaneously published in a separate hardcover edition by Viking.
Identifiers: Canadiana 20250190451 | ISBN 9781037802201 (hardcover)
Subjects: LCSH: Fairfax Financial Holdings Limited. | LCSH: Watsa, Prem. |
LCSH: Holding companies—Canada. | LCSH: Success in business—Canada.
Classification: LCC HD2810.12.F35 T46 2025b | DDC 332.60971—dc23

Book design by Dylan Brown
Typeset by Terra Page
Cover design by Dylan Browne
Cover image: © pixelrobot / Adobe Stock

Printed in Canada

10 9 8 7 6 5 4 3 2 1

To my sons, Harry and Sebastian, with love.
And to Maggie, for your infinite support.

The actual business of insurance is not that differentiated. What differentiates our company is culture.

We believe capitalism is a force for good and that we should never succeed at the expense of our principles.

Our motto—Fair & Friendly—became our answer to the question: How do we do the right thing in business?

Prem Watsa

CONTENTS

PREFACE

"I mean really," intones Prem Watsa, "who could have seen that coming? I sure didn't." It has been several years since Fairfax Financial Holdings, the company he founded in 1985 and still controls, ran out of problems and distractions. Everything started running the way Watsa always vaguely imagined it could and he is still wide-eyed, drinking it all in.

It's not like Fairfax is having its first taste of success. Fairfax is no forty-year-old overnight success story. The Toronto-based company, which is built on insurance assets around the globe but has been better known for its investment arm, was sitting on an enviable long-term record of growth. It became a market darling in the 1990s, when a group of hard-core value investors bought their way into the insurance industry and turned their company's shares into a red-hot growth play. Investing prowess and astute, bearish calls on financial markets made Watsa into a celebrity for a while, which added a paradoxical layer to his reputation as a quirky, brilliant, and secretive recluse with absolutely zero interest in a public profile. People did not know what to make of him. They figured Fairfax might be a cult.

After 2000, for different reasons—some self-inflicted—the company struggled to produce strong, predictable profits. What Watsa was watching in 2022 were the clouds parting fully with dramatic effect on a corporate transformation that had begun six years earlier. Had investors been watching closely, they might have caught the slow-moving metamorphosis in veiled glimpses and flashes. The insurers had become solid blue chips. The investment moxie was back on display. Investors did not see it, mostly because they had stopped paying attention. Fairfax had fallen off the market's radar.

The investment team at Fairfax was legendary for making a lot of smart big-picture calls and turning them into lucrative trades, and none of those was bigger than the Big Short. No, Watsa and Fairfax were not in the Hollywood movie, but they played the whole mortgage madness and Global Financial Crisis as well as anyone. That story is well known. Less well known are a number of brilliant moves or trades in recent years that have helped speed up the company's transformation.

There is one move we will call the Big Turn. It's the mid-2010s, and the economy is still feeling aftershocks from the financial crisis. Inflation is dead. Fears of deflation are in the air, which means central banks are cutting rates to zero and buying up bonds and other assets to prop up the economy. Fairfax is rightfully nervous. Deflation might settle in, inflation may mount a comeback—either way, the bond market increasingly becomes an unsafe place to be, and insurance companies invest a lot in bonds.

Central bankers still say they never saw it coming. Fairfax did. It had been waiting years for this. When inflation did explode in 2022, it smashed long-term bond prices, blowing a hole in the balance sheets of financial institutions and destroying between 10 and 30 percent of the book value of insurers who were exposed. Fairfax, which had deftly stepped aside from the bond market, dodged the carnage and had stacks of cash ready to then aggressively buy bonds and surf the rise in yields.

History will likely write this convulsive turn in rates as the moment of death for a forty-year-old bull market in bonds. Fairfax had successfully called the Big Turn. Classic value investing is predicated on avoiding big losses and making smart moves that exploit dislocations in financial markets. The Fairfax team nailed both and played the turn like masters. No one has made a movie about it, but it belongs in the investors hall of fame. Watsa modestly insists it's just good value investing.

Truth is, there are no evil banker villains or mortgage frauds in the Big Turn like there were in the Big Short. Instead, the drama lies in the bond market—and even the best screenwriter would be challenged to make yield curves sexy. Think about it: There is a reason the makers of *The Big Short* decided the best way to retain the audience's attention in a movie about credit default swaps and asset-backed mortgage securities was to have Margot Robbie explain it to them naked in a bubble bath, glass of champagne in hand.

The legendary Big Turn helped put wind in the sails for Fairfax shares. Between the fall of 2022 and the end of 2024, the stock rallied 217 percent, outpacing the red-hot tech leadership of Amazon (+94 percent), Microsoft (+84 percent), and Apple (+83 percent). The rally tells us the stock was back on the radar of some smart investors, but most others were either no longer paying attention or simply didn't want to believe it because they had been burned before.

Fairfax lives for the long term. The company has taken a meandering path, but it has been true to its strategy from day one. It's all laid out in Watsa's first letter to shareholders, and you can track it over forty years to learn that when Watsa talks about future plans, he's looking further out than you might expect a company to be looking. In fact, it is next to impossible to really understand Prem Watsa in the past or present without understanding what he has been imagining Fairfax will be in the future, long after he is gone.

Fairfax had always been a company with a rich, colourful history, and as the 2020s continue to roll along, the Street has been rubbing its eyes and squinting, realizing the firm shows signs of offering an even brighter future ahead of it. Conveniently, the company has opened up to tell its story in detail for the first time as it hits its fortieth anniversary. There is a rich trove of lore to reveal and countless misconceptions to clear up. Watsa and his leaders here explain all.

It's an extraordinary story of a Canadian company's performance—with legendary compound annual stock returns of more than 19.2 percent since day one, compared to 11.3 percent for the S&P 500 over the same period and just over 8 percent for the Toronto market. It's definitely a turnaround tale. It's also an immigrant success story and a rare narrative of compassionate capitalism about a company that dared to build its mission on the principle of doing the right thing. Also, for a story about an insurance holding company, there were times when things got pretty weird, like that time Wall Street hedge funds hatched a plan to kill the company and hire Bob Dylan to sing while they danced on Watsa's grave in the Hamptons.

Here is another amazing strategy we will call the Big Long, which included a bunch of moves, each involving different ways Fairfax could buy up more of Fairfax. One trade involved total return swaps. Swaps again. Imagine your favourite movie star in the bubble bath with a glass of champagne: It went like this. In 2020, Watsa and his team found some banks to help them design an unusual trade. Instead of buying the shares back like ordinary companies do, Fairfax took out swaps on its own shares. Through swaps, Fairfax never actually bought the shares; instead, it spent a lot less to buy the rights to the upside—or downside—in the share price, which had collapsed in the pandemic and could not possibly, Watsa reasoned, fall even further. The wind we were just talking about would soon hit the stock's sails.

The outlay is the interest cost owed to the banks, which buys and sells the stock on Fairfax's behalf. In 2024 alone, the trade netted $1 billion. It is up $2 billion to date and still paying off today. If there were an Oscar for Best Trade Involving TRS on Your Own Stock, this would win it. Who even makes a trade like that? Again, Watsa isn't interested in playing it up for the spotlight. "It's just solid value thinking. We simply could not believe how cheap our shares were, so we acted." In the past, Fairfax had made its name on riskier bets on market collapses, but with its new playbook, the value masters had refined their strategy to lower their risk without lowering their payoff. Was there a movie about it? Nope. Magazine cover story? Not yet. Just a few very smart investors chatting on financial sites.

Nowhere in Paul Rivett's job description was it written he was expected to take late-night calls from demented corporate saboteurs waging psychological warfare by reading out passages of Harry Potter stories in sinister voices. Rivett arrived at Fairfax in a legal role that would evolve over the years to see him become Watsa's second-in-command as president. He first walked in the door in 2003 to discover the company was under siege by a who's who of Wall Street hedge funds. They wanted Fairfax dead, but Watsa was still hoping they were confused, would get bored and just go away. Rivett uncovered a much more serious threat than the weird Potter calls and pushed Fairfax to fight back. He also opened a channel with the media, which included dialing my number as editor of the *Financial Post* in Toronto.

We met in the boardroom of Fairfax's office near Union Station and Rivett laid out some of the ugly insider details of a concerted attempt at corporation assassination. There was no table pounding or demand for supportive coverage; Rivett just asked that we keep an open mind and be on guard for false allegations. The hedge funds knew reporters would be likely to publish their allegations, especially when one of them wore the Street cred of taking down Enron. Participants in the attack were painting Fairfax as the next fraud of the century, and their plan was getting traction with the media.

The media found Fairfax a confusing company to cover. It still is. Our reporters could never get them to talk. We had been running the same file photo with stories for years because we could not get Watsa to sit for a fresh shoot. I left the meeting with Rivett better informed, and I went back and started reading Watsa's extraordinary annual letters to shareholders again, as I had gotten out of the habit since my reporter days. For someone painted as an uncommunicative recluse, it struck me that he sure worked harder at disclosure and transparency than any other CEO I knew. Those letters became an important part of this book. The first half of *The Fairfax Way* tells the corporate story, while the second digs deeper to help the reader understand a complex and misunderstood company, and to appreciate what makes Watsa and his team tick when it comes to value investing, as well as management strategy and culture. The letters are rich source material for both halves of the book and I've drawn on them regularly throughout as a way to reveal just how well he narrated the story, in real time—it's all there.

I had always learned a lot about market history, cycles, and risks from reading the best CEO letters, like Watsa's and Warren Buffett's. And I knew Fairfax had an uncanny ability to make a lot of money when bear markets came a-mauling. Walking into that meeting with Rivett, I was also already familiar with the hedge fund allegations because our reporters were getting those calls from mystery sources with bombshell allegations. One low-profile brokerage was the source of most of the concerns, which were being amplified by the hedge funds through cooperative media outlets, predominantly in the U.S. I had no idea how ugly the long war with the shorts had gotten behind the scenes. Our reporting team always had trouble getting a clear read on complex vulnerabilities like finite insurance, insurance covers, reserving shortfalls, and the like. Fairfax had a reputation as a notoriously difficult company to understand. Shunning the media had not helped its cause.

Almost twenty years after my meeting with Rivett, Watsa sat down with me for a long Q & A on the magic that capitalism can create when you build a solid business, treat people right, and give back. It dawned on me that a lot of what people found weird about him and the culture at Fairfax was that these people truly felt business can and should be a calling. That conversation on building wealth and doing good by doing well turned into more conversations and, eventually, this book.

It is about time. This is one of Canada's most successful companies ever, but most Canadians have never heard of it. Those that have heard of Fairfax very likely do not understand how the company actually builds value for the long term. Fairfax started in Canada but is now the nation's blue-chip company with the most exposure to markets outside its borders. The company is worth close to C$60 billion. Watsa himself is worth billions but most people have never heard of him either. He does not do *Dragons' Den*. He has never owned a professional sports franchise. But his company measures employee retention in decades, not years—people never leave.

Under his leadership, Fairfax has zealously set an ambitious mission to build a company with a culture that will see it thrive long after we are all gone. It's about being fair and friendly and treating people right. Think of it as their secret weapon, a competitive and enduring moat that fuels stronger performance. Watsa was never quite ready to have the Fairfax story fully told—until now. I am delighted to be the one to tell it.

The company's early days saw a tight, small group of Bay Street portfolio managers and traders snapping up increasingly larger insurance companies, working their own take on the Warren Buffett recipe for success at Berkshire Hathaway, where the holding company of the legendary Oracle of Omaha held insurers and leveraged their store of cash to exploit his supernatural nose for winning stocks.

Fairfax's particular recipe involved buying struggling insurers on the cheap, a short-sighted value strategy of frugality that necessitated later paying the price with a longer, bumpier road to consistent profitability. What made that uneven performance work for a long time was the company's uncanny success with investments, which offset the struggling insurers, sometimes spectacularly. Two decades in, that relationship reversed when the rehabilitated insurers turned the corner for good and the investment side spent some time in the ditch.

In 2022, what Watsa was recognizing was the emergence of a Fairfax with not only both major sides of the business humming but also a third engine of sustainable earnings power firing up. This is what Fairfax had always been working toward in its characteristic searching fashion but had found elusive. This new-era Fairfax is something that the market is beginning to get its head wrapped around.

"It dawned on me that with all our hard work and patience, we had actually transformed the company," he says. "We never had a fixed plan of exactly where we would end up. We let opportunities guide us. But this felt like it. We had never been in that position before, and it was amazing to see. Now we want to set it up to last another hundred years—or more."

PART ONE

THE FORMATIVE YEARS

From India to Canada

Chapter One

WATSA'S ROAD TO VALUE INVESTING

"This is our religion, this is our way of thinking." —Prem Watsa

Prem Watsa developed a persona in the early Fairfax days of the 1990s as a Canadian mash-up of Warren Buffett and Howard Hughes. Some of that is at least somewhat true.

Like Buffett, he was a talented investor who ran with the classic value crowd, shaped by the philosophy of Benjamin Graham who believed the best way to make a fortune was to buy good stocks at deeply discounted prices, wait around until the market woke up to that fact, then unload them at a nice profit. Wash, rinse, repeat.

Watsa certainly borrowed a few pages from Buffett's playbook, most notably the idea of buying insurance assets to pool for cash to invest. So, there are enough parallels between the two investors that calling Watsa Canada's Warren Buffett is apt enough as shorthand. It's easier than explaining how the company he runs has an insurance, reinsurance, and insurance runoff empire with assets around the world, but he is also a high-profile investor in financial markets who once in a while attracts a lot of attention when his bearish calls bear fruit, and he also owns a lot of the restaurant chains you see when driving on Canada's highways and has invested in hockey and golf equipment, pulp and paper, copper mines and guest beds, container ships and travel resorts, wedding gifts and funeral homes, chemical companies and Florida timeshares, plus an airport in India; banks in Ireland, Greece, and Egypt; out-of-favour media companies; pulses; food additives; and toy retailers. The one investment of his that investors are most likely to be aware of, at least in Canada, is the iconic turnaround investment that is still alive but never quite turned around—the company formerly known as Research in Motion (RIM). Yeah, he is the guy who tried to buy BlackBerry and backed its big comeback plan.

There are more similarities. Buffett and Watsa both built holding companies to own insurers on one side and run high-profile investments on the other. But their strategies are not the same. Besides, Watsa is quite content being known as Canada's Prem Watsa. To be more precise, he is quite content not being known at all.

As for the Hughes part, he was never, and still isn't, someone who seeks the limelight, especially through the media. "We've worked very hard purposely to avoid speaking to the media. The same goes for speaking about ourselves," Watsa explains, "because we are convinced it's much better for our company to have low expectations, then try to perform and to let our performance speak for itself." Far from hiding away, he has always been active on boards, managing investments for SickKids children's hospital, working to raise money to give a leg up to youth through post-secondary education with the Horatio Alger Association, and running the treasury for his church. Watsa was all over town making speeches, but if reporters, accustomed to being the ones who get to turn down pitches, cannot get you to sit for an interview when they want one, then, yeah, you're a recluse. So that public persona stuck.

It was not just the media; Watsa also shunned stock analysts and, unless they were necessary, investment bankers. And because he focused only on long-term growth, didn't have an investor relations department at Fairfax, and fashioned a corporate culture that espoused doing the right thing—with no swearing no less—he was cast as an eccentric as well. The company and its culture were so unusual to people in some quarters, they took to calling Fairfax a cult. I mean, really: No swearing on Bay Street. WTF?

To understand Watsa and the Fairfax Way, you can look through twentieth-century corporate history and discover all kinds of disciplined capitalists who successfully built wealth to last and enjoyed giving back. Watsa holds a special place for people like John Templeton, who ran one of the most successful mutual funds ever, lived frugally, and was a generous philanthropist. To Watsa, arriving in Canada as a young adult with no background in business, these new influences shaped his mind as an MBA student and his early career as a portfolio manager.

To understand Watsa on a deeper level, however, you have to back up. You need to meet the little Indian kid from modest beginnings in Hyderabad, the one who became a billionaire overseas and who remains better known in his birth country than in Canada or in the U.S. where Fairfax has its largest footprint today. In India, people celebrate him as an inspirational story of entrepreneurial success. The Watsas were not historically poor but he did not come from money. As a famous capitalist who made it in the West, when he visits, he is scrummed by reporters for off-the-cuff quotes about the direction of the economy or Fairfax's investments in India. Current company investments in the country sit at about $7 billion and Watsa has said he expects to double that in the coming years. (Note: All currency amounts are US$, unless otherwise noted. The company started reporting in C$ but shifted to US$ in 2003.)

THE LITTLE KID FROM HYDERABAD

To meet that little kid from Hyderabad, we need to take the story more than 13,000 kilometres away from Fairfax's head office in Toronto's Bay Street financial district. And while we are at it, to set things up, we will set the scene by dialing back history to the mid-1800s.

In the years leading up to India's transition to a formal colony under British rule, the East India Company administration loosened restrictions on the activities of Christian missionaries from Europe. Emboldened, a group of German and Swiss Protestant theologians—operating as the Basel Missionary Society (BMS)—sent a group of three missionaries to Mangalore (now Mangaluru), a community of about thirty thousand located about nine hundred kilometres south of Mumbai on the Arabian Sea.

BMS made schools and education a key plank in its conversion efforts, with Christian teachings featuring in the curriculum. As might be expected, their efforts as foreigners were met with a lot of resistance. Strategically, they directed particular attention toward the lower castes, or classes, as Christianity promised an escape from the rigidity of India's religion-driven social hierarchies.

Within a few years, the missionaries made their way to Udupi in North Canara where they made the acquaintance of a schoolteacher by the name of Ramachari Watsa. Prem's great-great-grandfather turned out to be a prized convert, not only because he was positioned as an educator to spread the faith but also because he was a Brahmin, an influential upper caste.

"Attracting a Brahmin in 1857, particularly a teacher, was undoubtedly a feat for the BMS, which at the time sorely needed some such success," writes Ryan Touhey, a historian at the University of Waterloo (where Watsa served as chancellor) and author of *Faith, Fortitude and Family: The Watsas*. Ramachari, who adopted Suvartappa as his Christian name, converted along with his family, spawning a lineage of Christian faith in the Watsa family, as well as an intergenerational line of passionate educators. Prem would carry the faith with him and personally benefit greatly from his father's career as an educator.

Suvartappa Watsa became a BMS school headmaster, and his son Christanuja would later join the BMS Seminary as both a scholar and a missionary. Together with his wife, Margretha, Christanuja had eight children, including David, who also followed in the BMS path, becoming headmaster of a middle school.

David was the grandfather Prem never met. Tragically, both he and his wife, Krupa, died young, leaving four young children—she first in childbirth, he later from typhoid. Until their own deaths, the grandparents cared for the orphaned kids, the eldest of whom was Prem's father, Manohar. After the grandparents both passed, all four children, ranging in age from seven to fifteen, were placed separately with adoptive parents.

It was a rough upbringing, but Manohar excelled at school, earning a scholarship for himself that allowed him to also fund his brother. He then won admission to the elite Jesuit St. Aloysius College in Mangalore (his prowess on the cricket pitch along with his academics gave him a double edge on acceptance) and followed in the family footsteps by doing teacher training in Chennai (formerly known as Madras). From that point, Manohar became a peripatetic, strategically moving around the country and studying abroad in the U.K. to advance his education and administrative responsibilities in order to accelerate his career.

Prem's father had high expectations of himself and of his children. "My dad's work ethic was an inspiration—he went where he could help out. He always wanted to better himself as a teacher and also create more opportunities for his children."

When Manohar moved into the role of vice-president with a line to becoming president at Hyderabad Public School (*public* in the traditional British meaning, called *private* in a North American context), Hyderabad became home. He married Irene in 1940, and they had two sons and two daughters: David (first name, Ranjan) in 1942, Navo in 1945, Prem in 1950, and Krupa in 1952.

"I remember my father as a no-nonsense kind of guy—really disciplined, ambitious, and tough. He pushed me. He expected us to study hard and work hard. If I got marks of 90 percent, he would ask what happened to the other ten." So life was classes and homework with some sports in between. Prem had no problem with that. It suited him, since he wasn't big on going out to parties.

Manohar's executive position meant automatic admission for Prem at an exclusive school, and it was perfectly obvious to the young student that his new bona fides put him in a good position to write the competitive exam for the super-elite Indian Institute of Technology (IIT). It was the good fortune of the boy to have had access to the quality of education that, combined with his brains and hard work, opened doors that would otherwise have remained closed. Prem was determined to make the best of his excellent luck.

As he advanced on an impressive educational path, the young Watsa carried with him strong values that had been moulded at home. It all started, he says, with family and an awareness of the need to help others. "Family is absolutely at the heart of my values. My mom and dad cared about their own family and their extended family, which was mostly on Mother's side since my dad was an orphan. Religion played a part as well. We were Christians. Faith has always been important, and living by its principles is a primary definition of living a successful life. Second is marriage and family. Business comes third. We did not have a lot of money, but we did okay. We learned to care about people, family values, treating people well, and looking after others who were less fortunate.

"That was my experience. I think that is common in poor countries. It was the same in Greece or Italy. It's a function of the fact that people are not doing as well. I think it's tougher in Canada and the U.S. to have those values as strongly because most everyone is doing well. In India, there was never a question whether you needed to look after your parents. One of the reasons people in North America put their parents in a retirement home is that they can actually afford to do that."

In his book on the Watsas, Touhey identifies how those values were further strengthened when they were combined with the immigrant experience, fostering a resilience and optimism that drove families like the Watsas to make the absolute best of their opportunities in a new land. Prem says this force helped drive his entrepreneurialism when he discovered that outlet in Canada.

"Immigrating to new countries requires fortitude, curiosity, a willingness to persevere, and an entrepreneurial spirit," writes Touhey. "It also requires the optimist's conviction that with hard work and dedication, better days surely lie ahead. This is certainly the picture that emerges from this period of the family's history. Much as their ancestors had made unorthodox decisions as to how to better themselves and their families, supported by a bedrock of deep Christian faith, Manohar, Irene, their children and now grandchildren were a living testament to the endurance of these qualities. But above all there was the bond of family."

In Prem Watsa, this combination of values, rooted in an Indian experience together with all the economic opportunities in Canada, would ultimately yield a driven entrepreneur with an ingrained commitment to doing the right thing—a cheerleading capitalist with a generous heart and a desire to give back.

"My upbringing shaped how I developed a sensitivity to people, and I think that was what influenced me to come up with the idea that you can build a company that was good for everybody," explains Watsa. "I don't know precisely where it came from, but when we launched the company, it just seemed like the obvious thing to do. Our company's motto, fair and friendly, is a reflection of that kind of thinking, and family values. For me, that was developed in India, in my formative years as a young man."

KEEP TRYING DIFFERENT DOORS

For all the doors available to him, Watsa had to work hard to make it through them. To his and his father's delight, he got accepted to IIT Madras in Chennai directly from high school. At Manohar's urging, he entered the chemical engineering program in 1966 and studied hard, and while he was no cricket whiz like his father, he found time for field hockey and chess, as well as tennis, which he still plays. He excelled as a champion at table tennis.

One fly in the ointment: Watsa proved to himself for a fact what he had already suspected—he did not actually want to be an engineer, which was not what his father wanted to hear. The education served him well, regardless. And there was something wholly extracurricular and far more profoundly fortuitous about this time. Her name was Nalini Loganadhan, and the two students were immediately smitten.

"The thing that really attracted me to him, in addition to the fact he was very handsome, was that he was always confident, always trying to find ways to help," recalls Nalini, who was studying English literature and liberal arts at Stella Maris College. "And that has never changed, no matter how much success he has had in business. It's just naturally in his nature, which is an exceptional quality." She was impressed by his manners. "After we met a few times, we knew we loved each other, he immediately told my mother that he wanted to marry me."

Canada was not part of the plan at this stage. Watsa graduated in 1971, and having cooled on chemical engineering and with marriage plans requiring a path to an alternative career, he chose another door—another prestigious school called the Indian Institute of Management Ahmedabad (IIM) to bolster his qualifications. He failed to get in. He tried again and passed. The door was open. Things were falling into place for a future in India. But Manohar had other ideas.

Prem's older brother, David, had recently married Margaret, a British teacher who had come to India on an assignment and decided to stay. But as the two explored options, her own pull of family grew and soon a move to London, Ontario, in Canada was made to reunite the couple with Margaret's three sisters and bring new opportunities to her husband.

With David settled in London, where he took a job with a Caterpillar dealership, Manohar pushed Prem to join him. Prem was starting to recognize the potential of a career in business, and his father saw limited options in a highly socialist India. As Prem's son Ben puts it, "My dad left India because there was no opportunity. His dad saw that and pushed him." Still, Prem was not sold. "I said, 'No, I don't want to do that,'" he recalls. "I told my father, 'I want to get married. I just got into this great program. My life is made!' I had zero desire to leave India. But at age twenty-two, you listen to your dad." He had not even seen that door as an option, but with his dad's words ringing in his ears, Prem was quickly running for it.

AN EXIT STRATEGY AND A PERSONAL SUPERPOWER

With the guiding hand of his school administrator father, an MBA application was put together for a business school in London. Watsa's IIT transcript carried a lot of weight, as did his acceptance into IIM. He was accepted. He had no idea that the local school was Ivey School of Business, regularly ranked as the best in the country and a top fifty worldwide. Classes started less than a month after his acceptance, and Watsa had not even begun the daunting process of applying to immigrate.

In 1972, there were 582,837,973 people in India, 5,049 of whom would arrive as landed immigrants in Canada, a nation of 22,218,463. One of them was Prem Watsa. You can excuse Canadians if they failed to notice the wide-eyed twenty-two-year-old graduate student with eight dollars and a university acceptance letter in his pocket stepping off the plane in Toronto in September 1972. They would not have noticed anyone; most of them were glued to their TV sets watching the legendary Canada–Soviet Union ice hockey "Series of the Century." The engineering graduate who did not want to be an engineer also did not know anything about ice hockey. He left the airport breathing a big, long transatlantic sigh of relief that just would not quit. He was still spinning because getting into Ivey had actually proved to be much easier than what he had faced getting out of the country.

Weeks earlier, his first move had been to New Delhi to apply for a student visa, and with his acceptance letter in hand, he figured the hardest part was behind him. It was anything but. "The immigration officer explained he did not want me to go on a student visa because government officials expected I would turn around and apply for landed immigrant status," recalls Watsa.

"Instead, he said I had to apply to become an immigrant from Indian soil, and the odds of being accepted were much lower. It was more like a lottery. It would also take a lot longer, and my first classes were starting in two weeks. But he just told me that I wasn't getting a student visa, and this was my problem."

Watsa left the office dazed and retreated to his friend's apartment where he was staying. Soul-searching, he discovered the inner resolve and a primal power of persuasion that would serve him very well in his adoptive country for the rest of his life. Calm in demeanor and standing at five feet ten inches, he is not an imposing man in stature. But his quiet intensity and the forceful optimism of his personality was already unmistakable. The people who work for him recognize that look of Watsa with its clear vision, passion, and good intentions. The one where he says, "Hey, why don't we do this?" It's Prem's superpower and it is hard to resist.

"In the end, I just shook it off and hoped for the best. I went back to the office the next day. The officer looked me in the eye and immediately had a change of heart." Watsa still needed to apply for full immigration status, but all of a sudden the officer was invested in making this happen for him, which made all the difference. "In the end, I think I got more of a gut check on his part than a background check. Then he telexed my brother in Canada to act as a sponsor and scheduled me a quick physical exam. It was all complete in two weeks. It was a reminder to me that luck can turn on a dime, so just never give up and always be grateful for good fortune."

Watsa never forgot that episode and years later he tried to hunt the officer down to thank him. Too late to find him alive, he connected with the officer's family and formed a bond. That move was made of gratitude, just as it was to recognize the efforts of his family history by commissioning the Touhey book. Not coincidentally, both actions were influenced by former governor general of Canada David Johnston, who sits on Fairfax's board. Johnston's lengthy and illustrious curriculum vitae includes authoring a book in 2023 called *Empathy*. In it, and to Watsa personally, Johnston advocated that people should take actions beyond merely experiencing feelings of gratitude or compassion.

THE IMMIGRANT'S EXPERIENCE

In London, a town of about a quarter million at the time, two hundred kilometres west of Toronto, David and Margaret put him up in their small flat in a relative's house. Prem, whose room was not much bigger than a broom closet, was in culture shock. "I'd come from India where there are people all over the place. I am used to a lot of people and lousy cars. In London, I saw no people. You see cars on the street, beautiful cars. But you can't see a single soul."

He did not have a lot of time to stand still and digest it all. In two days, he had to be in class. When he made it to class, he felt like a fish out of water. "No question, most of the students were wealthy and white, and they were looking really good in their suits. It was almost all men and there were a couple of immigrants. One Chinese fellow and an Indian who had already been in Canada for a while. And one woman."

The students in MBA programs were mostly from well-to-do families. With the Watsas, money was hard at first; Prem couldn't even afford to go to a movie or eat at McDonald's. Whatever he did manage to earn, he put aside to save for the wedding. "I'd go to university and I'd see these people having lunch in the cafeteria, and I'd think to myself they must be very wealthy."

Watsa says he did not waste any time feeling disadvantaged because he saw nothing but opportunity. He was confident that hard work and a little luck would pay off well for him. "The biggest factor in India might be who you knew, but in Canada the biggest factor was just you. Anything was possible." In the meantime, he just had to learn who the Maple Leafs and Canadiens were—and learn to wear long underwear.

"I had never seen snow before. When winter came, it was cold and I learned to wear long johns to stay warm. It was an experience—a real immigrant experience—and I always thought that was a good thing. A lot was new and in the years that followed, I picked up skills that I never thought I would have. As an immigrant, you have to do that: You're at the bottom. My kids were born here in Canada. I tell them they have one major negative in their upbringing—they weren't immigrants."

That meant his kids would not have to sell air conditioners door to door. When the snow melted, that is exactly what Watsa did during his first sticky southern Ontario summer. It was not what his chemical engineering degree had trained him for, but as an immigrant, you take your opportunities and make the most of them. He connected with another immigrant, Ihor Horich, a Ukrainian who was trying to make a go of it as a dealer for Lennox, the appliance company. Trouble is, Watsa had neither a car nor any money to buy gas. But he had hustle, which Horich recognized, Watsa recalls. "He says, 'You know, Prem, you gotta go and sell.' I'm not selling too much. I have no money coming in."

Watsa solved the first challenge by borrowing a car from his brother's brother-in-law. It wasn't yet the days of high finance, negotiating billion-dollar deals, but Watsa channelled his powers to help Horich see a way through his predicament to find a better arrangement. "I said to him, 'You have to pay me some gas.' And so he took me to a coffee shop and said, 'How can I pay you any gas money if you don't sell?' So he put his arms around me and said, 'Instead of giving you a 3 percent commission, I'll give you a 5 percent commission.' Then I started selling. I sold a lot of air conditioners." The same innate superpower of persuasion that worked so well with the immigration officer was getting stronger. You can imagine anyone opening their door to a sales pitch from this enthusiastic salesman would be opening their cheque book before long.

Between that and putting in odd work where he could find it—selling other stuff door to door, such as stationery, or pitching in at his sister-in-law's cheese shop—he socked money away while going to school. He had set himself a three-point plan on arriving: get his MBA, get established in Canada, and save up enough money in two years to bring Nalini over from India and get married. With a strong work ethic and discipline with money, he managed to hit goal number three a full year ahead of schedule.

It was easy for those around him to look at the focused and determined young man and see someone who would make a living and support a family. But no one saw a business titan in the making. What about Watsa himself? What was his attitude to money and the pursuit of wealth in his early twenties? "I didn't have one," he answers without hesitation. "Nothing. Zero. At first I didn't know a stock from a hole in the ground. I learned I could do pretty well with investing, so I basically just ran with it. When I arrived in Canada, I was mostly hoping for a good job and to make a good life for my family. I had no conception of building a lot of wealth and zero plan to build a big company."

Nalini's grandmother was an exception; she saw in Watsa someone who would make the most of his opportunities and thrive. She saw something in the young man's confidence and ability to meet challenges. And something in the way he cared for those around him. So, as Nalini made preparations to follow her fiancé and join the growing family presence in London for a Canadian wedding, her grandmother leaned in to whisper something prophetic in her ear.

"She said, 'Remember, this is the boy the family will depend on,'" Nalini recalls half a century later. "And that was a strange thing, when I knew that he was penniless. So I didn't know what would happen. Now I know. What I did see then was Prem appreciated the opportunities that his father's hard work had created for him. His father was a big inspiration to him. As an orphan, he had to make it on his own. That was a hard thing to do in India, but he was very successful. He did it with hard work and a drive to get ahead, and Prem paid attention." Nalini and Prem were married in Ontario in August 1973, and Watsa's parents, sisters, and their husbands were soon to join the growing Watsa presence in Canada.

BACK TO SCHOOL: "FORGET YOUR TEXTBOOKS"

Learning to love numbers, ratios, and portfolio management did not come naturally. "It was really tough," says Watsa. "It was a different way of thinking. In engineering, there is one right answer: You take your formulas, plug in the numbers, and there is your answer. In business school, you come with these sets of assumptions and you find this here is the answer if you do it this way, but that there might be another answer too. For the longest time, it drove me crazy. How can you have two right answers? That first year was especially tough. You have the case method, which is fantastic, where you break into small groups and there is lots of discussion. It was very tough to get used to. And to later have to stand up and make your argument to sixty other students, you learn you really had to be prepared."

Watsa was still feeling somewhat out of place, but in year two something totally clicked: investing. The reason it clicked for Watsa was the guy teaching the investments course—the former dean himself, Fred Jones. "I still remember the first class with Dean Jones. He says to us, 'Forget your textbooks. Here is an analyst report on Alcan Aluminum.' It was a real-life report and had just come out. It took equity analysis out of the classroom and into the real world. For me, it made it come alive. I was hooked."

All of a sudden, Watsa saw a real company headquartered in Montreal. You could buy shares in it and become a part owner to make money on it. Or lose money. And he saw the research work, modelling, and forecasts that investors were using to make their decisions. Ordinary investors were relying on that research, as were major mutual funds and people managing large pensions. Doing that kind of research seemed like a pretty good gig.

Watsa was not the only one whose mind was lit up by Dean Jones. After he retired in 1974, the business school revealed Jones's class had been the most popular in the MBA program. It was another bit of good fortune to have been exposed to the Ivey legend before he stopped teaching. "Every class was like that. It was fantastic. That is definitely when I discovered my interest in stocks and bonds and in investing generally. I did not see it coming, so when I talk to young people, I tell them just keep your eyes and ears open because you never know where that inspiration is going to come from. I sure didn't."

Dean Jones did more than bring the numbers alive. He taught the importance of having the right temperament for long-term success. "He had made a lot of money in the stock market personally, but he made a real distinction between investing and speculation. At that point, I didn't realize how much that mirrored the philosophy of Benjamin Graham. He told us not to speculate, whether managing other people's money or our own."

Speculation can become compulsive, and even if you win at first, you will likely end up losing everything, Jones cautioned his students. "I never forgot that lesson," says Watsa. "You saw it in the dot-com era and in many other periods of valuation froth and bubbles. People who were making a ton of money ended up losing everything. Even if they sold things and got out, they would turn around and try to bottom fish the same investments at lower prices and the values just kept falling. The tech mania of the last few years is the very same thing."

Watsa got his own taste of speculative thrills when he entered and won the stock-picking contest at Ivey by selecting high-beta risky shares and, by his own admission, "got lucky." He already knew that this was not how he would approach investing with real money. But he still had no idea that he would even work in the investing business. An MBA can be a valuable edge in landing a job, but there were a lot of industries in which it could be applied and he was open to taking the best opportunity that presented itself.

DEAR SIR, I AM WRITING TO . . .

"I had no idea where to look for work. Absolutely no clue. But I casted widely for jobs in finance and investing." The school was helpful in passing on word of new postings. It would even help with resumés and submit them on the students' behalf. However, the ones sent on his behalf weren't generating any calls. So Watsa leaned in to improve his odds.

"My school resumé made it clear that I had been in Canada for just a year and half, so I suspected my newcomer status might be working against me." He reworked his CV to play up his education, training, and abilities and left out the part about being an immigrant. And he added the fact that he was the winner of the Ivey stock-picking contest. From then on, he made sure to post every letter personally, usually direct to the CEO, and he got a call for each one sent.

Like so many decisions that can decide one's fate, his job search basically came down to a coin toss. As he was finishing school, two of his personally posted letters attracted interest. One was a firm offer from 3M to work as a financial analyst in London where he could be near his brother's family. The other was an investment analyst gig with Confederation Life in Toronto. "We ended up making the decision based on location, because Toronto is Canada's largest city and held more opportunities for my wife, Nalini, to work as well." Nalini soon found work in a local branch of the Canadian Imperial Bank of Commerce, starting as a teller.

Another curious reason the Toronto option won out is because four interviewees were called back for a second interview, but Watsa was the only one to show up. This is one of his more-often-told humble stories, one of Watsa's life tales that he draws on to count his blessings. Good fortune is a powerful force. So is gratitude. In the end, landing at Confederation Life in Toronto was one of the more fateful moves in his life; it ended up shaping his mind and opening doors to a new network and much bigger things that he had never imagined doing.

The story of the first job starts with a comedic—and racist—case of mistaken identity. Watsa is running east on Bloor Street to his fateful job interview at 1 Mount Pleasant Road, built for Confederation Life but now known as the Rogers Building. A squad car jumps the sidewalk, and Toronto's finest emerge, revolvers drawn, to apprehend the suspicious running brown man. Seems there had been a bank robbery reported nearby, Watsa learns, while pinned to the hood. The fact that he is wearing a nice suit likely works in his favour and he is quickly released.

Still sweaty and now about ten minutes late for his interview, Watsa composed himself in the lobby and made his way up in the elevator to a boardroom where he was surprised to discover he was the only candidate still in the hunt. The others might have been off robbing a bank. More likely, they had nailed better jobs in the time since the first interviews or were still gunning for spots at one of the higher-paying investment banks.

Confederation Life, a step down in both cachet and compensation, was the kind of investment shop where analysts could get great experience over a few years and then leverage that toward a bigger paycheque in the financial district at Bay and King Streets. But most preferred to leapfrog Confederation entirely and head straight to the big money. As Watsa says, "Who wants to go work at a life insurance company when you can go and work at Wood Gundy? I was learning on the go how things really worked. You might be qualified for the top-paying entry-level jobs but you were battling fifteen to twenty MBAs, all with good grades. And then there is me, who has been in the country for only a year and a half. So by then I was getting calls, but I did not get one for those plum roles. As an immigrant, often you have to do something different. You have to be hungry."

At that point, Watsa was very hungry, still sweating from his run, and he got the job. "It paid $11,000 [Canadian] a year, which was solid money. What I did not know was how pivotal getting that job would be for my career. I have often looked back and felt that I was very fortunate to have got this job. I could have gotten a job at a bank or another institution and I would never have been exposed to Ben Graham. So I consider myself very fortunate."

Before he started his first big job as a recent MBA grad, one more opportunity presented itself. Horich, the Ukrainian Lennox dealer in London, offered the young graduate a toehold in the appliance business.

Watsa's response: "I said, 'Well, you know, I got a job, Ihor.' And he said, 'How much are they paying you?' And I said, '$11,000 a year.' He said, '$11,000? You're not worth that.'"

As an immigrant, it's important to take your opportunities as they come. As an immigrant entrepreneur with an ambition to make a name and build some wealth, it's also important to keep reaching higher.

THE ROAD TO DAMASCUS—VIA KING AND BAY

Whatever Watsa may have lost out on in a fatter salary from one of Canada's big banks was more than compensated for by what he learned at the school of life. Like his great-great-grandfather, he was about to be converted—but by a different kind of missionary, one who followed the value investing preachings of a certain Benjamin Graham.

Confederation Life was not for everyone but those analysts who landed there could benefit from a master class in value investing. It was the best kind of graduate school: You keep learning and get paid for it. Dozens of new graduates got their starts at the firm, which tended to start them out as research analysts before they qualified as portfolio managers and went on to run investments for its insurers, pension accounts, and portfolio accounts. "They would train you for seven, eight, or nine years and by then your pay was well behind and they could no longer keep us," explains Watsa. "But it was top echelon for learning."

The major force behind the learning was one person—John Watson. A chartered financial analyst, Watson, thirty-three, had just been appointed vice-president and head of investments at Confederation. He would prove to be a key influence on Watsa. "John was my first mentor professionally and influenced me a lot in life because he was also a tremendous human being. I looked up to him and wanted to be like him. He had high standards and integrity. That made him a powerful force in my life when you consider that he was also my boss."

Watsa worked primarily for Tony Hamblin, another big influence who was destined to be a lifelong partner. But the firm's lean structure also afforded Watsa the opportunity to report to Watson directly, and it was like having the master professor emeritus as his personal career coach. As an analyst in a value investing shop, it was expected that you apply rigorous value principles in putting together a stock report. Watsa would share a draft of his best efforts with the boss, who then offered immediate direct feedback that quickly sharpened the younger man's skills. Dean Jones at Ivey may have sparked the flame of Watsa's investing passion, but it was Watson, by sharing the gospel of Benjamin Graham, who stoked it into hot fire.

It was only a few days into his new job that Watsa got a surprise bonus in his orientation. The new recruit had received his pencils, erasers, foolscap, and IBM typewriter. Then Watson did a walk-by and dropped a fat book on his desk with a thud and a terse command: "Read this!"

The book was *Security Analysis* by Benjamin Graham and his professor colleague at Columbia Business School in New York, David Dodd. "The first thing he said to me was 'Forget what you learned at business school.' I read it fifty times if I read it once."

The book became an instant classic when published in 1934 as the Great Depression was tightening its grip. It has since seen a new edition or reprint in every decade but one, with the latest edition being the seventh in 2023. Graham and Dodd set out to give investors an analytical edge by steering them to think of true investing as finding companies whose stocks were trading below the value of their actual businesses. The authors and their book are credited with launching investment analysis as an academic discipline within business education.

Graham and Dodd sought to distinguish investing from sheer speculation, which they argued had become rampant in general markets in the roaring 1920s, playing a major role in the market mania, crash, and the subsequent economic depression. *Security Analysis* became the textbook for a new way of thinking about stocks, where rigorous analysis and patience could win out over the obsession with short-term results. It served as an antidote to the volatility that was torpedoing portfolios in the Depression era. With *The Intelligent Investor*, published in 1949 and targeted to a more general investor rather than a stock analyst, Graham espoused the value philosophy in an easier-to-follow format. Together, the two books comprise the elemental canon of value investing.

"IT EITHER GRABS YOU IMMEDIATELY, OR IT NEVER GRABS YOU AT ALL"

For Watsa and his colleagues at Confederation, following Graham was liberating and empowering. It proved you could win with reason. Rationality would not win all the time, but being rigorous and patient could get you there more often than the speculators and impulsive traders. "It frees you up to stick to your own logic to find conviction," says Watsa. "You get rewarded for trusting yourself, then being patient and getting your reward. And you learn that you actually know a lot more than the stock market does."

An approach that meant you could win with a system brought Watsa under the spell of Graham's thinking. "I read that book from John Watson and I had my 'road to Damascus' moment. All of a sudden, things were obvious. The light clicked on—long-term value investing, downside protection, margin of safety, all of the things we take for granted were right there. I could see the approach really clearly and how the market works. I was so excited—so much so that I said to my wife, 'If we have a son, let's name him Ben.' She agreed, and now Ben is a value guy too. It's in our blood." In another of many parallels between Watsa and Buffett, the latter named his middle son Howard Graham Buffett: Howard after the child's own grandfather and Graham after the grandfather of value.

Some colleagues needed a bit of that powerful Watsa persuasion to get the light to turn on. "At first I was not entirely convinced," recalls Roger Lace, Watsa's lifetime colleague from the time at Confederation to today as chairman of Hamblin Watsa Investment Counsel, Fairfax's investment arm.

"It felt like we were turning the clock back a bit," Lace continues, "working from a book published in the 1930s. Later, in my encounters with Prem we went deeper, and he was really persuasive in helping me to see it. I'd been training on efficient market theory and had no particular bent in terms of style of analysis. But there were many discussions, and it was usually Prem arguing the thesis and convincing me and the others to see it that way. Between Graham, Watson, and Watsa, we all became convinced this was a smarter way to go. A light actually did turn on and I became part of that culture."

By putting a premium on rational thought, value investing could engender a certain conviction in any one course of action. And conviction, in religion or investing, can become fervent. In Watsa's early days, the value way of thinking definitely unlocked a fervour in him, and he embraced it with a passion that some colleagues found a little over the top, as Lace relates. Value fired up Watsa, and he had to learn how to tone it down a bit. In time, he sought to remove his own ego from the business and create a culture where egos were checked by all at the door. But wisdom comes with age, and when you're young, passion rules. Lace recalls:

> Prem was very outspoken, very enthusiastic, and he had an almost evangelical feeling about value investing. [He] had so much conviction that I think some people got tired of hearing about it. But not the true believers like myself and Brian Bradstreet. We had to do a lot of internal and external presentations as analysts. Prem pounded the table and did not take opposition lightly. Over the years, I suspect, a few people probably took him aside and said, "Hey, you're coming on a little too strong here," because he became a very good listener. He took his persuasive powers and learned to point people in the right direction without being too heavy-handed.

Paul Fink, a colleague at Confederation Life and later at Fairfax, once conjured up a vivid image of Watsa that combines the evangelical with ferocity: "He's like a pit bull when he gets hold of an idea. He's tenacious enough to talk a barnacle into jumping ship. Often, he's a little simplistic about things but it takes guts when the whole world's against you. And guts he's got."

Lace discovered that once they got into portfolio management at Confederation Life, Watsa showed everyone he would always fight for his convictions.

> He took some pretty big positions in some pretty unpopular areas. I was of the same mindset, but I'm the type of guy who would rather switch than fight. If my superiors put their foot down,

> I went out of the room with my tail between my legs and did what I was told. Not Prem. There were more and more guidelines and policies laid down from higher levels, but in the rare instance that you felt there should be some leeway, you were allowed to take it to the CEO or certain members of the board. It was almost a joke because every other day, it seemed, Prem would be marching up to the boardroom to argue about the smallest details. And they always gave in, which was quite amazing.

Between his sense of purpose and ability to make others see what he saw, Watsa was emerging as a powerful leader. He galvanized his colleagues around the intellectual appeal of value almost as a theology, with the former little kid from Hyderabad demonstrating the magnetic, proselytizing zeal of a newly converted preacher. Fifty years later, of his own proselytization, Lace cites two men as the forces that turned on the light for him and he is not sure who ended up the bigger factor. "I guess I would have to ask myself if that was Graham's doing or Prem's ability to convince people."

Watsa took the value gospel to anyone who would listen at Confederation, amplifying Watson's influence. But he did not get a big chance to win over a lot of converts. There were only three or four new recruits coming on board each year, and by his guess, only a 10 to 20 percent chance any of them would see the light on value.

"For most of them, the value approach just seemed too simple—too old-fashioned and out of date," says Watsa. "But for Roger, Brian Bradstreet, me, and a few others, we just had to read Graham and we concluded: 'This is our religion; this is our way of thinking. We are not going to go any other way.' It either grabs you immediately; or it never grabs you at all."

"COME ON OUT INTO THE REAL WORLD AND PLAY"

Nine years in at Confederation, Watsa started looking around more seriously for the next job, par for the course among high talents in a low-pay shop. The lure of working with John Watson remained strong, as did the chemistry of working under Tony Hamblin and alongside Roger Lace and Brian Bradstreet. Watsa had been promoted to VP by then, but he and Lace were both growing more frustrated. The blinkered thinking and bureaucracy of institutional money management led them to regularly blue-sky the idea of hanging out their own shingle. However, having recently bought his young family a home, Watsa was hesitant; he was looking for a new job that would offer some reassurance he could keep up on his mortgage payments.

An exit plan soon presented itself when Tony Arrell, a high-profile, value-minded money manager dropped an invitation to join him at an investment shop he ran called Gardiner Watson in Toronto. "You're not an institutional kind of guy," Arrell told him. "Come on out into the real world and play."

Watsa signed up but by the time he took up his post, Arrell had jumped to another shop. At Gardiner, Watsa connected or reconnected with some other key future partners: Frances Burke had come over from Confederation Life as well and later became head trader for Hamblin Watsa Investment Counsel; Mary Pritchard, later to be Watsa's executive assistant, was also there; and there was Francis Chou, who fatefully helped steer Watsa into not only creating Fairfax but also into making his most famous trade during the Global Financial Crisis.

Gardiner was in flux, and while Watsa scratched his head and wondered what to do next, his network kicked in. Tony Hamblin, his former boss at Confederation, had reached the end of his patience there. He had a good line on an opportunity at National Trust and tried to recruit Watsa to come along too. Watsa, meanwhile, had been spending a lot of time thinking about playing in the real world, which led him to bounce an idea around with Donald "Bud" Willmot, who was majority owner of Gardiner and one of Watsa's well-placed accounts.

Watsa countered Hamblin's offer: "Tony, we should really just start our own company. I have already kicked the idea around with Bud and he is ready to fund us for a few years and hand over his own money for us to manage." That was it. Hamblin Watsa Investment Counsel (HWIC) was born in September 1984.

HWIC picked up some good accounts quickly and after landing a few large fish in the U.S., the business was off and running with Hamblin (president and bonds), Watsa (equities), Burke (head trader), and Pritchard (executive assistant) in on the ground floor. They were soon joined by Roger Lace and Brian Bradstreet, making it six partners.

In recalling the years at HWIC, Hamblin once said Watsa proved over and over that he had a unique mix of talent, conviction, and ability to inspire others. "There is a big difference between a good analyst and a good portfolio manager. The one makes recommendations; the other makes decisions. And good decision-makers have to have the courage to buy stocks when they're down and the discipline to sell when they're up or not working out, and they have to do that with consistency. Prem Watsa is exceptional in that regard. There was always the same humour in the office no matter what happened. The interpersonal skills were remarkable."

For Watsa, their early success validated ideas in his head about building a business that was principled. Being profitable was important but the bigger issue was to establish a company that would be beholden to value thinking. As Hamblin later put it, "We both wanted independence. Our driving force was not to make a lot of money, but to do what we wanted to do, when we wanted to do it, in the way we wanted to do it. If it worked, good. If it didn't work, well, the fault would be ours." Soon, Watsa would be encouraged to take the notion of a principled company even higher as a broader force for good.

NOW WHAT?

This is a great Horatio Alger story even if we stop it right here. Young immigrant makes good, hustles, gets value religion, falls in with a good crowd, builds a home for his wife and three children, even co-launches his own value-minded investment firm on Bay Street in Toronto—all after arriving in Canada with eight bucks in his pocket. (Truth be told, there was a bank draft for about $300 in the other pocket, but that was from Dad and written out to Ivey School of Business for the first semester.) Now their company was landing $50-million accounts to manage. But Watsa was conditioned by this point to take advantage of the opportunities that fell his way. And the more he looked around, the more he discovered new opportunities.

Watsa likes to tell that eight-dollars-in-my-pocket story. It grounds him, and he hopes it inspires others, just like Horatio Alger. The same goes for the story of getting his first big job when no one else turned up for the final interview. Ditto how that fateful move brought him to John

Watson who brought him to Ben Graham. It's important to count one's blessings. Another story of inspiration and gratitude comes up often. In it he is twenty years old, still in India, and catching the train back to Hyderabad from school in Chennai. Crouched on the steps of the jam-packed third-class carriage, he is holding on for dear life and some guy sits down next to him and says, "Have you ever read Napoleon Hill's book *Think and Grow Rich*? You have to read it."

Hill was a pioneer in the modern self-help publishing world, practising an art of positive thinking that paved the way for the empowerment coaching infomercials of Tony Robbins and the "law of attraction" concept behind books like *The Secret*. It pretty much rewired the mind of the impressionable twenty-year-old Watsa who was searching for direction, having balked at becoming an engineer. There are a thousand get-rich-quick books that carry similar promises and Hill's own story is apparently more than a little fiction when it comes to certain facts, but its powerful message was clear and inspiring to the young student. Not long after he arrived at his destination, Watsa bought himself a copy of the book, and it became his own personal *Chicken Soup for the Compassionate Capitalist Soul*.

Hill's book instantly made the young Watsa an ardent capitalist, even though he had no money to speak of, and it was a motivating factor in convincing Watsa to study business after his engineering degree. It reinforced his sense that success was an attitude and that positive thinking and faith can carry you a long way. One of the key messages the book delivers is not to love money but, rather, to leverage it to escape from fear of poverty. That fear, Hill wrote, is one of many that hold us back from making more of ourselves, including but not limited to material wealth. And the system Hill touted as most able to underpin a betterment of society and broader civilization was capitalism.

"I will never forget reading that message and I have never stopped believing it to be true," says Watsa. "That thinking really resonated. It inspired me to think about how wealth and capitalism could be a vehicle for doing good."

In the book, Hill describes capitalism as the guiding force that helped the U.S. emerge as the world's leading economy. "This is a capitalistic country," he wrote. "It was developed through the use of capital, and we who claim the right to partake of the blessings of freedom and opportunity, we who seek to accumulate riches here may as well know that neither riches nor opportunity would be available to us if organized capital had not provided these benefits."

Watsa was still largely ignorant of business and capitalism, but his perspective had been reshaped. Hill's conception of which sort of qualities can enable one to think and grow rich reinforced Watsa's general thinking and ambition. The book describes a "definitiveness of purpose" as an essential characteristic to help a person develop the persistence to surmount whatever difficulties they may face. Definitiveness of purpose, coupled with the ability to make others see it and want to be included, could well be another way of describing Watsa's emerging superpower of persuasion.

His son Ben says another way to describe it is what people have called the "reality distortion field" when describing Steve Jobs in his days at Apple: One visionary person can inspire others around him through a mix of drive, passion, and charisma to see and share the same mission.

An important factor in Prem's conversion was what made him so receptive in the first place, adds Francis Chou. Also an immigrant from India—arriving in Canada two years before Watsa—and a huge fan of Graham and Berkshire Hathaway, Chou got bored with university and decided to teach himself investing while working as a Bell Canada technician. He proved to be particularly adept; his investing club would turn into a successful value fund, then a family of funds with enviable returns.

Prem's mind had been formed around strong principles and the power of reason led him to hunger for ideas worthy of clear conviction. He already had the character and self-discipline. What he lacked were the ideas to believe in and act on, reasons Chou.

"All his actions are based on strong principles. When you grow up in India, every class in every grade at that time was brainwashing you into socialism. He turned away from that when he adopted capitalism and the principle there was he felt capitalism was good for society as a whole. At that time, he would have been part of the 1.1 percent of Indians who thought that way. Normally when you grow up in a social system, you fight for that system because you've been brainwashed. But

Prem is guided by principles and he is very comfortable as a contrarian. So he flipped."

So we have Napoleon Hill and Ben Graham, Dean Jones and John Watson, Warren Buffett and Henry Singleton (whom we will introduce later). Each helped to bring Watsa into business, investing, and value thinking. Each celebrated the power of positivity, individual discipline, and the progressive creativity of capitalism when done right. Other inspirations followed and reinforced these ideas. Like John Templeton, for example.

Templeton, a legendarily successful fund manager and devout Christian, was an inspiration for Watsa's character as much as for his disciplined value approach to investing. "He had the best track record ever and he also had really good personal values, just like John Watson," says Watsa, who called Templeton a friend for nearly thirty years before he died in 2008 at the age of ninety-five. The two met when Watsa was exploring next steps after Confederation, but Templeton had just finished hiring a Canadian team. "If Mr. Templeton had offered me a job, I would have taken it and probably would never have left," he says. Templeton, at one point, was Fairfax's largest shareholder.

For Watsa, faith brings constant awareness of blessings in life, as it did for Templeton. While the lessons he first learned from Hill inspired him, at a deeper level religious teachings grounded him more profoundly. His father inculcated in him a lesson that Watsa has carried with him throughout his life: "Work as hard as you can, as though everything depended on you. Pray as hard as you can, as though everything depended on God." That quote would become a signature way for him to close off his speeches, often twinned with his favourite quote from the Bible: "For what shall it profit a man if he shall gain the whole world and lose his own soul?"

Many twists of fate propelled Watsa along his path, which is not unusual. What is remarkable is how he took advantage of them. Constantly sponging up and collecting ideas, he was forming a blueprint in his head of how to run a large enterprise using capitalism for good. But he did not have that blueprint yet. And he had yet to meet the business partner who would help him put those ideas into words and actions.

Meanwhile, he was fired up on ambition and reminding himself constantly of a message he had learned from that little book a stranger had told him about on a train: "If the mind can conceive, the mind can achieve." Watsa had identified in himself a certain definitiveness of purpose.

Though the values were baked in India, Watsa has enormous gratitude for everything he learned in Canada about how to create and build a business. The Hill book had tickled his imagination about what money could do, but at the time he still had no idea how those things worked. All that would come after he made his new home, studied, and surrounded himself with a valuable network in his adoptive country.

> All those lessons from that little book loomed larger once I started to study business and when I opened my eyes, seeing free enterprise first-hand in Canada. It was obvious to me that capitalism was the ideal engine for a successful society. I could see anything was possible here. In India, it was too tied up in restrictions and socialist five-year central planning. There wasn't enough capital or competition. And there was too much corruption.
>
> As for any business acumen I developed, that is all Canada. I didn't understand anything about capitalism or free enterprise until I came here. I basically had no clue about business or financial markets and didn't even have a plan to find anything out. But I was looking for a chance to make something of myself. Hard work and a lot of good luck, like meeting up with the right people, took care of the rest.

So far, these forces had led him to launch a new company with his old boss. But as soon as they launched, an exchange with another contact had Watsa running off stage left in a hurry to turn the business into something completely different.

THE BIRTH OF FAIRFAX

Fairfax was born of a fevered scramble. In later years, the company's preferred play was not to chase deals. It would build a reputation as an honest straight shooter. Then it would just sit back and answer the phone. In the summer of 1985, however, there was no sitting back. Watsa found himself in a mad dash in all directions at once.

The new investment firm was just taking its first steps, but Watsa was already taking a left turn with a side project that could reinvent the business. He was trying to do his first deal, one that to this day, having done multi-billion-dollar transactions, he is convinced was by far his toughest.

His target? What had captured his imagination were the near-bankrupt Canadian trucking insurance assets of a Richmond, Virginia-based company called Markel. Watsa knew next to nothing about insurance—or trucking for that matter. Neither did any of his four partners at HWIC, who were under the impression they were in the wealth management business and maybe had no business chasing after a broken insurer. The pursuit was a bit of a side hustle for Watsa, who, once he got his head and definitiveness of purpose around an idea, was determined to make it happen.

Where did the strategy come from? Blame it on "the Chouster" (rhymes with *rooster*). If the Fairfax story were a TV series, Chou would be the character who turns up a few times in the season and steals the scene. One fateful scene while Watsa was still at Gardiner featured a short exchange with Chou that ran pretty much like this:

Chou: "Prem, do you know how Warren Buffett makes his money?"

Watsa: "Sure." (*Rattles off some of the great value investments like GEICO, Coca-Cola, and American Express.*)

Chou: "Nope. The guy basically came up with the idea of investing the float of insurance companies."

(Watsa blinks. Light bulb above his head turns on.)

"I was so impressed I told the boys we have to hire this guy," recalls Watsa. Although he had been following Buffett and Berkshire for more than a decade, Watsa was obviously missing a few details. Chou's insight stirred his imagination with the idea that you could run a separate business and leverage its store of money to generate additional returns, as long as you kept cash on hand to pay off future claims. It seemed almost too good to be true for a talented investor. Gardiner soon hired Chou. (Fairfax would later hire him and help him launch his own funds, after which he went out on his own, returning for a stretch in the 1990s. In 2017, Chou launched his own mini-Berkshire, buying Stonetrust Commercial Insurance Company, a Louisiana-based workers' compensation insurer to complement his funds with float.)

Armed with this new insight, Watsa started to wonder after HWIC launched if it might make sense for the new company to invest in an insurer to leverage its float. Not long after, he heard there was a motivated seller who might be up for a deal.

THE SCRAMBLE FOR MARKEL'S CANADIAN BUSINESS

George Christoff, a stock salesman at Gardiner who also happened to be a director on the board at Markel Financial Holdings, had a front-row seat on the company's financial woes. The trucking insurance business was in one of its cyclical slumps and Markel Financial was on the ropes, with bankruptcy looming and regulators demanding a quick capital injection to protect the company's clients and stay afloat.

Christoff put Watsa on to Steven Markel, one of the key family members controlling the parent company and subsidiary. The two met for lunch at the 54th, predecessor to the legendary Canoe restaurant where bankers and business leaders have been making deals on the 54th floor of the TD Bank Tower for decades. By then, it was clear to Watsa the company was distressed, and he also knew he did not have the money to buy a healthy company. His value mindset warmed to the idea of a bargain. Out came the proverbial paper napkin, and Watsa put down some numbers that included rescue money for the company and assigned control to a group led by him, outside the freshly launched HWIC. Markel agreed and Watsa had his deal—all he needed to do was raise C$5.25 million to make it happen. Cue the fevered scramble.

"Adding insurance operations was Prem's side hustle," says Roger Lace. "I was moderately skeptical but my bottom line was that hey, Buffett did it, too, and he was a big Graham value investing guy. So if Buffett can do it, why can't we?" Lace and others at HWIC would be individual investors in the Sixty Two Investment Company Ltd., the control group. But Watsa needed a lot more money.

Watsa had to put his abundant powers of persuasion to work to drum up interest in owning a piece of a basically bankrupt trucking insurer. He was new at this game but one big thing in his favour was his good network from a decade in managing money. He was young but had enough of a successful track record that many people were prepared to bet on him—even in the face of uninspiring fundamentals.

First stop was a visit to Donald "Bud" Willmot, chairman at Gardiner Watson. "I was managing his portfolio of about $20 million [Canadian] and had gotten to know him," Watsa recalls. "But when I showed him the deal that I wanted to do, he looked at me and said, 'You know, Prem, I would go to Vegas and gamble my money before I put it on a trucking insurance idea like this.' My heart sank, but then he added, 'If you really think you can make it work, go ahead and do it. I will invest.'"

Another stop was with Robbert Hartog, a successful Canadian entrepreneur. Hartog would later serve on the Fairfax board as one of Watsa's most trusted advisors and a corporate "godfather" and role model to him as a novice chief executive and board chair. Hartog was also a generous philanthropist and might have offered Watsa C$400,000 over breakfast at the King Edward Hotel more as a charitable donation than an investment expected to yield a return. Watsa remembers getting ready to give Hartog his full pitch over freshly squeezed orange juice in the hotel dining room and being interrupted immediately, along the line of:

Watsa: "So, I'm looking for backing for this restructuring . . ."

Hartog: "Yeah, that's fine, Prem."

Watsa: "Do you want some charts? I can work up some tables . . ."

Hartog: "No, that's fine. I'll invest in it!"

Sometimes you invest in the person as much as the idea.

Other investor contacts fell in line: Winslow Bennett, Wally Bedolfe, Bill Bulger, Jack Herbert, Paul Murray, and John Nicol. Soon, he had commitments of C$2 million, structured as preferred shares that paid holders

8 percent annually to compensate them for the risk. Now he needed the other C$3.25 million, and he had a good feeling about where he would find it. He had already taken the temperature of bankers over at Canadian Imperial Bank of Commerce (CIBC), and they had been favourably disposed. So, a day before the other investors were coming over to sign off on the preferreds, he headed over to CIBC after work on a Wednesday to lock the deal down. By seven in the evening, CIBC had signed up. Everything was done. At nine, Watsa sat in his office at 67 Yonge Street. As he marvelled at his good fortune, a smile broke across his face. Then the phone rang.

It was Kenneth Davidson, CIBC's lead on the investment. Davidson was still driving home to Hamilton on Highway 403, but he had one of those big 1980s car phones pressed to his ear. He'd had time for reflection on the trucking insurance business and had had a change of heart. "I'm just not feeling good about this," Prem remembers hearing, still wincing at the words almost forty years later. "So I asked him, 'What will it take? Do you want a little more interest? More warrants?' He says, 'No, Prem, I really feel uncomfortable doing the deal. I just can't do it.'"

It was one of those rare moments when Watsa's persuasiveness failed him. With the benefit of hindsight, he wonders if he himself would have turned down the same deal if the roles were reversed. "I was thirty-five years old and had no experience. It's not like it was hard to see why he balked. Besides, the company was losing money badly and was near bankruptcy. Of course, neither of us could see then how quickly it would take flight in 1986." CIBC would miss out on a windfall, of course. But at that moment, Watsa was back to scrambling.

Distraught, Watsa made two quick phone calls, one to Hartog, always a key advisor, who counselled him to keep the deal in play. "Wait a bit," he said. "Maybe there will be another train." The other call was to Steven Markel, who desperately needed the cash to keep the regulators at bay. Watsa was not the only one hanging here. Markel quickly decided Watsa was still his own best bet for survival and urged him to go ahead with meeting the investors in the morning.

Watsa regained his ability to inspire, talking a few other suddenly nervous investors off the ledge to stay the course now that CIBC was out. That kept the C$2 million in his hands and a deal with Markel over pizza cleared a path to move forward by kicking the financing can down the road a bit. Half the money raised so far could go into the insurance company's capital. While Watsa had missed his deadline with the rest of the money, Markel Financial got its emergency cash, the regulators would be happy, and Steven Markel gave Prem another six months to secure the remaining C$3.23 million.

Time to knock on doors again at all the banks and lenders in Toronto. Months went by and everywhere Watsa got the same answer: No, no, and no. "At that point, I told myself you can just give up or you can start thinking of a solution that does not come from a bank."

An idea finally came to him as he drove the whole family out to the East Coast for a camping trip in August 1985. He pulled the car off the highway, checking his pockets for change. Watsa didn't have one of those big 1980s car phones—he needed to track down a pay phone. "It struck me I had never thought of the gang back at Confederation Life. That was basically my last chance."

Jim Martin, who had been part of his original hiring team at Confederation Life, picked up the call, liked what he heard, and asked Watsa to follow up with details. A written proposal would follow, which another ex-colleague, Paul Fink, would tease Watsa over, mocking its grand ambitions by referring to it as "The Watsa Manifesto." Despite the ribbing, both Fink and Martin were impressed enough to offer their own personal investments, which was a fabulous vote of confidence but ironically created an added hurdle: Now there was a potential conflict over mixing company and employee funds—which meant the whole deal had to go for full presidential approval. And guess who was about to reveal he hated it?

"I THINK THIS IS GOING TO BE A REALLY BAD INVESTMENT"

First, Pat Burns, Confederation's president, called an internal meeting and asked John Watson if he actually liked the deal or was just being nice to Watsa. Watson insisted he did, which was not the answer Burns wanted to hear. It would be another few weeks before Watsa and Markel got the chance to stand before Burns to try to sway the big man in person. They never really got a chance. Burns walked in, sat down, and proceeded to completely suck the air out of the room. "I want to tell you guys I'd never do this deal," he said, directing most of his attention to his own colleagues in the room. "This is like the property and casualty business—it's up and down. My brother was in P & C and almost bankrupted the company. I think this is going to be a really bad investment. If I were you, I'd never do it."

Watsa looked at Markel. Markel at Watsa. They both looked at Burns. "We almost had heart attacks," Watsa recalls. "We were looking at this guy and wondering what had just happened. The next train—our train—was supposed to be coming in. Then suddenly it wasn't." Then, just as suddenly, it was.

Burns turned to Watson and added on his way out of the room: "If you want to do it, that's fine. But I want you to know I wouldn't do it."

Watson nodded and waited patiently for Burns to close the door, then announced, "We are doing the deal. We said we were going to do the deal. We are doing the deal." Then he tossed over a condition.

"He told me I didn't have any money in the game," says Watsa. "He said, 'Prem, come up with $100,000, fast, because you need to have something to lose.'" Watsa countered with a humorous dig delivered more as a plea for mercy. "'Johnny,' I said, 'do you remember what you used to pay me? Where am I going to find a hundred grand?'"

The awkward laughter settled quickly. The clock started ticking yet again. It was Wednesday, September 21, 1985.

The scramble at this point was all in Watsa's hands. He drained every account he had, including his retirement savings. Two days later at 3:59 p.m., he had his certified cheque for C$100,000 at the lawyer's office. The deal had gone sideways many times, but this time it was done. Watsa was already a very talented investor. He was now showing signs his dealmaking was not too shabby, either, and hubris kept any doubts at bay. "It was definitely the hardest deal I ever did, but I never thought it was risky. I was dumb enough to not think it was risky."

The gang at Confederation Life was not dumb. They knew it was risky, and Fink picked up where he left off with the Watsa Manifesto ribbing, warning Watsa he had better not stumble because if he did not meet his terms, they would have him by the throat, or worse. "You know, Prem," Fink offered in a friendly reminder, "Confed is on the hook for this. The moment you lose your $3.5 million [Canadian], we're going to put you out of your misery, close the company, and get our money back. You lose, you're gone. No flexibility. We're going to pull the trigger."

Twenty-five years after the Confederation investment in Watsa, Fink looked back at the bluster and conceded that while business is just business, there was something underneath it all that gave the investors faith Watsa would be good for it, even if the trucking insurance venture collapsed on them. It was trust.

"What you have to realize about Prem front and centre is that he is a Christian of the old-fashioned kind—you know, honest, hard-working, charitable. So people who know him trust him. That's one of the reasons I did the deal with him, plus he had a great sense of humour. He was untested, but I thought for sure, somehow, some way, he'd pay us back even if he didn't have to." Mind you, he added, "If he'd told us at that time that this stock would go from $3 to $600 within ten years, we would have thought he was loopy."

One thing people forget, Fink explained, was that being kind and modest doesn't make you a "fraidy-cat": "If you ever play tennis with him, he's out there to kill you. But when he did injure you unto death, he would call an ambulance as soon as he could. So he was a good guy to bet on." Capturing the moment with the aforementioned sense of humour, Watsa showed up on deal-closing day with a statue for Fink of a man with an extended arm aiming a handgun. "That gun was pointed at my head," quips Watsa.

Watsa didn't mind the pressure. In fact, he thrived on it. He was great at investing, the company was well capitalized, and he was calling the shots with help from the Markel family. He even had the company's float and portfolio to manage. How hard could insurance be?

"That was it. We finally had a company we could control. Sure, it was a crappy insurance company but we had $25 million [Canadian] in investments that we could manage and we could go out and win business. That's how we began."

PART TWO

THE DEALMAKING MACHINE

Putting the Pieces Together

Chapter Two

LET'S BUY SOME FLOAT (1985–1988)

"1985 was a very significant year for your company. As your new Chairman, I would like to review the major developments and also indicate to you our plans and objectives for the future." —*Prem Watsa*

Meet the new boss. With that understatement, given that the company had just stared death in the face, Watsa greeted shareholders in early 1986. A year before, bankruptcy had been knocking at Markel Financial's door. Now, with new backers, Watsa made it clear it was itching to quickly expand.

Watsa used the short one-page letter to introduce himself and the new board. He succinctly shared the company's investment philosophy and spelled out what he intended to achieve at the time and in the future. His annual letter, he related, would serve as his primary communication tool. Even today, this inaugural letter should be required reading for investors thinking about becoming Fairfax shareholders, because it laid out a mission that has remained remarkably unchanged throughout four decades of ups and downs. It was also short, in contrast to later letters that clock in at thirty pages or more with detailed disclosure on a dizzying mix of moving parts.

Watsa made it clear the HWIC team knew little about insurance, but having two members of the Markel family, Steven and his cousin Tony, as partners meant there was a constant in savvy insurance management that would blend perfectly with the investing brains over at HWIC. In the early years, the two companies collaborated on management and even made joint acquisitions before ultimately deciding it was better to go their own ways.

In discussing the future, Watsa's letter made it clear they were a bunch of classic value investing people looking to build something over the long term; insurance was just a part of it. The truth is they had no idea where the company's future was headed, and they liked it that way. He stressed there was no master plan, and the team would do its best to take advantage of opportunities as they presented themselves. Again, this was the classic playbook stuff of value contrarians with a holding company.

"Our investment philosophy is based on the value approach as laid out by Ben Graham and practiced by his famous disciple, Warren Buffett," he wrote. "This means we buy stocks of financially sound companies at prices below their underlying long-term values. We expect to make money over time, not in the next month or two. In fact, in the short term, stock prices could go well below our cost. In our purchases, we are always trying to first protect your capital from long-term losses before attempting to make money."

Watsa also tipped investors to expect rich disclosure on all activities, but they would have to get used to waiting for it. "Our major objective will be to run the company for the long-term benefit of all shareholders. As shareholders ourselves, we plan on providing you with the type of information that we ourselves would find useful. This annual report is our first stab at more complete disclosure."

In tone and substance, his words echoed the formal correspondence a young Warren Buffett introduced with his investors in his pre–Berkshire Hathaway investment fund in 1956. Buffett promised investors, all family and friends, that he would speak clearly and simply in explaining Berkshire's philosophy and discussing the performance of the fund. Like Watsa later, he stressed the goal was to explain everything that he himself would want to know. Implicit was the wish, having answered all the questions before they could even be asked, that he be left to himself to invest wisely without being pestered with questions or requests for additional updates.

Watsa also explicitly set the targets on financials in that first letter: "How should you judge our performance? We think all companies should be measured on their after-tax return on common shareholders' equity. In Canada, the average company has earned about 13% on shareholders' equity over many decades. Our objective is to earn a long-term return averaging 20%, while maintaining the financial strength of the company."

Watsa made it clear that the 20 percent target should not be "onerous" in the first few years, given the benefit of tax-loss carryforwards. "Over the years, though," he cautioned, foreshadowing future tinkering with the targets, "20% after tax is a very challenging objective." In other words, he was saying we expect to be on fire out of the gate but do not be surprised when we outperform by a smaller margin in the future.

"It is really important to not just have targets but to put them down in writing and make them transparent," he says today. "It shapes how you make decisions and priorities year to year. I think it's unlikely that we would have been as successful as we were with our performance if we hadn't enshrined them as targets." And there were many tough years when they missed those targets and had a lot of explaining to do to shareholders. As we will see, the targets were also revised over time.

Another thing Watsa made abundantly clear from the get-go (and it would be hammered home in every letter to follow) was that management intended to retain control of the company and had vowed to never sell it, at any price. The initial investors, including Watsa, had a class of shares that gave them ten times the votes of ordinary shareholders, which meant they could chart a long-term course without feeling pressure from impatient or activist investors who might try to take the company over and bust it up.

Watsa let shareholders know that in the "extremely unlikely" event Fairfax were sold, all shares would be treated equally. Shareholders, he cautioned, should however never expect to receive this "attractive one-time bonanza" even if an offer landed at twice the current market price. In return, shareholders would be able to look forward to "some excellent long-term gains" that might hopefully emulate Berkshire Hathaway's. It was a contract of sorts—a commitment to never sell offset by a promise to reward shareholders for sticking around.

A DRAMATIC WIN ON TRUCKING

In the fall of 1985, the guy running the company was like the dog who finally catches the car and asks himself, Now what? Watsa was chairman, but he hadn't even been on a corporate board and didn't know how to pass a resolution. Having Hartog as a mentor would prove invaluable. Watsa was also CEO, but he had never run a company. "And I sure didn't know anything about how to run an insurance company."

In Watsa's head, the operating strategy would always be to buy companies with great management and leave it in place to run things with a lot of autonomy. The stop-gap move initially was to rely on the Markel family, but his team knew they needed new people in place. The Markels were investors now, but they had their own parent company to run. So, Watsa hunted down some experienced help while Steven Markel babysat the corner office until Keith Ingoe was brought over from Halifax Insurance to run the Markel Financial operations.

Soon, the company faced its tests and at first passed with flying colours, learning the value of patience in a weak pricing environment when it opted to retrench instead of chasing market share. Those moves paid off dramatically when the competition foolishly did the opposite.

There were only two main players writing trucking insurance in the country: Markel Financial, which had narrowly escaped bankruptcy, and United Canada Insurance, which was on the ropes itself. "We decided to be disciplined," explains Watsa. "Most insurers aren't as investment-oriented as we are. They are market-share-oriented and keep trying to expand during soft markets. We had learned it was better to drop unprofitable business in these periods and focus on profits." They were ready to wait out United—but they did not have to.

United Canada, sitting on 40 percent market share, recklessly blew its brains out to expand after Markel Financial's brush with bankruptcy. Death came to United in a matter of months, which was a gift from the insurance gods to Watsa et al. "I knew they were on their last legs, but we couldn't have predicted their quick demise. They offered to sell to us, but why would we buy them when they had built market share writing unprofitable business against us? And now we could just go out and take market share for free."

In 1986 alone, Markel's revenue soared from C$14 million to C$41 million, and earnings swung from a loss of C$1 million to a profit of C$6.5 million. Industry conditions were turning down and performance would suffer in 1988, but it was an auspicious debut. "There is no question that the insurance cycle is on the downswing," Watsa told shareholders, lowering expectations for the coming year while also reminding them that it was the company's strategy to avoid writing business unless there was the prospect of an underwriting profit. In this early experience, it must have looked to shareholders like these investment guys, newbies or not, were as good at steering insurance operations as they were at buying stocks and bonds.

MORE FLOAT, PLEASE

The initial capital investment that brought in new management had raised a total of C$9.1 million in September 1985, consisting of a C$5-million private placement by Watsa and key insiders, plus C$2.6 million from the Markel Group parent company and C$1.5 million from other investors. The private placement was done in preferred shares and warrants, which were convertible into common shares that held voting control. The stock debuted at C$3.25.

About C$6 million of that initial financing went to shoring up Markel Financial's capital. With business absolutely exploding in the summer of 1986 after the demise of United Canada, the company was running out of money, in a good way. To feed its expansion, Watsa and his team sold investment bankers on the opportunity to raise equity in July, less than a year from launch, and this time the total was C$20 million. The stock offering price had more than tripled to C$10 and the shares would hit C$12.75 by year-end.

At this point, the team might have forgotten they were still wet behind the ears; they were a confident, even brash, bunch. A short internal memorandum attached to the draft prospectus for the C$10 offering spelled out industry conditions and comparable metrics at other insurers. At the end of the seven pages of discussion, the company included an appendix with financials from two companies that it hoped to emulate—Berkshire Hathaway and Teledyne, both legendary companies. It was akin to a young hockey player including stats from Wayne Gretzky and Alexander Ovechkin on the back of his rookie hockey card as benchmarks of what he hoped to achieve.

"We had barely succeeded in repackaging a broken insurer," Watsa says. "Those were two companies I admired most. It's not like we were confident we would play in their league. No way, but we figured we had a good chance to build a decent business that was inspired by them. As far as investing goes, Berkshire was always the biggest influence. With Teledyne, it was Singleton's talent for allocation in acquisitions but especially with share buybacks."

Teledyne and Berkshire were rarefied company to aspire to join. It was an unmistakeable sign that these insurance rookies were aiming high. Rick Salsberg, Watsa's *consigliere* and one-man legal and acquisitions team from Torys LLP, recalled Fairfax's remarkable mix of modesty and inexperience together with cocky ambition. Sometimes it was their strength in the early days; sometimes it was their weakness.

"Prem was always a value investor, and in the beginning that also applied to insurance companies that Fairfax bought," said Salsberg in an interview just months before he passed from cancer at age seventy-nine. "The very best insurance companies weren't really available to us because they were too expensive for our budget, and, regardless, the fact they weren't selling at bargain levels meant they didn't fit the value investing style. We were somewhat innocent in that we felt the insurance part wasn't the hard part. We figured we could just buy the assets and then the hard part was going to be done making money on the investment side. So we were thinking, 'Let's just get this insurance company and start investing the float.'"

Investors would get subordinate voting shares to minimize diluting control of the multiple-voting shareholders. Watsa laid out the structure in detail in the 1986 annual report, again explaining the connection between management control and the share structure:

> Why did we sell subordinate shares which have only one vote and retain multiple-voting shares (10 votes) for ourselves? Mainly because we wanted to control Markel Financial and manage the company to provide an above-average, long-term return to shareholders. Our multiple voting shares are not traded and can be sold in the public markets only as subordinate shares. Also, a takeover offer for our shares, if accepted, immediately triggers a similar offer for all the common shares outstanding.

Completed in July 1986, the deal put another C$5 million in the bank for operations, plus C$1.5 million to cover expenses. The rest was shopping money, and just two months later the team made its first acquisition.

In buying Sphere Reinsurance Company of Canada, Markel Financial started to diversify, introducing a new line of business to the holding company. The price was C$4 million plus a note that paid C$2.8 million, contingent on the health of its reserves. Watsa was learning, with the help of Salsberg, the importance of structuring deals to guard against hidden reserve problems at the beaten-down insurers they were picking up.

In late October, an amalgamation was executed with Morden & Helwig Ltd. (M&H) at a cost of C$2 million in cash and C$6.9 million in shares. As the largest claims adjusting firm in the country, M&H brought gross revenue of C$30 million and 570 employees under the Fairfax umbrella. It brought even more diversification.

With most of its acquisitions, Fairfax regularly explored the potential for new assets to be turned into decentralized vehicles for further expansion. With M&H, it set to work hatching a plan to build up M&H into a global claims company, either together with Markel Group's claims business or, later, by buying into the U.K. market. To that end, M&H was taken public in 1987, raising another C$20 million and a full purse for more acquisitions. The initial mad scramble to refinance Markel Financial was slipping into the past. The company paid out Confederation Life, Watsa's investors, early with a sweet profit, and he got his statue with the pointed gun back from Fink as a souvenir.

M&H was a deal machine within the Fairfax deal machine. That addition showed a lot of promise, but ultimately it would struggle from inconsistent performance. By now, Watsa had already made it standard practice to lay out the rationale behind Fairfax's acquisitions in his annual letter to shareholders. Then as now, he included a frank discussion of risks, so when certain assets struggled, investors could always go back to the letter and be reminded that Prem had at least warned them.

In his 1988 letter, he noted the latest string of M&H acquisitions and first extolled: "We now have a very sound base for expansion in the U.S. and the growth potential of our claims adjusting operations over the next few years could be very exciting." There followed a cautionary note: "**NO** guarantees though!" The bolding was Watsa's—and it was prescient.

The company now had three assets in three distinct lines of business, which was great for diversification. The original trucking insurance operations were now running next to the reinsurance assets and a claims business with lofty ambitions for expansion. With the new direction, the holding company needed a unifying name that was not Markel.

MARKEL BECOMES FAIRFAX FINANCIAL

The new corporate moniker was created in 1986 by Brenda Adams, who came from the old Markel to Fairfax where she served as corporate secretary. The Markel name would still be used for the original trucking insurance business as well as new lines of insurance through acquisitions. However, Fairfax Financial Holdings became the new name for the umbrella holding company.

Never a fan of marketing spin and promotion, and ever eager to give voice and credit to employee ideas, Watsa quipped to shareholders, "You may be surprised to know that [the new name] did not come from a 'name' consultant." Like Berkshire and Teledyne, Fairfax Financial was created to be a dealmaker first and to shift to organic growth later. The mission to build through purchases was right there in Adams's idea for the company name. Although coded in the wordplay of a portmanteau, it riffed off the company's recently formulated motto of "fair and friendly acquisitions":

- *Fair* reflected the expectation that the company would treat its customers and employees fairly, and it would do the same with management and employees at the firms it courted as targets;
- The second *F* stood for *friendly* for the way it would do deals, with no raiding, big layoffs, or backing out of agreed terms; and
- The *Ax* was for acquisitions, the deals that would act as blocks to build the house of Fairfax.

The full context of fair and friendly culture, in Watsa's words, runs like this: "Fair, because in all our dealings we try not to take advantage of anyone. Friendly, because we try to go the extra step to treat everyone with more than just professional courtesy, and because we don't engage in hostile acquisitions. That's our culture."

Early in 1987, its second full year, Fairfax moved a few blocks in the downtown Toronto financial district, taking up offices with HWIC where they remain today, across the street from the 54th restaurant at 95 Wellington Street West. Before they had even unpacked, they were already chasing down several more deals that would close that year:

- Otter Dorchester Insurance Company, through Markel Financial. Specializing in agricultural insurance, Canada-based Otter Dorchester brought with it another C$11 million in gross premiums and came at a price of C$2.6 million.
- Lindsey & Newsom. Fairfax's M&H and Markel Group split a purchase of L&N, a Texas-based claims firm that also operated a training school for adjusters. Price tag: $14 million.
- Shand, Morahan, and Evanston Services, a professional liability insurer. Fairfax and Markel Group of the U.S. split the cost.

Shand, Morahan, and Evanston was a big fish. Global giant Alexander & Alexander was in a weak spot and prepared to sell it for book value. Steven Markel and Watsa figured out their offer strategy on a flight to New York: $30 million cash and a $47-million five-year note that would shrink if the business showed strains and had to pay out reserves. This strategy of Watsa and Salsberg to use contingent notes would become a standard way of protecting Fairfax from negative reserve surprises.

Fairfax was the effective lead (with 35 percent, Markel Group with 35 percent, and investment bankers pitching in). It was growing up fast. The new acquisition earned premiums of $105 million in 1987, before joining Fairfax, and had assets of more than half a billion dollars. HWIC was happy to see the $280-million portfolio at Evanston come along with the asset purchase. For shareholders, the script was already getting hard to follow with so many deals. They had not seen anything yet.

In this period, Markel Group retained a 20 percent interest in Fairfax Financial. Watsa and Steven Markel were keen to see what they could grow together with Shand and M&H. By the time 1988 was behind them,

Fairfax's average return on equity capital (ROE) over the first three years of the company's life was a robust 26.1 percent, versus 11 percent for the benchmark Toronto Stock Exchange 300 (later reconstituted as the S&P/TSX Composite). As the numbers grew, the business press started to pay closer attention. The company had arrived with a splash.

MEET WATSA, THE MARKET GURU

The folks at HWIC had ridden the stock market roller coaster before, but 1987 brought a new kind of nausea, one that scared some people away from the market for a long time. By the end of a single harrowing trading session, October 19 would be known as Black Monday. The Dow Jones Industrial Average closed an eye-popping 22.6 percent lower than where it finished the previous Friday. It was the worst flame-out since the Great Depression and speculation ran rampant that a new depression was in the cards.

Market collapses are nearly impossible to time. The tendency is for stock markets to generally stake incremental gains, with lots of smaller ups and downs. When it's time to retreat, it's often short and brutal, but rarely as bad as this was. Then again, stocks had been soaring, and when everything is going up, the value crowd gets nervous. Watsa and his colleagues had been watching the Dow rocket more than 40 percent over the previous seven months, and as contrarians, they had already been preparing for trouble.

The Black Monday event would earn Watsa kudos as an uncanny savant in bubble watching. Before the crash, while investors stampeded into the market in hopes of easy money, he and the HWIC team sold down half of the company's stock portfolio and booked a lot of profit. In the years that followed, Fairfax would go on to make a lot of prudent macro calls on financial markets, the best known of which was a big short against the U.S. housing market in the lead-up to the Global Financial Crisis.

Watsa drew on Ben Graham's calm and reason in a way that also reassured shareholders to look past the turmoil to better returns in the long term. The worst thing investors could do, value investors will preach, is to sell out after a big crash. Sure enough, the market snapped right back.

"Can this be 1929 repeated all over again?" he mused to shareholders in his 1986 letter. "Unfortunately, we don't know the answer . . . What we do know is that short-term fluctuations in the market have always resulted from the twin emotions of fear and greed and have nothing to do with the underlying business fundamentals of the country or company."

The time would soon come when Watsa and his HWIC team would get labelled as "perma-bears," but the thirty-seven-year-old executive's ability to read the macro environment in the late 1980s led him to see constructive conditions for solid gains. To him, it looked a lot like a repeat of the post–Second World War boom times. Before the extreme run-up and crash, he had observed: "Where does the stock market go from here? We don't know but if we had to guess we think there are many long-term secular forces that could result in the stock market experience of the 1950s being repeated. We think there is a good possibility of the Dow Jones rising significantly in the next five years. We continue to find good long-term values that meet our criteria."

Black Monday threw a wrench in the gears, but investors who refused to be ruled by fear or greed and followed Watsa's lead did well staying bullish. It turned out that while valuations had been overheated, a big contributing factor to the panic was the introduction of electronic trading in index futures, which caused defensive hedges to unintentionally amplify the extreme volatility. The shock wore off and markets rallied.

A bigger concern Watsa wanted to share with investors was the swelling bubble in Japanese stocks. General asset prices, especially in Japan's real estate and financial markets, were inflated by loose monetary policies in the mid-1980s. A classic speculative bubble ensued where manic investors bid up prices and fortunes were made until it all came crashing down in the early 1990s.

Watsa had been presciently sounding the alarm on Japan, but as with many of his calls, he was dead right—but early. So there was a stretch when market watchers dismissed him as a Cassandra doomsayer. The Japanese crash served as an ugly reminder that we could see another Great Depression and Watsa remained vigilant. Ben Graham's experience living through the 1929 crash and its aftermath taught him that investors needed to act early, for if they were not bearish in 1925, he cautioned, they only had a 1 in 100 chance of surviving the Depression. Graham himself learned the hard way, getting wiped out and having to rebuild his holdings.

Watsa regularly repeated Graham's warning to shareholders. And he had been sounding the alarm on the risks in Japan for several years before they were validated. It must be said that even the best stock market crystal balls can be 100 percent accurate while remaining rather imprecise on timing. Watsa never veered from his conviction that Japan was going to hit the wall with a crash of magnitude but even he was quick to acknowledge the challenge predicting precisely when.

"The major risk we see is a collapse in the highly speculative Japanese stock and real estate market," he wrote to shareholders in his 1987 letter. The Nikkei index had just followed its 43 percent surge in 1986 with another 15 percent gain. Watsa stuck to his collapse call but said to shareholders, "If any of you know when that will happen, please let me know!" The Nikkei lifted off for another 40 percent gain the following year, prompting Watsa to exclaim, "So much for our expertise in Japanese stocks! If this continues, Japan will be the only equity market of consequence. Count me among the skeptics."

The Nikkei continued to defy the odds for yet another year, jumping 29 percent in 1989 before the bubble popped and it collapsed. It would not regain its 1980s peak for an astounding thirty-five years. Good call from Fairfax.

Chapter Three

GROWING PAINS AND MEA CULPAS (1989–1992)

"We were optimistic. We thought 1989 was going to be a difficult year; it was much worse as you will soon find out." —*Prem Watsa*

Whether the news was bad or good, shareholders were quickly learning that their CEO and chairman would never sugarcoat or bury the bad news.

The opening lines of his 1989 letter, above, expressed Watsa's personal frustration. There were several things taxing the patience of the young executive. At the top of the list was the company's core trucking insurance business. Fairfax had expected softer pricing and lower volumes of new policies to erode performance—that was all part of cautiously riding the insurance cycle. What it had not expected was the trucking insurers deciding to go rogue and almost crash the company.

It was not apparent at first what was happening at Markel Financial. An attempted diversification into the bus, taxi, and rental car businesses was not doing well. And Watsa's small leadership team did not appreciate that the company had failed to adequately pull back on writing unprofitable business—in contradiction to Fairfax's clearly stated strategy of managing down cycles by retrenching, never expanding. "We failed miserably," Watsa told shareholders. But these factors could have been addressed and reversed. There was another, even bigger problem: an ill-fated foray into the world of construction surety that could have proven fatal.

The internal numbers came in steadily worse at the insurer, eventually ballooning to a C$14-million loss and a combined ratio of 133.6 percent when the target was 100 percent. (Insurers are measured by an annual ratio of losses and expenses to revenue premiums written—where 100 percent is breakeven. Above 100 and you're losing money. The further below it you are, the more profitable you are.) Concerned, Watsa put a trusted executive, Rick Salsberg, on the case to get to the bottom of it.

Salsberg, the company's former outside legal counsel at Torys, had been swayed by Watsa to come aboard in a broader capacity that included nonlegal responsibilities. Salsberg was treating it as a fixed one-year sabbatical from his firm to see if he liked it. Watsa persuaded him otherwise. Salsberg ended up staying that year and never left until his passing in 2024.

Salsberg's official position of VP of corporate affairs didn't begin to capture what he did for the company. He was lead on acquisitions, legal counsel, advisor on everything, and a key architect of Fairfax's treasured Guiding Principles. "He could solve any problem—the tougher the better, and we had some tough ones—and always with a sense of humour," offered Watsa at Salsberg's funeral service in 2024. "Hiring Rick was one of the single best decisions I've ever made, not only in business but in my life. He became my most trusted friend, and I never, ever took a significant step without his advice."

So it was Salsberg who got the nod to find out what was going on at Markel Financial. It did not take long to figure it out, he explained: "I went to head office and picked up on the excited office chatter about the booming surety business the company was chasing." Surety was basically a banking function, but the gang there wasn't approaching it with a banking mindset.

Like any line of insurance, surety was easy money—if no one makes any claims. Markel Financial failed to cover itself. "They were insuring builders' projects would get finished, and if not, the insurance company would have to finish them up." An incompetent move in any circumstance, it had the potential to be lethal folly with a downturn in commercial real estate looming. Claims were already starting to come in as builders stumbled and failed. "The liabilities on these surety contracts were around $40 million [Canadian], way more than the full value of the insurance company. A whole lot of them were in really bad shape."

Salsberg spent the first quarter of 1990 finding the fire, putting it out, and then getting a new senior management team in place, something a fair and friendly holding company was loath to do. It was messy but it could have been so much worse, Salsberg recalled. "The company could easily have gone under at that point. It was scary times."

Fairfax would make proper provisions, purchasing reinsurance for the surety operations, which sent the combined ratio to a sky-high 343 percent. "We only ended up needing 25 percent of the reinsurance. But we still had to pay for it," offers Watsa. "For the first year or so, we were pretty nervous. Until the building is built, you can't get out, so you just cross your fingers. Luckily, they turned out to be quality building companies."

Total gross surety losses by the end of 1991: C$21 million. Lesson learned. Crisis averted. Offered Salsberg, "It was frightening, but we managed to do it within the financial capability of the company—and we never had an incident like that again."

DECENTRALIZATION REFINEMENTS

With just a few years under his belt running a company, Watsa was developing his management style: He stepped up, owned the mess, learned from it, made changes, and then shared his education with shareholders. The letter to shareholders was where he would celebrate the company's wins, share kudos for his leaders, as well as explain the company's blunders and how they could be fixed. In this case, Watsa explained in his 1989 letter that the decentralization strategy itself had not failed—Fairfax had failed its strategy.

> We have emphasized in the past that our companies are run independently by our presidents. While the advantages of this approach are many, the downside is that things can happen in any of our companies of which we may not be aware. This happened to us in Markel in 1989. Why did this happen at Markel? Could Fairfax have responded sooner? Do we need to be more centralized, more hands-on in our operations? All good questions. On reflection, I think the major reason for the problem was that while our individual companies were run in a decentralized manner, they were still all reporting to me.

The company quickly put in new reporting lines. Subsidiary companies in the holding company would deliver business plans and corporate updates to specific executives in Fairfax's tiny head office. "This method of operation we feel will make it unlikely that our experience at Markel will be repeated and, if it were necessary, we would be able to react much sooner," wrote Watsa.

Further organizational reporting changes would be made in the future, as the company tried to balance its desire for decentralization and an unbureaucratic small head office against the growing size and complexity of its subsidiaries. It also showed the vulnerability at Fairfax of not having an experienced senior executive with oversight of the insurance operations. That leadership would come much later.

So the explosion out of the gate was followed with some missteps. The first three years had been easy by comparison. Markel Financial would take several years to turn around. Meanwhile, Shand, Morahan was far from firing on all cylinders. Losses had run the combined ratio up to 119 percent, with runoff expenses from past underwriting and the rebuilding of reserves to blame. This asset would be sold in 1990 to Markel Group when the two holding companies dissolved their partnership.

THE SAGA OF MORDEN & HELWIG

Morden & Helwig, the claims manager, was doing well in Canada but its push into the U.K. and the U.S. was challenging and unprofitable. It would get the close scrutiny from head office that Markel Financial had lacked in the late 1980s, but it proved stubbornly difficult to turn around.

Watsa labelled Morden & Helwig's 1989 performance a "disappointment." The following year, after Lindsey & Newson was consolidated into M&H, he wrote, "We continue to expect improved profitability from the U.S. operations." Close readers of the letter by now would understand that Watsa was a relentless cheerleader and it was a big deal if he voiced his expectations like this. The language was as stern as his demeanour would allow.

The frustration was elevated when these assets underperformed the next year as well. "This is not acceptable to management and they are focused on turning this around in 1992," Watsa pledged to shareholders.

When still no progress was made, more help was dispatched south where expansion had proven a disaster. Watsa kept his faith in a future return to profits but reminded shareholders, "To date, I have been wrong!"

This asset would prove to be an ongoing headache, except for a few years in the late 1990s when cash flows were improved with oversight from Francis Chou (him again). Whatever restructuring, added assets, rotating management, and name changes (to Lindsey Morden and then to Cunningham Lindsey) were thrown at it, it would remain a frustration.

Yet, while grand ambitions for a global claims business were being set aside, much larger successes with core commercial lines of insurance and reinsurance would soon eclipse those struggles. Eventually, in 2004, Watsa had dropped the once-hopeful claims adjusting section from his letter entirely, and in 2007 he announced Fairfax "came to terms with our unsuccessful stewardship" of the company.

It's instructive to look at losses from an asset allocation perspective. Value investors want to buy cash flow at a discount. But cheap acquisitions can also become black holes. Fairfax poured a lot of money into the claims company, investing in it at $20 a share when the business looked like it had turned the corner. Then again at $8 after it stumbled again. In 1994, it sold the U.K. operations, and Fairfax put more money in as a show of "long-term" faith in future profits. "You didn't expect the long term to be so long, did you?" he mused to shareholders, sharing their pain. "We didn't either!"

In selling a controlling stake in Cunningham Lindsey in 2007, Fairfax had to privatize it by buying up stock at $3.25 that it had taken public in 1987 at $10. Any CEO would chalk it up as an embarrassing loss, but this value CEO used the moment to instruct investors on allocation opportunity cost, especially when you use your stock on acquisitions. Typical Prem, he weathered the sting with a wince tempered by a wink: "To really rub salt into the wound, some of you long-term shareholders will remember that we purchased Cunningham Lindsey in 1986 for $2 million [Canadian] and 578,000 shares of Fairfax." Those investors would have been richer by about $180 million had they kept the stock—and that doesn't include twenty years of compounding. Unfortunately, Fairfax still wasn't free and clear in the end: It was still a holder of some of the firm's equity and debt. Some experiments just didn't pan out, and there were several more.

THE GORY DETAILS FROM FCA

Similarly, Fairfax's investment in FCA International Ltd. taught it an effective lesson. Fairfax paid C$22.5 million to gain control of the second-largest credit collection agency in North America in 1989. In that deal, the founder, who had an excellent record running the firm up until the recent few years, wanted out. Watsa, of course, had a soft spot for motivated sellers.

As a passive investment at Fairfax rather than as a held operating company, FCA escaped the full scrutiny of Lindsey/Morden, but its spotty nine-year record was there in the annual report if investors wanted to track it before Fairfax dumped it at about breakeven. Typical Prem, once again blaming no one but himself, said almost a decade later: "I would rather not comment on one of my major mistakes in the past decade, but as full disclosure is one of our objectives, here are the gory details," he told shareholders, before explaining how directing the money into Coca-Cola shares instead of buying FCA in 1989 would have grown into an investment of a quarter billion dollars. Instead, the C$22.5 million investment was still worth C$22.5 million. "Another great investment by your chairman!"

LOVE AND HATE—AND WALWYN

Let's stick with the losers for a bit longer. Another lower-cost but higher-profile diversification would play out in investment banking, but within a more compressed time frame. Much like Fairfax's investment in BlackBerry many years later, the purchase and sale of Walwyn attracted unwanted media coverage like vultures to carrion. "To our surprise," Watsa would quip, "this purchase really took the press's fancy and Fairfax made the headlines more than once!!!" Translation: Please leave us alone!

"It's funny," observed David Rooney, who served a very short stint as the company's only CEO not named Prem Watsa in the Fairfax head office structure in the late 1980s. "Nobody was interested when we bought an insurance company in Chicago earlier this year for $77 million." It would not be the first time investors paid disproportionate attention to the minor dramas in Fairfax's Canadian backyard, even as they ignored the enormous success the company was enjoying elsewhere in and outside the country.

Paul Fink, one of the several former Confederation Life staff who came on board with HWIC and Fairfax in the early days, got wind in late 1988 that Financial Trustco was looking to shop its 37 percent controlling interest in Walwyn Inc., a blue-chip Bay Street brokerage. Fairfax snapped it up for C$13.4 million, in partnership with Confederation and veteran banker Tony Arrell (who would take on the CEO role) as partners.

The price was cheap, cut down by the Black Monday sell-off that had scared investors into sticking their money under the mattress. Watsa, always looking for growth vehicles, mused that Walwyn could prove to be a launch pad for more acquisitions in the brokerage business, but it would sour more quickly than a glass of milk in the hot sun.

Fairfax tapped Fink to snap up more venture capital assets as a one-man investment banking unit called Fairbridge. Seeing opportunities in every direction, Watsa also set up a real estate banker in the mix. You never know where you will get traction—or trip up. In 1988 and 1989, there was talk of traction.

"We believe that over the long term Walwyn will be an excellent investment for Fairfax," Watsa told investors. A year later, doubts emerged, but with good humour, he voiced his muted confidence in the venture. "We expected to lose money in our first year," he wrote to shareholders. "We were not disappointed!"

Abruptly the following year, it was already time to cut their losses entirely. "We are no longer in the high-profile stock brokerage business," declared Watsa. "This is the last time you will read this section in our reports—and I'm sure you are very happy! (I am!)"

Unlike with other assets, he showed zero patience for waiting for this investment to pay off. He was not too wowed by the business opportunity as a diversification. And he especially disdained the personal limelight and general gossip about Bay Street personalities. In less than two years, Walwyn merged with Midland Doherty with help from Mackenzie

Financial. That triggered the exit of Tony Arrell, Watsa's value-minded choice as leader and the same guy who had lured Watsa to Gardiner. Fairfax, suddenly eager to make its own exit, found a buyer for its stake in Watsa's former employer Confederation Life.

"Our venture into the stock brokerage business cost our shareholders $3.5 million [Canadian] plus the opportunity cost on this capital for two years. It is highly likely (and personally very much appreciated) that you will not see your Chairman's name in the local newspapers soon!" He would later raise the total estimated hit to C$18 million.

The investments by the banking team were also a source of regret: "We said in last year's report that Paul Fink was not planning any further investments until the current ones mature. And did they mature!" Faced with writedowns, he made sure the blame lay with him and with market sentiment (investors weren't stampeding back into equities after the 1987 crash) rather than with his colleagues' investment prowess: "You can be sure we will never get into a venture capital investment again. Unfortunately, it was a costly lesson—we prefer to learn from the mistakes of others." Beating his critics to the punch, he added, "The investment banking losses were mainly due to your Chairman's bright ideas! Like Warren Buffett, we have found that when good management tackles an industry with poor prospects, it is the industry's reputation that remains intact."

SMART BUYS FOR THE LONG TERM

For Watsa and his small leadership team, the constant testing of different sectors and lines of insurance, such as claims and collections, was all part of an imperative to grow the core commercial insurance business beyond trucking. They soon found some great buys where other U.S. firms were getting out of Canada.

Federated Insurance Holdings of Canada, which wrote property and casualty premiums with farming and other commercial accounts, was a smart buy in late 1989. Despite the fact they didn't actually have the budget, Salsberg and Watsa flew down to Federated's parent office in Minneapolis to talk with the chairman, Chuck Buxton, who had grown tired of running the Canadian assets. (Buxton was known to be quite vocal in his distaste for having to translate all his financial statements into French for Canadian regulators.)

They chatted. Salsberg and Watsa liked what they learned. At nine in the morning, the Fairfax duo sat on one side of the boardroom table with at least ten guys facing them on the other. Salsberg whispered to Watsa that they should thin the crowd to keep it simple. They managed to reduce the crowd to the two of them plus Buxton and his president. The dialogue was decidedly more *Fargo* than *Barbarians at the Gate*. After the crowd had thinned, Buxton, not one for long-winded speeches, broke the silence something like this:

Chuck: "Well, what are you guys going to pay us?"

Prem: "Twenty-eight million."

Chuck: "Okay."

Prem: "The only problem is we don't have the money."

(Chuck stares blankly.)
(Prem smiles with characteristic definitiveness of purpose.)

Chuck: "And how much *do* you have?"

Prem: "We only have eight. But we have an idea."

Chuck: "I'm not into high finance, but I'm sure we can arrange something."

Salsberg wrote up a formal letter of intent. In the early days, that is often all it took. Fairfax was set on never backing away from terms, even without a formal offer. And so it would offer a letter and call it binding, with the formal agreement to follow. If a deal hit a snag after that, Salsberg said Fairfax's typical counter would be "Okay, you have our offer. We're afraid that if you're not sure, we will just find the door." Fair and friendly did not mean loosey and goosey. But when the deal is done, fair and friendly means it was done—Fairfax is enormously proud of the fact it has never walked away from a deal or altered its agreed-to terms.

Two hours after they started, they had a deal. Buxton went off to play a round of golf, while his president signed off on the details. The offer called for just C$8 million in cash, for Fairfax's benefit, plus two C$10-million notes, which Fairfax could pay out of future cash flows. One of the reasons the talks went so well was culture. The companies were a good fit. Watsa lauded Federated's family approach: Salespeople sold to consumers in their homes, direct without brokers. Negotiations were fair, friendly, and furiously fast. Federated, based in Winnipeg, remains a key asset for Fairfax thirty-five years later.

The Salsberg-Watsa negotiating style was working. "We got it all done on one trip," recalls Watsa. And he was already paying attention to another target out on the West Coast in Vancouver, Commonwealth Insurance. Commonwealth's ultimate owner, a troubled New York–based owner of financial assets called AmBase Corporation, was caught up in the savings and loan crisis. It was looking to shop its U.S. subsidiary Home Insurance Company, which held Commonwealth directly.

The seller's eagerness to do a deal gave Watsa hope. And the asset's stability, in both its finances and leadership, whet his appetite even more. Channelling his inner Buffett, he had rebuffed an earlier phone call from a First Boston banker who was fishing for bidders on Commonwealth, responding, "We don't do auctions, but if you're ever ready to sell it to us, we'll talk." The next call from First Boston came with a direct offer and a bargain-rate price tag.

In future years, Watsa might have looked for a way to gobble up both Commonwealth and its parent Home Insurance at the same time. But his eyes were not that big yet—and let's remember he still did not even have the money to buy Federated. The only question here was if he and Rick could find a way to buy Commonwealth. One thought was to work with Markel Group again as a partner. That thought led to a discussion and another, even bigger thought.

FAIRFAX AND MARKEL GROUP GO SEPARATE WAYS

Watsa wanted Commonwealth. His American partners at Markel Group did not. All of a sudden, he and Steven Markel had a big decision to make. The two entrepreneurs had a lot of history together. The question now was do they keep things the same, get even closer, or split. Commonwealth would prove to be the flashpoint.

The Markel family's original plan in selling to Watsa was to get out of Canada. But that plan had been waylaid by the fact that the two founders were having so much fun building new cross-border ventures together. Complicating things, Markel Group still owned 20 percent of Fairfax, and Watsa considered Steven a co-founder and partner.

Bottom line, each wanted to be a builder, but it's hard to meld a vision on culture, never mind decisions on capital allocation. And both those issues would have become a taller challenge because the pace of acquisitions was accelerating. The biggest single barrier to sustaining the partnership was the Markels' embrace of a formal, centralized approach to management. Watsa says there was realistically only one way to go with the two firms: "We decided to disentangle them completely so that each of us would have greater freedom to pursue our growth." Watsa wanted to see his company grow under one corporate culture. While the two companies shared many attributes, Fairfax's decentralized culture stood apart.

The two dealmakers sat down and did their best to come up with a fair and friendly breakup that would also allow Watsa to pounce on the Commonwealth opportunity. The Markels wanted Shand, Morahan and paid $45 million, plus its 1.6 million shares in Fairfax, and handed over its interest in the Morden & Helwig claims business. Fairfax took the cash and bought Commonwealth for C$57.5 million, about C$10 million under book value. For now, Fairfax was essentially a Canadian company built from the castaway pieces that U.S. insurance companies no longer wanted.

"It changed the game for both of us," says Watsa. "Shand, Morahan was a great success for Markel. Commonwealth was a great success for us. Steven and I remained on each other's boards until 1998, when our purchase of Crum & Forster put us in direct competition with them in the United States."

Markel Group, which had been farming out asset management to Fairfax's HWIC, got itself a building block that would transform itself into a successful mini-Berkshire with its own internal strength in investing. The two companies have had similar long-term success, even evolving to a somewhat similar structure today with multiple strong engines of growth from the insurers, fixed income and equity investments, and a venture engine of diverse long-term investments.

Markel's history is an interesting parallel to Fairfax's. The company, family-owned and founded in 1930 as Markel Corporation, always had a focus on trucking insurance before going public in the 1980s and diversifying in the 1990s. Its shares first traded just months after Fairfax's debut at a price of $8.33 a share on the Nasdaq and the company changed its name to Markel Group in 2023. It closed out 2024 at $1,726. Markel Group's frank and quirky letters to shareholders are also popular reading for the well-rounded value investor.

LEARNING TO MANAGE VOLATILITY

Some real negatives had obviously piled up for Fairfax in the early 1990s. Not only was the insurance industry in the fifth gruelling year of a soft market on pricing but also financial markets were not great, with serious underperformance in value stocks. Markel Financial would take several years to fix in Canada after hitting its surety pothole. Strong investment gains usually stepped up to offset the losses on operations, but lately much of that strength was in one-off gains stemming from the sale of assets to Markel Group in the co-founders' split. That windfall was masking some real problems.

The year 1990 proved to be a major stumble. Watsa was looking further down the road to better times, while investors were getting nervous. Fairfax managed to record a profit of C$23.1 million, but the entire gain was attributable to the sale of assets to Markel in the U.S. For shareholders measuring their return over a one-year period, 1990 was the first year they took a serious bath. The stock retreated more than 40 percent. The only mention of that tumble in Watsa's letter was the fact that Fairfax found its share price so cheap, it bought back 25 percent of the outstanding shares. The stock had been down 60 percent at one point, as investors fretted over the earnings stumble in the trucking insurance business. In future years, Watsa would feel compelled to remind investors to be rational and relax, because things go up and they go down in the short term.

Rattled nerves were largely calmed by the stock's near-double bounce back the following year. But doubts were settling in and the media had questions. Unaccustomed to being on the back foot, Fairfax schooled the media a bit on its obsession with short-term stock swings. Watsa took a moment to share for the record his thinking—and irritation—in the following year's letter. If Fairfax was going to think long term and ignore volatility, it figured shareholders should do the same:

> A word about our press and/or investor relations department. We have none. We believe in making full disclosure through our annual report, our annual meeting, our interim financial statements and, when appropriate, periodic announcements. Further public comment is rarely necessary or constructive. We believe that Fairfax and each company within the group should be judged by its long-term results and not by "good" or "bad" press. That is why we regularly have a "no comment" for the press.

In 1992, the insurance side again racked up deep losses, and with the one-time offsets drying up, investments were also a disappointment. "The inevitable happened. For the first time since we began in 1985, we did not earn a return on equity in excess of 20 percent," wrote Watsa. He had repeatedly acknowledged it was a high bar, but one they were not prepared to abandon. Investors might do better, he suggested, to look for an average return of more than 20 percent if measured over a five-year period, not year to year.

For all the challenges, Watsa was far less concerned about suffering a few off years than about building the company's future cash flow, earnings, and book value. Fairfax would exit this period in the early 1990s as a different company. It had suffered on some failed diversifications but had also added some healthy insurance assets for the long term, at great prices no less. Federated and Commonwealth quickly emerged as gems.

The stock had become more volatile, but investors who could handle the volatility were reaping the rewards. From 1985 into the early 1990s, the stock compounded at a Berkshire-level annual rate of 37 percent. The company had become one to watch.

Watsa stressed that investors should fixate less on the top line or earnings per share and instead pay more attention to book value. "We expect to encounter as many problems in the future as in the past—and perhaps more—but we hope to continue to compound book value per share at rates in excess of 20 percent over the long term," wrote Watsa, who maintained the future was bright, if sure to be a little lumpy.

"It continues to be as uncertain and unpredictable as it always was. However, with good people and good fortune, we continue to labour towards our long-term objective of earnings in excess of 20 percent on shareholders' equity by running Fairfax and its subsidiaries for the long-term benefit of customers, employees and shareholders."

Perhaps getting the sense that Commonwealth and Federated would generate some actual underwriting profits in the year ahead, Fairfax leadership formalized a plan to start sharing the wealth. Starting with a target of 1 percent of annual pre-tax operating income, Fairfax shared $200,000 with a variety of Canadian charities in 1991 and would grow that percentage and total substantially over the years.

In 1992, Fairfax made a few significant changes to its corporate structure. One, the company purchased HWIC outright. The investment company had been winding down its pension fund managing outside Fairfax, and moving it fully under the Fairfax roof simplified the holdings and freed up resources to focus on investing the float and capitalizing the insurers.

Two, Fairfax also purchased 49.9 percent of the Sixty Two Investment Company, the initial investment group that refinanced Markel Financial. Essentially, Fairfax was buying out Watsa's initial partners and retiring some of those shares like a buyback. That class of stock was not traded and Fairfax paid out the investors at a liquidity discount of 15 percent.

Reflecting on what those investors had made possible for the company, Watsa was humbled: "Looking back, these investors must have been special to have financed an almost bankrupt insurance holding company led by a chairman with no corporate experience at all. There may, after all, be some truth in the definition of an entrepreneur—'Unreasonable conviction based on inadequate evidence'!"

Chapter Four

THE GO-GO YEARS (1993–1998)

"WOW! What a year! In many ways, 1993 was the best year we have had since we began in September 1985." —Prem Watsa

Time to start shopping again—if only Fairfax could find something to buy. It had been several years since the company had done a big deal. It had been paying down debt, which freed up more cash. All they needed to do was find something they wanted to buy. "While we have examined many situations," Watsa noted in 1993, "nothing has come of them." Things were about to change.

When Fairfax opened its wallet, the Street got excited. It meant stock and bond offerings to fund the deals, which was good for business if you were an investment bank. It was also good business for the portfolio managers and brokers buying and selling stock. At this point, the Street was not caught up in the Fairfax story. That, too, was about to change. And the stock's leap of 145 percent in 1993 was a signal that investor interest was picking up in a big way.

When the opportunities began to fall into place, Fairfax kicked off a spending spree that made the company over several times, all while making it a market darling on Toronto's Bay Street. The deals fuelled growth, and bullishness drove the shares to higher highs. Analysts fell over one another in a scramble to boost stock price targets and investors climbed on the bandwagon.

The coming deals in the mid- to late 1990s would boost the size of Fairfax's home Canadian base, but the most dramatic expansion took place in its neighbouring market to the south. Quickly, the U.S. became by far Fairfax's largest base of operations. The company also gained an early global foothold in reinsurance. This pattern of growth spurts would repeat itself in waves over the decade: If you turned away from Fairfax Financial for a few years, you would not recognize it when you looked back again.

Watsa had always made a habit of not courting a public profile. In these days, the company still did not do a quarterly call. Watsa was no recluse, being active with charities and church, but to the media whom he regularly turned down for interviews, he developed that reputation. The business press wanted to know more about the company behind the growth juggernaut. And the mysterious Mr. Watsa became well known for his hot investing hand and bold macro calls. "It was never my motivation to become a hot name on Bay Street," he relates today, disinterested as always in the bright lights of media attention. "I would rather build a business."

The acquisitions rolled out in three major waves, totalling seven large companies in a six-year period. A few of them would turn out to be gems. A few of them were dogs. But even the dogs contributed some valuable assets that remain a large part of the Fairfax story today. Welcome to the go-go years.

WAVE ONE: RANGER AND LOMBARD (CONTINENTAL CANADA)

"I'd say Prem's first significant failure was Ranger." —Andy Barnard

For such a transformational run, Watsa et al. could not have made a bigger blunder as their first step. The Ranger Insurance Company deal represented a lot of firsts for Fairfax: their first solo deal to buy a U.S. asset; the first deal that included a debt underwriting; and the first stock offering in years. It was also the company's biggest purchase to date.

Hindsight tells us otherwise but in real time it looked like a great buy, largely based on Fairfax's success to date in integrating new assets. It was building its network in insurance, and in yet another first, this was the initial deal for its due diligence team of internal experts. Fairfax felt confident in its purchase.

The Houston-based niche energy sector insurer wrote premiums for propane distribution, oil and gas, trucking, and agriculture. True to its policy of being patient and then pouncing on opportunities,

Fairfax's small team scrambled quickly to do two related financings to get the deal done. Watsa praised the nimbleness of his group. "We had barely heard of Ranger prior to October 1993; we had no plans to issue any shares and would have salivated if told about a public debenture issue."

Operations at Ranger were mildly unprofitable but projected to quickly hit breakeven. At $125 million, the price tag was considered a reasonable premium to book value of $105 million. The purchase was enhanced with protection in the form of contingent notes. "Fair price, like beauty, lies in the eyes of the beholder," offered Watsa, reminding shareholders that Fairfax's competitors had not exactly jumped at this opportunity and there was a chance his team might not be seeing straight. "In insurance there is always the possibility that something from the past can come to haunt you." Kudos to any investor who took out a highlighter and ran it over those words.

To fund it, the company issued two million shares at C$55 each. That almost covered the tab, but Fairfax also tapped U.S. investor demand for an additional $100-million ten-year debenture. The company was fast becoming a favourite for investment bankers. The additional cash was used to retire bank debt, pay off the final cost of buying the Federated assets, and contribute another $75 million to cash on hand.

Ranger wasted no time in messing up. Commonwealth and Federated were looking great, while Ranger had a combined ratio of 114 percent in its first year. The next year, 1995, it had a "gruelling" year, with a growing hit from past under-reserving and a ratio of 118 percent. "This was very disappointing to us and you have every right to question our judgment—again!!" Watsa told shareholders in his 1995 letter, owning the flak. One could never accuse Watsa of hiding the company's mistakes. "We continue to report to you, once a year, the pluses and minuses about our company. We do this so that you can get a balanced view of our results but also to keep ourselves honest. Managements that fool their shareholders tend to fool themselves. Every year we work on improving your understanding of our company and we will always be receptive to ideas you may have about further disclosure."

At Ranger, Pete Wallner was swapped in to pick up from the struggling Tom Friedberg as CEO and Watsa expressed his optimism that the company was turning the corner: "We think we have licked the reserving problem and perhaps gone too far. We'll know by next year."

"I hope I don't have to eat humble pie again!"

The next year's letter explained how that call worked out: "I was wrong, again, on Ranger in 1996. The key is *I* and not Pete Wallner and his management team. The problem of the past continued to haunt Peter and Ranger with a combined ratio of 123.5%."

Wallner had been able to improve operations a bit but additional reserving and discontinued business lines put him further behind. This was the proverbial long-tail risk of buying insurers that had blown their futures trying to pay for bad premiums written in the past. It was, as feared, coming back to haunt them.

Underwriting losses hit $85.5 million in two years. Watsa could only hope that Ranger, now with another new CEO, could put its past behind it and would not require more reserves to meet past claims. The eternal optimist, he hoped for the best but his conviction was on shaky ground by now: "I hope I don't have to eat humble pie again!"

He didn't—until the following year, 1997. Ranger ran at a loss of 112 percent, but its continuing business ran at 100.5 percent, almost break-even. Net income was $10 million. Hope was renewed, but it was more like Lucy, the football, and Charlie Brown. Watsa took another kick for three points himself: "We feel comfortable that Ranger's combined ratio in 1998 will be in the 100% area."

Missed it and not by a little. Ranger delivered a combined ratio of 146 percent the next year. Fairfax had lost patience. Looking back, Watsa suspects that with today's depth of talent and experience, Fairfax might have turned things around, but at the time the company just did not have access to top talent in their new American market. It also did not have an Andy Barnard on board yet.

The CEO moved on to another Fairfax company and yet another leader was installed, with the same result. In 1998, Watsa lamented that Ranger delivered "the worst results of any company under our stewardship over the past 13 years!" Watsa put his forecasts on hold and announced the firm would need to be aggressively downsized: "Ranger has been a problem child for us for five years now—it shows you that in spite of good intentions, insurance can be a very tough business!" What made that child such a problem was a mix of bad premium writing in the past, poor management over a long stretch, and, in the present, a terrible market with soft pricing. As Watsa would lament years later: "We thought the soft market wouldn't go down further. We thought we had the right guy in charge and we went through hell. In this business, operating management has to watch over every single exposure, be fanatic about the details or else you're in real trouble."

Big as it was, Ranger could not hold back the bigger story, which was one of accelerating strength. Ranger was super frustrating but it was a sideshow. As any of the dyed-in-the-wool value masters will say, don't let your losers slow you down; you only need a few big winners to outperform.

Swallowing a whale

Fairfax would tap its same internal due diligence team to dig into the finances of Continental Insurance's Canadian operations, this time with a much-improved result. As in past acquisitions of the Canadian assets of U.S. or global insurers, the decision on any sale would be made at head office—in this case, New York. But Watsa started off his own due diligence by reaching out to the subsidiary's CEO, Byron Messier, directly. He was always aware of the value of management, and Ranger had reminded him to think people first.

Messier would be key because if Watsa was successful in getting Continental Canada, he wanted to keep the firm intact with strong leadership. The two leaders found themselves in sync but only after getting past one big concern on Messier's part. "Byron thought they were too big for us," says Watsa.

Messier had just returned to Continental Canada, where he had two decades of previous experience, and had a strategy in place to quickly boost performance. He strongly suspected Fairfax was overreaching. In Canada, Commonwealth and Federated wrote combined net premiums of about C$150 million. Continental Canada wrote about C$400 million in commercial lines by itself, suggesting this could be a small fish swallowing a whale.

Watsa did that thing he does and won Messier over, telling him he could run the show, decentralized, as long as he got the combined ratio to 100 percent or less. Salsberg and Watsa made another trip to New York for another classic Fairfax fair-and-friendly-but-take-it-or-leave-it offer with no competitive bids and an end-of-day deadline. An element of heightened tension was that the parent company was itself on the block and a new buyer might choose to hold on to the Canadian subsidiary.

CEO Jake Mascotte, a motivated seller, handed the file off to a vice-president, who worked out a price with Watsa and Salsberg by early afternoon. Mascotte sent him back to get a better deal. He also suggested they all pick up on discussions the following week, which prompted Watsa's fair and friendly but hardline reply: "We won't be here next week."

Mascotte's side, intent on getting a sweetener, countered with an ask for an additional C$10 million contingent on Fairfax getting the Canadian asset to average a 100 percent ratio over the coming five years. Salsberg and Watsa figured there was a good chance that condition would not be met. Besides, if it were met, they'd be happy to share the wealth. Mascotte and his CFO tweaked the letter of intent and signed it before dinner.

Then the lawyers got involved, indignant that management had signed an offer without their input. A few weeks later, the deal was done for C$155 million, about C$8 million below book value and eclipsing Ranger as Fairfax's largest deal to date. A headline from *Insurance Media Watch*, a trade journal, echoed Messier's initial assessment: "Small fry Fairfax to buy big fish Continental."

Only days later, the whole U.S. company was sold to CNA Insurance. "The first thing they did was use every trick in the book to try to break our agreement," recalls Watsa. "They wanted to keep Canada, but it was too late."

In the future, these two deals would become archetypes for the kinds of deals that Fairfax either wished to replicate—or avoid repeating at all costs. Continental Canada, renamed Lombard Insurance, was well on its way to covering Fairfax's acquisition cost, turning a net profit of C$101 million in its first two years. Lombard would become one of the prized assets in the Canadian portfolio of insurers.

Ranger, meanwhile, would become a code word for what happens when best intentions go horribly wrong. In the future, Watsa would talk about the prospective fate of new acquisitions and quip, "I hope this is another Lombard and not another Ranger."

Bigger deals, bigger impact

The earlier acquisitions brought Fairfax the initial foundation of core Canadian operating companies—Markel Financial, Federated, and Commonwealth. In 1993, the company booked C$5.3 million in insurance underwriting profits and total earnings after tax of C$8.9 million. Net premiums were C$164 million.

Then the numbers exploded. Once Ranger and Lombard were absorbed, the company-wide number rocketed more than fivefold to C$850 million. The deals were getting a lot bigger. Fairfax was getting a lot bigger. And it was happening quickly.

Here is a snapshot of key metrics showing the burgeoning size of Fairfax and how much the two major purchases expanded it in just fifteen months.

The Ranger and Lombard Impact (at Dec. 31 1994)		
Fairfax total	**C$ million**	**Increase**
Net premiums written	850*	5.2 times
Investment portfolio	1,551	3.8 times
Shareholders' equity	392	2.4 times

* Includes annualized net premiums from Lombard, acquired November 30, 1994.

Source: Company annual report

To buy Lombard, Fairfax issued another million shares, this time at C$76 a share, diluting the total outstanding to nine million, up 50 percent from 1993. Long-term debt also soared, from C$72 million to C$225 million. For Fairfax, growth was important, but how it grew was a crucial consideration from an asset allocation standpoint, especially as the price tags grew.

"We should note here," Watsa told shareholders, "that we are careful about issuing shares. We shun companies which make acquisitions at twice book value and finance them by issuing their own shares at a discount to book value. If our shares were not selling at fair prices, we would not have issued them and thus, would not have purchased Continental Canada. You will remember, we have never been interested in becoming bigger—only in earning attractive long-term returns on shareholders' capital by treating customers, employees and shareholders fairly."

The ideal value tactic here was to issue shares at a multiple of book value, then turn around and make acquisitions at a discount to book value. From this perspective, before Fairfax learned that it had some very expensive long-tail reserve problems, the Ranger acquisition strategy looked brilliant. Thinking like value investors do, Fairfax also knew it had increased its shares outstanding by 1.5 times, but yielded a boost to net premiums of 5.2 times and a gain of 3.8 times to its total investment portfolio. It looked set to be a big winner—as long as it did not have all kinds of long-tail liabilities that would suck away earnings for years. Oops.

The growth trajectory certainly got the attention of Bay Street by the mid-1990s, with broad participation of the big brokerages on the share offerings, noted Watsa. Having brokerage sales teams talking up your stock gets your stock talked about, not that Fairfax was either courting new shareholders or fond of paying the underwriting fees. "We thank them for an excellent job," wrote Watsa. "After not issuing shares for seven years ending in 1993, we have raised almost C$500 million from share issues in the past three years. No wonder the investment dealer industry is doing well!"

Raising money from share offerings was funding the binge, but Watsa felt compelled to caution shareholders and bankers alike that the company would not be shopping so much with freshly issued stock that diluted the company's per-share book value: "[We] request them not to extrapolate this recent frenetic activity in their future plans!"

In reality, the actual frenetic activity was only getting started in earnest. After the Ranger purchase, Rossa O'Reilly, stock analyst at CIBC World Markets, captured the enthusiasm that would run up and down Bay Street for most of the decade, saying it "should be an excellent fit for Fairfax, doubling its size and rendering it capable of writing insurance through the U.S."

Analysts were baffled with the valuation challenges inherent in assigning stock target prices and tracking Fairfax's quarterly performance. They were accustomed to tracking top line (revenue) and bottom line (earnings per share). But both of those measures were awfully lumpy by nature at Fairfax, so analysts would regularly be way off on quarterly earnings estimates. They also learned to emphasize Fairfax's preferred measure of long-term growth in book value per share, but investors tended to be more short-term focused. A more Pavlovian response prevailed—the more companies Fairfax bought, the more investors got excited and the higher they bid the stock price.

WAVE TWO: ODYSSEY (SKANDIA AMERICA), CTR, AND SPHERE

> *"Prior to buying Skandia America, Prem had bought out-of-favour companies that had lost a lot of money from soft markets and that no one wanted to be involved with. He definitely specialized early on in buying things from the bargain bin, with companies that had highly motivated sellers." —Andy Barnard*

In the next storm wave of activity, several new assets came into the mix. Amidst the flurry of moves, one particular asset emerged as something special—OdysseyRe, as Skandia America Reinsurance would be renamed. It was a big buy in itself, giving Fairfax a growing U.S. profile. But it also delivered a dramatically larger presence in reinsurance, including a launch pad to the global market.

The Skandia/Odyssey[1] deal stood out for other reasons as well. The Lombard deal had come off clean, with management intact just the way Fairfax liked to operate. This latest deal was anything but

[1] Reference to Odyssey refers to OdysseyRe (Odyssey Reinsurance Company), which later became Odyssey Group.

straightforward. First off, Skandia America brought a lot of bad-brand mojo baggage: The company had been slipping down the ranks. A rebrand would clear the way to a new start but not before the company also received a makeover in assets and management.

It would also need to integrate a lot of outside pieces. In the aftermath of a few more quick transactions—you might call it a roll-up—Odyssey emerged more like an insurance-industry Frankenstein's monster, stitched together with parts from other purchases. At its core, the assets were strong—it was just a messy bit of meatball surgery. As part of the mix, it needed a new heart in the form of culture.

Odyssey's sliding performance gave Fairfax what it loved—a bargain price tag from a motivated seller. In May 1996, the deal settled for $228 million in cash, or two-thirds of book value, with another contingency note to cover Fairfax for reserves surprises. Odyssey arrived under the Fairfax umbrella with $200 million in annual premiums and an investment portfolio of $1.1 billion. Ranger and Lombard had had a dramatic impact, and now by some measures, Odyssey was doubling Fairfax all over again.

Fairfax had some stumbles putting the pieces and people together, but this story, unlike Ranger, has a happy ending. Odyssey would soon emerge as, in Watsa's words, Fairfax's "crown jewel." At least as important, the deal ended up bringing in the missing piece of the company's management lineup—a brilliant insurance operator and strategist named Andy Barnard.

Barnard would be the one to build Odyssey into that crown jewel, and later he became the architect of Fairfax's reinsurance business. In 2011, Fairfax welcomed him as its first global insurance leader in the holding company's tiny management team, which was well represented by investment people but not insurance.

Back in 1996, Barnard was impressed with Watsa's pitch. But he was number two at Transatlantic, a strong reinsurance player based in New York, and he wanted nothing to do with running Skandia America for Fairfax. One glaring problem was the fact that he knew the company far too well: "I was well aware of how the company was mismanaged and had become a forgotten soul in the industry. I was working at a very powerful company that was on an upward trajectory and I was already in a top role. Did I want to go to a broken-down, disrespected shipwreck that needed a lot of work?"

As Salsberg recalled, "Andy quite rightly thought this was a joke. In the end, he and Prem connected and the fact that it was a tall challenge actually convinced him to come."

Watsa's powers of persuasion

Salsberg himself had fallen under Prem's spell. He had seen how Watsa had an uncanny way of making his enthusiasm contagious. It was a matter of setting clear, ambitious goals and showing faith in others to get there together by being the best versions of themselves. He does it with kindness, never intimidation.

Barnard and Salsberg were Watsa's two most important hires. When Salsberg started working with Watsa as outside legal counsel, he saw things coming together at Fairfax and appreciated he was valued and could play a major role. But he'd only signed on for a year as a kind of sabbatical from his firm. Watsa wooed him by framing it as a new challenge. Recalled Salsberg, "I told him, 'No.' I knew what I was doing at Torys. I might have too much to do but I know what I'm doing. I didn't know what I'd be doing at Fairfax."

Watsa just did that thing he does: He looks into your eyes and says, "Come work with me. We need you." It worked with Salsberg, who'd had months to test drive Watsa as a boss. "I wouldn't start to get a deeper understanding of his vision and skill set until later, but it was always wonderful because he always made everything so easy," said Salsberg. From the moment Watsa had walked into his office at Torys, Salsberg saw things he hadn't seen in other clients. He wasn't a volatile screamer for one. "He never used bad language; he never got angry. His mind works all the time and things are always positive. He would just say, 'How do we do this? Let's think it through and find the best way.' It was fun doing the work."

For Barnard, the wooing took three months before it paid off. The two had no history to draw on. As the deal was coming together, Watsa asked around for names, and he particularly liked what he had heard from Paul Ingrey, a legend in the reinsurance business. Ingrey offered up three names as the best to chase: Andy Barnard, Mike Wacek, and Jim Migliorini. In time, Watsa would get all three, but Barnard was top priority.

Three dinners into the courtship, the story goes, Barnard took a ride back to the Toronto airport from Watsa's driver Mason Hoxha, who shared some blunt feedback to get off the fence and take the offer: "What's wrong with you? This is a very good company. This is the best job you'll ever have." Barnard confirms the exchange but downplays it as a "minor factor" in his decision. The major factors? One was Watsa's approach to decentralization. Another and perhaps the biggest was the size of the ambition and the understanding he would get the right support. "At the end of the day," says Barnard, "it was the challenge of the turnaround and the fact I was not going to get a crack at the CEO job at my current company any time soon. It was a risk I wanted to take, but I was comfortable that I was going to be given a lot of leeway to develop the company with my own vision."

In a series of dinners and discussions, the two discovered they had a lot in common on ambition, how to build companies, and how to treat people. "I knew he was opportunistic and that he gave his CEOs a lot of latitude in building their own companies, which was really attractive," Barnard recalls. "It was clear he was contrarian. I was aware of his previous deals, many of which were really shrewd. And I also remember a lot of conversations about how to handle adversity and losing money. You know, 'Are you going to do a knee-jerk and flee the business when you run into trouble, or can you manage your way out and focus on the long term? And what is the best way to get the most out of people?' His philosophy was very much in sync with my own." Barnard signed up for an unusually long ten-year arrangement and never left.

In his letters to shareholders, Watsa habitually states that hiring Andy Barnard was the single best decision he ever made. Extensive interviews with Fairfax leaders make it obvious they find it impossible to imagine Fairfax being what it is today without Rick Salsberg and Andy Barnard.

Odyssey itself is a bit of a microcosm of Fairfax, in how it was assembled and integrated and then built up in a decentralized manner. Richard Sauer, author of *Selling America Short: The SEC and Market Contrarians in the Age of Absurdity*, once described Fairfax as "the final foster home for companies no one else would take." Barnard's ultimate achievement was to turn Odyssey and the rest of them into one big family.

Backstory: How Skandia became the next whale

The Odyssey acquisition proved to Fairfax that it could expand its business and culture into the U.S. and start looking seriously at global expansion. It also proved that big things can happen when you think big, because the deal they started with was a lot smaller, before all the Frankenstein stuff.

Skandia America was a perfect example of a company gone adrift due to poor management—a large, bureaucratic, top-down global firm with a faraway head office in Sweden that was completely out of sync with its operations. Up until now, Fairfax had mostly been buying up the Canadian subsidiaries of American insurers. This time, it was the North American assets of a Swedish insurer.

Skandia America's history is a great case study on how not to run an insurance subsidiary. Barnard had witnessed that first-hand when he worked there. He knew the disconnect between Stockholm and North America; it had left him dumbfounded and disillusioned and was the main reason he had left back in 1985.

"Sweden was basically directing American management to withdraw from all the areas of business that had caused it problems," he explains.

> Anyone in insurance should know that you manage a cycle by reining in when pricing is bad. That's the time to sacrifice market share and sales commissions. Stockholm was out of touch with the U.S. market and reflexively panicked at precisely the wrong time. When a lot of costly claims are made, the demand for insurance grows and prices pick up. That is the time to get aggressive and sell more insurance. But head office would direct its U.S. managers to freeze sales or even exit business lines that had caused them problems. Meanwhile, conditions would have changed dramatically, so you had prices going up 200, 300 or 400 percent. There was tremendous opportunity, but the Swedes didn't want to hear anything about that.

Skandia's reputation for bad timing was notorious. Brian Young, who was promoted to Odyssey CEO after Barnard graduated to a Fairfax-wide role in 2011, saw the same mistakes. In fact, the whole industry saw Skandia the same way. Young recalls an industry contact relating how the Fairfax purchase led to the loss of a "reliable bellwether." That man was Jim Stanard, founder of RenaissanceRe, and it was a full decade after the transaction when he quipped to Young, with ironic yet genuine remorse: "I'm really disappointed Prem bought Skandia. We used to see which direction they took and we would just do the opposite."

Let's back it up a few months to December 1995 to see how the deal went down. Most offices were winding down for the holidays, but Watsa was in his office on Wellington and the phone was ringing. It was Jim Dowd, CEO of Skandia America. The two had done a small deal in 1989, when Watsa sold Skandia most of SphereRe's assets; Fairfax had been having trouble finding the right entry into the reinsurance market. Dowd now said the Swedish parent company was set to pull out of North America completely. Would Fairfax be interested in the Canadian assets?

It's hard to ever accuse Watsa of thinking small. With Continental (renamed Lombard), Fairfax the minnow had already swallowed a whale. So Watsa's response to the question was to ask another question: "What about Skandia America? Is it for sale too?"

Dowd digested that thought, fully aware it was the company he himself was running. "Yes, but it's too big for you."

Fairfax was bigger now, countered Watsa. "Have you seen our statements lately? I think you'll find we're of sufficient size."

Fast-forward to a trip to Stockholm for Dowd and Watsa, and the whale is swallowed. Dowd stayed on during the transition to ease things through all the distractions, which were set to multiply. With such a big deal, it made sense for Fairfax to digest it slowly. Then the phone rang with another opportunity. Things were about to get a lot messier: There was a new business for sale that would fit nicely with Skandia and turbocharge the nascent reinsurance business line.

On the line this time was Tony Griffiths, a close advisor to Fairfax who had gotten wind that a French insurer was looking to spin off its reinsurer subsidiary, Compagnie Transcontinentale de Réassurance (CTR), an established reinsurer with a global reach. With so much on his plate, Watsa had to be swayed to even take a meeting on it. What he learned intrigued him, so he reached out to his brand new in-house insurance leader—who had yet to even have his business cards printed.

"I was roughly a week into my new job with Odyssey when Prem rang me up," recalls Barnard. "He asked me about CTR, and I was enthusiastic. In my previous job, I had been very active as an architect in building out the international reinsurance business. So when the opportunity was there to complement Skandia, which operated only in the United States, with a company that operated around the world, it was really attractive. So we did the deal." The price: C$175 million.

Barnard was quickly earning his keep. Watsa now had someone who could listen to the heads of the operating companies and better understand if they were actually making sense. Someone who could look at a battered French reinsurance company for Watsa and recognize that while it might not survive, its assets could be folded into Odyssey and give Fairfax an immediate global reach in a new line of business.

It was Fairfax's first move into the U.S. market and now its first move into the global market. It might make more sense together, and now Watsa had someone to run it all. He insists he would never have done the deal without Barnard on board.

Whatever would happen with the various pieces acquired, Watsa's big strategic bet here was to be a player in a new line of business. "Reinsurance is now a very significant activity for Fairfax and our future will be very dependent on the performance of our two recent acquisitions," he told shareholders.

For Barnard, it played to his strengths: "It was Prem's first significant foray into the reinsurance business, but for me, it was right in my wheelhouse."

Initially the two businesses were kept separate, but as feared, CTR quickly turned out to be too expensive to rehabilitate. Like Odyssey, it had large exposures to long-tail risk from asbestos and reinsurance recoveries. Unlike Odyssey's liabilities, however, CTR's were too large to fix. Much of its business was put into runoff, and its salvageable assets were rolled up into Odyssey as a global workforce.

Odyssey, the Frankenstein's monster of insurance, had just gone through yet another dramatic growth spurt, all in the space of a year. And Fairfax was ballooning along with it. In one year, Fairfax's net premiums jumped 1.7 times, its portfolio grew 2.5 times, and shareholders' equity tripled. Fairfax was beset with acquisition indigestion and insisted it would take a rest. "Don't be surprised if we make no acquisitions in the next five years," Watsa told shareholders when the CTR deal closed. Then the phone rang again . . .

In June 1997, a $217-million deal for Sphere Drake of London was announced. The reinsurer was a troubled company that soon proved to be beyond saving but brought in an additional $900 million to the investment portfolio. "We had to shut Sphere down but we held on to a few pieces of it and folded that up into Odyssey as well," says Barnard.

Odyssey's rapid transformation remade Fairfax. This acquisition and its related deals, such as those for CTR and Sphere, were game changers in terms of size, geography, and lines of business. Additionally, Odyssey became the model in terms of adapting subsidiaries into a unified culture.

The investment team at HWIC certainly was not complaining. The Fairfax portfolio now sat at C$5.8 billion, compared to C$404 million back in September 1993 before the first two waves of the buying binge started.

WAVE THREE: CRUM & FORSTER AND TIG

"There is always the risk of growing too quickly." —Prem Watsa

The late 1990s were end-of-an-era years for Fairfax. The manic phase of acquisitions was playing out, and investors' blind faith was already turning to skepticism in some corners. Watsa and his team already faced a tall task of turning around a bunch of impaired assets—and that task would become almost Herculean when coupled with a soft market and a run of natural event catastrophes of near-biblical proportions.

Just to make things worse, stock markets were volatile in a warm-up to the tech wreck of 2000. So, while operating losses were piling up on the insurer side, returns from the investment portfolio were struggling to pick up the slack as they had for much of the first dozen years. HWIC was about to push a lot of money to the sidelines for safety, which acted as a further drag on returns.

For Fairfax, the mission did not change. This was a bumpy build of a company that intended to pay the price in the short term to be successful for a long time. But investors were suddenly a lot less patient. They didn't want to pay the price. They were eager to see the new assets get cleaned up, today.

Many of these shareholders had come aboard during the go-go years and had not been groomed to think long term; instead, they thought of Fairfax as a hot growth stock and everything was great as long as everything was going up. Most insurers were suffering a rough patch, but none more so than Fairfax's subsidiaries. It was not clear if Fairfax was in a short-term slump or being relegated to a lengthy stay at the back of the class. Was Fairfax itself a Ranger or a Lombard? Actually, even Lombard looked terrible at this point. But at least investment gains were still propping up earnings. The HWIC investment team had recorded realized gains of C$1 billion since starting out in 1985, and about C$650 million of that had come in 1997 and 1998 alone.

That billion dollars is "one of the reasons we entered the business many years ago," Watsa told shareholders. "We come to the insurance business with an investment mindset as opposed to an insurance mindset (focused on increasing market share), a key long-term positive for Fairfax." Of course, Watsa also cautioned that these gains were very hard to predict and investors in Fairfax would always do well to look past the lumpiness of short-term results. The reality was that short-term gains were actually masking ballooning losses on the insurer side. Things were not being cleaned up quickly, as investors had hoped.

In 1997, Fairfax first published a detailed table in Watsa's letter to shareholders that tracked the combined ratios of each subsidiary. The table gave added clarity on the terrible performance, which stayed that way—until it got even worse. Investors were growing skeptical, and probably the only thing that could distract them would be Fairfax rebooting its buying binge.

Watsa's phone rang again. Word of who to call when you are selling a broken asset on behalf of a motivated seller had clearly gotten around.

It was a Xerox executive in the U.S., who was running a fire sale of struggling insurance assets acquired earlier in the copier company's ill-fated efforts at diversification.

TWO MORE TRIPS TO THE BARGAIN BIN

It was February 1998, and Watsa was putting the finishing touches on his 1997 letter to shareholders, many of whom were eager to hear how Fairfax was doing with its turnarounds. Watsa put his writing aside, took the call, and then called Salsberg right away. The two flew to New York and, par for the course, had a deal, pending financing, by the afternoon. "We have never hired investment bankers for ourselves in doing deals. Then or today," Watsa says. "And we never had an M & A department. It was usually me and Ricky."

Salsberg and Watsa were unable to secure their customary exclusivity agreement, but they got a handshake. And when word of the deal leaked out, the Xerox executive kept his word, and the deal was done March 11, 1998. For a price of $680 million, Morristown, New Jersey–based Crum & Forster was welcomed to the Fairfax family.

Crum brought net premiums of $939 million in commercial lines of insurance (a similar profile to Lombard in Canada) to Fairfax, as well as an investment portfolio of $3.3 billion. Resolution Group (later renamed RiverStone) was purchased the following year, adding another diversification, this time into runoff, which is the windup operation where written-off assets are managed on life support until their obligations are retired. Fairfax had learned first-hand how important this part of the insurance business can be, especially with companies like Ranger, CTR, and Sphere Drake, parts of which Barnard explains had truly become a "black hole of liabilities."

In his growing role, Barnard was eager to spend less time on black holes: "Fairfax acquired RiverStone and its reserves, as well as the team that managed it. It was a very strategic acquisition for Fairfax because it created an in-house capability to take care of discontinued businesses. Troubled assets take a lot of attention, and if you're up to your eyeballs in managing problems from the past, it gets a lot more difficult to look forward."

Crum would be one of Fairfax's bigger management challenges in the following years. But they eventually polished it into a gem. Meanwhile, Fairfax went digging again in the discount bargain bin and pulled the trigger on yet another major deal—TIG Holding. The price tag: $847 million, with an investment portfolio for HWIC of $3.9 billion.

TIG was a mix of the good and the terrible. As always, optimism was high in the beginning. It has always been Watsa's nature to hope for a turnaround. But in the end, it was another case like CTR: Some valuable assets were rolled up into other assets, and a large part of it was pushed into runoff. One ironic upside was TIG became a major supplier of impaired assets to RiverStone. That's not the kind of synergy you try to build a business on, but at least they were paying themselves to clean up their own mess.

TIG was made up of two companies. TIG Reinsurance was strong and immediately slated to be rolled up into Odyssey. Dallas-based TIG Insurance, however, was a flapping red flag from the get-go. "TIG Insurance had a very flawed business model, and I don't know that Prem appreciated how flawed it was," says Barnard. The strategy called for a virtual business with everything, including sales, outsourced. The model is known as MGA (for managing general agents), and an outside sales team has the delegated authority to write the company's premiums.

"It created all these incentives with the broker to write business with less regard for its profitability and more for volume and sales fees," Barnard explains. It didn't take long for Watsa to pull the plug on the business and put it into runoff at RiverStone. In retrospect, Watsa says the reinsurance asset was valuable enough in itself to make the transaction a positive. But the deal ended up delivering less than expected.

It was only fitting that the last two deals in a frenzied six-year run of acquisitions were outsized and controversial. Crum would tax Fairfax's patience and finances for years before becoming one of its top performing assets. TIG would quickly unravel but contribute some prized assets to soften the blow.

To finance Crum, Fairfax issued one million shares at C$475 a share and a $400-million debenture offering. For TIG, Fairfax issued another two million shares at C$500 each. All those new shares created two problems. One, Fairfax wanted to buy them back but was headed into a cash crunch. And two, even more new shareholders came aboard with high hopes that the stock would recover its ability to soar. How would they feel if the stock market darling turned into a dog?

Close readers of Watsa's letters would see hints that a period of indigestion would weigh on performance and shareholder patience alike. Sometimes it is easy to mistake the weight of casual words of caution in the letter. But vague or not, if they are repeated, you can assume Watsa has a clear message for everyone, such as in his comments in 1996, in the midst of the go-go years: "We welcome our new shareholders and emphasize again, as we did in 1993 and 1994, that our company is run for the long term. So don't be too concerned about short-term (read quarterly) surprises but I'm sure they will come one of these days!" If that is not an actual profit warning, it is certainly blunt advice to be cautious. For shareholders who weren't getting the message, he repeated it yet again in 1998, with added colour and exclamation points.

> Please don't forget what we said in our 1996 Annual Report: "We have been fortunate not to have had any short-term (read quarterly) surprises but I'm sure they will come one of these days!" And, unlike prevailing practice in the financial markets, you will *not* get a "profits warning" announcement from us: To further dampen your expectations, we suggest you read our old Annual Reports that list all the mistakes we have made in the past (even I don't do that with a full stomach!).

On the upside, the two deals continued to transform Fairfax into a major U.S. insurance company. The Canadian asset base was strong but now very much overshadowed, and the global footprint was getting very interesting, especially in reinsurance. Fairfax found itself in 1999 with a roughly equal three-way revenue (premiums) split between Canada, the U.S., and reinsurance.

MEANWHILE IN ASIA . . .

With all the investor attention on North America, the company had its head up looking for other opportunities. Fairfax started planting acorns for future growth in India. In 1998, it bought Euro-America Insurance Ltd. for HK$22 million, changed its name to Falcon Insurance, and recapitalized it at ten times the purchase price. Importantly, it made sure the asset was not broken and had strong management out of the gate. The less indigestion going forward, the better.

"In case you think we must have been suffering a sudden case of the Asian Flu, we bought this company because Kenneth Kwok agreed to come in as its CEO," wrote Watsa. "Kenneth has had a long and successful track record running a Continental subsidiary in Hong Kong and was well known to Byron Messier and his team at Lombard." The global strategy was still just a big idea with a small footprint, but it had become something for shareholders to watch.

TOPPING OUT: THE END OF AN ERA

As 1998 came to an end, anyone could see that Fairfax was emerging as a completely different company that had taken on a lot of risks to grow at a frenetic pace. The record of Watsa and Fairfax was so far largely unblemished and analysts showed every sign they expected the company to pull all the additions together and clean them up profitably.

If an investor ignored the escalating combined ratios of the insurers, the rest of the picture still looked exceptionally bullish at the end of 1998. Fairfax hit its ROE goal of 20 percent, trouncing the return of 3.2 percent for the Toronto market. Net income rose 67 percent, book value per share was up 47 percent, and the stock managed a 69 percent return. What could go wrong?

Over the first thirteen years, the stock had compounded 48 percent annually and book value, 41 percent. Fairfax was an almost unprecedented success story, and Watsa said he would be happy if the company continued to have success at half the speed. "There is only one Canadian company and two U.S. companies whose stock price has compounded at a rate faster than ours," Watsa told shareholders.

In classic Fairfax dad humour, Watsa had fun extolling Fairfax's ability to be nimble and seize opportunities without following a rigid master plan: "While this growth is mind-boggling even for us, the bad news is that it was not based on a 'vision' statement or long-term plan that we have for Fairfax (I have checked but have yet to find it!)." He was also cautioning that the frenetic amount of M & A that was fuelling growth could not last and investors should moderate their expectations: "This growth cannot be extrapolated in the future (we will own the world if it is!)." Some observers wondered if a vision statement might actually have been a good idea if it led to fewer trips to the bargain bin. One of Canada's more astute investing writers, Jonathan Harris at *Canadian Business*, would muse presciently, "You have to wonder if Watsa's bargain-basement purchases are going to get him in trouble."

For now, these deals were ticking Watsa's boxes in a big way. "We were always opportunistic," he says. "It's not as though we had planned to expand into the United States, but these two companies became available at about the same time, so we said, 'Okay, let's take a look at them.' Though they were a big bite for us, they fit our parameters, meaning we didn't get into auctions, the prices were below book value, the terms were attractive, and we could finance them."

The grand total of growth in key areas of business from this jet-fuelled go-go buying binge between 1993 and 1998 was an eye-popping thirty-seven-times increase in net premiums written (to C$5.5 billion), a twenty-three-times lift to the investment portfolio (to C$18 billion), and a six-times expansion in book value per share (to C$225). Many investors who came on board must have thought the go-go was going to keep going and going. Bullish stock analysts with aggressive target prices were counting on it.

BUBBLE WATCHING WITH PREM

In the 1990s, Watsa started to give over more space in his letter to market conditions and threats from valuation bubbles and other factors. Even investors who are not shareholders can profit by reading the letter for a guru's insights on inflation, deflation, tech stocks, value-versus-growth strategy, fixed-income trades, and the housing market. And as the 1990s played out, he became increasingly bearish. Repeatedly, he turns to Ben Graham's words of wisdom for investors to follow, such as the need to stay the course and think long term if volatility strikes: "The investor with a portfolio of sound stocks should expect their prices to fluctuate and should neither be concerned by sizeable declines nor become excited by sizeable advances. He should always remember that market quotations are there for his convenience, either to be taken advantage of or to be ignored."

Regarding Fairfax shares, Watsa always emphasized his expectation that the growth in share price would track the growth in book value, but that investors could expect periods when one or the other would lag. Over time, however, he said this correlation would revert to the mean. Watsa also regularly reminded investors that the outsized gains to date in share price, book value, and other measures would not be repeated. The company was going to buy insurers until it felt it had the pieces in place to create a strong engine of organic growth. Things would settle down and some of the target metrics would be adjusted. The plan was never to remain a binge-buyer's growth stock.

While other CEOs might talk up their stock's potential for future gains, Watsa stood out for cautioning investors about froth in his own shares in the go-go years. As early as 1995, the share price's ascent into triple digits prompted the value-minded CEO to teach a valuation class:

> With Fairfax at $100 per share, many of you are probably wondering if this is as good as it gets. Is the stock overvalued and can it drop significantly? This is a good question and you will have to come to your own conclusion based on the facts that we have disclosed in this Annual Report.

The facts in question? Watsa added for consideration several points, including general price volatility, which could "easily" result in a 50 percent decline. Sounding a note of caution, he observed the stock was trading at twice book value, at the top of its recent range. But he also noted that book value is conservatively stated and intrinsic value is higher than book. So investors had to do their own math to figure out if the stock was in nosebleed territory.

He has always been fond of Graham's rational advice that an investor "should never buy a stock because it has gone up, or sell because it has gone down." Here, he concluded similarly: "So I really don't know what the stock price will do in the short term—never have—but I suggest taking the long view." A close read of the letter could easily be seen as a wink that shareholders should be increasingly ready for volatility in the short term. It's not a suggestion to sell, just a reminder to disciplined investors that things go up and they go down—even Fairfax shares.

In 1990, the last time the stock suffered a steep decline, there might have been fewer freaked-out investors because they knew better what they had signed up for. Those were the kind of investors Watsa and Fairfax wanted. But there were a lot of new investors along for the ride five-plus years later, and they might not have been as keen to ride the volatility. He took stock of the long-term investors on his shareholder list: "Have we been successful in attracting this type of investor?" Yes, he offered, pointing to trading activity statistics for proof. Long-term investors bought and held—they did not trade in and out. Noting that Fairfax ranked 293rd on turnover (shares traded as a percent of available shares to trade) on the TSE 300, he concluded, "Exactly where we want to be!!"

Nevertheless, all the new shares being issued meant new shareholders. The company had issued three million shares to purchase Ranger and Lombard (Continental) and another 1.1 million in securing Odyssey (Skandia) and CTR. A further three million for Crum & Forster and TIG followed. That meant a lot of new investors. "We hope your results will not be too dissimilar to the shareholders who purchased our stock in 1986," he told them.

After a volatile year when the stock swung between $285 and $403, many of these new investors got jumpy. Not getting much news through the business press, they started ringing the company. Watsa and his small team at head office wanted to be left alone, and he took to his letter as a way to drive that message home:

> This is perhaps a good time to discuss stock price fluctuations—particularly for the benefit of some of our newer shareholders! Stock prices *have always* fluctuated—and *will always* fluctuate. This applies to stocks in general but to Fairfax in particular . . .

> Some of our more recent shareholders have reacted to these fluctuations with persistent telephone calls to our head office asking about the effects of El Niño, the Mexican earthquake, the Asian crisis, etc., etc. We have to emphasize that our company is run for the long term; short-term stock price fluctuations are meaningless and as we have only thirteen people in our head office, we do not have the time to answer these telephone calls.

Instead, he encouraged them to attend the annual meeting and ask any questions directly. And if they found it too stressful to play the patient value game, Watsa said he'd be happy to see them sell: "If you cannot handle the short-term fluctuations, then perhaps we are not the stock for you." You won't come across many CEOs who will suggest you dump their shares and buy someone else's stock.

WARNING LIGHTS START FLASHING FOR STOCKS

While sounding a caution on his own shares' valuation, Watsa was growing concerned about the broader market as well. In Fairfax's first decade, Watsa painted a picture of a 1950s-style market backdrop where most boats were rising. No longer. "For the first time since Fairfax's inception in 1985, we are becoming concerned about the overall stock market environment," he told investors in his 1996 letter. "With many warning lights flashing, we are being more cautious than usual in making any new stock investments."

These concerns echoed those in Federal Reserve chairman Alan Greenspan's famous "irrational exuberance" speech of December of the same year. Readers of Watsa's letter were getting an advance warning on a growing valuation bubble that would soon inflate technology stocks in particular and cause a spectacular crash.

Of course, Fairfax was early. They were almost always early. When stock markets roared ahead in 1997, Fairfax took its "warning lights flashing" assessment and raised it to "red alert." They sold down holdings in U.S. and Canadian stocks, leaving equity exposure at its lowest level to date by the end of the year. The timing is always the hard part. This would have been a good time for Watsa to reuse the quip included in his letter about the exact timing of the Japanese bubble in the '80s: "If any of you know when that will happen, please let me know!"

The company was also early on another type of investment risk—collateralized bonds. At this point, Fairfax was flagging bonds backed by credit card debt and also anticipating the future disaster in asset-backed bonds tied to residential mortgages, which triggered the Global Financial Crisis. Fairfax was still a few years early on the tech wreck call. The mortgage disaster? That was still a decade away.

THE STREET GOES GA-GA FOR FAIRFAX

One of the common characteristics of bubbles is they inflate faster near the end before they pop. Typically, you will see a narrowing of leadership where a few heavyweights do all the lifting of the indexes. The late '90s were no exception, with the S&P 500 racking up consecutive frothy advances. Curiously enough, Fairfax shares were even hotter, driven by all the growth through dealmaking. Keep in mind that 8 percent is considered a solid annual gain for the broader market and consider the S&P 500 was sitting on a four-year run of 34, 20, 31, and 27 percent advances, respectively. Fairfax was nervous about the broader market but was exploding itself with 46, 196, 10, and 69 percent gains over the same period.

By this time, Fairfax was a true market darling. Bay Street analysts covering Fairfax were among the hardest working because the company kept transforming, deal by deal. Every new deal required more company analysis, fresh modelling, revised price targets, and new research reports.

Until there were signs of a downturn in performance, or any indication the assets Fairfax had bought were hiding insurmountable problems, there would be fresh buy recommendations and higher target prices on the stock. At this point, Watsa could do no wrong.

In the spring of 1996, imagine you are Melanie Ward, an analyst with the RBC Capital Markets team at Canada's largest bank. Covering Fairfax stock, which is in yet another sprint, Ward is finding it a busy file, and she is not alone. From C$98 at the end of the previous year, the stock zooms to C$180 by April's annual meeting. She acknowledges the challenge of forecasting the extremely lumpy earnings per share, which is the Street's preferred metric of charting results, and suggests investors take a breath and let the stock settle down.

"While this appreciation has been phenomenal, we do not expect this to be repeated at the same pace over the next few months. It is very difficult to forecast Fairfax's future results due to the erratic nature of the company's growth and earnings from acquisitions," Ward reported, calling the stock a "hold" with a C$198 one-year target price.

She was also quick to add a conditional "pending an additional acquisition" on her report. That proved prescient, as Watsa and Salsberg were busy at that very moment hammering out their offer for Skandia America. The last thing an analyst wants is to be behind on the story, and this one was moving fast.

In July, just after the Skandia deal was done, Ward upped her target to C$200 and also issued a three-year target of C$300, factoring in investors' blossoming love for the stock in her math: "We believe Fairfax's acquisition expertise, coupled with the growth in the investment portfolio has led investors to pay higher price-to-earnings and price-to-book multiples."

The shares took out the first full-year target in six weeks when the CTR deal came to light. And took out the three-year target just eight weeks after that. Fairfax was threatening to become the 1990s version of a modern-day meme stock. "Anybody who expected this stock to reach $260 is a magician," said Mark Maxwell, analyst at CIBC World Markets. "I don't think anybody expected it, not even Watsa. It's amazing."

Ward and Maxwell had lots of company. The Street loved Watsa and adored Fairfax when everyone was making money. Analysts came up with a name for the higher multiple that investors were now willing to pay for the shares associated with the wheeler-dealer CEO—they called it a *Prem-ium*. "The market, in light of the track record Prem has been able to produce, is taking the best-case view of what he will be able to do with Skandia and imputing that into the current share price," Maxwell told the *Financial Post*. "Prem Watsa knows how to make money. This last acquisition [Skandia America] was a stunner."

The "Watsa as market wizard" thesis bit both ways. Analysts also flipped that factor around to say that the dependence on a market master's hot hand could prove a vulnerability to the company if he were run over by a bus without anyone to replace him.

By the summer of 1997—after Fairfax bought Sphere Drake—things got even more bubbly on Bay Street. Rossa O'Reilly, analyst with CIBC World Markets, tallied up the latest additions in float, investment portfolio, and premiums, and with the stock at C$390, issued a target of C$465. That target price equated to eighteen times earnings, more than double where it traded at the end of 2024, and a whopping 3.2 times book value. Even in the post-Covid-19 era, it was common to see analysts using a multiple of less than one times book in setting target prices on the shares.

Fast-forward to September 1998, and the shares were trading at C$429. Quentin Broad at First Marathon Securities initiated coverage of Fairfax with an eye-popping twelve- to eighteen-month target of C$810. In a December update, after the TIG deal closed, he nudged the target higher to C$860, ten times what the shares were trading at in early 1996.

YOU CAN FIX ALL THIS IN EIGHTEEN MONTHS, RIGHT?

"While we remain cautious over the rapidity of the successive acquisitions, we remain very comfortable with management's capability to integrate them over a period of 18 months to two years," wrote Broad in his report, which expressed confidence in Fairfax continuing to meet its goal of a 20 percent return on equity. The First Marathon report is entitled "Got a TIGer by the Tail." In hindsight, it might have been advisable to remind investors that tigers can maul, especially if they, like TIG, are run on a toxic business model, are under-reserved, and happen to be overexposed to long-tail insurance risks.

The report's C$860 stock target carried a typical twelve-month time frame. The shares would take another twenty-three years to reach it. Heading into the end of the century, just like that, the go-go party was over.

Chapter Five

THE LONG ATTACK OF THE SHORTS (1999–2005)

"It took us some time to figure out that this group of shorts, these hedge funds, were trying to destroy us." —Prem Watsa

In the first year of the twenty-first century, Watsa noted with curiosity that the company had attracted a new kind of investor in Fairfax—"a few short sellers!!"

Shorting is often used by investors as a hedge, to balance against their long positions in stocks. More commonly, it is known as a straight bearish bet that pays off if the share price falls. Fairfax's CEO and chairman expressed his team's disappointment with the performance of the past two years, and as for the shorts, he quipped with humour and mild curiosity in early 2001, "We had 47,100 shares sold short (i.e. hoping to benefit from a decline in our share price) as of December 31, 2000—and I thought we attracted long term investors only."

It was easy to ignore the bearish sentiment at this point. The stock had attracted only a few investors ready to bet against Fairfax, and it shouldn't be surprising that a few investors saw a good bet against a stock that had climbed so far so fast. Remember, Watsa himself had mused in his letter about high valuations and 50 percent retreats for Fairfax shares. But in the next few years, the number of shorts would grow dramatically to include a who's who of Wall Street hedge funds including "catastrophe capitalist" Jim Chanos. They were convinced the stock was going to zero, and it appeared they intended to feast on the corpse.

As a money manager, Watsa had no problems with short selling. In fact, he was just a few years from solidifying his reputation as a master of the "macro" short call by cashing in on the tech wreck with short sales of his own. But the coming battle with the hedge funds was something different. The hedge fund shorts were looking for the next Enron-style fraud and soon grew sure they'd found it in Fairfax. Where others saw complexity or underperformance in Fairfax's financials, the shorts diagnosed lethal liquidity strains and accounting cover-ups. Their aggressive, concerted, and high-stakes attack would drag on for four years, exacerbating Fairfax's challenges at the worst possible time.

The 1990s acquisition-fuelled growth surge had given Fairfax many of the pieces it needed to evolve into a large-scale insurance operator. And it had given investors a wild ride and made a lot of them rich. The plan's next act was to quickly fix the potholes and make these assets profitable. It did not work out that way. Fairfax struggled, and impatient investors punished them harshly for it. No longer a market darling, the company began the new century as a market pariah. Throw in the return of a soft market in insurance, a historic market crash, several epic years of catastrophes, and an expensive accounting restatement—plus an insane sideshow of hedge funds out to profit from the company's demise—and you have a madly rich chapter in Fairfax history. Let's break it out into five major storylines.

1. THE GO-GO IS GONE

The last year of the twentieth century started well enough from an outside perspective. Fairfax did not look like a candidate for short sellers. Bullishness still prevailed on Bay Street, but you could feel the winds were changing, as if Fairfax was going to quiet down for a bit after all the excitement. Analyst stock target prices were taking haircuts but were still up in the C$800 range, about C$200 above where the shares were trading.

In a bearish turn, the stock had pulled back 29 percent since the March 10, 1999, release of the 1998 annual report, which carried Watsa's usual frank discussion of risks related to the new assets. Of TIG, he allowed, "In the insurance and reinsurance business there is always the possibility of reserve development from the past and reinsurance recoverable bad debt coming to haunt us." He also offered another observation: "There is always the risk of growing too quickly."

Those comments could have been read as a warning, but Watsa also seemed his usual decidedly upbeat self on the plan to get the new assets into shape. Even in 2000, the optimistic Watsa scoffed, "Many observers believe because we purchased these companies at a discount to book value that they were 'damaged goods' or have some unfixable problems." He continued, "We believe strongly that it is not a question of 'if' but only a question of 'when' both companies achieve their goal of 100% combined [ratios] or better. [Crum] and TIG's experience in the next few years will likely be similar to Lombard and not Ranger."

The will was clearly there, but in a short period of time TIG would very much resemble a Ranger. A glass-half-full perspective could still point to the valuable asset TIG provided in its emerging reinsurance business; even if it could not be saved completely, it could be salvaged for parts. Crum, meanwhile, was a multi-year headache that threatened to become a Ranger only to end up an absolute gem of an asset for Fairfax. Watsa would never sell it today. But if you ask him if he'd ever buy a company in that kind of shape again, he wouldn't need to mull over his response: "No! Never!"

Fairfax, as always, kept its head down and worked on improving its business, as investors and the Street grew a bit wary. Most of them, anyway. Bullishness dies hard. In April 1999, Quentin Broad at First Marathon Securities (author of the "TIGer by the Tail" report) issued a new gushing report after the annual meeting entitled "Why Do We Like Thee—Let Us Reiterate the Reasons." But even Broad was getting the feeling his bullish thesis was becoming a lonely one. "Unfortunately," he wrote, "the market does not appear to be listening."

Broad laid out the tall challenges that he still believed Watsa could successfully address: "Ranger has now proven to be a disaster. Sphere Drake in London is having problems, the jury is still out on the rest of the acquisitions." Turns out, the jury would come back with its verdict in the next quarter. It would be damning.

"One of these days"

Careful readers of Watsa's annual letter might have been more on guard than most. In his 1998 letter, he included a reminder that Fairfax does not groom market expectations by tipping analysts to incoming bad news. However, when he repeats comments on adverse scenarios, it can be a clue that those concerns are more than purely hypothetical. As we have noted, a version of this comment appeared a few times: "We have been fortunate not to have had any short term (read quarterly) surprises but I'm sure they will come one of these days!"

As prophesied, "one of these days" arrived August 5, 1999, when Fairfax released its second-quarter numbers and Broad's "jury" came back to weigh in. Like other analysts, Rossa O'Reilly at CIBC World Markets dug into the financials when they hit news wires after the Thursday market close, working on a report for investors to be issued Friday morning. The numbers were bad all around.

As Watsa had said before, "Things can change very quickly in the insurance business." Analysts had lately focused their concerns on Crum as a major drag on performance, but they were digging into all the insurer assets to weigh the hot trouble spots: TIG, Ranger, Odyssey, and Sphere. There were many. Even Commonwealth was having a freakishly terrible year and went on to post an abysmal full-year combined ratio of 186.7 percent.

O'Reilly slashed his target price from C$550 to C$390, dropped his recommendation from "strong buy" to "underperform," and hit send on his research note on Friday about ninety minutes before trading started. Fairfax shares opened into massive selling pressure. The stock collapsed by an eye-popping C$114 to end the day at C$274, chopping almost 30 percent off the value of the company. It was the worst one-day price drop the Toronto market had ever seen.

Some market participants shrugged it off as a result of so few shares being traded. "It's not a very liquid stock so it's not hard to move it up and down," offered Steve Horrocks, a trader with Charles Schwab. Others called it a bizarre overreaction. "I'm sitting here in shock," said Kim Shannon, then chief investment officer at Merrill Lynch and long-time Fairfax watcher.

From that point on, Bay Street and investors played a guessing game: Had Fairfax bottomed out or was it facing even bigger problems ahead? Tom Jarmai replaced Melanie Ward at RBC Dominion, initiating coverage in September 1999 with an "underperform" call and target of C$150. For investors who had bought at C$600 with C$850 target prices in mind, the prospect of a 75 percent decline left a memorable sting, which some of them never forgot.

"We feel satisfied that we have adequately warned you"

At one point, the sell-off took the stock nearly 70 percent lower in 1999, convincing Watsa to break with precedent and actively reach out to settle rattled nerves. The company had suffered a similar downdraft in 1990 and shrugged it off. Watsa asked for the same stoic patience in 1999 and showed a bit of frustration with investor reluctance to focus on the long term.

"While I have refrained from discussing fluctuations in our stock price—up or down—this recent significant decline prompted me to write this letter to you," he began in the November special edition of his shareholder letter. (The usual letter is sent in March after the previous year's financials are released.) It was essentially a news release but more personal. These special edition shareholder letters became fairly common in these turbulent years.

The message Watsa hammered home in that letter, as well as in the letter attached to the annual report a few months later, was that Fairfax would always accept short-term volatility in earnings and share price for the benefit of long-term results, something he stressed was "the single most important statement about understanding the Fairfax philosophy."

The frustration with shareholders was palpable as Watsa told them some of the earnings drag was attributable to the cost of shorting the market and insisted, accurately, that the trade would pay off when the market tumble arrived, so please keep the faith. He also noted that the last time Fairfax shares had tumbled so far, the company bought back a lot of shares and was doing that again, buying nearly one million in 1999 and early 2000. It was a bit of a dance for the CEO, who wanted to ask for more discipline and patience from shareholders as well as contritely let them know he, too, was very disappointed with the performance.

"So do annual stock price fluctuations connote high risk? Was the price decline in 1990 or in 1999 because Fairfax was a very risky company? Not at all!" While the drop in earnings had hammered the stock, he reminded shareholders that book value was growing well and the stock would track that trend over time. "We feel satisfied that we have adequately warned you about the possibility of fluctuations and have always emphasized the long term," he wrote. It's safe to say he was more excited than his fellow shareholders about the opportunity to buy back shares on the cheap.

Watsa expressed his frustration with a public commitment that put Fairfax leaders on notice: "While we have always emphasized underwriting profit, today, at Fairfax, there is a renewed focus on achieving a 100% combined ratio by each President. Anything else is *unacceptable*." (Watsa's italics.) He didn't say it directly, but it was becoming apparent that shopping for insurers in the bargain bin might not have been the best strategy.

Watsa offered up another plea to refrain from bothering management with phone calls and to read the extensive disclosure on risks: "Any further comment is unnecessary and distracting. Our belief is that results will prevail in the long term and short-term promotion of Fairfax is neither necessary nor desirable. We have consistently advised you that Fairfax is run for the long term, that quarterly earnings surprises will come and will not bother us (no profit warnings from Fairfax), and that you should be prepared for stock price fluctuations of 50–60% as they have happened before for Fairfax—and almost every other company listed on the TSE or NYSE at one time or another."

2. THE SEVEN LEAN YEARS: LONG TAILS, POTHOLES, AND BROKEN PROMISES

Watsa was more contrite and made zero excuses for Fairfax's financial performance when he wrote his full annual letter three months later. With 1999 now in the rear-view mirror, Watsa was candidly blunt with his assessment: "[The year] was a disaster for almost all our underwriting operations. There is no other word for it. I am embarrassed by these results and apologize for them." The stock's full-year decline was 55 percent. Net income dropped 68 percent. Not a good year all round.

Fairfax could have tried to blame the weather, with cause. But it did not. In an average year, there were one or two catastrophes for the industry to contend with, but 1999 saw ten and these took a bite of nearly $200 million out of Fairfax's earnings. "Almost makes you nervous watching the weather channel," quipped Watsa. A bloodbath in bond markets and the lack of any lumpy realized gains to even things out left the company painfully exposed.

By the time the results and Watsa's apologies were out, Fairfax's reputation as the Street's market darling was firmly behind it. The share price and targets ran up on a good quarter and then slid again when more bad news followed. Fairfax's lumpy earnings increased the volatility as investors tried to read the short-term tea leaves. It would soon become clear this was a serious losing streak; the only thing in question was how long it would last.

How Lean? By the Numbers	
Cumulative underwriting losses (1999–2005) (in C$ billion)	
Insurance and reinsurance	1.1
Runoff	3.1
Other costs	0.2
Total underwiting loss	4.4
Total losses including expenses	5.5
Net income	0.0

Source: Company annual report

The period of underperformance would be continually stretched out further. Watsa tried several times to put a name to this chapter as a way to formally consign it to history. Labelling it the "atrocious three years" failed to stick as the slump persisted. It doubled in length before tacking on yet another year and finally became known in company lore as the "seven lean years." Shareholders got regular, candid apologies, but what they wanted to see was a fix. The main culprit was the bargain-bin acquisition strategy.

Up until this point, the steady pace of acquisitions had ensured Fairfax showed growth in earnings, premiums, and earnings power from book value and float. Acquisitions were off the table now, with the exception of TRG Holdings, a runoff specialist, in 1999.

Without Fairfax's takeover-driven growth, the Street now crossed its arms and tapped a foot, waiting impatiently to see how quickly the company could get its insurers' combined ratios into shape. It was show-me time. Unfortunately, Fairfax was getting further away from profitability, as it poured cash into bolstering reserves. Things would have been dangerous if the investment side had not done so well during the 2000 crash and the grinding bear market that followed.

Watsa's apology and appeal to investors in his November 1999 letter had stoked an impressive short-term rally. The previous good times were still fresh in investors' minds who chose to see the glass as half full. Quentin Broad, now at NBF Securities, assured clients that a turnaround was in the works. In a reflection of the Street's growing impatience, however, he gave Watsa et al. a shorter leash to fix reserving shortfalls at TIG and Crum: "We would expect these initiatives to start making themselves visible in mid to late 2000." He was asking NBF clients to stick around for a fix in the next six months. After that, all bets were off.

The stubborn turnaround would frustrate everyone. Things were certainly not, as Broad expected, visibly improving at TIG or Crum by mid- to late 2000. And while Watsa's optimistic nature never flagged, he was blunt in expressing his frustration with Fairfax's lack of success. It didn't help that the entire industry was in a terrible funk; this was not just a Fairfax slump.

"Nobody—and I mean nobody—truly knows what you are buying when you buy an old book of insurance"

"Against the backdrop of the worst insurance market in 30 years, it has taken longer for us to recognize and fix the problems of the past—much longer than we had expected," Watsa wrote in his 2001 letter. "There is no question that I was too optimistic when we purchased [Crum] and TIG about industry conditions in 1998 and 1999 and our ability to turn around these operations."

Watsa and his investment colleagues might have been telling themselves at this stage that they should have listened to all those people who warned them insurance could be a dangerous business. Jeffrey Bronchick of Cove Street Capital, a Fairfax shareholder, summed up the danger of long-tail risk in a piece for Jim Grant of *Grant's Interest Rate Observer*: "Nobody—and I mean nobody—truly knows what you are buying when you buy an old book of insurance."

Combined ratios at Crum and TIG were running at 146 percent and 128 percent, respectively. Expectations had been for 110 percent and 105 percent, which already indicated big losses. The numbers were grim, and Watsa asked shareholders to read his words twice to let them sink in and then apologized yet again: "It is quite astounding how wrong one can be in this industry." Investors might have welcomed the blunt honesty, as well as the context that the stumble was industry wide—but that did not mean they liked the message or 2000's additional 7 percent slide in the company's stock.

Watsa remained upbeat as he addressed the gloom in the room, noting investors might be worrying: "What's wrong with Fairfax? Can it survive?" He noted that some big investors were scrutinizing Fairfax as a distressed asset. "Our low stock price attracted many 'deep value' investors who purchased our stock just as they purchased bankrupt Loewen Group bonds," he wrote, in a reference to the Vancouver-based funeral services operator that filed for bankruptcy protection in 1999. "For most of 2000, Fairfax was worth more dead than alive and, given our results, it was easy to see why! 2000 was a very difficult and disappointing year for our company and its shareholders—and I was too optimistic as I said earlier."

The following year, the company made Tony Griffiths, who had already served on the boards of several Fairfax subsidiaries, a director on the holding company's board. Watsa acknowledged, joking-not-joking, "Given Tony's extensive turnaround experience in Canada, the timing of his election to our Board may not be inappropriate."

The challenges were a mix of classic long-tail risk from exposure to worse-than-expected claims related to asbestos and environment issues, combined with the challenges of changing handling practices for claims and underwriting during the transition to new ownership. So the apologies continued.

In 2001, book value dropped by 12 percent, and the shares slid another 28 percent. Before things got any worse, Fairfax issued 1.25 million shares to shore up its financial position. The deal was done at C$200, the first time the company had sold stock at below book value—something Watsa never wanted to do. But retaining financial strength was paramount, and strains were evident.

Fairfax leaders are always quick to concede that part of the challenge was self-inflicted. All fingers point to the habit of buying insurer assets on the cheap without appreciating how much a buyer could get hurt by the liabilities. Experiences like Ranger, TIG, and Crum taught them the hard way. But when you're building for the long term, you persevere, even if investors turn away.

Year after year, there were more apologies to shareholders.

When it looked like the lean years were finally done, Watsa shared his deep frustration, though he felt like the company was finding closure: "The last seven years have been very disappointing to me personally, to the management of the company, to our Board and, of course, to you, our shareholders. We never expected to have a dry spell that would last this long."

3. BLAME CANADA? THE "ULTIMATE LONG-MEMORY STOCK"

For Fairfax, one casualty in this period was investor loyalty. There were signs the company was making progress and building value—2002 and 2003 saw back-to-back record profits and 11 percent and 29 percent increases, respectively, in book value. The insurer subsidiaries were still in rough shape, but Fairfax was actually outperforming the broader industry at this point, with Andy Barnard making great strides at Odyssey. "Fairfax seems to be getting up off the floor while many insurers are falling to their knees," observed John Zemanovich of Raven Investment Management in early 2003.

Even at the end of the lean years, Fairfax still sported Berkshire Hathaway–like compound annual gains if you kept to a twenty-year perspective (book value at 25.9 percent and stock price at 22.7 percent). Companies would kill for that performance. But the past few years had investors feeling otherwise. Those unlucky enough to buy the stock at the start of the lean years and hold on for all seven years were sitting on a loss of close to 70 percent. Another serious overhang on the stock was the war with American hedge funds who were hoping to profitably cash out their shorts when Fairfax collapsed in some kind of hoped-for accounting fraud.

Among Fairfax's critics in this period, the view was that the team at HWIC held a hot hand for making investment gains during crashes but couldn't deliver consistent operational results at its insurers. And once that kind of thinking took hold—true or not—it became hard to shake. Andrew Pastor, an analyst for Toronto investment firm EdgePoint, which holds Fairfax shares, looks back and sees a shadow cast on the company from this period that has endured into the 2020s. Fairfax made a dramatic turnaround in the few years leading up to Covid-19, he says, but investors overlooked it because of what he describes as a collective, lingering blind spot—specifically among investors from Canada. It's not all about the lean years, he reasons; it's more about psychology—and Canadian investors.

"While long-memory stocks exist in every market, the dynamic is magnified in Canada," he wrote in his company's 2022 year-end equity comments. He reasoned that the country's stock universe is so small that the investment community arrives at herd perceptions, good or bad, and holds on to them. Fairfax is now a global company but with its head office in Toronto and its shares trading primarily on the TSX, it is subject to a parochial investor bias.

"If you have been burned on a stock in the past, it can take years before you ever look at it again," Pastor wrote. "Fairfax is the ultimate long-memory stock. It went from market darling to pariah. What should have been a comeback story was missed by investors afraid of getting hurt again."

Long-memory investors remember Watsa's missed promises of this period. He was optimistic as usual and his outlook didn't line up with the results. Investors heard a lot of apologizing. Canadians apologize a lot—we *are* a sorry lot. Maybe the little guy from Hyderabad was becoming too Canadian? In 1999, he vowed in his letter, "We have to prove to you (and ourselves) that we can achieve these results in 2000," only to offer his rejoinder the following year: "I was too optimistic in my report to you last year and was wrong." And the year after that he did it again, labelling Fairfax's results as "atrocious."

Turnarounds are hard. Fairfax was frustrated. So were investors. Meanwhile, analysts were under pressure to forecast performance for their clients. Fairfax became the kind of stock you just did not want to put a price target on at this point. And those who did often found themselves on the wrong side of their call, which created new long memories. Analyst Tom Jarmai at RBC jumped back on the bandwagon in December 2000 in anticipation of the release of strong full-year numbers. The stock soared 50 percent in a month as he doubled his 2001 earnings projections. These kinds of rallies raised investors' short-term expectations of a return to go-go growth. What they got was more disappointment—and even longer-lasting memories.

What's more, this was not only a case of fixing problems from the past. A month later, Jarmai said the numbers showed that new post-acquisition insurance underwriting was so poorly reserved, it was eating into his projections for current and future earnings. Frustrated, he dropped his call back to "underperform," and the stock dropped 14 percent in a day, shaving C$400 million off the market capitalization.

Year to year, it was impossible to know if this was going to be a one-off bad year, a "three atrocious years" losing streak, or worse. There were those solid two years in there—2002 and 2003—which kept the faithful's hopes intact. Generally, however, the whole lean period was something that Fairfax was happy to forget—and some investors still cannot.

4. FAIRFAX EARNS ITS STRIPES FOR BEARISH BETS

Warren Buffett has his so-called Noah rule: "Predicting rain doesn't count. Building an ark does." In value investing terms, that means it's great to see a bear market coming, but it will not do you any good if you fail to protect yourself. And if you can also make money from it, all the better. Watsa lives by the same rule. In 2000 and even more so during the Global Financial Crisis in the second half of the decade, Fairfax ran a master class in weather forecasting and a graduate seminar on ark-building.

Watsa and Fairfax had taken to warning investors in 1996 and 1997 about dark storm clouds gathering above the markets. As usual, they were early with their forecast. The team spent four years reducing exposure to stocks, a period in which the S&P 500 doubled. Acting from conviction often means you miss out on the hot money, as Fairfax proved in being early on its crash call on Japanese stocks in the late '80s. When the tech-driven U.S. market soared yet again in 1998, they decided to keep playing defence, and with an epic bubble building, they added a little offence as well with a bold, bearish bet.

It was a material macro call, so they let shareholders know what they were doing with a special October 2, 1999, edition of Watsa's letter. Fairfax informed investors that it had taken equity holdings down to minimal levels and was sitting mostly in cash and the safety of government bonds. That was the defence. On offence, the company bought "puts" on the S&P 500 that would allow it to pursue safety but also to profit from a decline in the index. "We have attempted to prudently protect our shareholders' capital from this pain," wrote Watsa.

The initial purchase of $700 million in puts was at an average index level of 1012, effective between August 1999 and June 2001. Every 100-point drop below that level would increase the value of the puts by $70 million. Total cost of the puts was $72.8 million. If Fairfax was too early, the puts would expire, worthless.

Watsa tracked the ballooning valuations in tech stocks and continued to warn investors away: "If history is any guide, when the music stops, these stocks will be down 90%, unless they are taken over by another high-valued company." Many tech equity analysts had all but given up on modelling companies on earnings—or even sales. New era "metrics" made their way into use, such as the farcical "price-to-concept" ratio. In an example of the irrationality that had set in, Nortel, at the time still by far the largest heavyweight on the Toronto market, had snapped up Qtera Corporation for C$3.5 billion even though Qtera had zero revenue, never mind any profit.

It was a teachable moment for investor discipline, and Watsa was generously giving lessons. He explained that making bearish trades in the middle of a manic market top was very expensive. He also knew conviction is a value investor's best friend: Just be sure you're right, ignore the stupid money, and wait—even if bubbly stock prices keep bubbling.

> We have been very wrong over the past three years as the S&P 500 has done very well—but we will not *speculate* and buy things that don't make any economic sense. We do not believe in "New Eras" and feel that most participants in today's equity markets in

> the U.S. will suffer significant *permanent* loss. It is very likely that the high price for the S&P 500 and Dow Jones reached in this cycle (which may have already taken place) will not be seen again in the next 10 years.

Again, one of the toughest things in value investing is not being able to spot a great buy or a grossly overvalued market—it's having the resolve to wait and not give in to the crowd. "We felt we were from another planet," Watsa told shareholders in 2000 as the dam burst. It was, of course, a great call. The S&P 500 peaked at just over 1500 in March 2000. It did not decisively break through that level for another thirteen years.

When doomsday becomes boomsday

One of Watsa's biggest fears was a repeat of the Japanese market's 1989 collapse. That infamous bubble saw the Nikkei stock index peak in 1989 and remain down about 50 percent a full decade later. The Japanese stock market took eighteen years to bottom out, at 82 percent below its peak, and thirty-five years to finally attain a new high. The HWIC team had built a "nuclear" or "doomsday" test into its investment portfolio, designed to ensure the firm's regulatory capital could withstand a hit of 50 percent in its stock holdings, 30 percent in preferred shares, and 20 percent in bonds. As 2000 loomed and the tech bubble inflated, Watsa ratcheted up his rhetoric. "We are concerned that our 'doomsday' scenario may be tested some time soon," he wrote in his 1998 letter. The next year, he elevated the warning: "We expect a full testing of our 'doomsday' scenario soon."

The HWIC team had spent a few years loading up on options to gain on a tumble in U.S. stocks. Some of Fairfax's short positions—on a basket of tech stocks as well as the broader index—had already expired, worthless. Undeterred, Fairfax bought more, confident a crash was imminent. Other crash preparations included keeping its stock exposure to a very small 8 percent of the investment portfolio and most of that was outside North America.

The tech crash finally hit in early 2000, and stock markets were hammered through late 2002 and into 2003. Fairfax's bets on falling stocks and indexes paid off handsomely, turning doomsday into boomsday, while investors and Fairfax's competitors alike suffered massive losses. Boomsday gains pushed investment returns at Fairfax to a 100 percent gain over the three worst years of the downturn, all while major indexes plummeted by as much as 40 to 60 percent. And nimble trading led the HWIC team to pounce on bargains, lifting the surge after four years to a whopping 187 percent. "We hope we can do as well when we are positive about the markets!!" quipped Watsa in early 2004. Fairfax had cemented its reputation as a stock that investors could flee to for safety and gains when the rest of the market went into the dumpster.

5. DISASTERS STRIKE: AN EPIC RUN OF CATASTROPHES

The windfall from the tech wreck couldn't last. Between the soft markets, unprofitable insurance operations, weaker investment returns, and the steady outflow of cash to bolster reserves at TIG and Crum, the lean years were biblical in scale. In that context, the addition of a plague of catastrophes—natural and man-made—feels about right.

The 9/11 World Trade Center attacks resulted in the largest loss in the U.S. property and casualty industry, just under $50 billion. Then there were back-to-back years of major natural disasters. Four hurricanes struck Florida in 2004, handing Fairfax a $222-million hit. The next year, three more storms hit—Katrina ($431 million), Rita ($84 million), and Wilma ($201 million).

Fairfax's strategy was always to prepare so that it could afford a hit of up to one year's investment income in the worst case. "In the property and casualty industry, catastrophe losses can be lethal," cautions Watsa. "Hurricane Andrew in 1992 more than eliminated all the profits Allstate had made in the state of Florida in the over fifty years it had been in business." The hit to total Fairfax group profits from the major catastrophes in the early 2000s was enormous.

THE HEDGE FUNDS: WELCOME TO THE BIG APPLE

Now that we have set the table with all the good (profiting from the tech wreck) and the bad (almost everything else), let's get to the ugly. The struggling insurers and investor impatience were initially the main event but a minor sideshow distraction was about to take centre stage in terms of drama. Fairfax's struggles to get TIG, Ranger, and Crum into shape had drawn some attention. And the company was about to bring itself more by taking its shares public on the spotlit financial stage of the New York Stock Exchange.

As the previous century came to a close, a full three-quarters of Fairfax employees were in the U.S. and the same proportion of revenue came in U.S. dollars. To raise its profile in its new operational base, Fairfax made the decision to add that U.S. listing in December 2002 and move to U.S.-dollar reporting for 2003. The IPO would also raise much-needed cash for the holding company.

Would Americans understand the stock any better than Canadians? Unlikely. The mix of dozens of subsidiaries and majority- and minority-held investments combined with lumpy realized-versus-unrealized investment gains, tax losses, recoverables, and charges for runoffs, reserving, or catastrophes led to some vigorous head-scratching. In the go-go 1990s, that complexity might have baffled investors, but it fed the perception that Watsa was some kind of infallible market wizard or Canada's Warren Buffett. He was mysterious and could do no wrong. When momentum turned the other way, some investors suspected the complexity was hiding dark secrets. The fact that Prem Watsa was widely considered an inscrutable recluse and Fairfax wouldn't talk to the media or do analyst calls just amplified that perception.

With all that in mind, the business media in Toronto were curious to see what the Americans would make of Canada's infamously enigmatic investor and his company ahead of Fairfax's NYSE IPO. One story in the *National Post* was headlined "Does Anyone Understand This Stock?" Fairfax, wrote Scott Adams, "is still one of the most difficult beasts to understand in the stock market and not just the Canadian market but now the U.S. market, too." Derek DeCloet, a *Post* columnist, ran with that same angle, writing a mock memo to New York's investment community to let them know more about the odd company about to trade on the Big Board.

> To: Wall Street
>
> From: Canada
>
> Re: Reclusive rich guy
>
> We feel compelled to warn you about the strange company we are sending into your midst . . .

Aside from media curiosity, there was no suggestion that Fairfax was about to get any notice, never mind a short-selling ambush. The timing was actually good: Fairfax was enjoying a bounce-back period in the middle of its lean years and its shares had been rallying in Toronto. Watsa even issued a bullish special edition letter entitled "We Are Back!" in early November, touting signs of a turnaround in the making.

The shares made their quiet debut during the holiday season. In its first fifteen days, the stock averaged less than 180,000 shares a day. On January 13, 2003, a Monday, the first shot was fired. Peter Eavis of TheStreet.com put out a column musing, "Has Fairfax fallen into a deep hole it can't climb out of?" The story suggested grossly inadequate reserving and mounting debt could see Fairfax "face the mother of all liquidity crunches over the next 18 months." The points raised were coming from a research report by Morgan Keegan analyst John Gwynn, which was released Friday of that same week. Meanwhile, the NYSE's most recent weekly list of highly shorted stocks showed two million Fairfax shares had been sold short.

When the Morgan Keegan report was released, Watsa was pulled out of a Friday dinner meeting in Stratford, an hour north of his former Canadian hometown, London. "We thought this guy must be kidding," he recalls. "We never heard of him before, never heard of Morgan Keegan before." He returned to his meal, bemused but confident it would blow away the next week. Mostly, he felt there was sloppy thinking behind the analysis of liquidity threats and under-reserving. How could anyone take it seriously?

> It was so obviously wrong. If they'd spent five minutes on our annual report, they'd have realized that we are a very decentralized company and each of our companies is separately capitalized and financed. So at any one time, we could take a company public.

> We could even sell it if we had to. We never needed to do that, but we did take Odyssey public and we took Northbridge public. And we were able to refinance our bonds at Crum & Forster. If you had bothered to read our annual report, you'd have recognized that we had a lot of options in front of us.

But the genie was out of the bottle. Monday was Martin Luther King Jr. Day, so markets were closed in the U.S., but in Toronto Fairfax shares opened into a freefall. Watsa's phone was ringing constantly and he found himself on the line with the Toronto Stock Exchange, which wanted to know what on earth was going on. So, with one eye on the stock as it plunged 40 percent to $57, Watsa and his team drafted a statement. The news release carried the same underlying tone of dismissive incredulity: "The valuation methodology for reserves employed in a recently issued research report on Fairfax suffers fatally from the inherent limitations admitted by that report and a complete lack of knowledge of the factual details necessary to produce a reserve calculation."

For now, Watsa was able to calm the panic. The shares zoomed back up to $85 by the end of the day's trading. But this was just a warm-up: Gwynn would write another sixty-plus research reports on Fairfax in the next few years. Welcome to one of the uglier hedge fund wars in Wall Street history.

A SHORT HEDGE FUND WHO'S WHO

Since launching his New York–based SAC Capital fund in 1992, Steve Cohen was recording 40-plus percent annual returns, and now it appeared he was looking to pad those numbers with a big drop in Fairfax shares. Adam Sender, an SAC alumnus, had spun out his own fund Exis Capital Management and seemingly saw the same opportunity. Dan Loeb, whose Third Point hedge fund had been running since 1995, was another Wall Street big gun who appeared to smell blood. It seemed they were all reading Gwynn's research and sharing notes.

Rounding out the list of major shorts was the colourful Jim Chanos, sometimes known as the "catastrophe capitalist" and lauded with sleuthing out and profiting by betting against various frauds, most notably Enron Corporation, through short sales.

Chanos made his name as a stock analyst in Chicago when he smelled fraud in the cash-flow financials of Baldwin-United, the name behind the venerable American piano maker. By this time, Baldwin was making a different kind of music, morphing into a closed-end fund selling a kind of insurance annuity that made it a market success story with $24 billion in assets in 1982. Chanos dug in and discovered Baldwin was paying fat commissions to its sales force out of the cost of the annuity and hiding the shortfall.

His "sell" call made him a lone voice of warning while Baldwin's CEO was being celebrated by Wall Street analysts and the business media. When Baldwin bought a new firm, to keep its fraud going, regulators reined it in, and the crackdown spiralled into a $9-billion bankruptcy, the largest at that time in U.S. history. Chanos was just twenty-four years old. His reputation was made. On an insurance fraud no less.

THE FORMIDABLE MR. CHANOS: "WE THINK THIS IS A ZERO"

Reputations were about to be put on the line in the battle with Fairfax. From Wall Street's perspective, it didn't look like much of a fight: In the ring, the legendary architect of the Enron takedown and his tag team of hedge fund heavyweights takes on a reclusive former door-to-door air conditioner salesman from Hyderabad via small town Ontario. That's how the hedgies framed it. The U.S. media lapped it up.

With Enron, investors, analysts, journalists, and regulators had looked but failed to see fraud. Chanos saw it. Then he started shorting it and rode it down to zero, walking away with half a billion dollars for his efforts. So when Chanos said there was now serious trouble at Fairfax and bet his money on it, people took it seriously. As late as the summer of 2005, Chanos remained certain Fairfax would follow the Enron script: "We think this is a zero."

Chanos and the other hedge fund heavyweights, as well as stories in TheStreet.com, *Fortune*, and other media were all singing from the same song sheet when it came to Fairfax. And the song sheet in question was a series of research reports written by John Gwynn at Morgan Keegan. The boutique investment firm was a small player and Fairfax was Gwynn's first file at his new employer. As he built his bearish thesis on the stock, it became clear a loose community of hedge funds were already sharing and coordinating their short strategies, even before the stock's IPO on the NYSE.

Of course, there is a natural alignment of interests between investment banks and big investors, whether they are bullish and long or bearish and short. Everyone is looking for an edge and sometimes information is swapped, sometimes with a wink, sometimes with an email. There are also regulatory rules about sharing and trading on information from research reports before they are released publicly. Let's just say this community played loose with the rules. And the media is always interested in getting a scoop on the next Enron. Was Fairfax it?

"IT TOOK US SOME TIME TO FIGURE OUT THAT . . . THESE HEDGE FUNDS WERE TRYING TO DESTROY US"

Author Matt Taibbi deftly covered the campaign in his book *The Divide: American Injustice in the Age of the Wealth Gap*. In a single breathless paragraph, he captures the absurdity and menace in what reads like a screenplay pitch for a messy Wall Street thriller:

> The Fairfax fiasco is a tale of harassment on a grand scale, in which the cream of America's corporate culture followed executives, burgled information from private bank accounts, researched the Canadians' sexual preferences for blackmail purposes, broke into hotel rooms and left threatening messages, prank-called a cancer-stricken woman in the middle of the night, and even harassed the pastor of the staid Anglican church where the Canadian CEO worshipped on Sundays. They worked tirelessly to scare away investors and convince rating agencies to denounce the firm, and in general spread so many lies and false rumors to so many people using so many different false names that they needed a spreadsheet to keep track of their aliases.

Was it always the plan to bring down Fairfax at any cost? We may never get an exact picture on why this war unfolded the way it did. John Gwynn was eventually fired for sharing his research reports with hedge funds prior to their release, then he passed away in 2009.

Some media accounts frame Gwynn as an analyst who worked hard at finding a company that genuinely might be headed for a wall. He may even have held the conviction that Fairfax was already going down. Either way, he was prodigious in sharing his take in more than sixty pieces of research—what Fairfax labelled a "relentless drumbeat of false, misleading and recklessly unfounded reports." He may have gotten it all wrong because he had not understood the company.

Gwynn focused on what he alleged were deficiencies in reserves, goodwill, shareholders' equity, tax obligations, revenue shortfalls, reinsurance recoveries, and other issues. He dug at some of the liquidity measures Fairfax was already working at addressing, which gave the assertions a veneer of truth. And yet, looking past his more reckless, unsubstantiated claims, he seemed to have a fundamentally bad read on the situation. As Watsa explains, Gwynn failed to understand Fairfax had all kinds of levers and tools to address just about any financial challenge. A number of factors were straining its finances, but the only serious things Fairfax was guilty of was being misunderstood and financially strained.

The costs of runoff and reserve building were giving Fairfax a terrible case of acquisition indigestion, but it was manageable. The company had purchased an additional reinsurance "cover" from Swiss Re to absorb losses from reserving. In an emergency, it could float or sell off larger stakes of its assets, or even entire subsidiaries. Its finances were fully insulated. Perhaps another company in its position would have done a fire sale to make a quick cleanup of quarterly results and promote its stock. But Fairfax was patiently managing its own way, refusing to panic, playing the long game for future strength.

What became evident is that Morgan Keegan did business with the hedge funds by handling their trading. The brokerage later settled with Fairfax, but denied any involvement in a campaign against the company. Gwynn and the shorts, however, appeared to have a shared interest in coordinating their efforts to inflict maximum damage to support major short positions. As Taibbi offers, "The record suggests that their collective belief that enough bad press and negative market momentum would crater the firm was even stronger than their belief in Fairfax's actual problems."

BAD TIMING FOR ANTELOPES

The hedge funds may have misread Fairfax's vulnerabilities, but it would be easy for any investor to see real strains. Fairfax had broken assets to push into runoff, which was an expensive process. Other assets in better shape still required buckets of cash from the holding company to offset reserving shortfalls. That redirection of cash ate into the emergency kitty at head office, which was meant to be kept at $800 million in those days, and the hedge funds were watching every dollar in and out as it shrank.

The strains were real, says Bill McFarland, at the time Fairfax's auditor with PwC and later the company's lead independent director. "Everyone was after Prem," he recalls. "They only had $2 billion in equity and very nominal income, so there was no cushion for problems. No dollars for a rainy day." Watsa needed cash and he also needed time, from an auditor's perspective, because a company needs to show a record of stability to give regulators confidence in their operating stability.

The added stress and distraction wore everyone down, recalls Roger Lace: "That was a very rough period. Prem always made the point that the company was very diversified and had a lot of flexibility, but there was heated discussion on which options we should choose to beef that up. The short sellers were the lions and tigers looking for the weak antelope in the herd. There was weakness there, for sure, and they pounced at our maximum vulnerability."

With the big cats circling, the annual bleed of cash into covering reserves at Crum, Ranger, TIG, and other subsidiaries forced Fairfax to make some moves to regain financial flexibility and retain cash reserves on hand at the holding company. Fairfax had a "management holding company survival ratio" for its cash cushion. That meant having enough cash to pay administrative and interest expenses with no dividend stream from any of the insurers or reinsurers for a four-to-five-year period. Adding to the drama, Fairfax was feeling pressure to protect the financial strength ratings of the main insurance companies. And a spate of catastrophes added to the squeeze.

Watsa and his senior team met regularly, drawing up lists of all the options that could provide added financial flexibility. Extra reinsurance that Fairfax could draw on was picked up from Swiss Re. There were assets to be IPO'd (Odyssey and Northbridge, a new amalgamation of the Canadian insurance assets), while retaining control. Equity offerings were mulled over, to be placed with Fairfax-friendly investors rather than publicly, which drove the hedge funds crazy.

Uncharacteristically tense meetings took place at head office, as management drafted their emergency list of to-dos. They ended up doing pretty much everything on their list, including three equity issues, the creation and IPO of Northbridge, and a major bond and convertible underwriting for Crum. They won their needed wriggle room and avoided a potentially deadly ratings downgrade. They did not have to sell any assets and they won back a lot of investor confidence. But it was hard on the team to figure out how to play all that defence.

"There was a lot of internal tension—more than we had ever experienced before," adds Lace. The hedge funds did not back off. Instead, they portrayed Fairfax's financial strengthening moves as panic. "It never affected me in terms of my long-term faith in Fairfax, but you could see how it looked with the shares down and bad news in the press. You look at that and you could easily believe it was all going to hell. We made a lot of good moves and got through."

The annual letter started to give over pages of detail on the state of preparedness at Fairfax, along with discussions on the running totals of debt, reserving, cash on hand, and access to credit. That disclosure helped their case. So did the added clarity on the value of the subsidiaries as Fairfax opened up to investment bankers during the equity and debt offerings. Curiously, this added disclosure of the inner workings at Fairfax gave Wall Street a much rosier view of the company's finances. Until then, it had only been able to guess.

"Eyes have been opened to Fairfax's accomplishments over the past 15 years," offered Jeffrey Bronchick of Cove Street Capital when the Odyssey IPO closed. "This may, in fact, be the first real look at Watsa and Fairfax the U.S. has ever had."

Now that they were publicly traded, Odyssey and Northbridge could raise more money individually if needed. Investor appetite for the two stocks helped stoke more optimism in Watsa and Fairfax. The manoeuvring continued—Fairfax realized it had sold a bit too much of Odyssey in the IPO and bought back enough through a convertible offering to reach 80 percent and maximize tax benefits. Both subsidiaries would be reprivatized several years later when Fairfax had lots of cash on hand from its Big Short–style bets on the Global Financial Crisis. The overriding goal was always cash on hand and financial flexibility.

The IPOs reflected positively on Fairfax in a less obvious way as well. The subsidiaries now had a market value via the stock market and it was much higher than the prices Fairfax had been carrying on its books. Instead of accounting skullduggery hiding inflated holdings, the company books were actually understating their value. Finally, there was still more upside. Odyssey did not have brand recognition in its home U.S. market. Being publicly traded helped to change that. None of that convinced the hedge funds to walk away: In fact, they turned up the heat.

"A FULL COLONOSCOPY"

Even loyal Fairfax shareholders could be vulnerable to the bad press and the stock was under steady pressure between 2002 and 2006. "You have to remember that a lot of what was wrong with the stock at that time was the short sellers trying to convince the world that there was a serious problem," says Wade Burton, today president of HWIC but then an analyst with Cundill Funds of Vancouver. "And there clearly was not a serious problem, but enough people say enough things about anyone and people will believe them."

Cundill, led by legendary Graham-follower Peter Cundill, had already been a Fairfax shareholder. And as Burton, then thirty-one, was doing research for one of the firm's value mutual funds, he found Fairfax kept turning up as a strong buy on his screens, despite the strains. "I saw a company that tripled in size between 1999 and 2003 and was doing it with a lot of debt. There was a lot of speculation that they were underreserved and a lot of people on the Street hated the stock. So I did a full colonoscopy on the financials."

Complexity made that task hard work. You had to understand how Fairfax operated as a holding company and how it handles risk. In insurance turnarounds, there is a lot of runoff—upwards of $200 million a year in Fairfax's case—and cash flowing up to the holding company from the subsidiaries, as well as flowing out from the holding company to meet various obligations.

"In the end, it really came down to Prem," says Burton. "First of all, I needed to establish that he knew he had these assets that he could sell to repay the holding company debt if necessary. And second, I needed to learn if he was a fraudster as a lot of the short sellers were saying."

Watsa passed Burton's test, and Cundill invested a lot more in Fairfax, taking the lead in a subsequent underwriting that beefed up financial strength to insulate it from the hedge funds. Impressed with the company, Burton was later courted by Watsa and joined the Fairfax team.

Average investors didn't have the expertise or access to do their own deep dive on the company and were stuck wrestling between their faith in Fairfax management and the scary allegations coming from well-known hedge funds. The faithful and the detractors squared off and muddied the waters. To market watchers, it was becoming impossible to even guess at who had the upper hand. "Quarter after quarter, both sides wait for someone to blink," Justin Fuller, an analyst at Morningstar Inc., told the *Wall Street Journal*. "There is just a bunch of rabid fans and equally rabid short sellers, arguing at full volume," observed Derek DeCloet, columnist at *The Globe and Mail* in November 2004. "Those who follow the insurance company closely tend to believe it's either (a) absurdly undervalued or (b) headed for bankruptcy."

Meanwhile, the cooperation between short sellers and Gwynn appeared to turn down a dark path. As the hedge funds found themselves unable to make their bets pay off, attempts were made to sink the company by more unsavoury tactics. "It took us some time to figure out that this group of shorts, these hedge funds, were trying to destroy us," explains Watsa.

FAIRFAX FIGHTS BACK: ENTER PAUL RIVETT

As a young lawyer on Bay Street, Paul Rivett, later president at Fairfax, had worked on a number of deals involving the insurer. He liked what he saw and came aboard to join the corporate legal team in 2004, by which time the run of negative stories and rumours was in its second year. It bewildered Rivett but also had him thinking about what great timing it was for him to snap up the company's stock for his retirement fund.

"They're great people. I can't imagine it's that low," Rivett recalled thinking. Once aboard, he began to notice how orchestrated the campaign of stories, the research coming out of Morgan Keegan, and the short-selling strategies were. He recommended and then led a preliminary investigation confirming that the same false allegations and flawed research findings were being repeated in different stories to create a false chorus of doom. He was also acutely aware that Fairfax's policy was to ignore the media altogether and he set out to convince Watsa to fight back.

It wasn't Fairfax's style to get into fights and the hedge funds were counting on that continuing. "They saw us as an easy target," Rivett explained to Bethany McLean at *Fortune*. "We don't talk to the media, our stock is thinly traded and this is a reputational business." He reasoned that if Fairfax didn't tell its story for itself, the vacuum would be filled by the bad guys. "We were being beaten around, not just in the U.S. but also in our own backyard," Rivett recounted years later. "It took a conscious effort to get Prem to hire a PR firm, just for basic damage control, and even more effort to get access to editors and reporters so that they could hear our side and get the facts right."

Recalls Watsa, "Paul was instrumental in making me realize that as you get big, you become of interest, and if you don't talk to the media, you're seen as secretive, sinister, with something to hide. So when these guys dumped on us and we had no friends in the media... They had never read our annual reports. Since then, we've wised up."

As the shorts' campaign dragged on, the next uncharacteristic—but prudent—Fairfax move was to hire some big guns. Adopting a don't-bring-a-knife-to-a-gunfight attitude, it enlisted Michael Sitrick, a high-calibre fixer whom *Fortune* once called "one of the most accomplished practitioners of the dark arts of public relations." Sitrick and Watsa? An extremely odd couple to say the least, but these were extraordinary times.

These were new tactics for everyone at Fairfax. Salsberg remembered being thoroughly creeped out when he met with people to discuss providing additional help on the legal and investigative side. Some of them were "scary," he said. "You couldn't feel comfortable that they would abide by the rules. If we hired them and they didn't, we'd be tainted."

The decision was made to go with Marc Kasowitz, an aggressive trial lawyer at New York–based Kasowitz, Benson, Torres & Friedman. The law firm also did investigations but, said Salsberg, "played by the rules when they did things like going to bars and listening to conversations to help us build the lawsuit."

The A team was in place. Up until then, Watsa's thinking was always, "The facts will out." Spyro Contogouris was one of the key factors that convinced him patience could backfire dangerously.

"THE CASE OF THE HEDGE FUND HITMAN"

Contogouris was a freelance research analyst in his mid-forties, working out of New Orleans as M14 Reconnaissance LLC. In a 2007 *Bloomberg Markets* feature headlined "The Case of the Hedge Fund Hitman," Anthony Effinger profiled Contogouris, who had colourful past dealings involving Houston real estate and Nigerian natural gas. His investment in the latter, which collapsed, indirectly led to his meeting fund managers who had bet against that investment and they included portfolio managers working directly with Steve Cohen at SAC. Contogouris had discovered a market for the kind of financial investigative work he seemed to enjoy in the shadows, making a lot of money for short sellers. "We do work based on speculation—and last I checked, it wasn't illegal." His SAC connections and other efforts led to his introduction to former leading SAC portfolio manager Adam Sender, who had formed a new hedge fund, Exis Capital, funded primarily with SAC seed capital. It also brought him to Chanos and prominent hedge fund executive Dan Loeb. During this period, he worked out of the New York offices of Exis, a client, with his colleague Max Bernstein. While the short sellers' campaign, the Fairfax Project, could count on sharing information and coordinating with analyst Gwynn, it appeared to be Contogouris and Bernstein who took the lead on the misinformation and intimidation, according to allegations which were denied by both men. "Contogouris would peddle his fantastic fiction to anyone and everyone in the investment, regulatory, law enforcement, and financial media who would take a meeting," alleges Michael Bowe, a lawyer who represented Fairfax as part of the Kasowitz team. "Many of those," Bowe says, "were set up by the hedge funds clients, who presented him as a brilliant independent analyst and not their paid operative. He would bring to these meetings a big architectural tube containing an enormous schematic of Fairfax's organizational chart that would take up an entire conference room table when unfolded. On it, he had added entities, lines, and notations of the frauds he claimed he had discovered but were not disclosed by Fairfax."

In addition to props, Contogouris would reportedly often also bring along a solo, small-town accountant who made his living doing the books for individuals and small businesses. In the meetings, however, he was presented as a skilled forensic accountant with expertise in complicated insurance companies. "In these presentations, they would declare with certainty that 'Fairfax is the greatest known insurance fraud of the 21st century.' The two would lay out a case where Fairfax, like Enron, had billions of dollars of undisclosed off-balance sheet debt, undisclosed losses, and multiple foreign subsidiaries engaged in masking these deficiencies and other frauds."

A ROGUE'S GUIDE TO INTIMIDATION

Watsa's resolve and humour during the attacks were legendary inside Fairfax. His wife, Nalini, recalls, "One of the guys in the office said, 'Well, Prem still laughs in the office so things can't really be that bad.'" That is just how his mind focuses, she adds. "He works as hard as he can, and he sleeps like a baby. He never worries about anything that he doesn't have control over. He just insisted, 'The truth will out.'"

But many staff in the office of fair and friendly Fairfax did worry and lose sleep. And the longer it went on, the nastier it got. "When they came after Prem, I remember talking to Rick because I didn't understand what was happening," recalls Nalini. "It was so scary, and I told Rick I don't know who these people are. They were calling me at home too. I asked him to please look after Prem because I thought Prem was sometimes a little bit naive. I was afraid something would happen to him. The way they came after him, I told Prem I will never get over it the rest of my life. I knew he had done nothing wrong, but the things that were said and the stories that were written, I cannot forget." At the time, Nalini had enough on her mind, dealing with the scare of a cancer diagnosis.

"It seemed sinister," offers Bowe. "Unidentified men visited Watsa's home when he wasn't there, began questioning his wife about his activities, and then left her a package with documents intended to suggest he was involved in fraud. They followed Watsa, surveilled his house, and left strange uncomfortable voicemails on his home phone. Someone would also gain access to Watsa's hotel room when he was visiting a subsidiary in Connecticut and leave the book *Tipping Point* on the pillow of his bed."

Many staff were targeted. Using the alias "Dick Tracey," someone warned Watsa's executive assistant, JoAnn Butler, that her boss was stealing money and set to flee the country or be put in jail. They warned she would be an accessory and locked up to live out her last days behind bars, says Bowe. Seeing Butler targeted made colleagues sick to their stomachs.

Some efforts stand out from Fairfax's allegations in legal filings. All the defendants, including Morgan Keegan and Contogouris, denied the allegations. Some of the actions were admitted, such as delivering materials to Watsa's reverend, but the parties defended their intent.

In the years after the suit, almost all of the parties were dropped by the courts from Fairfax's action for jurisdictional or other procedural reasons. Morgan Keegan eventually settled in 2018 for $20 million and Fairfax was awarded a jury verdict of $10.9 million against some of the defendants. Fairfax continues to appeal some of the courts' decisions. Fairfax's allegations in the 2006 suit include:

- Senior executives were regularly followed, visited at their homes, and fed a stream of financial records in manila envelopes that purported to contain or relate to frauds. They were threatened with prosecution if they did not agree to co-operate with Contogouris.

- Several attempts were made to hack the Fairfax website and multiple fake websites were set up in the name of Prem Watsa to disseminate false reports.
- Parties connected to the short sellers called senior executives and read odd things to get into their heads. Rivett recalls getting evening calls from them reading passages from *Harry Potter*. These performances were allegedly so popular with certain of the short-seller clients that they asked to be conferenced in when they were made. "It felt as if they were trying to wage a psychological warfare campaign," Rivett said.
- When the flood of Morgan Keegan research reports were failing to achieve the desired effect, the investigators' M14 Reconnaissance was used to issue more incendiary and creative research reports that drew parallels to money laundering, Enron, and other frauds.
- The hedge fund hitmen were thorough enough to know Watsa is a man of strong faith and they worked that angle as well, in dramatic form. One day in 2005, a letter was delivered to Reverend Barry Parker at St. Paul's Anglican Church. It began, "Dear Father. The attached documents are being sent to you out of my concern for the Church's finances" and described the "mystifying, spectacular rise" of an "insurance medusa" who had swindled money from his own company and was a danger because he was advising on the Toronto Anglican Church's finances. "Be aware, be skeptical and ask Mr. Watsa to make a full confession." Attached was food for thought in the form of a thirty-page write-up on a well-known fraudster entitled "Marty Frank[illegible] Greed and $200 Million Fraud."
- One day in 2006, Contogouris allegedly pretended to be a reporter and got past security at RiverStone, a Fairfax subsidiary in London, and began informing executives that Watsa had sold their firm and he needed some inside information to assist. The next day, he found and warned former Fairfax CFO Trevor Ambridge that criminal prosecution awaited if he did not accept a "fair and friendly" meeting to share confidential information. Like a spy caper, it turned into a double trap as Ambridge played

Prem Watsa with his parents, Manohar and Irene, at his graduation from the Indian Institute of Technology (IIT) in Madras in 1971.

Just weeks after she arrived in Canada with his parents, Nalini married Prem on August 25, 1973, in London, Ontario.

A young Prem Watsa.

The Hamblin Watsa team celebrates their first bonus cheques. (Left to right, standing): Roger Lace, Tony Hamblin, Mary Pritchard, and Prem Watsa. (Seated): Frances Burke.

Andy Barnard (left) with his protege, Brian Young. Both joined Fairfax through the Odyssey acquisition. Young succeeded Barnard as CEO of Odyssey, before moving into a global role under Barnard and overseeing all of Fairfax's insurers.

Order of Canada ceremony, 2015. Watsa was named a Member of the Order of Canada. Also pictured: David Johnston, who was appointed an Officer in the Order in 1988 and promoted to Companion in 1997.

Watsa says Indian Prime Minister Narendra Modi deserves high praise for the way he has opened up the Indian economy, raised living standards, and reduced corruption. Photo taken June 28, 2018.

Prem and Peter Clarke at a company event. Clarke is a celebrated example of nurturing talent to promote from within. Working his way up through all parts of the business since he came on board in 1997, Clarke was Chief Operating Officer in 2022 when he was appointed President, which makes him CEO-in-waiting.

Financial "tombstones" are common ways for companies and their underwriters to commemorate major financings. Watsa gifted this one to Paul Fink to celebrate the refinancing of Markel Financial Holdings in 1985. He found humour in Fink's threat to take Watsa down if he didn't deliver on a successful turnaround. "It was aimed at my head," explained Watsa.

A bust of Sir John Templeton (1912–2008), a legendary fund manager whose fundamental analysis blended value and growth strategies with a global focus. Watsa holds him in very high regard—personally and professionally. He keeps it in the Fairfax boardroom.

IN MEMORIAM

Rick Salsberg (1945–2024), pictured with Watsa. As a lawyer at Torys LLP in Toronto, Salsberg acted for Fairfax in the early days before taking a one-year sabbatical to join the company—a leave he never returned from. Watsa considered him his consigliere. He said he never made a decision without consulting Rick. Fairfax created an annual prize in his name "to the one person who most represents our culture" as well as a memorial leadership lecture and prize for graduates of the University of Toronto's Faculty of Law. The latter is to be awarded to the student "who has displayed the greatest interest in extra-curricular work of an academic nature."

IN MEMORIAM

Ramaswamy Athappan (1945–2024). While Watsa typically referred to colleagues by first name, Athappan was always "Mister." The two met in the 1990s and Athappan joined Fairfax in 2006, building the business in Singapore, and then more broadly in Southeast Asia under Fairfax Asia. He was lauded for his character as a leader, mentor, and advisor. He was also extraordinarily successful at insurance. As "one of the world's best underwriters," Athappan's contribution to Fairfax was recognized by Watsa with a new prize to be awarded to a Fairfax company for underwriting excellence. Fairfax has also created the Mr. Athappan Underwriting Academy in Singapore to train others in his methods.

Vinodh Loganadhan (1954–2025). In a milestone year of personal losses at Fairfax, the company lost a senior leader and family member. As VP of Administrative Services at a small head office, Loganadhan was essentially Watsa's Chief of Staff: "He was our go-to guy for just about anything that happened at Fairfax and we were the fortunate beneficiaries of his wonderful sense of humour and his sage advice on many diverse matters," says Watsa. Vinodh was also Nalini's brother—making him family as Prem's brother-in-law.

Watsa in action on the tennis court, where the mild-mannered leader took no prisoners. As Paul Fink described: "If you ever play tennis with him, he's out there to kill you, but . . . he would call an ambulance as soon as he could."

(Left to right): Ben, Prem, Nalini, Christine, and Stephanie Watsa on vacation in Greece in 2024.

Watsa was elected Chancellor of the University of Waterloo in 2009 and re-elected in 2011, serving in the role until 2014.

Fairfax senior leaders at their 35th anniversary gathering at the Corinthia Hotel in London, July 2022.

along to draw out the scammers and a meeting was planned to flush out their identity, while Contogouris worked to get the FBI and Britain's MI5 involved under false pretenses.
- In the summer of 2006, Contogouris and others allegedly spread rumours in the bond market and among regulators, first that Fairfax had failed to complete a financing and then that Prem had transferred the assets into Nalini's name and fled the country.

For those habituated to the Gordon Gekko culture of Wall Street macho profanity, records of emails between the shorts might not have raised eyebrows. But the contrast with Fairfax, where swearing and egos were discouraged and a "confrontational style is not appropriate," is stark. One email between hedge fund investors appeared to relish the prospect of sexual assault by the hedge funds. Another to Contogouris exclaimed, "Die, Prem, die!" Yet another: "I want his head in a box."

One exchange, between a shortseller and Contogouris, began with the latter pleading on July 23 with his client for a break from Fairfax to work on another file: "Brain is Fairfax fried." The response was that Fairfax was job number one until the company was dead: "NOOOOOOOOOOOOOO. FAIR #1 UNTIL WE C THE CORPSE."

IF YOU CAN FOOL THE DEBT RATERS, THE WHOLE HOUSE CAN FALL DOWN

Fairfax did not have to be financially squeezed to be vulnerable. There was an obvious drag on the stock, leading to emotional exhaustion and an enormous operational distraction during a difficult time. Even more threatening was the risk to reputation and debt ratings.

"Our one major worry was that people would no longer deal with us," explains Watsa.

> It never used to be that way, but now everybody looks at the stock price to get a sense of confidence in a company. Business won't come to you if your stock is going down. Banks won't give you a

> line of credit if you haven't borrowed from them before. The press starts asking what's going on.
>
> Worse, if Crum & Forster lost its A- rating, its customers wouldn't want to deal with us, the brokers wouldn't want to deal with us, and we wouldn't be able to write as much business, if any business at all. If you are BBB in the United States, you have a very hard time writing insurance.

The confidence factor definitely made the company vulnerable, argued Fairfax shareholder Staley Cates at the time. "It's one thing if the shorts attack a company with a certain kind of product, but in the world of insurance—where it's really about confidence and the rating agencies are so important—and if it ends up scaring the rating agencies, it can actually tangibly end up scaring the customer," said Cates, the recently retired vice-chairman at Southeastern Asset Management.

Emails that emerged in legal filings and the discovery process show Andy Heller of Exis Capital talking up this strategy of undermining confidence in Fairfax's backyard—"the way to get this thing down is to get them where they eat, like the credit analysts and holders," Heller emailed short investor Jonathan Kalikow of Stanfield Capital on February 22, 2006. "We're taking this baby down for the count. [Adam Sender] and I are going to toronto in 2 weeks for a group lunch."

Heller, Sender, and the other hedge funds of course denied Fairfax's allegations in the complaint. And it's not clear if that lunch ever took place, but, regardless, you would not have found Staley Cates at the table. Southeastern were deep value investors, big fans of Watsa, and loyal Fairfax shareholders. Like Burton over at Cundill, Cates and his guys did their own due diligence and found these years to be a great time to invest in Fairfax. The problems were well known, Cates reasoned: "He had to fill reserve potholes after saying he'd never have to do it again. Historic stuff was still coming in ugly." Their faith came with the clear risk that Fairfax could face a squeeze if reinsurers stumbled in a downturn in 2001, but they were confident Watsa could navigate it if it happened.

"Lots of people are nervous about this one," Cates told *Outstanding Investor*. "But to be fair, . . . those of our clients who know Prem aren't worried at all. In fact, they are downright pumped about the opportunity." It was a classic case of contrarian value conviction. Cates calculated Fairfax shares were trading at 50 percent of their fair value and Southeastern would step up as lead investor in the 2004 offering of $300 million. "One of the best indicators . . . that we're doing the right thing for our clients is when everyone thinks we're morons," quipped Cates. Having fans like Cundill, Southeastern, and Markel Group on hand to step up and invest gave Fairfax the luxury of not having to tap the broader public market for financings—much to the frustration of the short sellers.

"SHORTING FAIRFAX MIGHT BE VERY HAZARDOUS TO YOUR WEALTH"

While most of the vulnerability chatter centred on Fairfax, some of the company's biggest fans were seeing, even early on, some hurt coming the other way for the hedge funds. Cates looked at the short activity in Fairfax trading at the end of 2001 and wondered if the hedge funds even understood their risks. "It's not that the shorts aren't reading the footnotes. They just don't believe 'em—or maybe they expect things to worsen." He suggested short sellers had not done their homework and cautioned that they had picked the wrong stock to target: "Shorting Fairfax might be very hazardous to your wealth." How hazardous? "You can definitely get killed."

It can take a lot of money to run a short campaign and if supply is thin, it can get tricky and very expensive. Always generous with his expertise, Watsa schooled shareholders with some investor education tips on short sales at the April 14 annual general meeting in 2003: "Now, these are very brave people because ours is a very illiquid company; our shares are held by long-term investors. There's not much traded." The upshot was that the shares were hard to find in order to sell short and limited supply meant upward pressure on the price. The hedge funds certainly weren't going to be able to borrow shares from Cundill, Southeastern, and Markel for their short sales.

The longer the campaign ran, the more expensive it got. "Fairfax had an enormously expensive borrow," explained Andy Heller, chief operating officer at Exis Capital. "If Fairfax didn't go out of business in three years, the trade was a loser. If I'm paying 35 percent a year to borrow the security, just do the math." In order to call their trade a winner, many of the shorts would need to run Fairfax down to zero. And they were still convinced they could do it.

SHOWDOWN: FIVE DAYS IN JULY

The long war of the shorts, dragging well into its fourth year, would come to a spectacular conclusion in the fateful summer of 2006. For months, lines were being drawn in a true battle royal. Fairfax found itself in a fresh bit of unwelcome controversy that played into the hedge funds' hands. A broader SEC crackdown on so-called finite insurance had sent insurance companies scrambling to get a clear view on their accounting and disclose their exposures. The key concern of regulators was an abuse of finite deals that could be used to window-dress balance sheets to make reserving look healthier. AIG and others came under heavy regulatory fire for this accounting practice.

Tired of losing money, the hedge funds were becoming confident they were on the verge of a decisive knockout blow. A series of media stories was planned for July, which they hoped would prove fatal by themselves. The timetable for a crackdown on finite insurance was expected to provide artillery support. As the story is often told, those were the factors the hedge funds expected to prove decisive in taking down Fairfax. As Michael Bowe reveals, there would also be a surprise bomb ticking.

Bowe says investigators had been tracking an escalating amount of chatter since February. The other side was talking about a big day coming and it would come in July. As for the secret weapon, that was all the work of Contogouris, who seemed to have finally broken through with enough false information to regulators and the Feds to put Fairfax and Watsa in their crosshairs.

The investigation Bowe was leading in 2006 had gathered a lot of alarming insights, but the thing that alarmed him the most at this moment was how the conviction of the short sellers had suddenly escalated. Bowe's team was listening and watching. They heard the boasts that Adam Sender had a giant party planned. It would be a big deal. Bob Dylan was going to sing. Seriously. This was a hard rain coming for Prem. The war was expected to be wrapped up in July, and the celebration was due to take place on Labour Day in the Hamptons. By June, Bowe says they still didn't have a handle on exactly what was making the shorts so cocky, but it was time to hit the alarm and keep Dylan from stepping onstage on the east end of Long Island.

The report Bowe was putting together would have taken until October or November to finish, but the noise was telling him they didn't have time. "The campaign was so active that it was not hard to get information," he says. "It was all over the place." It was already early July. Bowe reached out immediately to Watsa and laid out his fears. Legendary for his patience and kindness, Watsa is more fair and friendly than fighter. But he is also a master tactician. "Prem is by far the mildest CEO I have ever met," offers Bowe. "He is also fearless when principles are at stake."

Watsa, *listens then thinks for a few seconds*: "How quickly can we get a lawsuit together?"

Bowe: "I can write it up in two weeks."

Watsa: "Let's do it."

(Bowe begins furiously typing the first of 100-plus pages, detailing the whole ugly four-year saga that has played out away from public eye.)

Bowe hit his deadline. Fairfax was finally ready to tell its side of the story. Then things hit a major roadblock.

By this time, it would appear that thanks to Contogouris, so many accusations were flying that the U.S. Securities and Exchange Commission, the Federal Bureau of Investigation, and the U.S. Attorney for the Southern District of New York had opened full investigations on Fairfax. That put the onus on Fairfax, being under watch, to flag its intentions to the Feds before Bowe and Watsa could proceed with a statement of allegations.

Meanwhile, the rumour mill was overheating. According to a *Forbes* story, Fairfax CFO Greg Taylor handled forty-one calls in a single day from nervous investors wanting to know if it was true that the company's office had been raided by regulators or the Royal Canadian Mounted Police, or that Watsa had already admitted fraud, or that he had fled the country on the corporate jet with his wife and as much cash as they could carry.

On Saturday, July 22, Roddy Boyd, a reporter with the *New York Post*, published a story that raised convoluted questions about transactions that allowed Fairfax to raise its stake in Odyssey back up to 80 percent from 74 percent, in order to enjoy favourable accounting and tax benefits. (Fairfax had unwittingly sold a little too much of Odyssey in its IPO.) On July 25, Boyd published another story, this time relating to the timing of Odyssey's disclosures on finite insurance exposures. Neither story got the kind of share price reaction that the shorts had expected.

As Boyd was putting together that second story, Bowe was putting the final touches on Fairfax's lawsuit. As required, he shared a copy of the complaint with the Feds and it hit a nerve. "We immediately got a call from the Southern District of New York," says Bowe, "and they told us not to file the case." Seems they found the allegations to be serious and worthy of investigation, but since it all overlapped with things the Feds were already investigating about Fairfax, they wanted Watsa and Bowe to take a number and wait. Time for another huddle with Prem.

Watsa elevated a few things to clarify with Bowe. He wanted to know if the regulators were committed to investigating the Fairfax allegations, whether they would push back against the hedge funds immediately, and how long legal action might take. We can expect it to be a year or more, replied Bowe, adding that even if the Feds did something, they might never share that information with Fairfax. "Prem just paused," relates Bowe, "and then he said, 'Okay, call them back and thank them. Tell them I'm sorry, my board has directed me to file this lawsuit because I need to protect my shareholders. We are going to file the case but we would be happy to co-operate with them in any way possible to help with their investigation.'"

Bowe was absolutely stunned. "If the government tells you not to do something when you are under investigation, you don't do it! Prem is just a great man, and he acts from principles. No other CEO in the world, I think, would have done that but Prem is so principled and it's like, 'This is the right thing to do and I'm doing it.' When we called them back, they were absolutely apoplectically screaming at us."

It gets nuttier. Bowe got an order to show up at the Attorney for the Southern District of New York office at nine the next morning to walk them through the allegations. Across the long table, the attorney general and team were in the middle, flanked by FBI and SEC representatives. Bowe watched the faces on that side of the room as they realized Contogouris was the leading man and bad guy of Fairfax's story. The lawyer concluded that all the juicy tips in the Feds' cases were also being fed by Contogouris, who he believed was actually their confidential informant. They appeared to have fallen for the convincing false roadmap to fraud laid out in the architectural tube. The Feds started off thinking that the Fairfax guys were the con men, Bowe figures, but were coming to the realization that their star source might be the one playing that role..

"He had totally bamboozled them into believing Fairfax was engaged in this wild fraud," alleges Bowe. "It was insane. I walked through the evidence with them and we convinced them that they had been had. Then they turned around, and they started investigating the hedge funds."

Only then did Bowe learn about the bomb that might have taken down Fairfax. While the whole exercise was turning into a farce, it came out that all three arms of government had bought into the wild fraud scenario to the point that they were poised to issue grand jury subpoenas in July or August to Fairfax and Watsa, says Bowe. Contogouris had apparently been earning his pay, inveigling his way into the corridors of power. A grand jury is designed to be top secret but even a whiff of it, helped along by certain well-placed parties, could have proven lethal to Fairfax's reputation. With zero idea that was in the works and by filing the lawsuit on principle and against the implicit instructions of the U.S. Department of Justice, Fairfax had managed to defuse a bomb.

The grand jury never happened. The shorts' campaign had fired all its other cannons but for one media story. The coverage, greatly anticipated by the hedge funds, so far had received very little reaction. The hedge funds were getting edgy. And they had no clue a counterstrike was coming. On July 26, Fairfax detonated its own bomb—a blockbuster statement of claim seeking $6 billion in damages and laying out in eye-popping detail its summary of allegations concerning the entire hedge attack. This wasn't how guilty, failing insurance fraudsters were supposed to behave. The tables had turned: Finally, the media had legal allegations to tell Fairfax's side of the story. "The noise level immediately died," says Watsa. "Not a word. Just like that. The shorts who thought they could drive down our share price and ruin our reputation made a really grave error."

To be accurate, the noise level did pick up one more time. A day after the suit was launched, Fairfax capped the week with a major restatement related to finite insurance. Fairfax had inherited some finite contracts through its acquisitions, but the SEC had a close look and gave Fairfax's accounting a clean bill of health after a writedown. Other firms, which were abusing finite insurance, were caught and fined.

Despite the restatement, investors did not flinch. The tide had shifted and the stock was rising again. The shorts retreated with their losses, Adam Sender walked away, and Bob Dylan never sang "A Hard Rain's A-Gonna Fall" in the Hamptons. Investors who bought into the hedge funds' story were bitter. Kalikow of Stanfield, for one, wasn't feeling great that he'd let Heller encourage him to invest alongside the shorts. The big fraud reveal, with media co-operation, in July was supposed to be the knockout blow. When the big gotcha turned into a nothingburger, Kalikow emailed Heller, casting the whole bearish operation as a slipshod undertaking. "No one can explain to me the fraud. Is money actually missing or not?" Kalikow said. "Now this trade is a disaster. All the news that was supposed to take this lower hasn't." Kalikow asked Heller why a company engaged in a massive fraud would file a richly detailed rebuttal with full disclosure. Kalikow did not wait for a response, choosing to answer that for himself: "They wouldn't." A lot of people lost a lot of money betting on Fairfax's demise. Kalikow, who counted among the smaller investors, later stated his loss had been in the $60–70 million range.

Fairfax heaved a giant sigh of relief. Salsberg took account, and all he could think was that this could have been avoided if Fairfax had had a fortress balance sheet in place. Today, Fairfax has annual operating earnings of around $4 billion and also keeps rainy-day cash of $2.5 billion on hand, plus a few billion in untapped lines of credit. It also has a long record of reserve redundancies. The hedge funds never would have taken a run at them with that kind of strength.

"Back then, people said your reserves are terrible," Salsberg said. "But no one can really know that. They can say whatever they want and with reserves there is no quick answer that is going to prove that we are right. So they can tell a crazy story. But were we in the best shape at the time they started—with cash reserves and everything in its best shape? No. We realized we had to do better. If we were Berkshire Hathaway, no one would have taken a run at us."

It was not the last time a hedge fund took a run at them. During the latest, in 2023, Fairfax's financial house was rock solid, if not quite Berkshire solid. Fairfax offered Muddy Waters Research, the research shop that supported the shorting, a chance to air its concerns and be answered on the company's quarterly conference call. Muddy Waters, which has made some successful moves in the past, got things completely wrong. Its research fizzled; Fairfax's stock dropped, then fully recovered.

EPILOGUE

The Fairfax lawsuit not only protected the company but also had broader repercussions in securities law, insists Bowe. It got the ball rolling on massive insider trading investigations in the United States. Armed with evidence from the efforts of Fairfax's lawyers, U.S. authorities launched the largest insider trading investigation in history, one that would captivate Wall Street for years and lead to the high-profile prosecution of many hedge fund managers, Bowe explains. SAC Capital pled guilty to wire fraud and securities fraud, paid a $1.8 billion penalty and agreed to dissolve its hedge fund. The legacy of Watsa's actions can be seen in the shift to regard short sellers who publish falsehoods about public companies as being engaged in illegal manipulation on par with other corporate frauds.

"That was all Prem," Bowe says. "Prem basically started a process that changed how short sellers operated and forced hedge funds and short sellers to behave in increasingly more legitimate ways."

One by one, whether due to jurisdiction (filing the case in New Jersey) or statute (the legal strategy was to target all parties in a racketeering charge), most of those named were eventually dropped from the suit. While the named parties dropped off, Fairfax has always stood by its allegations. The company insists it would have been successful if the case had been tried. The defendants, as might be expected, always denied the allegations. In the end, the company insists airing the dirty laundry was victory enough. The company quickly added a few billion in market value and popped again when Contogouris was arrested by the FBI on an unrelated fraud case. At the trial, a former SEC chief economist testified the turn was clearly due to the fact that the suit exposed and discredited the campaign led by Contogouris, says Bowe.

"The lawsuit was mired in legal technicalities, but it was hugely successful in that there was enough detail that the people could see what was going on," said Salsberg. "And at that point, the nastiness stopped because it was now obvious what they were doing." As a lawyer, Salsberg offered an 'insider's' shrug and observed, "When you are in court, often nothing works the way you expect it. That's why we have only brought cases twice, when we felt there was a broader issue of fraud that needed to be addressed." (The earlier example saw Fairfax take legal action to spark reforms to insurance "spiral" practices that affected its Sphere Drake subsidiary in London.)

Fairfax and Watsa, very much alive, had moved on. There was a company to run and a preference to see the whole chapter as a successful test of company resolve and corporate culture. "We became much stronger as a result of it," offers Watsa. "Mr. Templeton always said there is an opportunity behind every problem. We pulled together. We became closer and none of our leaders left because of it."

Throughout the battle with the hedge funds, senior executives recall seeing Watsa always level and collected, showing grace under pressure. You could never tell that anything was wrong, recalls Fink. Bumping into Watsa in the elevator one early morning in the middle of the war, he asked his boss how he was holding up.

Watsa, *beaming*: "Paul, as the Good Book says, consider your trials pure joy."

Fink, *shaking his head*: "I always thought you were losing it. Now I know you're totally gone."

Before he reached his own ninety-nine year term to maturity, the acerbic Charlie Munger, Warren Buffett's partner at Berkshire, left the world scores of wise quips on investing and life in general, including the upside of attitude and the perils of self-pity. One fits Watsa's experience with the shorts nicely: "The idea that life is a series of adversities and each one is an opportunity to behave well, instead of badly, is a very, very good idea." Looking back, Watsa says his faith gave him a lot of strength: "I would not diminish it. Things got very out of hand there. It got personal, and it threatened the financial health of the company. But I have strong faith as a Christian and under adversity it just got stronger. You just work as hard as you can, as though everything depends on you. Control what you can control. Work hard. Sleep well at night. We didn't lose any senior leaders. There was tension but never any internal backbiting."

Meanwhile, his eyes were again resolutely looking forward on building a more profitable company. By the time the long war with the shorts was settled in 2006, he was already preoccupied with a bigger threat hanging over the entire market and economy—asset-backed securities and a looming mortgage crisis.

In his 2006 letter, Watsa only mentioned the suit buried at the end, under "Miscellaneous" no less. Rather than gloating, he offered a terse, sober, and principled takeaway on behavioural standards: "Using manipulation and intimidation, as we have alleged, for profit or otherwise, should never be tolerated." Fairfax was happy to be done with it all, including the aggressive PR consultants and legal investigators.

The media moved on as well, at least in Canada. In the U.S., several reporters continued to paint Fairfax as the bad guys who got away with something. If someone like Jim Chanos says there is a fraud, some reporters are going to give him the benefit of the doubt. Chanos, for example, had been a crucial source for Bethany McLean in her work on Enron, which included co-authoring the bestselling book *The Smartest*

Guys in the Room: The Amazing Rise and Scandalous Fall of Enron. McLean surveyed the war's aftermath in a 2007 feature for *Fortune* entitled "The Inside Story of a Wall Street Battle Royal" and offered that Fairfax was not only guilty in the end of being too hard to understand but also perhaps the bigger bully in this Street fight. By that point, the shorts had abandoned their cause, suffering great losses; Gwynn dropped coverage of the stock; Contogouris was no longer working for the hedge funds and was arrested by the FBI on the aforementioned unrelated wire fraud charge. He pleaded not guilty and federal prosecutors later dropped the charges. Perhaps most importantly, Fairfax had successfully wrestled its operations back into profitability. In her piece, McLean wrote of "the distinct possibility that Watsa and his company are not, in fact, victims—in which case the story is perhaps even more disturbing." And she added, "it appears [the hedge funds] have been muzzled by a blunt instrument—litigation." Journalists desperately wanted to be ahead on another spectacular Enron story, but this was a false fraud built on lies.

You cannot say the Canadian media did not warn Wall Street. Fairfax was not your average holding company. It's not a big surprise that in 2009, the company decided to delist from the NYSE spotlight altogether. Later, the company's shares were made available for trade on the pink sheets of the Nasdaq for U.S. investors in U.S. dollars.

Watsa and Fairfax got away, but some U.S. market watchers figured they might have got away—with something tricky. Richard Sauer, an SEC assistant director who had been at Copper River, one of the parties named in Fairfax's suit, summed up the whole dispute like this: "As had happened at least twice before, Prem Watsa confounded his detractors with his Houdini-like ability to get out of tight situations. The bears thought they had him handcuffed, in a straitjacket, nailed into a coffin and dropped into the ocean. Then he appeared at their shoulder, dry as a bone."

Chanos, for the record, also moved on. He later concluded the shorts had made a big mistake in hiring Contogouris: "As soon as we found that out, we fired him." As for losing the bet, he says, "Our batting average is about 65 to 70 percent. So a third of the time, we're wrong."

The storm had officially passed. Fairfax was coming out the other side in good form. The insurers were in good running shape. TIG was finally gone with the good assets rolled up into Odyssey—which now sported a healthy combined ratio of 95 percent. Sphere was being wound up. Crum was fixed, running a combined ratio in the 92–93 percent range.

It was time to play catch-up, Watsa told shareholders: "We have some way to go to make up for the biblical Seven Lean Years that you have suffered." At about $200 million, underwriting profits would hit a record in 2006. Meanwhile, the investment team, its hands no longer tied, was working up some bold magic with its version of the Big Short.

Chapter Six

BETTING ON DISASTER (2006–2009)

"We see an explosion coming." —Prem Watsa

In the early days of 2007, Watsa huddled with Brian Bradstreet, HWIC's bond whiz, and the small investment committee at HWIC. The basic approach was always the same, so Watsa looked around the room and asked the usual question: "What's the best idea we've got?"

Bradstreet bit his tongue. He still loved the big trade Fairfax had going. But they were taking an enormous bath on it so far, to the tune of almost a quarter billion dollars. "At any other place, I would have been kicked out on the street," he says. But the best investors are often early—and Fairfax was usually early.

These are the scenarios that repeat in the history of Fairfax. It pulled out early from bubbly Japanese stocks in the '80s, leaving a lot of money on the table as the market made its final manic surge to the peak. It lost a lot of money preparing for the tech wreck, until it finally cashed in huge. So, here it was again with a big, expensive contrarian call that had yet to pay off.

With hindsight, it looks easy from the outside. Smart investors see a serious problem, make a trade, sit back, and then hit the jackpot. But sitting in these kinds of trades carries a cost—to your nerves and likely to your short-term profits. As the quarters and years roll by and the losses mount, you have to keep asking yourself if you are actually right. Will it pay off? Is it time to take a loss? Or do we double down one more time?

Even legendary investors have found themselves unable to hold on to a winning hand when the waiting is so expensive. Famed investor Julian

Robertson closed his Tiger Management hedge fund in March 2000 at the peak of the bubble. He had seen the risks but ran out of patience—and money—shorting runaway tech stocks for two years. He quit his marathon a few feet short of the finish line. So did Laurence Tisch, CEO of the Loews Corporation holding company. Tisch spent four years shorting stocks in the same period and gave up by 2000 after booking $2.5 billion in losses, just months before the peak.

The big trade Fairfax had going was a short on financial companies with exposure to the growing bubble in mortgage securities. In a trade like this, there is a fine line between being a hedge fund and a conservative insurance holding company. Either way, they were making a bold, aggressive bet on a negative outcome. But, significantly, Fairfax came at it from the perspective of caution, as a way to protect the capital of its insurers. It was looking for insurance on a major disaster they were sure was coming. Their crystal ball just could not say when.

Bradstreet still had his teeth locked firmly on his tongue. The others were looking sideways, waiting. So it was the soft-spoken Chou who piped up. "Buy more credit default insurance," he told the room.

"We swallowed hard and purchased some more," recalls Watsa. With $341 million already invested, paper losses (they would only record an actual loss if they sold the securities) had reached $211 million by 2007. The value of the position kept going the wrong way into June 2007. That summer, however, all hell broke loose, as predicted, and Fairfax was surfing in cash.

This was Fairfax's version of the Big Short. The book and movie made a legend of investors like Michael Burry, a smart contrarian investor who figured out a way to profit handsomely from the Great Financial Crash—reportedly $100 million for him, plus another roughly $750 million for his clients.

Fairfax made close to $4.2 billion on its (even) Big(ger) Short, but no one made a movie about it. If they did, the perfect guy to do the champagne-bubble-bath-explainer scene on credit default swaps (CDS) would be Brian Bradstreet. He was the trade's chief architect. Unlike Margot Robbie, he sports a white beard that would blend into the bubbles, making the eyes of his poker face stand out.

THE TRADE: "AN INSURANCE POLICY THAT MAY TRADE DIVIDENDS"

First, a quick refresh for historical context. In the lead-up to the Global Financial Crisis, banks, mortgage insurers, debt raters, and the real estate industry had all helped to profitably push consumers into a lot of unsound mortgages, which were in turn packaged into mortgage-backed securities alongside traditional healthy mortgages. It was like a virulent infection in the financial system that weakened it from within.

In movies and in TV interviews, strategists commonly try to position themselves as the ones who called a big crash. Most of that is bluster. It's easy to say after the fact, and if you did call it, did you act on it? Wade Burton says seeing the problem was actually dead easy: "Everyone knew there was a monster problem, but only a handful acted on their convictions—and none more so than Prem. You could see the CDS spreads showing where it was going to go." It didn't take brilliance to see the warning signs; it took brilliance to act and take advantage of them, he says. Back at his old shop, Cundill, similar discussions took place about trading the impending crisis through mortgage-related securities. No one, he says, could agree on what to do about it.

In the world of Ben Graham, rule number one is always to not lose money. That time was now. As Bradstreet explains, Fairfax's starting point was how to protect itself, not make billions of dollars. Fairfax could see the mortgage market dislocation happening, and the challenge was how to gauge its potential impacts on other parts of the financial system—before Fairfax got side-swiped. He and the team determined the link to reinsurance was the overriding threat to Fairfax.

So, what's reinsurance, really? Insurance is simple enough. The insurer sells premiums to individuals or companies to cover risks. The insurer can then offload some of that risk by buying reinsurance from another insurer. You cover the client, and you pay someone to cover you. The recoverable (i.e., the money owed to pay out a claim) is the loss on your business that you can offset with coverage from a reinsurer. Fairfax is one of the major insurers that operates in both insurance and reinsurance.

"In the old days, we bought a lot of insurers with long-tail liabilities, where you just don't know what you might be exposed to," says Bradstreet.

"There was a lot of reinsurance attached to those assets. The value of the recoverables sitting on our balance sheet was about $6 billion or so, which was a multiple of our common equity. So, if anything went wrong with our reinsurers, that recoverable would not be recoverable. We would have to come up with new money to pay those claims."

Fairfax had never had to worry about a scenario where the reinsurers themselves went bankrupt and were unable to pay Fairfax. As they explored the looming disaster, the scenario quickly went from "What if?" to "When?" The clock was ticking, and Fairfax did not have a $6-billion cushion on hand for a rainy day.

There were all kinds of signs the storm was coming, recalls Bradstreet: "We ourselves on the fixed-income side were being offered Ponzi-type stuff to invest in that came with an AA or AAA rating. So I began to fear that the reinsurance companies we were relying on to pay us might buy this junk and get into trouble, and we would not get paid. That would blow us right out of the water. I was losing a lot of sleep, trying to think about how to minimize the risk, especially since both the stock and housing markets were already overheating."

So that's where it started: How does Fairfax hedge its exposure to reinsurers—in particular AIG, Munich Re, and Swiss Re? "I started studying the financial statements of these companies," says Bradstreet, "and sure enough they all held these asset-backed, mortgage-backed, high-yield bonds that were pure risk. AIG was the one that scared me most. I thought they were doing crazy balance sheet stuff."

Fear is a good motivator, and HWIC learned it had to step back and look at its exposure more broadly. "We were able to buy a lot of CDS on AIG, Swiss, and Munich," Bradstreet explains. "But a lot of the firms we had exposure to did not exist anymore. They were assets held in trust accounts, so you couldn't buy CDS on them. So we had to get creative, which is something we are good at. You have to be good at seeing problems before others do, and you have to be able to find ways to protect yourself against loss."

What those first CDS trades failed to do was target where the ultimate threat was coming from, beyond AIG and the other reinsurers. "We had to ask ourselves what we were explicitly afraid of. That big fear was the exposure these reinsurers had to the mortgage market. We were able to buy some protection on Fannie Mae and Freddie Mac. We bought big protection on all the mortgage insurers and mortgage lenders."

Fannie (Federal National Mortgage Association) and Freddie (Federal Home Loan Mortgage Corporation) are federally backed U.S. agencies that guarantee home mortgages, and both collapsed in the Global Financial Crisis in September 2008. When Fairfax was investing against Fannie Mae, that lender already had $80 of exposure to toxic loans for every $1 of common equity. A single match could burn this house down, and a giant firestorm was headed straight for it.

It was not like people were unaware of the threats. It was obvious there was a real problem in the years leading up to the crash. Media outlets were full of stories about NINJA loans, where houses were being sold with fat mortgages to people with no income, no job or assets just to feed the demand for mortgage-backed securities. Zero down payments, subprime lending, soaring house prices, and easy money for those packaging up the bonds to sell as mortgage-backed securities: It was a recipe for greed and disaster. Simply put, Fairfax found a clean way to buy bankruptcy insurance on their reinsurers, as well as on the insurers and mortgage lenders behind them.

Before the big payoff finally arrived, Fairfax had been in the hot seat. "It can get very lonely being value investors," offers Watsa. You can tell other investors you are building an ark to survive the next storm, but they are just going to point up at the clear blue sky and call you nuts with all your crazy CDS doomsday bets. So you wait.

"We thought it would happen in 2005, 2006, 2007 . . ." says Watsa. "Some of our own people wondered what we were doing. Why weren't we just sticking to our expertise and buying good stocks instead of investing in what seemed like a new and exotic investment?" It ended up being transformational, burying any lingering financial-strength concerns related to the hedge fund allegations. "When others were awash in red ink, we made a ton of dough. No other insurance or reinsurance company came close. Our reputation was not only restored, but it rose higher than ever."

Those who tracked Watsa's letters could have followed the whole saga from home. Putting complex CDS trades into action might have been beyond an average investor's ken, but they could have saved themselves some hurt. "Some of you wondered—sometimes loudly—why we bother with these hedges and credit default swaps," he wrote in his 2006 letter. "Besides our comfort in having this protection, we continue to think that this insurance policy may pay dividends—perhaps sooner than you think." In hindsight, he was early as usual. And dead right.

"WHAT HAPPENS IF WE HIT AN AIR POCKET?"

In his 2006 letter to shareholders, still a few years from the full crisis impact, Watsa was digging into the risks of the booming market for asset-backed bonds. Readers were treated to a lecture by a master educator who laid out the HWIC thesis in advance for investors.

This was not a forensic "what went wrong" analysis. It was a "what is about to go wrong" heads-up. Newsletters with commentary half as smart might charge a few thousand dollars for their insights. Watsa's thoughts are free, even if you aren't a shareholder. So are Warren Buffett's and any other CEO's.

The great letter writers of business tend not to write books, offers Lawrence Cunningham, author of *Dear Shareholder: The Best Executive Letters from Warren Buffett, Prem Watsa and Other Great CEOs*. The letters have a higher purpose than ghost-written, hardcover, vanity tell-all memoirs. Their authors tend to be passionate educators.

"The best shareholder letters are those that treat readers as business partners, by offering deep insights," Cunningham says. "These writers share their perspectives on core business topics across the spectrum, spanning from general staples of the business school curriculum, such as accounting, competitive strategy and innovation, to employee morale and executive succession."

Way back in 2003, Watsa included his "auto dealer explainer" in his letter, walking readers through the moral hazard of playing a securitized shell game with credit risk. He wanted shareholders to understand what he himself was worried about, at a time when few people saw a threat.

> We have been concerned for some time about the risks in asset-backed bonds, particularly bonds that are backed by home equity loans, automobile loans or credit card debt (we own no

> asset-backed bonds). It seems to us that securitization (or the creation of these asset-backed bonds) eliminates the incentive for the originator of the loan to be credit sensitive.
>
> Take the case of an automobile dealer. Prior to securitization, the dealer would be very concerned about who was given credit to buy an automobile. With securitization, the dealer (almost) does not care as these loans can be laid off through securitizations. Thus, the loss experienced on these after securitization will no longer be comparable to that prior to securitization (called a "moral" hazard.) And here's the rub. These asset-backed bonds are rated based on their historical loss experience record which will likely be very different in the future—particularly if we experience difficult economic times . . .
>
> This is not a small problem. There is a $1.0 trillion in asset-backed bonds outstanding as of December 31, 2003 in the U.S. (excluding first mortgage-backed bonds). At the end of 2002, more than 65.5% of these bonds were rated A or above. In fact, as of December 31, 2002, there were more than 2,500 asset-backed issues rated AAA—significantly more than the 13 U.S. corporate issuers currently rated as AAA. Who is buying these bonds? Insurance companies, money managers and banks—in the main—all reaching for yield given the excellent ratings for these bonds. What happens if we hit an air pocket?

By this time, Fairfax had already started buying CDS in trades put together by Bradstreet and HWIC trader Enza LaSelva. So here was Fairfax carefully evaluating its risk exposure and investing in short positions despite the short-term paper losses. Meanwhile, investors were leveraging up on housing and piling into tech stocks. The air pocket was forming.

PROFESSOR WATSA'S "TREATISE" ON CDS

The stakes were rising, so Watsa, ever the educator, revisited the subject two years later. This time, he laid out Fairfax's swaps strategy. Frankly, it is terribly dense to an average investor, but you have to love that it's there for transparency's sake, even if for many, it's like opening the kimono and you still aren't sure what you are looking at.

Aware of the density factor, Watsa would, tongue firmly in cheek, refer to it as his "Treatise on CDS."

> Just a brief overview for you on our credit default swaps, which are 5-year to 10-year fixed income derivatives, which fluctuate with credit spreads, that we purchased from major banks. Here is an example. To purchase a 5-year $100 million credit default swap on a company that sells at a 30 basis spread over treasuries, one has to invest 150 basis points (30 basis points/year x 5 years), so $1.5 million purchases protection on an underlying $100 million of credit exposure of the chosen company over the next five years. The maximum loss to the purchase in 5 years is $1.5 million if the credit spread stays at 30 basis points or tightens even further.
>
> On the other hand, if the credit spread on this company doubles to 60 basis points, the credit default swap can be worth as much as $3 million, and if the company goes bankrupt, that swap can be worth up to $100 million. We have a diversified list of companies, mainly financial institutions, with respect to which we have paid approximately $250 million to purchase protection on underlying credit exposures. Accounting rules require these credit default swaps to be marked to market on a quarterly basis and the resulting valuation adjustment to be treated as a realized gain or loss.

All clear? Even if you do not get the technical aspects, you can see the way $1.5 million could turn into $3 million or even $100 million. And the guys were ponying up $250 million, instead of $1.5 million. If swaps are a bit intimidating, let's look at how it paid off between 2003 and 2008. And we will throw in the equity hedges (mostly plain-vanilla short positions on the broader S&P 500 as a bet on a general bear market) as well, which tell a similar story. Fairfax made it clear it had the patience to suffer recorded major losses (half a billion dollars over a four-year period!) to cash in on much, much larger gains. The astounding combined total windfall from both sets of short calls was more than $4.6 billion. And you can see what Watsa means when he said, "We had to endure years of pain before harvesting the gains."

The Bearish Double Windfall		
Recorded (losses) and gains (in $ million)		
Investment	**2003–2006**	**2007–2008**
Equity hedges	(287)	2,223
Credit default swaps	(211)	2,435
Total gain (loss)	**(498)**	**4,658**

Source: Company annual reports

EARLY DAYS OF WATSA THE PERMA-BEAR

The Global Financial Crisis was more than just a crash: It devastated the banking sector, sinking Lehman Brothers and Bear Stearns, and triggered massive bailouts as well as monetary and fiscal intervention to keep the financial system intact. Major stock indexes plummeted by half in a matter of six months. The full-year drop for the S&P 500 was almost 40 percent in 2008, and the aftershocks were felt for years.

Sorting through the devastation, Watsa took sober stock with shareholders: "All of the investment risks that we worried about and have written to you about for at least the past five years simultaneously reared their ugly head, as the 1-in-50 or 1-in-100 year storm in the financial markets landed in the fall of 2008. There were very few places to hide, let alone prosper." Of course, he was speaking for other investors—Fairfax did find a place to hide and prospered very nicely.

HWIC's contrarian success helped shape an enduring perception of the company as one that could frustrate investors for lengthy stretches, then make everything better by finding rainbows when everyone else was getting washed out in a hurricane. Closing the book on this scary chapter in financial history, Watsa told shareholders in 2009 he was happy to leave behind the drama and financial weapons that paid off so well: "Our adventure with credit default swaps is over—but we will remember it as one of the more significant events in our history!"

It's important to remember that investors who had been reading Watsa's detailed annual letter would not have been surprised by the crash. The only question had been when it would happen and how bad it would be. It's remarkable to look back at his letters in the years leading to the crash and see the warnings. Investors might have dismissed the doomsaying as the bearish musings of a perma-bear. But his only fault was being early.

- From 2003's letter: "We have almost half of our investment portfolio in cash and short term investments. The unprecedented conservatism in our portfolio reflects the uncertain times that we live in and also positions us to take advantage of attractive investment opportunities."
- From 2005: "As we have mentioned *ad nauseum*, the risks in the U.S. are many and varied. . . . Animal spirits are alive and well and downside risks have long been forgotten. We continue to be fascinated—morbidly—by the recent Japanese experience."
- From 2006: "As Warren Buffett has said, 'you pay a high price for a cheery consensus.' We continue to worry about the unprecedented issuance of collateralized bonds, mortgages and loans (we hold none!). We see an explosion coming but unfortunately cannot predict when."
- From 2007: "*Caveat emptor*!!"

The big macro calls on CDS and the S&P 500 shorts brought a massive windfall. But so did the investment returns for stocks generally in this period leading up to 2010. While other investors were still selling or afraid to buy, Fairfax eliminated its hedges and stormed back into equities, reaching record holdings in the U.S. and Canada.

Fairfax was making up for the lost time of the lean years, sitting on five-year annual returns of 17.1 percent versus 0.4 percent for the S&P 500. Its bond returns were 2.5 times those of the benchmark over the same period. Not surprisingly, Fairfax stock went into overdrive, breaking out of its malaise when it only managed one year in the black.

Fairfax Shares Play Catch-up	
Annual change in Fairfax shares	
7 lean years	
1999	-55.7%
2000	-0.7
2001	-28
2002	-26
2003	+87
2004	-11
2005	-17
Crisis rally	
2006	+38%
2007	+24
2008	+36
2009	+5

Source: Company annual reports

A year after the lean years ended, book value per share, the company's preferred measure of growth, sat at $137. It would soar 169 percent in the next four years to reach almost $370. Over the seven-year drought, Fairfax had made zero money. In the three years that followed, it earned $3.7 billion after tax. In investors' eyes, Fairfax was back. Watsa was back. Of course, he'd be quick to remind them he never left and has been very busy building the company effectively for the long term, including after he is gone, thank you very much.

There was a lot of ground for shareholders to make up. Excluding dividends, investors who hung on through the full lean years lost about 68 percent on their shares. The subsequent rally was good for a 144 percent rebound, but through the full eleven years, you would still be down about 24 percent, so no one at HWIC was getting cocky. Actually, they did not have the time to be cocky. They had a problem that they had never experienced before—too much cash on hand.

"WHAT DO WE DO WITH ALL THE MONEY?"

The windfall was landing right in the middle of the broader storm in the markets, which was a great time for value contrarians to put it to work, recalls Roger Lace, chairman at HWIC. "It was a nice challenge to face," he recalls. "We had to deploy billions of dollars quickly before the market went up again. What do we do with all the money? Prem wisely took the approach that we had to get out there and look for deals."

Initially, they pulled their hedges and went long on beaten-down blue chips like Johnson & Johnson, U.S. Bancorp, Kraft Foods, and Wells Fargo, all Buffett favourites that Fairfax intended to hold on to long term. In the short term, they were also buying municipal bonds backed by Berkshire Hathaway itself. In between trades, they had to contend with a lineup at the office front door of cash-strapped operators of distressed assets looking for some emergency backing.

It was a bit of an uncharacteristic buying frenzy, which wasn't the way Fairfax normally operated. "Perhaps we missed some things we should have bought, and perhaps we bought some things we shouldn't have, but on the whole it was the right thing to do," says Lace.

The blue chips served Fairfax well. The four stocks mentioned above were already up $281 million by the end of the following year. The big four in Canada, using convertible debentures or warrants—common during periods of distressed asset investing—were H&R REIT, Canadian Western Bank, Mullen Group, and GMP Capital. Combined, Fairfax turned $316 million into $592 million by the end of 2009, good for an 87 percent gain.

There were also a bunch of investments Fairfax made bad calls on. The team at HWIC thought it should have done better, but you can't win them all. On top of a billion dollars in mark-to-market and realized losses, Fairfax declared a long list of asset impairments that were, in accounting speak, beyond temporary. These bad bets included Level 3 ($226 million) and Frontier Communications ($84 million) and struggling Canadian media stocks Torstar ($175 million) and Canwest ($121 million).

Watsa's approach was to be patient and give operators their best shot, even when other investors or their bankers would have pulled the plug.

It's the same patience he would later show underperforming companies like BlackBerry, a generosity that attracted grumbles from Fairfax investors. "I'm not happy with all the things we bought," says Watsa. "But we don't run away from problems even if it means that we sometimes take a hit. It's case by case, but we want to be fair, friendly investors."

BUYING BACK CONTROL OF ITS INSURERS

With all the money coming in, Northbridge was reprivatized in early 2009 when Fairfax bought back the shares at C$39, five years after they had been IPO'd at C$15. They did the same with Odyssey later that year, buying back the public float for $65 a share after taking it public in 2001 at $18. Those stocks had done well for investors and there were rumbles of discontent from those who wanted to keep their shares in these successful performers. For Fairfax, however, the IPOs had served their purpose in adding financial flexibility and it was time to get those assets and growing cash flows back under one roof for all Fairfax shareholders.

It was a busy period for HWIC. After all the manoeuvring to retain financial flexibility in the lean years, the team was now acting from a position of strength, on the offensive. And between the gains from the short sales and quick gains on beaten-down stocks, the company stood apart. "Comparing levels at the end of 2008 and the end of 1998, most U.S. and worldwide stock market indices have not provided any return for the past 10 years," said Watsa in the middle of the housing crisis. For Fairfax, it was a different story. It had racked up a 19.9 percent average annual return on its common stock portfolio in that period. The S&P 500? A negative return of –1.4 percent. "Our reputation was restored; in fact, it was higher than it ever had been."

CEO CELEBRITY: THANKS, BUT NO THANKS

Whether Watsa liked it or not, Fairfax was back in the news. The media was gushing over Fairfax and its limelight-shunning CEO with the bold, bearish bets. In fact, *The Globe and Mail*, Canada's leading national news brand, would name Prem Watsa CEO of the year in 2008. "He called it," wrote Derek DeCloet, summing up Watsa's feat in three words followed by the kicker: "And he has $2 billion to prove it." Typically, CEOs would kill for that kind of publicity. Watsa, true to his atypical form, said, "No thanks." A year earlier, the CEO had doled out his own in-house award with a shout-out in his letter to shareholders: "Our man of the year is Brian Bradstreet who first came up with the idea to purchase CDS contracts in 2004 and then implemented it with Enza LaSelva, our fixed-income trader."

As for the *Globe*'s big cover story, Watsa refused an interview unless it changed the award to company of the year. It didn't. Ever generous with his time, he even offered to help the editors find a more suitable candidate. Peeved, the newspaper dropped the story's magazine cover position and moved the story inside to page 71. Nevertheless, Watsa was back in the news to the point that even the chattering classes were dropping his name. *Toronto Life*, a personality-driven glossy monthly, profiled him in 2009, again without landing an interview, as "the richest, savviest guy you've never heard of."

In those days, there were only a few times Watsa opened up to the media, and they were during the war with the hedges when Fairfax realized it needed to mitigate the flood of disinformation and false rumours. Perhaps the fullest interview was a candid sit-down with the same *Globe and Mail* business magazine, which carried a great photo of Watsa on the cover. In that "Prem Watsa Revealed" cover story, dating to February 2006, just months before the final blowout with the shorts, Watsa uncharacteristically opened up. Coming across as much less enigmatic than the media had made out, Watsa was asked by writer John Daly why he was suddenly available to talk. Watsa quipped with a smile and a wink: "Once in 20 years. Hey, you just got lucky." (Among the other few times Watsa opened up for a wide-ranging chat with the Canadian media were a TV conversation with Amanda Lang on BNN Bloomberg in 2018 and my discussion with him on compassionate capitalism in 2021.)

Recently, Watsa has relented and accepted several awards. Part of why, he says, is to accept some recognition on behalf of the full team at Fairfax. Members of the original team are passing on, and there is a lot to celebrate. So you will hear about Watsa receiving honours, but it is always jointly on behalf of the team, whether he is getting a Nation

Builder Award from the Empire Club of Canada or entry into Canadian Business CEO and International Insurance halls of fame. He was named a Member of the Order of Canada in 2015 and in 2020 received the Padma Shri from India in recognition of business and charitable success.

EARNINGS ENGINES: DON'T FORGET THE INSURERS

The media loves a big, bold "He called it" kind of investing story. But Fairfax, especially on the insurance side, would rather have seen the media writing about the sustained move in company-wide combined ratios from 105 percent to 95 percent or better. A new era of sustained profits from underwriting was actually more important for the very reason that it wasn't lumpy—it started to come year after year, feeding the float and compounding book value. That was the plight of the insurance business. It was less sexy than the investment side. Same story goes for Berkshire. Media headlines always favour how well Coca-Cola or American Express or Apple is doing over combined ratios at GEICO or Alleghany. Covering Fairfax, reporters just wanted to know if Watsa was worried about another bear market.

Misperceptions are sticky. Underwriting turned the corner in 2006. All the hard work was paying off—much later than promised. Even a problem child like Crum & Forster was having its own transformation after a decade of retooling. And yet you could not fault investors for being skeptical. The 1990s saw Fairfax manage to record an underwriting profit only twice, in 1991 and 1993, for a combined tiny gain of $6.2 million. Between 1990 and 1999, the combined underwriting loss reached a woeful $760.8 million, before getting even worse in the seven lean years. Underwriting losses overall totalled a whopping $4.5 billion between 1999 and 2005. (No wonder the hedge funds thought the company was a broken mess that just needed a nudge into the grave.) Over the following two years, however, Fairfax's three major insurer subsidiaries contributed a combined $2.13 billion in net earnings.

This was a new era for Fairfax. It proved it could run profitable insurers, even if some were not yet in top form. In 2008, the company-wide combined ratio was still high at 110 percent, but it was in much better shape than a lot of the slumping industry and headed in the right direction. Other insurance groups were not so lucky. Some were crippled by the financial crisis and market collapse.

"The P&C industry changed dramatically in 2008," wrote Watsa. "Mainly because of investment problems, the industry lost almost 10% of its $340 billion of capital. Many of the industry's leading lights are on the ropes. If these companies are consumed by a credit event or if the rating agencies lose patience, the current soft insurance market could become hard quickly. If this happens, our companies have the management and capital to expand, as they have in the past in these circumstances. If current conditions continue, count on us shrinking our business further."

GLOBAL EXPANSION TAKES HOLD

Unlike a lot of the big players in North America, Fairfax was increasingly looking outside the continent for opportunities. With all the drama surrounding Fairfax's core assets, it's easy to miss the company's baby steps into a larger-sized global footprint. The 1990s saw the purchase of Falcon of Hong Kong. In 2002, Fairfax bought First Capital Insurance in Singapore, and the following year rolled up additional local assets into the mix. The numbers initially were small, but these were profitable operations (the time for buying bargain-bin assets was over) and each was in a good position to expand regionally.

Watsa started to give over more space to Fairfax's Asian operations in his letter; in fact, the letter itself was getting rather long with Watsa covering the growing number of moving parts in the Fairfax empire. The deals were tiny compared to the mammoth deals of the late 1990s and, therefore, would not move the needle on financial results. But Fairfax was playing the long game, planting acorns instead of swallowing whales.

One of the targets for growth had always been India, Watsa's birthplace and a future economic giant. For years, Fairfax watched as the country made its first tentative moves in decades to open up the economy to foreign investment. The company seized its first opportunity in 2000, investing $10 million with ICICI, a commercial bank, on a joint insurance venture. Fairfax's plans for India were only getting started and ramped up dramatically in 2014 with the election of Narendra Modi as prime minister.

Other deals followed, with some of the assets rolled up under a new regional holding company, Fairfax Asia. At the helm was Ramaswamy Athappan, who died in 2024; he had enormous success building the company's presence in Southeast Asia from his base in Singapore.

"From humble beginnings in Canada . . . , by the end of 2007 we had insurance operations in Canada, the U.S., India, Singapore, Hong Kong and Thailand and reinsurance operations worldwide," said Watsa.

Investors could easily track several Asian insurers starting in the early 2000s and some were showing signs of future impact. By 2007, for example, Asian insurance premiums added up to $68.9 million out of a total $10.8 billion Fairfax-wide. However, the growth was more dramatic with Fairfax Asia's assets growing book value at a faster pace than the company's bigger core assets.

Another way to track Fairfax Asia's growth is through the size of the float it contributes to Fairfax. In 2009, Fairfax Asia's float was $127 million, about 6 percent of the float at Fairfax's core home base Northbridge asset in Canada. By 2013, it was $519 million, a full quarter of Northbridge's.

Even without acquisitions of foreign-based insurers, Fairfax's global footprint was already expanding through the operations of firms like Odyssey with foreign offices for the reinsurance business. But the addition of new firms based in Europe and Asia accelerated the shift. For a company that investors and analysts had trouble understanding in the past, it was now evolving into something even more sprawling and complex. While investors still suffered under the faulty impression that Fairfax's house was full of broken North American insurers, new drivers of financial performance emerged off the radar in places like Greece, India, the U.K., Ukraine, Malaysia, Brazil, and the Middle East.

A full quarter of Fairfax premiums were sold outside North America by 2009. And in the years that followed, Watsa regularly pointed out that the best growth opportunities remained outside North America and Europe, due to burgeoning middle classes and market under-penetration. With Asia and India now rich targets for expansion, Fairfax seized opportunities in 2008 to expand into eastern Europe, purchasing Polish Re.

Then it was the Middle East with a minority interest in assets based in Jordan and Dubai—plus the creation of a partnership in China and the launch of Fairfax Brazil. Other acorns of future growth arrived in 2010: a $217-million investment with KIPCO for a 41 percent stake in Gulf Insurance (a stake more than doubled thirteen years later) with broad exposure to the Middle East and North Africa.

The bigger moves in India wouldn't come for another four years, but ICICI Lombard served as a good warm-up. Fairfax was restricted by Indian guidelines to a minority stake in the firm and watched it grow from its launch in 2000 to become the country's largest private general insurance company by 2006, with 12.5 percent market share. Some of these acorns were already small trees.

Chapter Seven

DRIVING WITH THE BRAKE ON (2010–2016)

"We do not understand these markets and are staying away. Caveat emptor!!" —Prem Watsa

Looking around in the aftermath of the Global Financial Crisis, Fairfax's management team was collectively sharing a "Now what?" moment. The insurers were starting to throw off a lot of cash. They had put billions to work in investments. The company was in an unfamiliar sweet spot.

"In 2008 and 2009, Fairfax needed nothing," recalls Wade Burton. "We were well capitalized, the investment side had just made $4 billion during a global meltdown, and our insurance companies were going gangbusters." Burton's boss, Roger Lace, felt like the company had moved into a mature, less volatile period in its development: "It felt to a lot of us like there wasn't a lot left to be done. I was looking forward to coasting along for a few years and then moving into retirement. We were in for a bit of a surprise."

Next came fears about post-crisis economic aftershocks. Fairfax fell back into acting cautiously and playing defence. Stock market valuations crept up again, outpacing the strength of the economy while corporate debt strains emerged. Meanwhile, interest rates were still low and central banks resorted to emergency stimulus to prop up weak economic growth. Bradstreet, Watsa, and the team were worried the measures would ultimately lead to mounting debt strains and the onset of crippling deflation, ushering in a repeat of the Japanese experience of the late 1980s.

Fairfax took to hedging equities again, as insurance on its capital. The company started 2010 with 30 percent of its common stock hedged. By June, it had ratcheted that up to nearly 100 percent. "Our view was twofold," explained Watsa. "Our capital had benefited greatly from our common stock portfolio and we wanted to protect our gains, and we worried about the unintended consequences of too much debt in the system—worldwide!"

The team was still getting the job done in 2010, delivering an 8.1 percent gain to the portfolio, beating the broader indexes. But the cost of hedging wiped out almost a billion dollars, slicing the return by more than half to 3.9 percent. The windfall from the big crash was gone and a big investment in municipal bonds in the U.S. was unwinding, so earnings were fully exposed. Fairfax wanted protection from disaster, and it could no longer look to bonds to help out, as sliding inflation was dragging bond yields down. Equity returns were erased, and fixed income returns were close to zero.

As economic threats rose, Fairfax dug in and kept the hedges going. It even took out hedges on interest rates, preparing to protect itself—and to profit—from a move into deflation. Another collapse in equities or a decisive shift to deflation would have made those hedges pay off. Instead, the market just ground along under the dark clouds, making the hedges expensive with no windfall.

Fairfax stayed heavily hedged for more than six years, as it waited on a disaster that never arrived. The impact was like another run of lean years. Hedging losses piled up to reach a level on par with all the gains won during the Global Financial Crisis. By the time Fairfax put the kibosh on its ill-fated hedging programs in 2016, these protective insurance measures had managed to wipe out 100 percent of the operating income since 2010 ($4.4 billion). In 2016, the company's five-year return for its equity investments was minus 7 percent, while the S&P 500 advanced almost 15 percent. "We did it for protection," says Watsa, "but in the end I would have to call it a very costly protection!"

WAITING ON DISASTER: ASSESSING THE THREAT

This was a period of unprecedented strains in the global financial system. At a time when inflation crept down to zero and deflation emerged as a monster threat, central bankers were resorting to quantitative and qualitative easing after they ran out of room for rate cuts.

What's the big threat with deflation? Disinflation is a decline in the rate of inflation. Deflation, on the other hand, means a decline in the actual price level and carries with it the danger of an entrenched cycle where consumer spending crashes, layoffs rise, and investment is curtailed. The Great Depression of the 1930s and Japan's post-1989 crash both led to deflation, and the threat of a repeat was top of mind for history-minded strategists.

As a student of Ben Graham, Watsa believed that rule number one was to avoid permanent loss of capital in the investment portfolio and at the holding company level. Fairfax's macro call here was for both equities and inflation to fall. On the equity side, Fairfax shorted the major indexes and certain stocks. To "short" inflation, Brian Bradstreet devised a derivative strategy to profit from a shift from inflation to deflation. "Fighting the deflation threat cost us a lot of money," offers Bradstreet. "We were convinced that we would have deflation, because debt levels had gone up so much and rates were at zero." On the other side of these calls, the consensus view was that the credit crisis was safely in the rear-view mirror. Those who were nervous were especially nervous. Many strategists who had studied the Great Depression elevated this crash and its aftershocks to merit special, historic consideration. Watsa and Bradstreet were among them.

Fairfax was great on macro calls, but many think Fairfax blew this call; after all, they lost a lot of money on it. Is that not losing? We will never know how close we actually were to a major crash and deflationary economic wipeout. Unlike in the Great Depression, central banks around the world did everything in their power to make sure it didn't happen.

For the record, Fairfax did make money for a while on both its bearish equity and deflation bets in 2015. Large losses on equity and deflation hedges swung to gains of half a billion dollars and $36 million, respectively, in 2015. They felt their nightmare bets were starting to come true. In January of that year, the economies of seventeen out of nineteen countries in the Euro bloc were in deflation. Perhaps academic and pointless, it is still tempting to play armchair market strategist and wonder what might have happened if central bankers had not pulled out all the stops. Fairfax certainly felt it was driving into a repeat of its Big Short experience, and the trades were starting to pay off. The important thing to remember about Fairfax is that in both cases, it was playing defence first—not just betting on a windfall. Is fire insurance a dumb idea if your house does not burn down? It may come down to how much you paid for it and what you'd have left if it did burn down.

"You have to remember we were worried about the bigger issue of threats in markets and the economy," explains Watsa. "We would have been in trouble with all the equity we carried as capital. It was expensive, for sure, but we were being conservative. We need to remember what almost happened there."

Reading Watsa's letters during this period makes you wonder how close we got. Fairfax sounded like its "insurance" was going to save the company and pay off big time for shareholders. It could have been the call of the century—and another Great Depression. Let's all be glad they were wrong when Watsa told shareholders in 2013, "While it is very painful and costly waiting, we think your (and our!) patience will be rewarded." It wasn't.

In the end, Fairfax stuck to its bets until the election of Donald Trump as president of the United States. By 2016, the economic backdrop was showing resilience, and the prospect of tax cuts and other stimulative measures was strong enough to convince Fairfax to get out of the way. Looking down the road, Bradstreet, Watsa, and the investment team became convinced a broader turn in the interest rate cycle was about to begin. They needed to overhaul their strategy.

"Unfortunately," Watsa told shareholders, "the presidential election on Nov. 8, 2016 changed the world for us, so we reacted quickly by removing all our index hedges and some of our individual short positions and reducing the duration of our fixed income to approximately one year." A $1.2-billion loss on investments led to a $512-million loss overall for the year, just the fourth loss in the company's thirty-one years.

Of the Trump factor, he explained at the time, "Higher economic growth would result in higher profits for many companies, so that even though the indices may not go up significantly, we think a value investor like us can ply our trade again with less of a concern of economic collapse. When the U.S., a $19 trillion economy, does well, the world tends to do well!"

NO MORE SHORTING! "YOUR CHAIRMAN CONTINUES TO LEARN—SLOWLY!"

Fairfax did not lay blame elsewhere for its hedging stumble: Watsa took the heat with characteristic frankness and humility. He told shareholders not to ever expect another big short from the company with so much downside exposure. His big learning, as he would write with benefit of further hindsight in 2018, was that these kinds of macro bets ran fundamentally counter to the rational tenets of value investing. In value investing, patience rewards you. With short hedges, patience can kill you. There were better ways to protect the company.

"In the past, to protect our equity exposures in uncertain times, we shorted indices (mainly the S&P 500 and Russell 2000) and a few common stocks," explained Watsa, emphatically with a flurry of exclamation points. "After much thought and discussion, it became clear to me that shorting is dangerous, very short-term in nature and anathema to long-term investing. [Shorting] has cost us cumulatively, net of gains on common stock, approximately $2 billion! This will not be repeated in the future! We may use options with a potential finite loss to hedge our equity exposure, but we will never again indulge anew in shorting with uncapped exposure. Your chairman continues to learn—slowly!"

With hindsight, he later reflected that whatever they had thought about market conditions at the time, the HWIC team would have done better to stick to the basics. "There is no doubt we should have sold the hedges in 2011 and 2012 and just focused on what we were really good at, which was value investing," he says. "We should have stuck to finding good companies at good prices."

Salsberg chalked it all up to a company learning from its mistakes: "People could look at our performance and say those are not good results. We had to agree. It was a mistake on our part. We were really protecting against something that we thought was going to happen. We always explained why we were doing it, but in the end we had to admit the theory was not working. We didn't get it right."

At EdgePoint, Andrew Pastor classes turnaround stocks as "quality upgrade" opportunities for investors and says they come in three flavours. One is when the business model changes. Another is when new leadership transforms the company. In both, the catalyst is obvious, he argued in early 2022. The third, he said, applied to Fairfax, and its catalyst is less obvious and less common: "The hardest ones to spot are where the industry or management hasn't changed. In these rare instances, we're betting on the existing management to learn lessons from the past." With that analysis in hand, EdgePoint successfully bet on Fairfax's quality upgrade into "a durable growth company."

The lean years created a lot of lasting negative memories and long shadows for investors. Writing in late 2021 before the stock's recent turnaround, Nik Priebe, an analyst with CIBC World Markets, echoed Pastor in a report that Fairfax shares were trading at a depressed valuation primarily because of decisions made with the hedges: "We believe that the impact of historical investment decisions has cast a long shadow for Fairfax shareholders."

Any way you look at it, the whole hedging fumble was not up to Fairfax standards of performance and the drag was obvious, echoes Jake Taylor, CEO of Farnam Street Investments. He describes this second stretch of lean years and its effect on the company's investment portfolio performance as "a little bit equivalent to driving around with the parking brake on."

SHOPPING AGAIN—AWAY FROM THE BARGAIN BIN

Fairfax's M & A machine had been quiet for a while, aside from a series of smaller overseas acquisitions in 2008. In 2010, it made a significant move in its core U.S. market to pick up Zenith National Insurance. This acquisition stood out for the very important reason it was not picked out of the bargain bin.

Fairfax was a big fan of the company and its chairman Stanley Zax for about twenty years and was already holding a stake in the California-based employment speciality insurer. The deal brought Fairfax further diversification in its lines of business. More importantly, it didn't carry a long-tail risk of toxic underwriting. The tab was $1.4 billion to buy Zenith outright. Fairfax's existing holding in it was 8.2 percent at the time.

"Zenith will be the highest quality asset we ever bought," Watsa announced, explaining Fairfax had now "learned the virtues of acquiring high-value companies." No more turnarounds. The company wanted two strong engines of earnings growth. "We are now focussed on marrying our investment expertise with high-quality insurance companies with excellent underwriting track records."

Let's remember, though, that it's hard to curb one's value habits all at once. Zenith was high quality, but it was also a good deal because it was in the middle of cleaning up its underwriting book. The company had an impressive average combined ratio of 95 percent over thirty years, but as a workers' compensation insurance specialist, it had also been hit hard by the flood of layoffs in the aftermath of the Global Financial Crisis. It needed to retrench, pad its reserves, and clean up its book a little—and that would be messy.

Watsa included some words of caution on Zenith's short-term prospects for close readers in the "Miscellaneous" section of his letter, saying the new subsidiary would provide an attractive return "over the long term, although certainly not in the short term." Sure enough, the next year, Zenith posted a combined ratio of 137 percent and an underwriting loss of $24 million.

Investors might have cringed a bit at the performance of this "high-quality" asset for the next few years. Were we set for another Crum & Forster? No, it turned out to be all part of smart cycle management by Zenith. The company bulked up on reserves to recover from its hit and at the same time cut back premiums dramatically by 50 percent in advance of a pricing turnaround. The cleanup lasted three years, with ratios of 127 percent and 115 percent in the subsequent two years and clean sailing ever since.

"Prem was super patient in that stretch," offers Kari Van Gundy, long-time CEO of Zenith and now executive chairman. "That was a tough time for Fairfax, given they had paid a premium for quality with the acquisition." Looking back almost a decade after the deal, Watsa could not have been happier, observing that Zenith was not only profitable but also punching above its weight class: "No story has been as remarkable over the last half dozen years as that of Zenith. In 2019, Zenith contributed over $100 million of underwriting profit, the largest amount of our six major companies, despite having the smallest premium base."

Zenith was one of five acquisitions in 2010, adding to Fairfax's North American presence and also global expansion. The others included First Mercury (a Detroit-based specialty insurer) for $294 million; a 41 percent stake in Gulf Insurance (operating in the Middle East and Northern Africa) for $217.1 million; Pacific Insurance Berhad in Malaysia; and General Fidelity, a runoff insurer that was itself in runoff.

Another major asset to come under the Fairfax umbrella in this period was London-based Brit PLC, which was acquired for $1.88 billion in 2015. Operating as a Lloyd's of London speciality insurer and reinsurer of "complex risks," Brit delivered again on diversification with both business line and geography. ("Complex risks" can mean a lot of things, from an injury to Lionel Messi's hamstrings to an individual's or company's reputational risk. So, if your social media team messes up and the company gets "cancelled," Lloyd's has got you covered.) Brit also brought a strong record of profits ($229 million in 2014) and revenue growth ($1.7 billion in premiums).

In a friendly welcome to the family, Brit also came in clean with no surprises. In its first year, it climbed past both Crum and Fairfax Asia in underwriting profits. By 2022, it was contributing 14 percent of Fairfax's total gross premiums. (Of particular note, its Ki Syndicate 1618 digital platform quickly emerged later as a unicorn, writing $400 million in premiums in 2021, its first year, and more than doubling that in year two.)

HANGING OUT THE PRIVATE EQUITY SHINGLE

The dealmaking was back with a vengeance in these years, but with a new flavour. Watsa started encouraging people to ring him up if they were selling—big or small—or needed help managing succession in a family-held business or with a distressed lender's lifeline. And the phone rang a lot, especially about investment deals outside insurance.

The invitation to call him came with "a commitment to the founders that their companies would always be part of the Fairfax family and would never be sold." Some well-known local retailers took him up on the offer. For example, Fairfax in 2011 welcomed William Ashley and Sporting Life to the family. Golf Town followed.

Some of the push into more of a private equity–type portfolio of investments came from Paul Rivett—the sparkplug behind Fairfax's spirited defence against the short-selling hedge funds. Rivett, who moved up into the position as president of the company in 2012, was not a classic stock market value guy. He was an M & A lawyer in his genes and his experience was more in doing deals than the rest of the team. Suddenly, the company was doing a lot of deals with a private equity or venture capital flavour.

Soon, Fairfax was bridging the take-private of a funeral home operator, buying out family-owned retailers, investing in golf and other sporting goods retailers, and assembling a portfolio of restaurant chains. Much of the action was in Canada, with household brands like Sporting Life, William Ashley, the Keg, Bauer, Aviation Gin, and Swiss Chalet. There were sizable stakes in big-name companies such as Torstar, Resolute Forest Products, and RIM/BlackBerry.

Some complementary businesses were rolled up together, such as the restaurant chains in a partnership with the Phelan family that owned the Cara Operations group of caterers as well as Swiss Chalet. The roll-up would be IPO'd as Recipe Unlimited Corporation and eventually privatized back under the Fairfax umbrella with the Phelans as minority owners, who would later be bought out.

Outside Canada, a new partnership was created with Bill McMorrow of Kennedy Wilson, a U.S.-based real estate builder and lender. That relationship brought Fairfax closer into the network that rescued the Bank of Ireland. That group, which included Wilbur Ross and other investors, later teamed up again with distressed investments in Greece.

The phone didn't stop ringing. Fairfax would emerge in a decade with a new, growing revenue stream from some of their more successful investments, such as Recipe as well as Atlas Corporation, which owns the Seaspan container-shipping business. Recipe and Atlas would later be privatized. Both are part of a small group of large companies that provide the backbone to a steady, growing third stream of earnings to Fairfax.

INDIA, HERE WE COME!

Watsa had been biding his time to make a bigger move into India, and the election of Narendra Modi's Bharatiya Janata Party government in 2014 changed everything. Looking past politics, what encouraged Watsa most about Modi's tenure has been the commitment to open up the economy to competition, reduce corruption, and modernize life for a rapidly growing lower and middle class with universal access to basic requirements such as clean water, electricity, and education.

"For the first time in 67 years, India has an unabashedly business-friendly government," Watsa said at the time, predicting Modi would generate India's version of the accelerated development seen in Singapore after that country gained independence from Malaysia in 1965. "We expect Mr. Modi to be the next Lee Kuan Yew of India!"

As for a modern free-enterprise economy, there was nowhere to go but up. At the time, Canada's economy with 35 million people was about equal to India's at a population of 1.2 billion. Only a decade later, the two were wide apart—estimated at $2.52 trillion and $4.27 trillion, respectively.

Watsa brought Chandran Ratnaswami into Fairfax way back in 1995, with an eye to building out insurance as well as investment assets in the country where he was born. Ratnaswami has served as Fairfax's eyes and ears, and he has sat on most of the boards of companies where Fairfax has taken an interest. India was still decades from truly opening up, but Fairfax was keen to get in early. Ratnaswami recalled back in 2010, "A lot of people looked at Paul [Fink], Prem, and me and said, 'What's wrong with you guys? You're still a small company and there's so much growth available right here in North America. So what are you doing going after India?'"

One of the first big pushes into India came before Modi in 2012 when Fairfax bought a controlling stake in Thomas Cook India, the travel and foreign exchange firm. Initially, Watsa expected to use it as Fairfax's investment vehicle to acquire assets in India. When the new regime arrived two years later, Watsa opted to be more ambitious with the launch of Fairfax India, a publicly traded holding company based in Toronto and focused solely on investments related directly to India.

Fairfax India raised $1.1 billion, with $300 million of that coming from Fairfax. All of a sudden, Fairfax had multiple interests growing in India, with Thomas Cook (including a few firms it had just bought—Sterling Holiday Resorts and Quess, a facilities and personnel services operator) plus the controlling stake in its pure-play India vehicle Fairfax India.

At launch, the Fairfax parent controlled 28 percent of the equity and 95 percent of the votes in Fairfax India. (At year-end 2024, those numbers were 43 percent and 95 percent, respectively.) The plan evolved to expand Thomas Cook's footprint in travel, under Fairfax, while Fairfax India would concentrate more on heavy industry, chemicals, manufacturing, and infrastructure. Its prized asset currently is its controlling stake in Bangalore International Airport Limited.

THE RISE AND RISE OF ANDY BARNARD

One morning, Andy Barnard stood up in front of Fairfax shareholders at Toronto's Roy Thomson Hall and let them in on his big, hairy, audacious goal. Barnard figured it was time for Fairfax to acquire a new identity. Here it was, April 26, 2012, a full twenty-seven years since the launch of the company as an investment firm and he believed the insurers should get their due alongside the investment group.

Into his first full year as lead executive for all the insurance subsidiaries, Barnard was no longer focused just on Odyssey. He wanted the full team to get more recognition. His personal goal, he told Watsa, was "to have the company become as well-known for its underwriting results as its investment returns." It was a timely call: The insurers were already taking over the performance reins from the investment side.

Barnard was already a bit of a legend inside Fairfax by that time. He had pulled off a miracle in no time with Odyssey by building a global reinsurance business for Fairfax. The speed of Odyssey's rebirth was greatly appreciated by Watsa, given the financial tight spot Fairfax found itself in when the short sellers took a run at it in the early '00s. In 1996, Odyssey wrote $200 million in premiums, operated only in the U.S. and had shareholders' capital of $315 million. By 2010, premiums were almost $2 billion, it operated on several continents, and it had $3.7 billion in shareholders' capital. In 2012, when Barnard moved into the senior role, Odyssey accounted for almost half of Fairfax's business, and it wrote a third of its premiums outside North America.

As Fairfax lurched into its second lean-year stretch in 2010 to 2016, when hedging was the culprit, the insurers started to more than pull their weight. Company-wide underwriting generated $1.4 billion in profits in that period, with an average insurer combined ratio of 96.8 percent. Premiums nearly doubled to $9.5 billion, and the investment portfolio climbed from $20 billion to $27 billion. A few years later, Watsa took pains to explain to shareholders that the insurers were now golden. "In the past, as many of you will painfully remember, it took a long time for our insurance companies to consistently generate underwriting profits, so quite a bit of our net gains was dissipated as we took corrective action on our insurance operations," he wrote in 2018. "This is now behind us."

A year later, he made sure to give Barnard credit, beyond the usual recognition and not only for his record but also for how he achieved it. The numbers were great but Barnard was also moulding a stronger company. With current president Peter Clarke, he built in more oversight and accountability into management at the holding company level—without added bureaucracy. "During this time period we asked Andy Barnard to oversee all of our insurance operations and the results have been spectacular. So what has Andy done?" Watsa asked rhetorically before answering himself.

"First and foremost, he has brought his considerable experience to bear, helping our CEOs expand thoughtfully in the right places at the right times, while also encouraging the discipline so important to avoiding the big mistakes. He began initiatives, such as the Leadership Workshop and the inter-company Working Groups, that have become intrinsic aspects of our unique culture. He did all of this while being very respectful of our decentralized structure, with each of our Presidents responsible for their company's results."

Fairfax started to talk more and more like an insurance group that also made investments, rather than the reverse. But outside opinions can be slow to change. Trevor Scott, a Toronto fund manager at Tidefall Capital and a patient Fairfax investor, draws on a familiar metaphor to explain it. "Much like a large ship turning at sea, it takes time to change investor opinions and Fairfax is no exception," Scott surmised in 2022. "Although the company suffered from underwriting losses in 14 of the 20 years leading up to 2011, since then it has turned an underwriting profit in every year except one."

"ODYSSEY IS ODYSSEY. BUT IT'S ALSO FAIRFAX"

In many ways, Odyssey was a test case for Fairfax. It proved the Toronto company could land a big footprint in the U.S. and global markets, as well as establish a major presence in reinsurance. The next test was for Barnard to continue to harmonize the Fairfax culture across company and business lines, as well as geographic boundaries.

Each leader would drive their company's own culture, and the common glue came from the Fairfax guiding principles. What does fair and friendly look like? Can culture be a corporate differentiator? Can it add value and act as a competitive moat? The experience at Odyssey under Barnard validated Fairfax in thinking it could do all those things. "In the end, Odyssey is Odyssey. But it's also Fairfax," says Barnard. "I was already looking beyond Odyssey in building out the full reinsurance business, but after taking on the elevated role I was now looking at operations and culture across the full group of insurers."

Barnard introduced a lot more rigour, working with Peter Clarke, Paul Rivett, and others, in cross-company communication and collaboration. In a rapidly expanding company, there was more that could go wrong and a greater need to learn from each other and to put out fires before they happened. Regular calls were established for CEOs of the major insurer subsidiaries (the so-called G7) and another for the broader group of international companies.

PASSING THE TORCH

Barnard is quick to pass the praise down the line, especially to Brian Young who has travelled in his path for three decades now. The two have approached succession with a career-long time frame, a relationship where the senior leader might tap his protege for a future role a decade out. After they both arrived in 1996, Young replaced Barnard as CEO in 2011 and began transitioning into Barnard's role as global lead on insurance in 2024. In a period of twenty-eight years, Odyssey had only two CEOs.

Did Fairfax meet Barnard's goal to make insurance as well known as investments at Fairfax? Yes and no. The insurers have long been recognized as first-class blue chips. On the other hand, investments are always going to be more like sports with all the drama, wins, and losses. People love their sports. It's important to think about all those years people had so much trouble understanding Fairfax and appreciate that one big thing has finally changed—for all the lumpiness of realized and unrealized investments, the insurers are now delivering a fat, reliable chunk of profits and growth year after year. Shareholders have learned to keep an eye on Odyssey, Allied, Brit, Northbridge, Ki, and online insurance unicorn investment Digit and to worry a lot less about BlackBerry, Torstar, and the other ones that got away.

Andrew Pastor, the analyst at EdgePoint, has an anecdote that captures the odd-couple dynamic between the two sides of the business. He was lunching several years back with a certain Bay Street legend when the conversation turned to Fairfax. Pastor sold the investor on the prospect of a decisive turnaround in the making, which was driven by, yes, its high-performing blue-chip insurers. Dumbfounded, his lunch partner interjected, "You bought Fairfax for the insurance business? That's like buying *Playboy* for the articles."

A Little Recognition: Fairfax's Insurance Profit Machine	
1985–2011	
Insurers	16 annual losses in 26 years
Cumulative underwriting loss	$3.1 billion
Investment	2 annual losses in 26 years
Cumulative investment gain	$19.4 billion
2012–2024	
Insurers	1 annual loss in 13 years
Cumulative underwriting gain	$7.9 billion
Investment	2 annual losses in 13 years
Cumulative investment gain	$23.3 billion

Source: Company annual reports

Chapter Eight

COMING INTO VIEW (2017–2024)

"I think this is what Prem always set out to do." —Wade Burton

Few people saw it in real time, but history will reveal the year 2017 as the time everything shifted for Fairfax. The firm was thirty-two years old. Most companies are dead by that age; Fairfax was just growing up. Leadership had managed extraordinary things along the way and was getting ready to enjoy the sweet satisfaction of saying "We finally arrived."

Almost a decade earlier, many at the company thought their day had come. This time, it looked more convincing—even if it would be another five years before the transformation was obvious to everyone. "We were wrong when we thought we had a turnaround in place in the 2008 to 2010 era," offers Lace. "And we struggled for several more years due to the impact of hedging. But by 2017 and 2018, it became obvious we were emerging as a transformed company. We could see it clearly—even if a lot of investors were not ready to believe it."

The whole post-2016 era has been about this transformation slowly coming into focus in fits and starts. The pieces were falling into place, and a new Fairfax emerged. What made it so hard to see? Blame the hurricanes, floods, forest fires, and earthquakes. It was basic insurance catastrophe stuff, and it hit back to back with a vengeance; on its heels, there arrived a black swan event for the ages in the form of the Covid-19 pandemic. It took a few years for the dust to settle and the N95 masks to come off before the market realized what was hiding right in front of its nose.

For Fairfax, it was time to reset and fine-tune its value strategy. That meant letting deflation fears slide and preparing for a big turn in inflation and bond yields. It also meant it was time to finally say goodbye to ill-suited short sales in the form of equity hedges. "Despite our earlier success, it turned out our skills were not in short selling," Salsberg observed in hindsight years later. "It works differently from value investing where you buy and there is no nasty consequence for holding on for a while. With short selling, you have to realize you can't always outlive the market if the bet is going in the wrong direction. It's almost infinite how much you can lose." Watsa admits that this time, unlike with the big short, the whole hedging effort was a mistake. The failed bet served as a wake-up call that Fairfax had lost the script a bit on its own value playbook. There were smarter, cheaper ways to play both defence and offence. It was time to get back to value basics.

Ironically, Fairfax shares would hit the skids just as the company's financial picture was brightening. Investors failed to see that the company's insurers were racking up profits even in the face of massive catastrophe losses. In 2017 alone, Fairfax took a $1.3-billion hit from natural disasters and still recorded its strongest profit to date. This was a new-look Fairfax. Covid-19 froze the global economy, handing Fairfax a $669-million hit, and again, the company resiliently recorded a healthy profit. Investments were back on track without the drag of the "parking brake" of hedging. Investors, however, seemed to be sitting back and waiting for Fairfax to drive into some more potholes.

Still, the stock kept sliding. In 2020, the shares traded as low as $319 and a valuation of 0.55 times book value. That made no sense to Fairfax, so, like any smart value investor would, they decided to take advantage. From 2017 onward, the company put together a series of moves that accelerated its transformation, proved its investing groove was intact, and helped vault itself into the top echelon of insurance groups worldwide. They were done fixing things. It was time to go on the offence. Here are five ways they made it work.

1. MASTER DEALMAKING: BUYING ALLIED WORLD

Predictably, the deal to buy Allied World started with a phone call. This one came from Rob Giammarco, an investment banker. He had an idea for Fairfax, and it was a really big one. Fairfax had been making regular noises that its urge to merge was fading. Organic growth was a lot less risky—and cheaper. And in a decentralized strategy, it made more sense for the individual companies to be doing smaller, bolt-on purchases. But this deal was too good to pass up.

Introductions were made, culminating in an agreement for the largest deal in Fairfax history at just shy of $5 billion. It was signed on December 18, 2016, just as head office employees were nipping out early to get some Christmas shopping done, and was scheduled to close halfway through 2017.

Founded in 2001, Allied—a property, casualty, and specialty insurer and reinsurer operating out of Bermuda—was in great running shape when purchased, doing about $3.5 billion in underwriting. Its average combined ratio since launch was a stellar 90.7 percent. The only problem is the company lacked a strong investment record and there was internal disagreement on what to do next. On paper, it was a slam dunk. A quick calculation told Watsa that if you took its 3.9 percent return on investments and replaced it with HWIC's superior average performance of 7 percent, then the last fifteen years would have been delivering a return of about 20 percent versus Allied's actual return of 12 percent.

The only quibble might have been the price and how Fairfax paid for it: Watsa did not love the fact that Fairfax had publicly issued its own shares to fund the deal at a premium of only 6 percent to its own book value—while purchasing the asset at a premium of 32 percent to Allied's (1.32 times book value). Bargain value hunting habits die hard. The deal was dilutive, as well, increasing the total shares outstanding at Fairfax by 22 percent. But none of that could undermine that the upside to Fairfax was huge.

Overnight, the company went from middle- to heavyweight. It enjoyed a whopping boost of about 30 percent to gross premiums, investment portfolio, and shareholders' equity. On top of that, Allied was adding a huge amount of power to Fairfax's organic growth potential and the timing was perfect as the pricing cycle was moving into a sustained hard market in the aftermath of all the weather catastrophes.

Bulking Up: The Allied World Effect in 2017		
	Fairfax (in $ billion)	**Due to Allied**
Gross premiums written	13.3	30%
Investment portfolio	35.3*	29%
Common equity	10.9*	28%

* Combined numbers adjusted for financing and goodwill.

Source: Company annual reports

The folks at Allied had been exploring options for a while before Fairfax entered the picture. And they weren't too sure what to make of these fair and friendly types from Canada. Frankly, they seemed a little too good to be true. Allied had run into a wall, explains Lou Iglesias, CEO of Allied since 2019: "We were a small- to mid-sized, independent public company, and we started coming to the conclusion that even though we were growing globally, it was becoming somewhat difficult to compete with the bigger players. It's not like anything was broken—our capital was just more limited to step up—and we decided it might be a good time to merge or partner to get more financial strength. Or maybe we would decide to sell."

What he and the others feared most in putting their company in play was the risk that the assets would be carved up and people would either be cut or leave if they no longer fit in. "Any time you merge with a larger company, you can expect that a lot of your people won't be needed anymore and a lot of other people are going to jump ship," explains Iglesias. "We had a great platform and were growing. We wanted to continue our journey. It's obvious why Prem won us over. If someone comes and says, 'I want to buy your company; we're going to merge your business and get rid of most of your people,' you're not going to find that very attractive. Then Fairfax says, 'We want to buy your company, we love management, and we want you to stay on, keep all your best people, and you will have the ability to carry on your vision.'"

Watsa was especially attracted to Allied for its potential to expand. "We had a great lineup of assets in North America and the rest of the world, but Allied was absolutely transformational in terms of what it brought to the company," he says. "It has given us a really good sense of how we can continue to expand organically. Just as important, we were able to do it all in the Fairfax Way, retaining senior management and a great leader in Lou." Though there was a minor bit of shuffling with senior management, this was one of the cleanest deals Fairfax had ever done and had by far the largest impact.

Watsa was right. The hard market had arrived and the Allied team immediately put its foot on the gas. "I like to remind Prem that with premiums running at almost $7 billion in 2023, he basically got two companies for the price of one," says Iglesias. "It was a great strategy. Organic is best—you're not buying that added growth. Also, the ROE is better and there are fewer problems and distractions."

Shareholders had never seen an acquisition like this and the timing could not have been better. Hard pricing would be extended by the upheaval around Covid-19, and the top line for Fairfax's big five insurers doubled between 2017 and 2023. Investors were waking up to the realization that Fairfax was exploding and Allied was the new heavyweight insurance asset.

Organic, Transformed, and Hiding in Plain Sight

Premiums have more than doubled at Fairfax since 2017. Below are the top five subsidiaries, with almost all growth being organic.

	Gross premiums written ($ billion)	
	2017	**2024**
Northbridge	1.2	2.5
Odyssey Group	2.7	6.2
Crum & Forster	2.1	5.6
Brit	2.0	3.8
Allied World	3.1	7.1
Subtotal	**11.1**	**25.2**
Total *	**13.8**	**32.5**

* Total includes smaller Fairfax insurers.

Source: Company annual reports

An inauspicious debut

Pity the long-suffering shareholders who feared they were witnessing another Ranger when Allied first reported as a Fairfax company. The new addition landed with a fair-and-friendly thud—and an ignominious pool of Ranger-like red ink in Fairfax's full-year results for 2017. Allied's results were absolutely horrendous, delivering a combined ratio of 157 percent. Catastrophe losses wiped out more than half of its revenue from net premiums written.

What happened? Hurricanes and fires did almost all the damage, but in an accounting quirk, Allied's disastrous impact was inflated by the timing of the storms. Since the deal didn't close until mid-2017, only the second half's revenues flowed to Fairfax. The bad news was all due to second-half "Cats," which is insurance speak for catastrophes. And the bad stuff was really bad. In effect, in year one for Allied, Fairfax got half of the good stuff (six months of revenues) from Allied and a few years' equivalent of the bad stuff. There was another factor that spoiled the party with Allied's debut: They decided to cut back on the usual reinsurance purchased at Allied. That lapse proved to be an expensive one.

"The second half of 2017 reminded us yet again that ours is a risk business," Watsa shared in an understatement with investors. "During the third quarter of 2017 the insurance industry experienced some of the largest Cat losses in its history as a result of hurricanes Harvey, Irma and Maria and earthquakes in Mexico. During the fourth quarter, the industry suffered losses from the California wildfires resulting in total catastrophe losses of about $130 billion for the industry in 2017—close to the largest losses the industry has suffered in its history. Catastrophe losses cost us 13.7% of net premiums earned in 2017 versus 4.6% in 2016."

In dollar terms, Fairfax's combined hit to earnings reached an eye-popping $1.33 billion. The new acquisition had by far the largest exposure in percentage terms to all the big hits. On its own books, a full 53 percent of Allied World's net premiums were decimated, proof that insurance is, indeed, a dangerous business.

Year of the Cat: Why They Call It a Risk Business	
2017 losses due to:	**Fairfax (Allied share)**
Hurricane Irma	$372m ($154m)
Hurricane Maria	$282m ($125m)
Hurricane Harvey	$252m ($123m)
California wildfires	$185m ($87m)
Mexico earthquakes	$24m ($9m)
Other	$215m ($44m)
Total losses	**$1.33b ($542m)**

Source: Company annual reports

As a diversified group, Fairfax was proving to be resilient. Odyssey was able for the first time to weather a heavy disaster year and still make money. It closed out 2017 with a combined ratio of 97.4 percent, but it would have been a stellar 80.6 percent if not for the Cats.

Fairfax's once-impaired assets were now blue chip and after its initial misstep, Allied was about to join them. It eked out a profit in its second year despite another year of Cats, and within a few years, it was Fairfax's top performer on the top and bottom lines.

More bad timing kept the outlook cloudy in 2018 in the form of more Cats and also a late year sell-off in markets. Two stormy years behind it, it might have been time for a big reveal on its transformation. But the black swan madness of Covid-19 cancelled Fairfax's party.

2. PASSING THE COVID TESTS: "2020 WAS THE BLACKEST OF BLACK SWANS"

"The world stopped in 2020. Literally!" said Watsa in his letter. "Without any warning, the world's economies closed. And our insurance subsidiaries were hit by Covid-19 losses of $669 million! At the same time, stock markets crashed in March, 2020. It was a real-life stress test."

What stuck with Watsa from the pandemic was how it tested not just Fairfax's financial integrity but its company culture as well. It needed to do the right thing by its people across all its subsidiaries. And it needed to remain financially sound. It passed its big test on both counts and gained strength from adversity.

"As the Covid-19 pandemic hit in March/April 2020," wrote Watsa, "we had a meeting with our presidents saying clearly that we wanted no layoffs in any of our insurance operations due to Covid-19 reasons—and we didn't. We have a responsibility for looking after our employees—and I must say, with much gratitude to our presidents, we met it!"

The 2020 letter to shareholders didn't lead off with the usual discussion of financial performance: It kicked off talking about the human side of the pandemic. And it became a celebration of how Fairfax could manage through upheaval. Just as it did during the years-long attack by the hedge funds almost twenty years earlier, the adversity pulled people together. Another $23 million was directed to giving, raising the ongoing total to $239 million with an extra $4 million donated mainly to food banks in vulnerable areas of the countries where the company did business.

"These kinds of events have a way, especially if you take good care of each other, of bringing everyone closer. Covid did that," says Watsa. "A culture gets stronger when it is tested. We managed to avoid layoffs, but I think everyone had stories of friends, family and acquaintances who were not so well treated. We pulled together, and people were amazing with charity donations and other efforts to help in our communities."

The financial test

This was the kind of event Fairfax had always tried to be ready for. Cash on hand was there when they needed it, and an estimated $600 million was streamed down to the insurer subsidiaries that were side-swiped by a freeze-up in cash flow and supply chains. Other holdings needed help to get through the worst of the pandemic, including Thomas Cook India when the travel industry froze. "This is what we plan for," explains Watsa. "We know we are going to run into catastrophes. We expect that. But we also need to be prepared for black swans and trouble that we didn't anticipate."

The global hit to insurers was severe, but most of Fairfax's insurers came through the storm in good shape. People still needed to buy insurance. Brit was the only one severely hit by the pandemic, due to its exposure to the events cancellation business. It suffered a $240-million underwriting loss and saw its combined ratio balloon up to 114 percent. Company-wide, Fairfax's combined ratio was 98 percent (93 percent if pandemic losses are stripped out), which led to an underwriting profit of $309 million.

A year after the Covid-19 shock struck, Watsa expressed his relief at how most of the company's emergency funds had been left untouched. Fairfax had passed the stress test. "Because of cash and marketable securities in our holding company of almost $2 billion, no debt maturities to speak of in the three years 2020 to 2022, unused credit lines of $2 billion and well-capitalized insurance subsidiaries and major non-insurance subsidiaries," wrote Watsa, "we absorbed the effects of the pandemic and thrived. Our focus has always been to have a very strong financial position to meet the unexpected problems the world experiences—often, ones we have not witnessed before!"

Times were stressful. The interruption to business was devastating and open-ended. Zenith, a Fairfax workplace and employee insurer, was on the front lines dealing with chaos in employee benefits, human resources, and people's livelihoods. "It was definitely one of the most challenging periods in my career," says Kari Van Gundy, Zenith's outgoing CEO who held the position during the pandemic. "Think about payroll, our entire business is built off of it. The initial weeks were tough and we were busy trying to anticipate what happens with industries like retail and restaurants or travel where payroll was chaos."

How to invest in a pandemic

The trading team at HWIC was doing its best to take advantage of the volatility, but conditions kept shifting dramatically. At first, markets went into a free fall, so deep that Fairfax started picking up bargains left and right in the stock market. On fixed income, they started to buy into higher yields with distressed debt. Then massive government and monetary stimulus whipsawed the markets in new directions; in particular, it triggered a massive run-up in the price of various assets, especially high-risk tech stocks and cryptocurrencies. Just about the only stocks that failed to ride the stimulus wave seemed to be Fairfax and Fairfax India. Between the beginning of March 2020 and the end of December 2021, Fairfax shares were down almost 20 percent. The tech-heavy Nasdaq composite was up more than 80 percent.

The stimulus gave HWIC more to think about: How to play the expected upturn in rates and inflation? They were already in waiting mode for the Big Turn. But the central bank intervention and fears of economic collapse pushed interest rates back toward zero. It was a treacherous market to trade in.

"Central banks have really complicated things with intervention," reflects Bradstreet. "We could have added a lot of convertible securities and corporate bonds with high yields during the Covid period. It didn't happen. The central banks slammed that window shut with all the stimulus."

Bonds were still a bad place to be, but Bradstreet et al. still felt the turn was coming, so they waited in cash and kept their emergency kitty topped up. The difference now was that they had watched all the stimulus being pushed into the economy, and it meant that when interest rates and inflation finally did head up, they would likely rocket. For much of the rest of the market, rock-bottom rates were all many market participants had ever known; they didn't see the bomb coming.

Disasters and business cycles

The crazy business cycles in the insurance business have a way of evening out. The perverse upside of disasters was the positive impact they can have on insurance companies ready to take advantage. Many insurance companies were so beaten up from the crisis that they had to withdraw from the market, with the result being harder pricing for those in good enough shape to do business. It's the same scenario as after a damaging hurricane season, the 9/11 terror attacks, or even a global pandemic—ailing insurers get sidelined and business picks up for the strong. Fairfax came out of the coronavirus period with a strong wind at its back in what proved to be a lengthy hard market.

3. THE BIG LONG: IT PAYS TO INVEST IN YOURSELF

No matter how well Fairfax's insurers were running and the fact that its investment returns, now unshackled by hedges, were stronger, the stock stayed in the doghouse. Fairfax investment strategists were unhappy with the slump; at the same time, the longer these value investors stared at one of the best values they had ever seen, the less they could look away. Soon they were champing at the bit to invest in themselves. No more big shorts—it was time for the Big Long.

The Big Long was not a single investment—it was made up of ordinary buybacks, the CEO's personal share purchase, selling stakes in subsidiaries to raise money for additional shares, and an unusual swaps trade that allowed it to profit from a gain in the stock without having to even buy the shares. Each trade was a way to buy up more of itself. And each would pay off if the price was as cheap as Watsa and HWIC thought it was. Invest in what you know and try to get one dollar for fifty cents. Together, the Big Long trades marked a total break with the one-way bets on market crashes. Fairfax was finding a way to put all its creative strategies together and ground them in classic value. From a Graham margin-of-safety perspective, HWIC took comfort from its conclusion that the stock was now so cheap it had little chance of falling further.

How bad did the stock slump get? The shares spent a lot of time in the C$600 to C$700 range in the 2016–18 period, which wasn't much higher than it had reached when it was partying like it was 1999—which was literally back in 1999. Investors unfortunate enough to have bought at the top back then had faced the better part of two decades trying to get back to breakeven. In the aftermath of Covid-19, the stock reeled all the way down to the C$350 level several times. Investors wanted nothing to do with it. "I couldn't believe what we were seeing," says Watsa. "The fundamentals were all improving and the stock went south. It just did not make any sense." As contrarians, he and Fairfax were getting ready to buy as much as they could afford, in as many ways as they could come up with.

Many investors were convinced that with all its hedge-related losses, HWIC had lost its touch, and they probably rolled their eyes when Watsa did a bullish little calculation in his 2021 letter. He tallied up long-term growth in the company's book value per share and in the stock returns. He then reminded shareholders that those measures tracked one another over time and if the pattern stayed true, the stock was due to play some serious catch-up. "For our stock price to match our book value's compound rate . . . , our stock price in Canadian dollars should be $1,335. And our intrinsic value exceeds book value," he added for good measure, "a principal reason being that our insurance companies generate huge amounts of float at no cost."

Imagine being a shareholder and watching your stock slide to C$350 and then the CEO tells you a fair price would be about a thousand dollars higher. You could look at the company's recent record with hedging and dismiss him, but you might want to factor in the fact that the guy already told everyone a few months earlier that he'd ponied up $150 million of his own money in the stock. A lot of CEOs whine about their slumping share price and ask shareholders to step up and buy. Watsa stepped up himself. The stock mostly traded between C$450 and C$600 until finally lifting off in October 2022. By the time it passed Watsa's version of a "target price" of C$1,335 in January 2024, the stock was in full sprint, reaching C$2,000 before the end of the year.

You could teach a full MBA course on allocation based on all the moving parts of the Big Long. Here is a breakdown of those different moves, including a swaps trade for the ages.

- *Kick off a new era of buybacks.* Watsa started talking more about Henry Singleton, the legendary CEO of Teledyne who orchestrated the most aggressive and successful buyback strategy in corporate history. Watsa called him "the Michael Jordan of buybacks," and Fairfax was going to lace up its Air Watsas and play some serious buyback ball now that it was taking a break from buying companies: "Our long-term focus was clear. We had a much higher quality bar on acquisitions going forward and, as long as cash wasn't needed to shore up financial stability, the first investment we would consider was buying our own stock." In the past, Fairfax might have done a big buyback after its stock had stumbled and then gone back to using its cash for other things. What made this buyback strategy so extraordinary was that, even after the stock surged fourfold into 2025, Fairfax was still buying it back aggressively. The main reason for that is the earnings power is growing so fast that the stock's valuation remains relatively cheap.

- *Let the CEO's wallet do some talking.* "Throughout much of last year following the pandemic-induced market plunge, I made public statements to the effect that our belief was that the Fairfax shares were trading in the market at a ridiculously cheap price," Watsa told shareholders in his 2020 letter. "In the summer I backed that up by personally purchasing close to $150 million of shares." That kind of move from a CEO would normally be bullish, but it didn't get the stock moving. Who knows what shareholders were thinking. Maybe skeptics saw it as a desperate move to prop up a faltering share price. In 2024, Watsa sold 275,000 of the shares (out of a total 482,600 purchased in 2020) back to the company. Fairfax cancelled those shares, making it a big payoff for Watsa (he invested at an average price of C$400 and sold at about C$1,500) and an attractive buyback for the company (the stock went up another third since that repurchase).
- *Getting creative with swaps.* Late in 2020, Fairfax had invested most of its cash on hand, so rather than borrowing from the bank to invest, it got creative. The team turned to total return swaps (TRSs) to get exposure to a gain in its shares. TRSs are not a buyback per se, but they are another way to pay now to benefit from a rise in value of your own company. In this investment, Fairfax never owned the shares, though it continues to receive a stream of income as the stock rises and retains the right to extend the trade. If the CEO's big share purchase didn't convince shareholders to get back on the bus, the TRSs probably should have: "We think this will be a great investment for Fairfax, perhaps our best yet!" How good has that trade been? An initial notional amount of $733 million involved 2 million subordinate voting shares. At the end of 2024, the investment had returned $2 billion—and counting. With the TRS move as its cherry on top, the whole Big Long deserves a special place in the company's history of great investments and smart allocation strategy.

- *The Odyssey manoeuvre.* Same challenge here again—not enough money on hand to buy back shares. The solution this time was to sell 10 percent of the crown jewel, Odyssey Group, to raise cash for a buyback. The big brains at HWIC did some math and decided they could raise almost a billion dollars by selling that stake to two pension funds—the Ontario Municipal Employees Retirement System and the Canadian Pension Plan Investment Board. Fairfax retained the right to buy the stake back, and the funds were happy to hold it as they were rewarded with dividends. The value genius in this "Odyssey manoeuvre" was it was sold at an attractive 1.7 book value, a richer valuation than what Odyssey was being carried at on Fairfax's books, and then the company bought back its own shares at about 0.9 times book value. Fairfax surfaced value in multiple ways.
- *Buy your stock back in pieces.* As earnings and cash flow picked up, Fairfax did a sort of indirect buyback by boosting its controlling stake in various assets. These asset purchases increased Fairfax's share of earnings, which increased the value of the holding company itself. The company had stakes in many insurance (e.g., Gulf International, Singapore Re, Brit, and Eurolife) and noninsurance assets (e.g., Atlas, Recipe, and Eurobank). Following the timeless advice of Peter Lynch on buying more of what you know, this asset buyback strategy accelerated the importance of a third stream of profits, one that made Fairfax's results a lot less lumpy. At the new-era Fairfax, investment returns and insurance profits were increasingly joined by profits from shipping containers, banks, family restaurants, hockey equipment, and mattresses.

For a CEO and team who by their own admission had lost the value script a bit between 2010 and 2016, Watsa and HWIC were back in a groove with masterful allocation. What's more, they were investing with less risk. The TRS investment looks set to go down, as Watsa suggested, as perhaps Fairfax's smartest move ever. But the media never bothered to write about it.

Things were coming together on some unrelated major trading wins as well. This time, it was all about inflation and interest rates, and with the

Big Turn, Fairfax taught the rest of the insurance industry a master class on navigating rate cycles.

4. TIMING THE BIG TURN: GETTING THE INVESTMENT PORTFOLIO BACK ON TRACK

History will probably show that the initial trigger for the death of the bond bull market and the Big Turn trade arrived in 2016 with the election of Donald Trump. But it took years before everything lined up in 2021 to put it in motion. Until then, there was lots of waiting in store before Fairfax would again see juicy 5 percent returns from fixed income.

First, let's take a quick look at the stock return side of investments in this period. Fairfax paid handsomely to wind up its short positions, but the positive impact was felt right away. "There was an immediate pickup on performance once we got those hedges removed, even with the cost of exiting the trades," recalls Watsa.

Fairfax was feeling some relief, but Watsa was not about to give himself a pass for past underperformance. In fact, he was busy calculating how badly he had messed up so he could tell shareholders. As had become his habit, he would look at opportunity cost—in this case, how much more HWIC could have made if it had not cashed out some long positions on U.S. blue-chip stocks. These stocks, picked up after the mortgage crisis, were supposed to be forever holdings; Fairfax liquidated them for cash to cover its hedges.

On the plus side, Fairfax cashed out of those four stocks with a $1-billion profit. The downside was it had missed out on another easy $1.4 billion in the short term. Watsa called it "another cost of hedging" and "a costly mistake we will try not to repeat." It really needs to be stressed that a CEO calculating the unseen cost of forced decisions to illustrate to shareholders how poorly he has been doing is particularly uncommon and yet another reason to read this insightful letter each year.

The Big Turn and bonds

That's enough on stocks; the Big Turn was all about bonds. People like Watsa and Bradstreet are historians when it comes to interest rate cycles.

They have seen the cycles play out over much longer time frames. They were buying bonds in the '70s when inflation was sky-high. They were also at it when inflation and yields finally fell to the Paul Volcker dragon-slaying regime at the Fed in the early 1980s.

HWIC began to pivot in 2016 from extreme fear of deflation to a realization the bigger interest rate cycle may be about to turn back up. Either way, the bond market, especially longer-term bonds, which are most exposed to inflation, was keeping them nervous. The team had already started to liquidate its bond portfolio, taking the duration of the fixed-income portfolio down to about a year versus the former five to ten years. In other words, it found safety in the tiny-but-safe returns on the short end (T-bills), because it was better to have weak returns than risk major capital losses on the long end (five- and ten-year government bonds).

These big allocation moves can take a long time to play out. In the era of the Big Short, that meant losing a lot of money holding hedges for a few years until the predicted storm arrived. In the case of the Big Turn, Fairfax avoided most of the risk by staying out of the bond market. Its main cost was making peanut-sized returns, and it would be more than worth the price. Either way, such a move takes nerves and patience. As we have seen, value investors need to be good at waiting.

Again, investors could have followed along at home. The strategy was all there in Watsa's letter. In 2017, he made it clear that 2016's hunch had become Fairfax's core strategy. "Long interest rates have bottomed out and will likely go higher over the next five years," he wrote. "Perhaps significantly higher." The common wisdom on the Street was that inflation was down for the long count. Watsa, as usual, was contrarian and right—just early. Between a post-pandemic economic rebound and supply-chain bottlenecks, inflation finally started to fire up and the massive flood of fiscal and monetary stimulus fed it gasoline. The flames raged dramatically in the fourth quarter of 2021 and continued through 2022.

Yields soared along with inflation as the bond market suffered one of its worst bear markets ever. The losses blew a hole through the capital of individual investors and corporations. Long bonds were hammered in price and companies needed to either sell the bonds at a loss or recapitalize some other way. Insurance companies, most of which were ill-advisedly exposed heavily to long bonds in their portfolios, suffered mammoth losses in their book values of between 10 percent and 30 percent for the year. Several regional U.S. banks almost went down in the storm for the same reason.

Fairfax? It didn't get touched. It was one of the few big insurers worldwide to see an increase in book value. And all that cash sitting in short-term assets rolled straight into the bond market where yields were now attractive, so it had a head start on earning higher returns. Fairfax dodged a bomb and grabbed the prize.

5. THE GLOBAL STRATEGY GETS TRACTION

All those acorns Fairfax had been planting were growing up. "You can see that Fairfax now has insurance operations across the world," Watsa stressed to shareholders in 2019. He began to regularly hammer home the message that these markets were expected to grow much more quickly than those in the company's home North American market. They had two advantages—their middle classes were growing quickly, which meant there was more money to spend, and the markets were under-penetrated. By 2019, the footprint had grown a few sizes, with the acquisition of Allied World and Brit, plus entry into eastern Europe, Latin America, South Africa, Malaysia, Sri Lanka, Indonesia, Ukraine, Vietnam, Greece, and India.

This global strategy is one of the key things that sets Fairfax apart not only from Berkshire Hathaway—which is almost entirely focused on the U.S.—but also from all the other mini-Berkshires who have "done a Buffett" by mixing investing with insurance assets. These include Kinsale Capital Group, W.R. Berkley Corporation, and Fairfax's former partner Markel Group. Some of Fairfax's global assets have grown steadily over the years, only to rocket in significance when the company bought out other shareholders to bring all their financials under the Fairfax roof. For example, Gulf Insurance Group and Singapore Re are now major contributors to the top and bottom lines for insurance.

On the investment side, a noninsurance holding like Eurobank went from years of trying to stay afloat after the Greek economy collapsed to becoming a consistent top contributor to Fairfax's emerging third stream of earnings. Meanwhile, a few elephant holdings have emerged for future growth—the Bengaluru airport (controlled by Fairfax India) and Digit, a breakout unicorn that is becoming a star vehicle in Indian online insurance since Fairfax Financial invested in 2017. It holds a 49 percent stake in Digit with a cost of $101 million and value of $2.1 billion at the end of 2024. Fully diluted, its stake is 60 percent. Run by Kamesh Goyal, Digit has been a huge success in the past few years after launching in 2016. Similarly, Ki Financial, backed by Fairfax with Blackstone, was an enormously successful launch under Brit and is now rapidly scaling as an independent digital unit in the U.K. follow market.

Indian crown jewels in the making

A big chunk of the front section of Watsa's letter, after the obligatory topline review of performance and acknowledgements to leadership, by the late 2010s is given over to a discussion of India. Watsa continued to be a big fan of Prime Minister Modi and his efforts at modernization and, between the assets held directly by Fairfax and indirectly through Fairfax India, there were now a lot of moving pieces to update shareholders on.

There is overlap between the two Fairfaxes, but it's fairly clean. Investors in Fairfax Financial get exposure to India through Thomas Cook, Digit, and Quess, as well as through Fairfax India. The only insurance assets are held by Fairfax Financial, while Fairfax India's asset mix is mostly industrial, with exposure to chemicals, shipping, engineering, brokerage, and, most significantly, a 74 percent stake in Bangalore International Airport Limited (BIAL).

Fairfax India is light on staff and the parent company handles a lot of its investments for a fee, which Watsa says is much cheaper than duplicating all that capacity at the subsidiary. The structure does tend to layer one holding company on top of another, such that BIAL is being mostly held in Anchorage Infrastructure Investments, a Fairfax India holding company set up to pursue Indian infrastructure and privatization opportunities, so a shareholder of the parent would have exposure to BIAL through Fairfax Financial's stake in Fairfax India and that holding company's stake in Anchorage.

Under Chandran Ratnaswami, Fairfax India has generated strong returns since its launch in 2015. The annualized return on listed investments is 18.5 percent over the past decade. Almost three-quarters of investments are actually private. They carry a lower return of 7.3 percent over the same period, but the company notes that they are carried at very conservative valuations. Most of these are patient long-term plays; those that have been monetized carry an annualized return of almost 20 percent. Fairfax India's own stock, after an initial surge when the company was launched, has been a laggard in its first decade but has attracted value investor attention for the airport holding in particular.

Ratnaswami stepped down at the age of seventy-five in mid-2024, moving from CEO to executive vice-chairman. He was succeeded by Gopal Soundarajan in a shuffle that also saw a major milestone in succession as Watsa stepped down from his chairman role and was replaced by his son Ben. Ben is also slated to replace his father as chairman of the parent company when the time comes.

How Fairfax fell for Greece

In 2012, Wade Burton took the first trip by HWIC to see what could be made of opportunities in a restructured Greek economy. At the time, Greece was still the *G* in PIIGS, the acronym for the European economies (along with Portugal, Ireland, Italy, and Spain) collapsing under the weight of their own debt loads in the aftermath of the Global Financial Crisis. The times brought radical measures, including a 50 percent haircut to even the highest-grade government bonds, a move that crumbled the institutions that had bought them in search of safety.

Investing in another of the PIIGS had encouraged the value investors at Fairfax to do more. Back in 2011, Fairfax had followed Bill McMorrow of Kennedy Wilson—a California real estate management firm in which Fairfax had invested—into a rescue of the Bank of Ireland. Together with partners including Wilbur Ross, billionaire and secretary of commerce for the first Trump administration, that investment more than tripled in value as Ireland pulled itself out of crisis.

Greece has been a massive test of Fairfax's patience. Burton's team invested in:

- commercial real estate assets with Grivalia Properties (merged with Eurobank in 2019) and more recently in luxury hospitality assets with Grivalia Hospitality (owned 85 percent by Fairfax);
- a do-it-yourself retailer, Praktiker, which was recently sold to a Romanian firm;
- diversified power generator and metallurgy play Mytilineos (since renamed Metlen); and
- Eurobank, a stubbornly ugly duckling that eventually morphed into a cash-cow swan.

Eurobank is Fairfax's most dramatic value rescue. That it survived at all is amazing. That it grew to be a top equity holding and major stream of income in recent years even more so. As part of a group, Fairfax invested €400 million into Eurobank initially, at 31 euro cents a share. Fokion Karavias, its CEO, and Nikos Karamouzis, chairman, made good progress on the bank's finances, but the macro environment for banking scared investors witless as reforms and two banking recapitalizations were put in place by the European Central Bank. The round-one injection had been €2.9 billion. Round two was €2 billion (€350 million from Fairfax) at just one euro cent a share. The stock then fell by two-thirds. At one point, Fairfax was patiently sitting on its investment as the largest loss in its history. The good news was that it was overseas and wasn't called BlackBerry, so it escaped a lot of scrutiny and Fairfax stuck to its commitment.

"Many saw an inevitable failure but we saw potential," says Watsa. "And in Prime Minister Antonis Samaras, we saw the will to bring the country back from the brink. His will never wavered. In 2015, the country flirted with an irreparable catastrophe and we were called on to renew our bet on Greece. So we did. This time it was Alexis Tsipras, the PM leading the socialist left who made the dramatic, and we believe correct, call at the last second to work with the IMF."

The price of keeping the faith was to pretty much double the investment by an additional $389 million in 2015. The initial investment declined 73 percent in the first three years. Watsa did his cheerleading for patience in his letter even though the investment gave few signs it would emerge as the comeback kid. It was a classic value investment for the ages; even as the financials came fully around, the shares languished because no one wanted to invest in Greek banks anymore.

"We had to hold our breath several times," Watsa says. "The stakes were high. Many Greeks were pushing to leave the European Commission, and the EC itself had many members who were pushing to kick Greece out if it didn't make its own 'Grexit.' I never doubted Greece's potential." Watsa sees many parallels in the transformation of Greece with those that are taking place in India; he is a big fan of Kyriakos Mitsotakis, the current business-friendly prime minister now in his second term.

As a way to accelerate Eurobank's recovery, Fairfax used an interesting capital strategy in 2019 to merge Grivalia Properties' assets into the bank for strength, and then spin out €7.5 billion in non-performing loans. Later, with Eurobank on a stronger footing, Fairfax bought Grivalia back.

As of year-end 2024, Fairfax's 34 percent holding in Eurobank carried a market value of $2.9 billion, making it Fairfax's largest equity holding by carrying value (outside estimates based on its take-private valuation put the value of privately held Poseidon, which holds the Seaspan container shipping business, at as much as $4 billion). In the past three years, Fairfax's share of the bank's profits has totalled $1.2 billion. In 2024, Fairfax was paid $128 million in dividends.

"The people of Greece should have a statue up of Prem," offers Burton, knowing full well that Watsa would refuse it. "He stood behind the country."

A growing base in the Middle East and Northern Africa

Fairfax made one of its early steps into the Middle Eastern insurance market in 2008, and things have grown from there. A 20 percent stake in Arab Orient acquainted them with Faisal Al Ayyar, the vice-chair of the KIPCO investment group, the controlling shareholder of Gulf Insurance. In 2010, $217 million bought Fairfax a 41 percent interest in Gulf, which operated in seven countries in the Middle East and North Africa.

Fairfax's stake generated almost $200 million in premiums in 2011, rising to $477 million in 2018 and to $1.18 billion in 2022. In October of that year, Watsa's phone rang with a call from Kuwait. Sheikha Dana Naser Al Sabah, KIPCO's CEO, was looking at new investments and was willing to shed its 46 percent stake in Gulf to fund other commitments.

A few months of negotiations later, Fairfax paid $756 million—at a 2.4 multiple of book that would have made a younger Watsa blanch. The older, wiser Watsa, who already owned more than 40 percent, knew exactly what he was buying. Further tenders to minority shareholders have placed the holding at close to 100 percent, and the extended base of operations, now thirteen countries, will make further expansion in the region more likely when the phone rings again. Gulf wrote $2.74 billion in premiums in 2024, moving it into the big club of insurers under the Fairfax tent, ahead of Northbridge.

It is easy to underestimate how global Fairfax is already. The company tracks things like premiums, float, and profit based on where the firms are domiciled. These measures show the big Western players based in North America and the U.K. still account for 80 percent of consolidated premiums. If you look at where sales are actually made, a different picture emerges. Firms like Allied and Odyssey are active all over the world, so if you tracked total premiums as sold in North America and the U.K. versus the rest of the world, that number drops to 70 percent. That shift is likely to accelerate.

One area of global expansion that has been slower to gain traction is Africa. Fairfax Africa was launched on the Fairfax India model in 2017 but struggled to get its footing. Years later, the unit, which is publicly traded in Toronto, was restructured with new partners as Helios Fairfax Partners, and it has exited many of the original holdings and raised money for new private equity ventures. Watsa remains very bullish on the continent long term.

Not Your Parents' Fairfax: A Lot More of Everything

	2014	2024
Gross premiums	$7.4 billion	$32.5 billion
Underwriting profit	$552 million	$1.79 billion
Dividends + income	$404 million	$2.51 billion
Associate income	$106 million	$956 million
Operating earnings	$900 million	$4.8 billion
Investment portfolio	$26.2 billion	$67.4 billion
Book value per share	$395	$1,060
Share price	C$609	C$2,000

Source: Company annual reports

Everything at Fairfax these days says business as usual. Just fix your eyes down the road, keep at it, and pass the company on to the next leaders in better shape than it is today. Watsa continues to make the point that the company only took the best opportunities it could find and never navigated with a map or blueprint. But when he gets talking, you get the sense he feels the company is now accelerating on an open road with the GPS locked in.

Ask the younger leaders on the investment side and you get the sense they are jazzed about driving without the parking brake and sticking to their renewed faith in value basics. "I think this is what Prem always set out to do," offers Wade Burton. "Sure, we got off track a few times. But this is the original plan. The company has never wavered. The next ten years can be absolutely glorious for Fairfax. What we have now is awesome. The future looks incredible."

Ask the insurance leaders and they will tell you they already hit their stride more than a decade ago and have not let up. But now it's company-wide and in good hands for the next generation. "Sometimes the investments would be king, sometimes insurance would be king," says Sylvy Wright. "But I think this decade, it looks like both are kings and the time is now."

It feels good to have everything running in high gear, adds Brian Young: "There have been periods of intense activity building this empire. It is on pause now. From here it's all about execution and organic growth. It feels wonderful, it's the culmination of a lot of sweat and some tears, hard work, discipline, and patience. It has paid off. But it doesn't feel new to me. At Odyssey we have been consistently running profits since 2012."

For the long-term builders looking back, the biggest sense of accomplishment is having met serious challenges and come out on top by making adjustments for the long game. They passed their tests.

"Some of the most powerful lessons come from negative moments," observes Barnard, hearkening back to those first conversations with Watsa about how good companies manage for the long term when they run into troubles.

"We made mistakes. We got some things wrong—but we put them right."

PART THREE

THE VALUE MASTERS

Investing Strategy

Almost forty years into a ride of dealmaking and high-profile market bets, Fairfax became a hot stock again in the early 2020s. It had taken awhile, but word got out that Fairfax was reborn. The last time investors had seen the stock rally like this was the 1990s. This time, however, the bulls will tell you, has the hallmarks of something more solid in that it is built on earnings and not an acquisitions binge.

Do most investors understand Fairfax any better today? Probably not. Back in the '90s, the growth-by-deals story was easier to understand, at least superficially: Company gets bigger, everyone loves it, and stock goes up until it succumbs to acquisition indigestion. Same goes for the Big Short era a decade later: Company outsmarts markets with bearish trade, everyone loves it, and stock goes up until the company makes another bet that never comes good. Those perceptions may be true to outside investors, but they miss entirely what Watsa and his leaders were building inside the company for the long term.

To truly appreciate Fairfax, it helps to situate Watsa and the company in the context of the value crowd, where Fairfax is unconventional in the same ways a lot of other companies are unconventional. Viewed this way, you get a better idea of how they put their money to work in investing, in buying companies, and in how they approach the business of selling insurance. It's easier to see how they were trying to build a company for the long term. At the same time, the whole value context also makes it more obvious why Fairfax got off track a few times and why the curtain was slow to part on the company's big transformation.

Through this perspective, the unique contract Fairfax seeks with its shareholders isn't so unusual after all, and the strategy to buy frenetically only to stop on a dime makes perfect sense. All we have to do to appreciate why Fairfax still thinks its own stock is a bargain, even after it tripled in price, is to take a little trip down the connecting rabbit holes of book value and intrinsic value.

Chapter Nine

VALUE THINKING IN WATSAVILLE

"Good management is rare at best, it is difficult to appraise, and it is undoubtedly the single most important factor in security analysis."
—Philip Carret

The value crowd is a curious collection of contrarians who by definition run against the herd in a smaller herd of their own. Think of them as a community of mavericks.

Seth Klarman, a billionaire value investor with Boston-based Baupost Group, says these fellow mavericks are all driven to remain different and trust their own methods and instincts to outperform. In a 1999 *Barron's* piece, "Why Value Investors Are Different," Klarman described the best value investors as having a curious mix of supreme confidence and caution.

Benjamin Graham taught that, at the root of value investing, the market is a volatile voting machine in the short term and a weighing machine in the long term, and Klarman writes, "thus the investor must have more confidence in his or her own opinion than the combined weight of all other opinions. This borders on arrogance, the necessary arrogance that is required to make investment decisions."

That's where caution comes in, because the bargain price someone is offering could be the result of ignorance, emotion, or circumstance. The stock may even be overvalued, which means the seller knows more than you do. "This is a serious risk," writes Klarman, "but one that can be mitigated first by extensive fundamental analysis and second by knowing not only that something is bargain-priced but, as best you can, also *why* it is so."

What would a community of these cautiously arrogant value mavericks even look like, and what would you call it? Buffett famously came up with his own take, which he shared in a 1984 talk commemorating the fiftieth anniversary of Graham and Dodd's classic *Security Analysis*. Having studied the common traits of fellow top-performing investors over the years, he observed that all were value-oriented and had learned their craft at the feet of a "common intellectual patriarch"—Benjamin Graham. That connection, he explained, made them residents of a small "intellectual village," which he christened "Graham-and-Doddsville."

The best investors of Graham-and-Doddsville are "intellectual mavericks," writes William Green in his book *Richer, Wiser, Happier: How the World's Greatest Investors Win in Markets and Life*. What makes these people more successful, Green argues, is they win through the rigours of rationality and discipline: "They profit from the misperceptions and mistakes of people who think less rationally, rigorously and objectively." That good character guides them, Green asserts, to success in life as much as in investing.

Buffett's speech referred to specific investors but the term has come to refer to all followers of Graham. Prem Watsa is a resident of Graham-and-Doddsville. So are Brian Bradstreet, Roger Lace, Wade Burton, and the rest of the HWIC team past and present, along with, in some way, John Watson and some of Watsa's idols such as John Templeton, Henry Singleton, and two Philips—Carret and Fisher. Buffett himself is there too.

VALUE INVESTORS VERSUS VALUE OPERATORS

Value thinking extends beyond investing to how you run a company. Fairfax's decentralized model of operations, which pushes decision-making down to the subsidiary level to foster a culture of independence and accountability, was informed by strategies practised by other value masters. When Fairfax launched, Watsa had never run a business, never mind an insurance company. But he had a very good idea of how he wanted Fairfax companies to operate. He had soaked up a lot of that from the value crowd.

Author William Thorndike came up with his own metaphorical town, as a nod to Buffett. Its citizens, profiled in his book *The Outsiders: Eight Unconventional CEOs and Their Radically Rational Blueprint for Success*, were value-minded CEOs who excelled at the art of allocation. Thorndike examined the best allocators of capital and came up with a list of mavericks and contrarians who in character and deed would be very much at home in Graham-and-Doddsville.

His thesis is that the absolute best measure of successful CEOs is their ability to grow value on a per-share basis, exactly as Watsa prioritizes in Fairfax's Guiding Principles. These leaders achieved the highest level of success by deciding how to allocate capital in order to earn shareholders the best possible long-term returns.

What kind of personal characteristics did these individuals possess? Focus, modesty, and discipline, which meant avoiding the press, saying no to big flashy offices with lots of staff, and never overplaying the importance of short-term performance. They also typically drew "much comment and questioning from peers and the business press," explains Thorndike. So, yeah, people found them weird too. All of that sounds a lot like Watsa and Fairfax.

Of special note, these successful contrarian value operators shared a common love of decentralization as a way to empower employee talent and keep value creation in the hands of those building the business. They all hated the idea of head offices with layers of vice-presidents. Again, that sounds familiar.

Thorndike called his master allocators residents of "Singletonville," after Henry Singleton, whom Buffett once said "has the best operating and capital deployment record in American business." Not surprisingly, Singleton gets mentioned regularly in Watsa's letters to shareholders—sometimes referred to as "our hero." Watsa is a huge fan of Singleton's allocative mastery of toggling between aggressive stock-based acquisitions and even more aggressive stock buybacks. History has taught there is a wrong and a right way to do buybacks, and then there is an insanely right way to do it—Singleton's. We dig deeper into why that is when we explore Fairfax's allocation and buyback strategy in Chapter 11.

As an allocator CEO of operating companies and buybacks, Watsa is definitely a resident of Singletonville. As an investor, he also resides in Graham-and-Doddsville: His house crosses city lines, and depending on Fairfax's future success, his own neighbourhood could one day be known as Watsaville, not that Watsa would ever want anyone to call it that. It's not his style.

If Fairfax continues to execute its stock buyback strategy in the years ahead, Watsa might well become more commonly known as Canada's Henry Singleton rather than its Warren Buffett. That would make him less famous, since Singleton is not so well known. But that would be fine with Watsa.

THE MARGIN OF SAFETY

"This concept is the most important principle Graham ever taught investors," says Watsa. "Basically, whenever you want to buy something, try to buy a dollar for fifty cents. That's your margin of safety. It's less likely to fall more and if you have the pricing right, it is very likely to get back to its proper value, which gives you a 100 percent gain. You just have to do the math and figure out what a company is worth first. It's a totally rational exercise."

Graham's rule number one of smart value was do not lose money. Rule number two, Buffett has always said, was "See rule number one." Pretty much the worst thing you can do, Graham taught, is to overpay for a stock. In this sense, margin of safety is a cushion to protect you against the added risk of losing your money if a good company has more bad luck. Avoiding downside, value people will tell you, is more likely to generate consistently higher returns than shooting for big gains. Way back in his very first letter to shareholders in 1985, Watsa made it clear how Fairfax would follow Graham: "In our purchases, we are always trying to first protect your capital from long-term losses (as opposed to short-term price fluctuations) before attempting to make money."

Sounds easy enough: just get your one dollar for fifty cents. But how do you calculate that? There are lots of ratios that investors use in pricing stocks to tell you how expensive the stock is against earnings or sales or other metrics. Value buyers, Fairfax included, often put a lot of emphasis on book value. Book value captures the firm's assets minus the liabilities on its balance sheet. It is typically measured as a ratio of stock price to book value per share (BV/S). In valuation jargon, a company whose shares are trading 50 percent higher than its book value per share is said to be trading at 1.5 times book.

A margin of safety, to Graham, comes from an investor's expectations of future book value and what that means for the future earnings stream. It's easy to calculate a stock's current book value; where the analysis comes in is in assessing all those factors that could impact a company's ability to deliver. An investor needs to look at debt load, industry trends, and the firm's past record in weathering adverse conditions. You also have to be good at seeing what's coming next. A stock might be richly valued today, but about to become cheap. For Watsa, Templeton was a key influence, as he took a global value approach that always focused on identifying a cheaper way of buying future earnings. Just because you are a value investor doesn't mean you shouldn't screen for growth.

Just to make it more complicated, the valuation exercise also takes into account the opportunity cost of buying something else with much less risk, such as bonds or fixed income that pays a fixed return. Weighing all these metrics and forecasts is how analysts make their money. With *Security Analysis*, Graham and Dodd basically invented their own field of study. Watsa shares all the details of every acquisition in his letters, laying out the valuation model alongside detailed risk factors for each transaction.

It's not supposed to be easy. In the introduction to *The Intelligent Investor*, Graham cautioned the reader that his book is for disciplined investors and not speculators. Day traders need not apply. "This is not a 'how to make a million' book," he stressed. "There are no sure and easy paths to riches on Wall Street or anywhere else." The margin of safety is a thread that runs through Graham's book in that "intelligent" investors are those whose character allows them to learn how to identify that margin and control the self-defeating behaviours that lead one to speculate rather than invest.

THE REFORMATION OF GRAHAM

For the value crowd, the teachings of Graham endure but are not written in stone. Investors—Watsa and Buffett included—have picked the parts they feel are unassailable and dropped others. Value investors can revere the Graham canon without being literalists.

For example, Graham's playbook called for buying on the cheap with his margin-of-safety vest on and then waiting for the inevitable price recovery, whereupon he could quickly unload it on a "greater fool." Both Watsa and Buffett learned through experience that buying cheap was not always wise. They also learned for themselves that selling out quickly after prices recovered was often like shooting yourself in the foot. The greater fool might be the investor who did not hold on to a great stock for long-term gains—because compounding is where the magic happens. As Buffett likes to say, "Our favourite holding period is forever." Watsa feels the same.

Buffett was pure Graham for a while, then mixed it up. He had bought Berkshire Hathaway when the textile company was in sharp decline, as a so-called cigar butt Graham-style investment. (You take a few more puffs of cash flow before tossing it in the rubbish.) In retrospect, Buffett called buying the textile manufacturer one of his dumbest investments. But, being Buffett, he managed to take enough puffs to get Berkshire on track as his holding company.

Protective moats meriting higher valuations is not something Graham is known for. Buffett credits Charlie Munger with nudging him away from the bargain bin to buy "wonderful businesses at fair prices" instead of trying to buy "fair businesses at wonderful prices." Munger also convinced him to invest in tech stocks, culminating with their enormous investment in Apple. The rationale was all about the protective moat Apple had built around its consumer brand loyalty and retail ecosystem. At the time, Apple offered genuine value, in addition to the growth one would associate with tech stocks. Berkshire invested a lot in the company when its PE was still in the teens. As with Coca-Cola before it, Watsa says, Apple was a great investment because it was poised for rapid global expansion when Buffett got in. This was classic Templeton thinking.

Watsa made his own break from Graham orthodoxy. One way was learning that it is rarely worth the headache to buy broken insurers on the cheap in the hopes of escaping long-tail liabilities like asbestos-related claims. Another was to heavily overweight the intrinsic value of people and management in the calculus of asset valuation. Buffett paid his debt to Philip Fisher for that kind of thinking, while Watsa pays even more to Carret.

"Carret said it all: 'Management, management, management,'" says Watsa. "As a disciple of Graham, I was more value-oriented before—more mechanical or formula-based in terms of book value. But I evolved to really value management above all in investing in companies. Sleep Country was about management. Stelco was management. You don't have to be a genius; you can see it in the results. You can see it in David Sokol at Poseidon."

Elevating the intrinsic value of people and culture in its thinking was a big factor in guiding Fairfax in acquisitions, operating strategies, as well as investing decisions. So while a typical M & A team might look at employees as head count or a line-item liability slated for cost-cutting, the fair and friendly Fairfax team has them on the other side of the ledger as an engine of earnings power and a competitive edge for long-term growth. It's more of a belief system than calculus. It certainly kinder, and Fairfax believes it's also a genuinely smarter way to do business from a bottom-line perspective.

"There might have been a little dumpster diving in the early days when it comes to acquisition prices," offers Watsa. "And we may have had to try out a few leaders in turnaround situations at companies we bought. But we have always been focused on the fact that all business is, in the end, is people. You buy companies for revenue and earnings, but it's the people who deliver those things."

HEARD IT THROUGH THE GRAPEVINE: VALUING MANAGEMENT

The idea of putting a dollar value on a brand is guesswork. What about putting one on the quality of management or the experience of employees? Again, this is not a field Graham is well known for, but Philip Fisher became well-known for trying. Fisher, a San Francisco securities analyst born in 1904, started his own investment firm in the 1930s and, while enjoying a lot of professional success, retained a quiet profile until he published *Common Stocks and Uncommon Profits and Other Writings* in 1958.

In it, Fisher laid out an investing strategy for deep homework on how companies operate, influencing a lot of great value investors, including Watsa, to think about intrinsic value as a broader qualitative measure rather than the mathematical metric Graham endorsed. Fisher's highly influential technique—known as "scuttlebutt" or "grapevine" analysis—involved asking a series of key questions of company leaders and their clients to get at the intrinsic value of management. The questions covered a company's standing on reputation, innovation, research and development, labour relations, and organization structure. Fisher highlighted companies with strong margins but also with innovative cultures that could extend their company's competitive edge into the future.

"[Fisher] saw as a good sign any management who communicated freely with shareholders when the company was experiencing unexpected hard times," explains Robert Hagstrom in his book *The Warren Buffett Way*. "The management should also have an ability to develop good working relations throughout the company." Both attributes—being frank with shareholders and prizing internal communication—are near and dear to Fairfax's way of operating. In 1969, Buffett described his own approach as being 85 percent Graham and 15 percent Fisher. Fisher was more a growth investor than pure value, but his method of evaluation was totally in sync with value investors because it placed a premium on the intrinsic value of integrity and culture—as well as a focus on the long term.

Carret holds a special place in Watsa's outlook, having also developed a rigour around accounting for good management in the assessment of quality and value in investments. A value legend, he started up a fund in the 1920s and wrote several classic investing books including *The Art of Speculation* in 1975. Watsa has slipped in a few quotes from Carret in recent shareholder letters to stress the importance of great management, usually as a set-up before his regular roll call of leadership kudos at Fairfax.

In 2020, 2021, and again in 2024, when he suggested it become a permanent fixture in his letter, Watsa included a great quote from Carret that stands out by radically elevating the qualitative analysis of people over numbers and ratios (italics added):

> Good management is rare at best, it is difficult to appraise, and it is undoubtedly *the single most important factor in security analysis.* Find the company whose boss is heart and soul dedicated to profitable operations, and even more interested in the profits of five years hence than those of today! If he has sound business judgement, skill in selecting the other members of his team, the rare ability to inspire them to superior performance as well, the company's stock is worth investigation. There is no substitute for buying quality assets and allowing them to compound over the long term. Patience can produce uncommon profits.

These words echo what Watsa prizes in the management of prospective acquisitions, in the desired qualities of his own leaders, and in his own actions as CEO and chairman.

SHORT-TERM THINKING IS BAD FOR YOUR WEALTH

In a rush? Then value is not for you. Watsa loves to talk about how Fairfax's acquisition strategy boils down to keeping the company in good shape and then waiting for the phone to ring. Buffett likes to employ the baseball metaphor of a great slugger (for him, that was the Boston Red Sox's Ted Williams) who is smart enough to wait for the perfect pitch to come in exactly where he likes to hit it. If you wait long enough, your phone will ring and you will find a "fat pitch" stock or company that is a gimme. Patience can indeed, as Fisher would say, produce uncommon profits.

Watsa regularly cautions against short-termism and market timing in his letter to shareholders. "The focus on quarterly growth accentuated by quarterly conference calls has made the current stock market hypersensitive to short-term results," he reflected in his 2018 letter, a comment that could have been written in almost any of the past forty years. "It appears that most participants in the market are focused on forecasting the daily weather patterns whereas we like focusing on the seasons. We know winter will end . . . and spring will come, followed by summer. We just do not know the exact date and we may get some spring snowfalls!"

Watsa preaches the merits of investing for the long term—specifically, the power of compounding. That's where the magic happens in building wealth and why he urges shareholders to focus on cumulative returns on share and book value price in tracking Fairfax's progress. "It often amazes me how most people forget the power of compounding," Watsa wrote to shareholders back in 1987. In particular, he encouraged them to look at the effect on book value if return on equity is sustained at a high level. It's the antithesis of quarterly capitalism because time does the heavy lifting.

The late Munger used to say that the hardest part for investors is getting together enough principal to give compounding a good start, and then you can ease off the gas: "The first $100,000 is a bitch, but you gotta do it. I don't care what you have to do—if it means walking everywhere and not eating anything that wasn't purchased with a coupon, find a way to get your hands on $100,000." Watsa scrambled like mad to raise a few million to get Fairfax off the ground in 1985. The company's investment portfolio could conceivably hit $100 billion by the end of the decade.

INTRINSICALLY SPEAKING

Intrinsic value is one of those terms that gets thrown around a lot in value investing. As with people, it refers to something internal that you cannot really see from the surface, but that does not stop people from trying to put a precise number on what a company is worth.

The easy definition for *intrinsic value* is it's a current view of future earnings power. Watsa goes to lengths to make it part of the discussion in every letter to shareholders, but he never shares a precise way to calculate it for Fairfax. Graham had a calculation for it that tried to capture future earnings power based on discounting forecasted future earnings. Then you have Carret who insisted management is the "single most important factor in security analysis." How can you even try to put a quantitative value on a qualitative attribute? Can you measure intangibles like the future value of the collective experience of long-term leadership and employees?

You can get the sense that everyone in the investing world talks about intrinsic value as if they have a shared understanding. But even someone like Buffett will tell you how important intrinsic value is and then turn around and call it too much of a guesstimate to be reliable: "There's a lot more to intrinsic value than book value and P/E ratios," he told shareholders at Berkshire's 1996 annual meeting. "And anytime anybody gives you some simplified formula for figuring it out, forget it."

Can we safely forget about intrinsic value then? Absolutely not. Fuzzy as it may be, identifying the direction of future earnings power and cash flows is a crucial and fundamental part of value investing, and it influences how value operators manage their companies as well. Buffett was merely stressing that intrinsic value was more of a range than a specific price and it is an estimate through the eyes of an individual at a particular point in time. In other words, it's pure guesswork, but the more insights and analysis you put into it, the more valuable it gets. Let's pop down a little rabbit hole of six general points so you can understand why Watsa talks about intrinsic value all the time.

1. Where did the term come from?

From Ben Graham, that towering figure of investing history, of course. In fact, for all we know Graham offered the very first use on record of *intrinsic value* as it relates to investments. When he was writing for *The Magazine of Wall Street* in the 1910s, securities analysis was in its very early days as an academic discipline. Columbia Business School credits the first published use of the term *intrinsic value* to Graham's pamphlet "Lessons for Investors." In that piece he argued, "If the market value of a stock is substantially less than its intrinsic value, it should also have excellent prospects for an advance in price." Graham emphasized a calculation for intrinsic value based on earnings per share, the price-to-earnings (P/E) ratio, and a medium-to-long-term expected growth rate.

2. The best measure to track Fairfax stock growth

In the early days, Fairfax suggested investors track the company's cumulative return on equity (which was targeted first at 20 percent growth per year, then reduced to 15 percent) as a good measure of where stock returns would be over time. It later emphasized growth in BV/S over ROE. Both are good indicators of future earnings and expected stock returns, but BV/S was a lot less lumpy than earnings per share and more closely correlated to share price changes. Fairfax has always said that cumulative stock returns and growth in book value will move to their own beat for extended stretches but converge over time.

Okay, fine. But as the years went by, we learned that both those measures are too backward-looking. The better measure, the value crowd now reasons, is intrinsic value because it looks forward. In his 2014 shareholder letter, Buffett offers his trademark clear take on how investors should take it into account in relation to book value: "Of course, it's per-share intrinsic value, not book value, that counts. Book value is an accounting term that measures the capital, including retained earnings, that has been put into a business. Intrinsic value is a present-value estimate of the cash that can be taken out of a business during its remaining life. At most companies, the two values are unrelated."

3. Watsa's take

Fairfax's CEO weighed in with his own straight talk in a lengthy discussion on intrinsic value in his 1997 annual letter. (The whole letter stands out as essential reading for anyone who really wants to understand Fairfax's thinking.) By signalling that he believes intrinsic value (which doesn't carry a precise value) is higher than book value (which does have a clear calculation), he means intrinsic value will act to drag both book value and the share price higher over time. "We think our book value is not a very good representation of intrinsic value today," he wrote. "We think intrinsic value is much higher." Here he explains the magic of how all these things work together, before warning shareholders they will have to do their own math to figure it out:

> Return on shareholders' equity, i.e. return on book value, is the link between book value and intrinsic value as future earnings will be determined by the return on shareholders' equity. When a company like Fairfax earns more than 20% on shareholders' equity then, given that long-term interest rates are below this figure, the intrinsic value of the company will exceed its book value and its stock price will reflect its intrinsic value over time.

So while stock prices fluctuate in the short term—reflecting the twin emotions of fear and greed—in the long term they always reflect underlying intrinsic value. This is how we view the link between book values, intrinsic values and stock prices. We have given you a framework to value Fairfax but you will have to come up with your own number for intrinsic value.

4. The scuttlebutt on intrinsic

Using intrinsic valuation allows you to include things like great management, long employee retention, and culture in your analysis of a company. It may be impossible to put a price on those things, but they become a consideration. As such, they can provide a margin of safety on investments and create a competitive moat against competitors. Fairfax believes its fair and friendly approach to M & A and its reputation for treating employees and partners well are good for business. It also believes when you treat people well and use a decentralized approach, pushing decision-making to the front lines where people best understand the market, you will drive better performance than your competition.

5. The intrinsic value of the float

Having access to the float is an intrinsic edge in driving investment returns and cash flow. More on this later in this section, but the edge is simple: If you run a solid underwriting profit in insurance, the float offers the investment team not only a free loan but also pays the team to put it to work. It's like leverage, without borrowing the money. This is a big edge for companies like Fairfax that can generate strong compounded returns while it waits to see how the claims come in. Float works both ways: As it regularly ran large underwriting losses in its first few decades, the company took a long time to enjoy that value, so the float used to come at a cost, not a benefit.

6. Accounting rules are a wild card

Fairfax was happy with book value per share as a mirror of performance until two things happened. One, its profit mix evolved and, two, accounting rules changed. Fairfax follows several sets of accounting rules—with IFRS 17 being its group accounting standard—and adapting to mark-to-market guidelines over the years has added to the lumpiness of earnings. The rules also guide Fairfax and other companies to often carry the value of many assets at a price level much lower than their market value; that means a lot of value is not included in book value reporting. (Keep an eye on the letter each year, which will remind you of the dollar difference between carrying and market value of the company's investments. If assets are a billion or two higher than the accounting books are saying, those assets have the intrinsic value of delivering added returns and realized gains in the future.)

Buffett, in his 2014 letter, described the very same challenge this way:

> Book value has been a crude, but useful, tracking device for the number that really counts: intrinsic business value. In our early decades, the relationship between book value and intrinsic value was much closer than it is now. That was true because Berkshire's assets were then largely securities whose values were continuously restated to reflect their current market prices. In Wall Street parlance, most of the assets involved in the calculation of book value were "marked to market." . . . Today, our emphasis has shifted in a major way to owning and operating large businesses. Many of these are worth far more than their cost-based carrying value. But that amount is never revalued upward no matter how much the value of these companies has increased. Consequently, the gap between Berkshire's intrinsic value and its book value has materially widened.

THE INTRINSIC VALUE OF WATSA'S CHEERLEADING

Several times in every letter, Watsa can be found discussing performance in some way before tacking on an assertion at the end: "But the intrinsic value is much higher!" It is another way of saying that as good as things look, they are actually even better if you know how to look at them.

If the headline numbers are bad, redirecting hearts and minds to the intrinsic value can act as a balm to investor nerves in tough times. It is also a great way, regardless of short-term numbers, to encourage shareholders to tune out the noise and focus on the long-term future. Watsa's optimism is genuine—if you consistently build intrinsic value, that will set the pace for the share price to catch up over time.

On the occasions when Watsa urged shareholders to look past a poor stretch of earnings (for example, during the ill-fated hedging years of 2010–16), he would direct their eyes to the underlying growth of earnings power value. The investing results may have been wiping out profits, but intrinsic earnings power was coiled and ready to spring. Why? Premiums were up dramatically, the float was growing, and the future was bright. Nevertheless, frustrated investors were assuming that if earnings were weak, then the insurers must still be broken.

Here he was, musing rhetorically in 2016 that due to the strength of the insurers and the lifting of the equity hedges, the table was already intrinsically set for a turnaround, even before Allied was added to the mix. It would take several years before investors really believed him, but the call proved correct. This is a great example of how Watsa's letters can give shareholders a bullish heads-up, if they read them closely. Impatient investors might have had trouble believing it, however, after suffering through Fairfax's lengthy earnings drought. Investors saw a company stuck in a rut, while Watsa saw a transformation in the making. Imagine reading the following in early 2017—would it make you bullish?

> So why do we think intrinsic value of the company has increased? During this time period [2010–16], we asked Andy Barnard to oversee all of our insurance operations and the results have been spectacular. We made cumulative underwriting profits of

> $1.4 billion with an average combined ratio of 96.8%, with excellent reserving in spite of the largest catastrophe losses in our history in 2011. Through acquisitions and through internal means, our gross premiums almost doubled from $5.1 billion in 2009 to $9.5 billion in 2016, and our investment portfolios expanded from $20.1 billion in 2009 to $27.3 billion in 2016. So we have built a widely diversified, extremely disciplined underwriting focused insurance operation that should stand us in good stead in the years to come.

As a shareholder, you'd have to decide if this is a compulsive optimist hoping against hope for the best, or someone watching what was really going on and transparently sharing the good news. You'd also need to ask yourself how long you were willing to wait for profits.

In the same letter, Watsa picked up on what he thought makes the company so strong—the value of culture and decentralized management and how those drive growth in intrinsic value. He then links that value to an improved outlook. The net effect is to humbly cajole shareholders into staying loyal and to look past the rough stretch for calmer seas ahead. Watsa never wavers on the mission and messaging, with a little added humour (yes, Prem, profits *will* help) to keep the faith:

> The biggest strength of Fairfax continues to be its fair and friendly culture operating ethically in a highly decentralized and entrepreneurial structure. Companies in the insurance business worldwide . . . and in other industries . . . as well as management talent, are attracted to Fairfax's culture and structure. This is a huge reason why our intrinsic value will continue to be significantly in excess of book value! I know, I know, profits will help!! And believe me we are focused on replicating the investment performance which we achieved over many years so that we can again deliver attractive returns for you, our patient and loyal shareholders.

Chapter Ten

THE SHAREHOLDER CONTRACT

"... as we have only 13 people in our head office, we do not have the time to answer these telephone calls." —*Prem Watsa*

Publicly traded companies cannot control who buys their shares. And shareholders, unless they own heaps of stock, cannot control management. So it's always better if they are on the same page.

What would happen if a contrarian value company like Fairfax, with a very long-term focus, wanted to choose like-minded shareholders? There would be certain expectations on both sides. Call it a contract, even if it were not formally written down. What would a contract for Fairfax and its shareholders look like? On the Fairfax side, the company would ask of shareholders:

- Please read the Guiding Principles. Never expect the company to act against its values or culture.
- Accept that we are confident we can hit annual growth in book value per share over time, and that we are confident that over a longer time frame, our stock will keep pace and all of us will do well.
- Remember to share the same long-term focus we keep ourselves. Our earnings are often lumpy, especially due to either realized investment gains or losses. Don't expect us to groom analysts on earnings expectations.
- Don't get all worked up if the stock suffers the occasional, inevitable downdraft. We're disciplined, so you can be too. Please stay out of the way and let us do our jobs. (No phone calls, please.)

- Have trust in us to be transparent. We intend to be accountable, explain our performance, and update you on our general financial strength.
- On that note, please read our richly detailed annual letter to shareholders. We explain our performance in detail. We highlight risk factors, headwinds, and tailwinds. Sometimes we talk about swaps and stock bubbles. We own our mistakes. And we tell you who all the amazing people are at our subsidiaries. They do all the hard work and they never leave.
- Know that we have a dual-class share structure to retain management control for the long term. There will be no sale of our company, so do not expect to receive a bonanza on any such transaction.
- Believe us when we say we think our stock is undervalued. And note that we may hint to you when it is richly valued as well. Things even out over time.
- Accept that the company does not commit to strategic plans and prefers to take the best opportunities as they present themselves. We are patient but ready to pounce.
- Please bring good questions to the annual meeting, so everyone can benefit from the answers. We will answer them all. We will also provide you with food from Recipe restaurants, and our other companies will give you souvenir swag.
- Sorry, your chairman will never apologize for the large number of exclamation points in his letter!!!

That kind of theoretical contract would be a recipe for a great relationship, and it would not look out of place at a lot of other companies in Graham-and-Doddsville or Singletonville. When Buffett drew up his first partnership with family and friends in 1956, he laid out clear expectations of his investors. He let them know they would get the first 6 percent of returns and 75 percent of any upside beyond that, with the remainder going to him. He told them to think in five-year returns, not annual; that he wasn't tying his strategy to market or economic cycles; and that he would explain the investments in detail only once a year in his letter. Otherwise, he asked to be left alone. That was his deal: Take it or leave it, no negotiations. That's harder to get away with at a public company, but it would fit with Fairfax.

In his book *Common Stocks and Uncommon Profits,* Fisher described this shared expectation by using a restaurant metaphor. The former Stanford professor taught readers that investment managers and companies, just like restaurants, can engender strong loyalty by having the other party opt in to the relationship. You might make great sushi or hamburgers or dim sum, be bargain-rate or Michelin-starred, with white linen or picnic tables. Whatever you choose, stick to it and you can attract customers who are like-minded. Once they know what to expect, they will come back with expectations you can meet, and you won't need to keep explaining the menu.

Watsa set out to do that with Fairfax. Even in that initial one-page letter to shareholders in 1985, the new CEO asked rhetorically what investors might expect from the company by way of updates. He answered himself: "As shareholders ourselves, we plan on providing you with the type of information that we ourselves would find useful." In other words, trust us to treat you like a partner. Buffett has described his approach to disclosure by focusing on what he needed to know and explained in a clear way his sisters, Doris and Bertie, would understand.

WHAT HAPPENS WHEN YOU BREAK THE CONTRACT?

Shareholders might not be happy at times with Fairfax decisions or performance, but they have little to complain about when it comes to disclosure. On the flip side, if shareholders forget to stick to the "contract," they might get a talking-to. We saw some of that in the '90s and early '00s when the Fairfax CEO expressed frustration with shareholder impatience and excessive questions. In his 1997 letter, he declared: "The objective of our Annual Report is to provide you with enough information so that you can get some idea about (a) what Fairfax is worth; (b) our ability to meet our obligations (in other words, our financial soundness); and (c) how we have done given the hand we have been dealt." In other words, full disclosure doesn't mean constant disclosure, so please be disciplined and think long term. That is why he asked shareholders to find the strength to resist bothering Fairfax with distracting calls, but promised to answer them later. "So as a matter of policy, we will not be responding to investor calls about stock price fluctuations or other questions about Fairfax on an individual basis but would be delighted to answer your questions at our annual meeting."

You have to think that a lot of these shareholders had jumped on the bandwagon when Fairfax stock was in the climbing part of the roller-coaster ride. It was less fun riding it down and they wanted assurances it would stop soon. This was the same time Watsa got a bit wound up and went so far as to suggest these shareholders might want to cash out and buy someone else's stock, as we learned in chapter 4. It's hard to fire your shareholders: It's not in the contract.

SETTING GOALS AND TARGETS

At Fairfax, it has always been the case to tell shareholders exactly what the company wanted to achieve next but be light on details as to how. Fairfax did not work from a plan on what kind of acquisition they would make next, so they could not share that. But on performance, they were clear. After a few years, they went further in spelling out their corporate objectives, along with details on how they wanted to operate, in the Guiding Principles. The principles became the glue for the company's unique corporate culture. The first few principles—grouped under the bucket "Objectives"—summed up the core promise to shareholders. It could not have been more direct. If you don't like this approach, please invest elsewhere.

1. We expect to compound our mark-to-market book value per share over the long term by 15 percent annually by running Fairfax and its subsidiaries for the long term benefit of customers, employees, shareholders and the communities where we operate—at the expense of short term profits if necessary.
2. Our focus is long term growth in book value per share and not quarterly earnings. We plan to grow through internal means as well as through friendly acquisitions.
3. We always want to be soundly financed.
4. We provide complete disclosure annually to our shareholders.

The principles have seen only a few edits in their four decades. Out of the gate in 1985, the goal had been a 20 percent after-tax return on shareholders' equity, an aggressive target that Watsa cautioned would have to be revised: "In the next few years because of tax loss carryforwards, this is unlikely to be onerous," he said in 1985. "Over the years though, 20% after tax is a very challenging objective."

Putting down specific expectations was about transparency, and it was invaluable in keeping the company focused. Watsa could have set a 15 percent target, but he knew the tax carryforwards would make that too easy. He wanted to push harder. In a speech accepting an award from his alma mater Ivey School of Business in 1999, he shared how important it had been to challenge themselves:

> Our focus right from day one was to build shareholder value over the long term. Now, everyone says that—but we actually defined it. We said the average business in Canada or the United States made about 11 or 12 percent on shareholders' equity, and we wanted to make 20 percent. We wanted to be above average, but over the long term. The fact that we defined that 20 percent, I didn't know it at the time but with hindsight, the fact that we defined it and put a number to it was the single most important reason for us achieving the 20 percent. Because we were focused on achieving a quantifiable number, and it drove our acquisitions. It ultimately drove everything we did.

In time, that target was first modified with a reduction to 15 percent in 2002, followed by a shift four years later to the same annual 15 percent target but in book value per share (not return on equity) and "over the long term" rather than each year. "We will view the 20% objective with nostalgia because it has served us well over the past 17 years," said Watsa in his 2002 letter. The 15 percent rolling target on growth in book value per share is still an aggressive target for any company.

Changes in accounting rules were a factor in the target reforms, especially those regarding mark-to-market valuation of company assets. As Canadian accounting rules changed to force Fairfax to include mark-to-market in measuring its shareholders' equity, reported returns were clipped. Hence the move to calculating the target based on book value instead.

TO OUR SHAREHOLDERS: THE LETTER

Fairfax wanted mostly to be left alone. In return, once a year they would tell you more than other companies would. On a quarterly basis, they always kept disclosure light, and it was only in the second half of 2001 that steep losses were raising enough anxious questions to convince them to reluctantly start doing quarterly conference calls. A few years later, when things got crazy with the attack of the hedge funds, Fairfax finally started to welcome the calls as a way to counter disinformation.

The two key vehicles for disclosure and communication have always been the annual report, with its shareholder letter, and the annual meeting. These are the same priorities for others in the value club, including Markel Group and Berkshire. Buffett's AGM in Omaha came to be called the Woodstock of Capitalism. These days, Fairfax draws a big crowd to its AGM at Roy Thomson Hall in Toronto. When they are not expressing their perpetual displeasure with the lack of progress at a BlackBerry turnaround, shareholders get the chance to hear directly from holding company management as well as many of the CEOs of leading Fairfax subsidiaries and holdings.

For the best tool to understand what Fairfax is thinking, doing, or worrying about, read the chairman's letters to shareholders. The letter started out as a one-pager in 1985, hit double digits in 1996 and now runs around thirty pages of strategic insights, background context, market wisdom, bearish musings, dad jokes, and some strong hints on future direction.

Fairfax avoids formal guidance with analysts but has been very candid of late in the letter about the visibility of performance a few years out. Operating earnings are smoother now: Bond yields are finally up off the mat, insurance is delivering dependable profits, and there is steady income from noninsurance companies. As a result, Fairfax has started to offer some forward guidance (with the Watsa proviso: No promises!) to investors, something it said it would never do because its results used to be so lumpy with stock gains or losses. A few years ago, it said operating earnings in the $3-billion range looked likely to repeat in the near term. The next year, it boosted that to $4 billion and to $5 billion a year later. Investment gains come on top of that. As momentum and compounding go, and if earnings remain this high, a growing factor in forecasting will be how well they put all this new-found cash to work. This is a new era for Fairfax—in a five-year stretch alone, the earnings windfall could reach in the neighbourhood of $20 billion, depending on the lumpiness of realized investment gains.

While many CEOs default to rote summaries of the year's activities, the great letter writers take advantage of the informal opportunity to offer up what amounts to a free MBA seminar. CEOs are free to ad lib in an informal medium and weigh in on what they think is important. "There is simply no more authoritative source than CEOs on subjects ranging from leadership and management to capital allocation and corporate stewardship," Cunningham writes in his book on the best CEO letter writers.

So what does Cunningham think makes a great shareholder letter? "Outstanding shareholder letters are well-written, honest, and consistently focused. They reveal the good, the bad and the awful, not ducking hard problems. They embrace long-term thinking, manifested by charting results over long periods of time, which means acknowledging tough patches put in the context of stronger returns over longer time spans." Given that description, it's not surprising that Watsa's name features prominently in Cunningham's book title.

Waxing on the character attributes of the great CEO letter writers, Cunningham hits the same messages we heard from Thorndike praising the great CEO allocators, or Buffett admiring the traits shared by the citizens of Graham-and-Doddsville. The best value CEOs are no-nonsense, rational, transparent, and smart. "Above all, these executives hold fast to a long-term horizon," Cunningham writes. "They eschew conference calls and earnings guidance, preferring to speak mostly through their shareholder letters." If by now you still think Watsa and Fairfax are odd, you can at least appreciate they are in rarefied good company.

Watsa is particularly proud of his hero Templeton's impression of the letter and annual report. "John read a lot of them, and he told me our letter and report was one of the best because it was thin on promotion and it told you all the bad news up front. We didn't hide anything," he says.

Readers of Watsa's letters come away with a deeper understanding of Fairfax thinking on leadership values, company strategy, employee development, compensation, succession, and performance metrics. As with Buffett's letter, the discussion comes with a healthy dose of common sense and positive encouragement. Sometimes, it's like having a personal coach to keep you grounded and not caught up in the market's speculative flavour of the moment. A big part of the reason people read the letters and flock to annual meetings like Fairfax's—and by the thousands to Berkshire—is for the positive reinforcement that self-discipline and faith in your own rationality and patience can make you happier as well as richer. Also, where else are you going to get warnings on stock crashes five years before they happen and learn about people like Phil Carret and Henry Singleton?

CONTROL IS ESSENTIAL

Fairfax could have been run as a private company, but Watsa understood the value of being a public firm with access to capital, as long as it could retain voting control. As a public company, the company made its case early and often: It needed freedom to allocate capital for the long term and required safety from hostile takeover threats. How Fairfax managed to maintain control, of course, was through its dual-class share structure, which retained multiple-voting stock in management's hands.

The plan was always to retain control and pass on that control to the next generation. But Watsa still had a lot to say about the practice of treating all shareholders equally in the highly unlikely event the company were ever sold. Because a multiple-voting superclass of shares affords a larger say in company votes, they often carry more value in principle. Watsa has had uncharacteristically harsh words for management that would sell off their control stake at a higher share price than ordinary shareholders would receive in the same deal. He related the details of one such "atrocity" in the 1998 takeover of Oshawa Group by Empire Company. (The offer was $116 a share for the multiple-voting stock versus $36 for the subordinate shareholders.) Similarly, Canadian

Tire, an iconic retailer, had been the subject of unequal control propositions. In 1986, Watsa insisted that kind of situation "cannot and will not happen" at Fairfax.

While critical of the abuse of dual-class shares, Watsa has also been ardently defensive of the structure for its ability to provide protection from raiders for the long term. He has told readers about companies that had been picked off when they stumbled, robbed of the chance to right their own ships. So when news stories painted dual-class stock as a negative for shareholders, he countered with a staunch defence:

> There is much discussion in the media about corporate governance, board composition, etc., etc. Also, there has been some negative press about dual voting share structures. I must say that a major reason for Fairfax's track record is its small, non-bureaucratic board and its share structure that together allow us to be entrepreneurial and react quickly to opportunities, and to take the long view and not be worried about stock market fluctuations. In the past 18 months, we have seen two excellent companies in the oil industry—Nowsco and Morrison Petroleum, be taken over because their share prices were temporarily low and probably would have benefited from a dual voting structure. While there are many abuses of this share structure, as far as Fairfax is concerned it is a big plus!

Vulnerability to hostile takeovers can make companies do irrational, stupid things like buying indebted assets to make themselves less attractive to raiders. Watsa promised shareholders that while Fairfax might make bad acquisitions by mistake, they would never do it on purpose: "We are one of the very few companies in the P&C industry (for that matter, any industry!) that can escape the trauma of being swallowed up in the current merger and acquisitions activity . . . Thus, many of our much larger competitors in the U.S. (and elsewhere) are fearful for their independence and sometimes, as a defensive move, make uneconomic acquisitions. We will not *knowingly* make uneconomic acquisitions, and our managements can truly build for the long term unencumbered by fears about their company being sold."

Of course, for Fairfax that long term was very, very long. In 1995, Watsa made it clear he had a plan for the vision to outlive him: "You should know that I have arranged my affairs so that my death (not expected soon!) will not trigger the sale of any of my multiple voting shares. No short-term bonanza even at my passing away!"

It goes without saying that the whole shareholder contract idea is more likely to go smoothly if the company's management can deliver outstanding returns over time, with the inevitable dismal stretches kept short and shallow. In the go-go years, media commentators called the tightly held control structure "Prem Watsa's beneficial dictatorship," with a degree of respect for the outperformance the stock enjoyed in the 1990s. Anyone who held the stock through the first half of the 2020s would feel the same.

THAT TIME WATSA ASKED SHAREHOLDERS TO RENEW HIS ACTUAL SHAREHOLDER CONTRACT

Over time, issuing more subordinate shares dilutes the control of founding shareholders. Voting power of the multiple-vote shares slid from 80 percent to 41.8 percent in 2015. "I was very uncomfortable going much below this level of control as our company would then be subject to being taken over," Watsa told shareholders at the time. "That left us two choices: either change the multiple voting share structure, or stop making acquisitions using our stock as currency."

A board committee came up with an arrangement to protect minority shareholders while retaining the power of the multiple-voting shares. Coming in the middle of a period of underperformance, some shareholders resisted, but the shareholder proposal passed. "All in all, this is an excellent deal for Fairfax and its shareholders," Watsa told shareholders after it passed, "as it allows us to expand significantly, while retaining the very valuable corporate culture that we have built over the past 30 years."

Chapter Eleven

WHERE FAIRFAX PUTS ALL ITS MONEY

"You can get your head handed to you." —*Brian Bradstreet*

Fairfax operations are now spread out with 22,000 employees at 26 operating companies in 50 countries, but its investing acumen resides behind an unassuming door just a few steps from the reception desk at the head office on Wellington Street in Toronto's financial district. Inside, a Hamblin Watsa Investment Counsel staff of just forty runs the combined $70-billion investment portfolio. The HWIC group makes up about half of the total head office staff, which, in a classic decentralized structure, is a small group to begin with. The investments, together with acquisitions, are the only things Fairfax does not leave to its subsidiaries to run for themselves.

THE HWIC STORY

Small as it is, Fairfax's investment team used to be a lot smaller. In the beginning, it consisted of the original HWIC crew of just four—the two names on the door (Hamblin on bonds and Watsa on equities) plus trader Frances Burke and Mary Pritchard as Watsa's executive assistant. They were soon rounded out with Roger Lace, Brian Bradstreet, and bond trader Enza LaSelva. Additions much later on included Wade Burton and Lawrence Chin, who both crossed the Street from Mackenzie Cundill, a Vancouver-based value investment shop and a one-time major Fairfax investor. Some of the staff have been working together for more than half a century, dating back to their starts at Confederation Life. Of course, value types are known to love their jobs so much they prefer to be taken out on a stretcher over retiring. Munger was still at it at the tender age of ninety-nine when he finally passed away. By comparison, Roger Lace and Brian Bradstreet are mere youngsters, but Fairfax has been pushing hard on succession for fresh blood.

The baton has been passed to a younger team led by Burton and Chin, who structure their teams to tackle both fixed income as well as equities to broaden experience. If members specialize, it's more likely to be by geography than asset class, given the company's global reach. Quinn McLean, for example, serves on HWIC by overseeing fixed-income and equity portfolios in countries of the Middle East and North Africa, as well as in South Africa.

"Wade and Lawrence are keeping us young," says Watsa. "We have been able to bring along some great talent and they have picked up so much knowledge from people like Roger and Brian. It's the same thing we're doing across the insurers as well. You cannot build the kind of continuity with culture that will carry us another fifty, one hundred, or more years without constantly thinking about succession."

In the early days, as HWIC was still courting clients on the pension side, it had dual responsibilities to Fairfax and to outside clients, which for a while included its partner Markel in the U.S. So while it was wearing a lot of hats, Watsa himself was the only one working on both the investment and insurance sides of the company. He was compensated as chairman of a diversified holding company but collected most of his compensation from HWIC, and much of it was performance-based. That is how they do it in wealth management.

As Fairfax and Markel's U.S. parent went their own ways and the task of managing Fairfax's growing insurance investments grew, Fairfax made a few moves to simplify the corporate relationships. Part of the effort was to avoid any potential personal conflicts of interest; after all, it didn't make sense to have the CEO of a company making his compensation predominantly by providing a business service to a holding company he controlled. Fairfax was probably the only company where the CEO was being paid directly to manage the company's own employee investment portfolio.

By 1992, HWIC had C$1 billion under management, with just over a quarter of that coming from the insurers and the rest from outside pension clients. Fairfax opted to buy up HWIC for C$14 million and began an orderly plan to wind down its pension and other external money management, in order for HWIC to devote all its energy to Fairfax.

In that same year, Watsa also reworked his compensation package to a fixed salary of C$600,000 with no bonuses from HWIC or any other source. That set-up remains in place today, and it stands out as cheap against any benchmark, offers Chou: "If someone else had built what he built and decided to pay himself $20 million a year, no one would blink." He received $19 million in dividends last year, at the same per-share rate as other shareholders. (Watsa says more than 90 percent of his total wealth is tied up in Fairfax shares and his control stake will pass on to the family trust. He does not get a bonus and has no company stock plan.)

Since 2000, HWIC has worked exclusively for Fairfax and its operating companies, with the one exception that it handles the investments for subsidiary Fairfax India—for a fee paid to the parent company. There is sometimes chirping on the investment chats and social media about the fee Fairfax India has to pay its parent, but Watsa insists it would cost a lot more to build that investing capacity at the subsidiary. The added stated benefit of having investments pooled is they can each be managed based on a single thesis; the job of a team under Fairfax president and allocation lead Peter Clarke is to spread the assets around to capitalize all the operating insurers individually for maximum diversification and strength.

How much money are we talking about? The size of the kitty initially grew rapidly through acquisitions but these days the growth is organic. The total portfolio (at the end of 2024) is $67.4 billion and the float accounts for $36.9 billion of that.

THE MAGIC OF FLOAT

Collect now, invest, pay most of it back later: If you can get this basic concept right as an insurance company and you invest well, this is your secret to generate a lot of value. Once you collect your premiums, you have time to generate returns before you have to pay them out. And those returns are yours to keep compounding as new premiums are written.

"This has been and will be the gift that keeps giving, especially if we stay profitable with our insurers," offers Watsa. "It's what originally attracted us to pairing our investment success with insurance assets in the first place. The value of the float is not only its cost but also a function of how well it is invested. And higher yields are now going a long way to support higher returns."

The float can easily become a liability if a company is weak on either underwriting or investing. If an insurer runs into losses, it means taking money from earnings to offset them. Same goes if poorly written premiums in the past create a need to buy reinsurance or to keep topping up reserves year after year (e.g., TIG, Ranger, and Sphere). As for investing, a lot of insurers, tempted by a few basis points more than what government bonds were paying, invested heavily in mortgage-backed bonds ahead of the Global Financial Crisis. Most also kept their exposure to long bonds high in the post-Covid-19 period when a major return of inflation and higher yields led to enormous losses. Both cases served up painful lessons and HWIC skirted trouble in each case.

The cost of the float to Fairfax changes, depending on how well its insurers are performing. In his letter, Watsa regularly updates shareholders with a table on what kind of cost or savings it is getting from its own float. In the simplest terms, if Fairfax breaks even on the insurance side, the cost of the float is zero. That's the equivalent of a zero-interest loan. If insurer profits are well above breakeven at Fairfax, the company is essentially being paid to take the money and invest it to its own benefit, which adds a little juice free of charge to the power of compounding overall. That is more like negative interest rates, offers Watsa.

The problem in the early days was that the company had trouble paying for the past mistakes at the insurers it had bought. For example, looking back from 2001, in eleven of the previous thirteen years, the float had come with a cost. Since Andy Barnard took on oversight of all the insurance assets in 2011, however, the company-wide combined ratio has been below 100 percent in twelve of thirteen years, ultimately yielding a total net benefit to the float of $7.9 billion, or 2.8 percent a year on average.

Low interest rates and bond yields were just a few of the things kneecapping the returns on Fairfax's portfolio and float in the 2010s. In the mid-2020s, higher bond yields and highly profitable insurers are giving growth in the float an extra push, lifting interest and dividend income to a record in 2024 of $2.5 billion. Back in 2017, that income stream was just $560 million. The float has surged 65 percent in the past five years, almost entirely from organic growth.

VALUE INVESTING AND BONDS

Graham and Dodd wrote mostly about stocks but they still had a lot to offer value investors on fixed income, explains Bradstreet, Fairfax's legendary strategist. "They didn't write a lot about interest rates and bonds, but they wrote about credit analysis and the need to think about margin of safety in fixed income. What they did was stress the need to study the history of capital markets to better understand trends. To me, that means understanding interest rates, which are tricky. You need that context to understand bond values. There are business cycles and broader trends, then you have mega cycles that play out over decades. If you start valuing bonds over the longer term based on a short-term recession, you can get your head handed to you."

The last decisive turn in rates and inflation was in the early 1980s when Fed chair Paul Volcker beat runaway inflation into submission with a steady stream of interest rate hikes. Bradstreet and Watsa were managing portfolios at the time and had front-row seats. "We were all right there at that last big turn," Bradstreet recalls of the group's early days at Confederation Life. As yields shot higher to 10 percent, they started buying. As would become their habit, they were right but a bit early—which almost handed them their heads. "We thought it was a fantastic value to be buying with a yield of 10 percent. But prices dropped even more and yields kept shooting higher to 18 percent! We came close to estimating how high they would blow out but we just didn't have the experience to time it better."

As in today's market of resurgent yields, this kind of market turn served up a reminder to investors that bonds are not always the safe and boring way of earning money. First, they can get a capital loss from the drop in the price of the bond. Second, they have bought a bond paying 10 percent, and other people who bought shortly after are paying less and getting 18 percent to hold it. "We thought we'd get fired, but we just kept buying as yields rose to 11 percent, 12 percent, 14 percent, and higher, which softened the blow. It was bumpy." This is the period when your parents or grandparents remember paying 18 percent on their mortgages.

Fast-forward to the early 2010s. In the aftershocks of the Global Financial Crisis, central bankers cut rates to almost zero and flooded the market with liquidity. Yields dropped, in some cases going negative—investors would actually have to pay for the right to hold a sickly security. Fairfax was in the money for short periods on its "deflation swap" bets but mostly it was deep in the red. Fairfax had come to the conclusion that bonds were increasingly dangerous, especially at the long end.

"The game is over for long treasuries (almost!)," Watsa told shareholders in his 2011 letter. The company began a bit of a fire sale on its long bonds, and it concluded bonds simply no longer had much value. "We have already sold half our long treasury position at a yield to maturity of 3% . . . and we expect to sell the remaining soon."

The HWIC team spent a lot of time over the following decade mostly seeking safety in shorter durations. When the Big Turn finally began, they would be ready. But until then, they would usually wait at the short end, in cash. Earning next to nothing was the price of safety. "We were literally starving to death from low yields," explains Wade Burton. In the past, Fairfax had done well with long-term bonds as a value investor, finding tricks in a declining yield environment to lock in on great rates with extendable maturities (a master stroke by Bradstreet) at the previous posted rates. But those kinds of opportunities were drying up.

Bradstreet found other creative ways to protect Fairfax on bonds by buying treasury "locks" that allowed Fairfax to lock in on the rate and price for future purchases. Other standout trades included following Buffett into municipal bonds that carried a Berkshire guarantee and raising a few eyebrows by investing in mortgage-backed securities after the financial crash when no one else would touch even the non-toxic ones. Earlier, Bradstreet invested $1 billion directly in State of California bonds when bankruptcy worries made those cheap and did great with

Nortel bonds when the stock of Canada's largest company was crashing. (The telecom equipment company had enough cash to pay out priority bondholders, even as it was lurching into bankruptcy. Bradstreet got a steal.)

A LONG WAIT AT THE SHORT END: THE BIG TURN REVISITED

The winning trade on the return of inflation after the pandemic may be the smartest move the company has ever made, so it merits more discussion in an allocation context. When Fairfax started seeing the bond market as particularly dangerous in 2015, the biggest fear was still deflation; a comeback for inflation was far removed from their thinking. The force that abruptly made it front of mind was that unlikely actor, Donald J. Trump.

The first election of Trump as president in 2016 brought with it the promise of lower taxes and looser regulation. Fairfax responded a few different ways. First, it got a lot more bullish on equities. Watsa et al. thought valuations were already rich but were certain that rising profits would drive equity gains. On bonds, they felt all the stimulus and liquidity would eliminate the risk of deflation any time soon and could act as a spark to higher inflation. That meant a bloody bond sell-off that would push yields higher and set the stage for a new cycle for the bond market.

What were their competitors doing? Mostly continuing to buy long bonds (i.e., 7 to 10 years) because that was what they always did. They were reaching for yield, which is another way of saying yielding to temptation. In wealth management or the insurance industry, it's typical to try to match or slightly outperform the benchmark yields. As long as you get close to that return, you won't stand out from the herd. The Street view is no one gets fired for hitting their benchmarks, no matter how badly their funds perform. To Fairfax, that kind of thinking was an unacceptably low bar for results.

It was also standard for insurers to match terms between their investments and liabilities: If half of your policies to pay out had ten years left in them and half averaged three years, then your fixed income should be split in matching ten-year and three-year durations, even if yields were historically low. Bonds were considered low risk, so matching liabilities like this was viewed by credit rating agencies as a very conservative strategy.

That is where the conviction of value contrarians like Fairfax can really pay off—they wouldn't follow traditional thinking. You just need to have strong nerves and patience, and you need to be right. There were windows when Fairfax stepped back into the bond market but mostly it just waited. Confidently, Watsa predicted to shareholders as early as 2017 his non-consensus view that the Big Turn was coming: "Longer rates have bottomed out and will likely go higher over the next five years, perhaps significantly higher." That meant danger if you held long-term bonds.

His message to shareholders was all about how the company was protecting its capital: "We have no net long term bonds (the interest rates on any we have are hedged) and we have over $17 billion (50% of our insurance portfolios) in cash and short term investments." Other insurers were not taking these kinds of precautions. A lot of the investment community thought Fairfax had lost its mind.

The years immediately before Covid-19 were tough on fixed-income investors. Some of the earlier central bank stimulus was pulled out of the market and bonds experienced several periods of "taper tantrums" where prices tumbled and yields crept up to attractive levels. Then the pandemic hit. Yields on government bonds tumbled as investors sought safety, while stocks collapsed. Convulsions were renewed when central banks and governments flooded the economy with emergency liquidity, and the trades reversed directions.

The initial Covid-19 panic in March 2020 sent stocks down by a third—so far that Fairfax went shopping, seizing the best time to buy bargains when blood was running in the streets. On the bond side, the economic freeze-up created opportunities and Fairfax was eager to snap up investment grade corporate bonds at high yields.

Fairfax was in its element for making money when markets were in turmoil. It had lots of cash on hand and started screening for high-yield convertible bond issues, something HWIC likes to do during recessions. (Usually issued by distressed companies, convertible bonds pay a high yield to attract cash for operations and convert to equities later under a set formula. It's a way to get the stock on the cheap and be paid well while you wait for it to recover.) But central banks shut down these strategies when they flooded the economy with cheap credit. "As Covid hit, we had $34 billion of our $50 billion in investments sitting in cash because we couldn't find value," says Bradstreet. "We didn't get enough time to put it to work."

The team began to realize the backdrop for the Big Turn trade was getting more powerful. The inflation surge they had been thinking about since 2017 was going to be bigger than they had expected. With all the bailouts and government incentives to keep hiring and spending, the global economy was being front-end loaded for a resurgence in inflation. When it hit, central bankers would say its speed and force was a surprise. They expected only a transitory jump. Fairfax saw it otherwise. You could say that Trump's tax cuts got the rate-cycle turn primed, but the monetary and fiscal response to the pandemic added jet fuel.

The Big Turn hit in the fourth quarter of 2021 and ran through much of 2022, creating one of the worst bear markets for bonds in decades. As its bet came good, Fairfax rebuilt its fixed-income portfolio with higher-yielding bonds. The impact was immediate. "We had been so starved for yield for so long, it was amazing," says Burton. "I remember thinking 5 percent yields are manna from heaven." Other insurers, banks, and investors were caught. The price tumble in their bonds created huge losses, bringing down a few regional banks in the U.S.

What's crucially important here is not only the fact that Fairfax got in smoothly and profitably captured the turn by backing up the truck on bonds. That was the offensive part. The earlier defensive part was the real genius. Ben Graham would have awarded an A+ to Bradstreet and HWIC for avoiding a destruction of capital when long bonds got clobbered. Patience in the Big Turn delivered uncommon profits.

"We were one of the few insurance companies in the world to have an increase in book value per share (up 6%) in 2022 while most of our competitors had a 10%–30% decrease in book value per share, mainly due to the effect of rising interest rates on their fixed income portfolio," a jubilant Watsa told shareholders. "Years of refusing to reach for yield by going long duration paid off for us in 2022, as 50% of our investment portfolio was in cash and treasury bills at the end of 2021."

HENRY SINGLETON: THE MICHAEL JORDAN OF BUYBACKS

Buybacks make a lot of sense with the value crowd, including Watsa. But you need to get your decision hierarchy right when it comes to allocation strategy and timing. Buybacks can be a brilliant move or a super dumb one. It comes down to price, timing, and alternatives. It makes sense, Graham recommended, to buy them back if they are cheap. He would never advocate for buying back shares when they were trading at a high value just because a company had cash on hand to do it. Regardless of price, there may be more pressing uses for a company's cash, such as paying down debt, making acquisitions, investing in capital, or boosting dividends.

From launch, Watsa and the HWIC team indicated that Fairfax would always consider purchasing its own shares, as long as they felt the stock was cheap. The company also made it clear that while it would issue more shares from time to time to cover acquisition costs, it would want to buy those shares back over time to avoid dilution. When it came to building book value over time, the key measure was on a per-share basis. Growing book value is the goal, but dilution meant growth is worse on a per-share basis.

The company's first dramatic buyback came in 1990, after a plunge of 60 percent in the share price made the stock a steal in Watsa's eyes. Fairfax bought as much as it could and Watsa explained the strategy to shareholders in his letter the following spring: "We retired 1.84 million shares or 25% of the shares outstanding in 1990. We felt this was an excellent investment for Fairfax in relation to potential earnings and current book value per share." It also meant the earlier big issuance of shares the company had made—two million shares in 1986—was almost fully repurchased and at a much lower price, which is great for book value. A decade later, he would call it "one of the better investments we have made!"

On a per-share basis, book value rallied 24 percent the next year. And while investors waited for the stock to match the gain, he preached patience: "This, of course, means that the intrinsic value per share of our company has increased significantly." By 1992, 2.1 million shares were retired, a full 34 percent of total shares outstanding. "This is perhaps an appropriate time to discuss our share buyback philosophy," he offered to anyone who had not been paying attention. "We believe that at stock prices close to book value, it benefits our shareholders if we buy back our shares and retire them, as long as this is done well within our financial capability."

In banker talk, buybacks are known as normal course issuer bids. But sometimes they are anything but normal. What happens when a firm starts buying its shares and keeps on buying and buying and buying? Watsa was heavily influenced by Teledyne's Henry Singleton, who did exactly that.

"I followed them for a long time going back to my Confederation Life days," he recalls. "Teledyne was kind of like Berkshire Hathaway and Templeton; you just watched everything they did and read their letters and annual reports. They can teach you a lot." Curiously enough, Singleton, the company's CEO, would not only serve as hero and inspiration but also as a warning to Watsa because, in the end, the company was broken into pieces because Singleton hadn't set out a vision to continue it. Watsa's mission has always been to build for success that would outlive him—something for future generations. "Singleton's approach to buybacks is always in the back of my mind," says Watsa. "What he did was incredible and bold. On the other hand, he never felt like he had the management to hand over the company. It was broken up. And I never want to see that happen to Fairfax."

In his letters, Watsa regularly brings up buybacks, but in 1997 he first dropped a reference to Singleton that suggested shareholders should be paying attention. It would be 2017 before he started to bring the name up on a regular basis. In the late '90s, Fairfax was in the middle of a spending spree and had been issuing a lot of shares to pay for it. All those new shares weighed on his mind, so he shared a little history about Singleton as one of the legendary masters of allocation in the history of capital markets.

"Henry began Teledyne in 1961 with approximately 7 million shares outstanding and grew the company through acquisitions while shares outstanding peaked in 1972 at 88 million," Watsa explained. "From 1972 to 1987, long before stock buybacks became popular, Henry reduced the shares outstanding by 87% to 12 million. Book value per share and stock prices compounded in excess of 22% per year during Henry's 27-year watch at Teledyne—one of the best track records in the business. We will always consider investing in our own stock first before making any acquisitions."

It was a common market view in Singleton's time that buybacks were a sign of weakness—a desperation tactic to boost a weak stock. "To say Singleton was a pioneer in the field of share repurchases is to dramatically understate the case," argues William Thorndike. Watsa was clearly thinking about working the Singleton playbook in the late 1990s; he was kept from pursuing it more aggressively at the time because—as he was just beginning to learn—Fairfax was about to be sidetracked for the next twenty years fixing acquisitions, namely with paying for reserves at certain assets and then overspending on hedges to protect them. Fairfax would still manage to do some buybacks, but the company had much more pressing ways to spend its money, which included reprivatizing Odyssey and Northbridge after the financial crisis and acquiring Zenith and Brit. Watsa's discussion in the letter offered a sneak peek into his admiration for the "Michael Jordan of buybacks," but he would simply have to wait for the cash flow before he started dunking.

It wasn't until Fairfax had course corrected in 2016–17 and begun its transformation that Watsa started talking more about Singleton again. The insurers were in great shape, and the investments were entering a much more supportive backdrop, which was all bullish for cash flows. Meanwhile, the company had just issued a lot of stock (5.1 million shares) to get its Allied World deal done, so there was some dilution to mop up.

Watsa was ecstatic about buying Allied. But the value allocator in him wasn't thrilled with the fact he had issued all those shares, especially when they were issued at a premium of just 6 percent to book value to do the deal. On the other hand, once the deal was done and Fairfax stock was still trading at around book value, he knew what he wanted to do next. As a value guy, he knew that buying Fairfax shares on the cheap would indirectly improve his deal on Allied because when you buy Fairfax at book, you are now also buying Allied at book, as well as reducing your share count.

When he started to refer to the Jordan of buybacks as "our hero," you could see his Singleton playbook setting up. Noting the run-up in shares outstanding after the Allied purchase, Watsa told the story again along with a new plan: "Henry Singleton, at Teledyne, reversed this trend, as you know, and over the next 10 years we expect to do the same—use our free cash flow to buy back our shares!" If the media were still writing a lot about Fairfax, that ambitious ten-year plan would have been a good story. In 2018, a year after signalling his decade-long plan to put the Singleton playbook into action, Watsa let shareholders know it was not just talk: "We began that process by buying back 1.1 million shares since we began in the fourth quarter of 2017 up until early 2019—about half for cancellation and half for various long-term incentive plans we have across our company."

When Watsa recapitalized it in 1985, Fairfax had 5 million shares. Over thirty-nine years, for acquisitions and to beef up financial strength, they issued a total of 29.5 million and bought back a total of 12.9 million, including 1.8 million held as treasury shares. The running total of shares bought back and cancelled from the start of 2017 to the end of March 2025 is 5.4 million shares. The average price over that time has been $706, with a total combined cost of $3.8 billion.

As of March 31, 2025, the playbook scorecard shows a current total number of shares outstanding at 21.6 million, down 23 percent from the peak in 2017. Watsa has been transparent about Fairfax's intentions, but it's still a guessing game as to how long and aggressive this buying spree will get. A recent triple in the value of Fairfax shares might lead one to assume the pace will slow. And yet, with the book value soaring, the shares are still trading at a discount to Fairfax's competitors on a book value multiple and price-to-earnings. Watsa, like a broken record, continues to indicate that the shares are trading at a discount to what he figures is their intrinsic value.

Cheaper by the Book		
Fairfax valuation vs. other insurers (2024)		
Company	Book value multiple	Price-to-earnings
Berkshire	1.6	11
Intact	2.8	21.2
Chubb	1.7	12.2
Markel Group	1.4	8.7
W.R. Berkley	2.8	13.4
Fairfax	1.3	8.7

Source: Fairfax

BUYBACKS, TAXES, AND "ECONOMIC ILLITERATES"

Buybacks get a bad reputation, sometimes for good reason. Some see stock repurchases as the last resort of bad leaders who have no idea how else to deploy capital. Others note that they are too often done at overvalued prices or when a company should be doing something else like paying down debt. How do you do them right?

Buffett used to lump buybacks in with dividends in the things-I-will-never-do box. He later warmed to the idea, while Watsa has always been a buyback fan under the right conditions. Berkshire's take is that buying back shares at below intrinsic or book value is generally a good idea. They are critical when cynical or incompetent CEOs don't do it right. "It's gotten quite common to buy back stock at very high prices that really don't do the shareholders any good at all," Buffett said in 2016. "It's fashionable and they get sold on it by advisors." His colleague, the late great Munger, argued buybacks are simply a better form of allocation because CEOs are so terrible at spending on other things, like acquisitions: "Generally speaking, in America, when companies go out hell-bent to buy other companies . . . they're worth less after the transaction is made than they were before. Averaged out, it's a way down, not up. And I think that a great many places have nothing better to do than to buy in their own stock."

Government finance officials have a habit of seeing buybacks as an easy revenue grab, and tax policy often paints buybacks as efforts at management self-enrichment. Government bean-counters also see them as an indirect way shareholders can skirt taxation on revenue. The government gets a cut when companies issue dividends so, the logic goes, why not take a cut when a company does a buyback? The question is: Should it?

Watsa says buybacks offer a net benefit to the company in the long run, and whatever benefit flows back to shareholders will flow into the economy in some way. But depending on the price they are done at, buybacks can be net good or bad for shareholders. Buffett echoed that sentiment in his 2022 letter. In the face of rising calls for tax hikes in the U.S., he reasoned the public is getting hoodwinked when buybacks are cast as innately unfair: "The math isn't complicated: When the share count goes down, your interest in our many businesses goes up. Every small bit helps if repurchases are made at value-accretive prices. Just as surely, when a company overpays for repurchases, the continuing shareholders lose. At such times, gains flow only to the selling shareholders and to the friendly, but expensive, investment banker who recommended the foolish purchases."

Buffett threw in a caution to avoid listening to ill-informed or duplicitous politicians: "When you are told that all repurchases are harmful to shareholders or to the country, or particularly beneficial to CEOs, you are listening to either an economic illiterate or a silver-tongued demagogue."

WHY THE VALUE CROWD AVOIDS STOCK SPLITS

When a stock hits three digits, most companies start thinking about stock splits. The strategy might be to add liquidity or, more often, it is done to make smaller purchases available to retail investors. Either way, Fairfax is not a fan. Generally, the value club is against splits for a few reasons. For one, splits do nothing to help increase book value, return on capital, or compounding—so why bother? For another, the value people like to focus on the long term and aren't interested in a lower share price. If a high stock price keeps trading volumes down and the punters out, all the better—leave the long-term gains to long-term shareholders.

Likewise, a consistent price reference reinforces a long-term mindset because it stays obvious where you started from, on a per-share basis. Watching Berkshire Hathaway main shares make their way toward $1 million apiece is all the more amazing when you remember they traded at $19 when Buffett made it his investment vehicle. They have never split.

Watsa says the company started getting share split requests back in the 1990s when the stock first crossed the $100 level. He was eager to guide expectations—to never expect one. "With our shares now trading at three digits, we are often asked about stock splits for greater liquidity, higher stock prices, etc., etc.," said Watsa in 1995. "We have always replied in the negative. Our view is that stock splits do not make shares more or less valuable; they just increase the number of slices that you take from a cake but do not increase the size of the cake. Our focus is to increase the long-term intrinsic value of our company (the cake) and not change the number of slices." With buybacks, a shareholder's piece just gets bigger and you do not have to pay for it.

He also noted with bemusement a few years later that when the stock suffered its occasional swoon, investors seemed illogically to get more alarmed with larger dollar drops, even if the percent change was the same: "In fact, if our stock was split 100:1 (don't worry, it won't happen), many of you would not have noticed the fluctuation from $3.95 to $3.20 even though the percentage drop would be the same."

For traders who want to see a lower sticker price for Fairfax shares, to boost trading volumes and commissions, Watsa says don't get your hopes up. In fact, with his commitment to buybacks, you will probably see fewer shares in the years ahead. "Price isn't a problem," he says. "And liquidity is never a problem. That is only a concern of short-term traders who want to get in and get out. We're not catering to that. Our company is not run like that. You can buy it at your own peril if you want to come in and out. We are in it for the long term and we are buying back our stock for the long term."

Berkshire faced its own pressure to split and ended up with a compromise because it felt shareholders might be taken advantage of. Buffett watched as the Street started talking about creating smaller units of Berkshire shares themselves and selling them to retail investors who were shut out of investing by a six-figure price tag. He issued a new class B "baby Berkshire" in 1995 at one-thirtieth of the main stock, solely out of concern that investors would be squeezed into paying fees on those units. As for Fairfax, the recent introduction of fractional share trading could head off any demand for such a scheme, no matter how high the share price reaches or how low liquidity gets.

AN ABOUT-FACE ON DIVIDENDS

The hard-core view on dividends among value-minded CEOs is negative, and Watsa was one of them, until he wasn't. The less money you pay out of corporate coffers, the more you can use to generate a compound return on capital.

In 1992, Watsa gave a lesson on allocation in the age-old debate over buybacks vs. dividends: "Every one dollar retained by Fairfax (as against paying it out in dividends) has resulted in at least one dollar of market value, with no taxes paid by our shareholders. As long as this test continues to hold (i.e. Every dollar retained resulting in a dollar of increased market value) and we continue to earn 20% on our shareholders' equity, we won't be paying any dividends because it would be contrary to the interest of long-term shareholders—to whom we try to cater."

Watsa the allocator's message was clear: Buybacks are always better than dividends and shareholders face a tax on dividends as well: "We think this continues to be the most tax effective way of distributing excess capital." For years, Fairfax followed this line of reasoning. To make his critics feel better, Watsa the educator used to tease them about the secret dividend payment they might not have noticed—called buybacks. There was some pressure on the CEO in the 1990s to institute a dividend; Watsa at this point was not prepared to blink. Instead, he did the math for shareholders time to show them the personal impact.

- First, looking back at 1995: "You know about our dividend policy. Last year, though, we indirectly gave you a C$0.77 per share dividend by retiring 85,100 at C$81 per share for a total cost of C$6.9 million."
- Again a year later: "You may have missed that dividend that we paid you in 1996. By purchasing 3,500 at C$160 per share for a total cost of C$0.6 million, we indirectly gave you a dividend of 6 cents per share."
- Watsa revisited that calculation in the 2024 letter, showing that purchasing 1.3 million shares at an average price of $1,179 a share, or $1.6 billion, carried a hidden dividend of $73 per share for shareholders.

In 2000, however, Fairfax had changed its mind and actually started to pay real dividends; it was either that or pay the CEO a lot more money. That year, Watsa eliminated his bonuses from the performance of HWIC, moved to a fixed C$600,000 salary, and finally saw dividends in a new, personal light. With his family's financial interests in mind, he said the company would "examine instituting a dividend—yes, a modest dividend—in 2001." It would be set at C$1 to C$2 per share, he told shareholders. "While the payment of a modest dividend results in double taxation to most of you and is not as economically efficient as retaining all our profits and compounding at high rates of return (as we have done in the past 15 years), this was the only way I could think of to bring my compensation in line with your interests."

The dividend debuted at C$1 in 2001 and hit C$2 a few years later and $10 in 2010. Investors were cautioned not to expect it to stay that high, as it equated to about 2 percent of book value per share and a full 17 percent of earnings in 2014. "Over time these ratios should drop significantly," wrote Watsa, "as we like the idea of a stable dividend and do not anticipate it will change for some time." It didn't—until new-era cash flows revised thinking, leading to a 50 percent increase to $15 in January 2024.

In the interest of disclosure, he occasionally still reminds investors that allocation decisions do come with a cost to shareholders and the company; if Fairfax had not started to pay a dividend, book value would be much higher. In 2022, for example, he shared a new calculation that $3.4 billion had been paid in dividends to date, equal to $152 per share, and the same dollar increase would have translated into a 23 percent increase for book value, which suggests a missed opportunity for stock gains. He was not about to cancel the dividend, but it was one of those teaching opportunities Watsa likes to use to remind shareholders that every allocation decision carries a cost.

Over at Berkshire, Buffett may have changed his mind once on buybacks, but he never warmed to dividends. Drawing on Fisher's restaurant analogy, he has argued that Berkshire is known for not serving dividends and, therefore, should keep it off the menu. It is definitely not because the company is lacking in cash. His replacement as CEO, Greg Abel, will likely face some pressure to add that as a dish.

Chapter Twelve

A FAIR & FRIENDLY GUIDE TO M & A

"This activity is anathema to us and gives business a bad name." —Prem Watsa

"We have never done an acquisition as part of a bidding war, we have never made a hostile bid and we have never walked away from a deal that we agreed to or gone back at the seller to alter the terms," says Watsa. "The idea of being fair and friendly in building the company was not a marketing slogan—it was a standard of behaviour that we thought was right, a way of thinking that you could do the right thing and be successful at business at the same time. We knew we were going to be doing a lot of acquisitions out of the starting gate and we wanted to be fair. That's the Fairfax way." What was not the Fairfax Way was traditional private equity, as Watsa has explained:

> Private equity has to be careful on their time frame and getting in and out. They have to do a lot of firing management. We go in friendly and long term, supportive of management. We aren't watching every move they make. With our company and our record of culture . . . we attract people who want to repeat that. If they want to sell at the highest price, we would not be the first stop. But we will be if they want to take some money out, are proud of what they built and still want to run the company and see it grow.

The whole fair and friendly thing could sound a little warm and fuzzy for an M & A crowd more at home with the sharks or the swagger of gunslingers. But it was also all business. Watsa and Salsberg, the Fairfax M & A team of two, were tough negotiators and they expected that the standard would be shared by both parties. One cryptic entry in Watsa's 1998 letter did not name names but captured his distaste when the principal on the other side of a deal tried to revisit terms post-deal. "I would caution certain readers of this report," Watsa wrote, "not to mistake our approach to business as a sign of weakness—as it definitely is not!" Salsberg and Watsa shot down that gambit. Today, Watsa reveals the protagonist was on the Ranger side. In retrospect, it might have been better if either side had walked away. It would have saved Fairfax a lot of headache and money.

For Fairfax, the basic rules of engagement have never changed but they were codified and clarified in Watsa's letter to shareholders. In his second letter, Watsa laid out the acquisition credo as follows:

1. Buy companies with good management in place already.
2. Only buy companies that can hit a target of performance.*
3. Companies will be run independently and performance measured against the same target.
4. Fairfax stock is as good as cash. When stock is issued, Fairfax will be sure to get as much value as it gives.**

* *In early days that was a 20% return on capital. Today, it matches the company's goal for its own performance—a 15% return on shareholder equity or in book value over time.*

** *The preferred value approach in building book value was, if possible, to issue any stock at above book and buy assets at less than book.*

From time to time, Watsa has reminded shareholders what fair and friendly was not. It was more of a message to potential partners: If you are a corporate raider, do not call us to participate in a joint hostile takeover. And if you are selling, we might be interested but will not get into bidding wars. And if you want to buy us, don't bother trying. Fairfax wanted to entrench its reputation for fair and friendly in order to attract business from like-minded partners.

"This is a major advantage for Fairfax in today's world of corporate activism and short termism," wrote Watsa. "Companies are being destroyed, quite often, by the short-term focus of corporate activists who, in order to make a quick profit for themselves, aggressively demand that companies sell divisions or cut costs indiscriminately, or get taken over! This activity is anathema to us and gives business a bad name. We will never take part in it!"

One time, the company found itself on the defensive against speculation that an initial investment in another company was a first step to some kind of hostile shakeup. Watsa was appalled and took pains to remind shareholders and the market that fair and friendly had no exceptions: "While we disclose these positions, we should emphasize that we have never taken a hostile position in a company—i.e., a position where we seek to change management. If we did not like the management, we would not have bought the shares in the first place. Activist investors we are not!"

SO MANY WAYS TO BUY OR INVEST IN COMPANIES

Fairfax buys or invests in a lot of companies and employs a lot of different strategies in doing so. Over the years, the company has taken big positions in everything from hockey equipment to media, mattresses, time-shares, and airports. Some have been public companies; others private. Several have later been rolled up (golfing with other sporting goods; a handful of Canada's largest restaurant chains), while most operate independently. Some have become a big strategic piece of Fairfax's third stream of "associate company" earnings. Others are less strategic and are expected to be sold when conditions merit. And if a holding, such as Stelco or Mega Bloks, wants to sell to another party, Watsa might be reluctant to sell but insists he would never stand in the way of that CEO's decision.

Over the years, some patterns to the buying have emerged, which help shareholders understand the company's strategy.

Start-up plays. While venture capital moves are not too common with Fairfax, there have been a few start-ups. "We invest in whatever makes sense," offers Watsa. Some of the big ones have been in India—ICICI Lombard from 2000 and sold for about $1.6 billion in 2017 and 2019; Digit, a hugely successful digital insurer that went public in India in 2024;

and Quess, which came from Thomas Cook India. In Britain, Ki is another insurtech hit, connected with Brit. In North America, Altius, a mineral royalty play; AGT Foods; and Seaspan (the container shipper IPO'd as Atlas and then taken private as Poseidon with entrepreneur Dennis Washington and Atlas chairman David Sokol). Some of these plays were incubated internally, as was its pet insurance business that the Crum & Forster team built up and Fairfax sold off for $1.4 billion in 2022.

Turnarounds. Most infamous here is BlackBerry, a fallen angel that stoked investor frustration among Canadian investors in particular. Same goes for Canwest and Torstar, two shrinking media holding companies that never paid off. Fairfax has a long list of investments that never turned around and the company took pains in the post-2016 period to monetize and clean up its holdings. The process is still ongoing. Reitmans, the Brick, Sporting Life, Golf Town, Mega Bloks, and Resolute (formerly Abitibi) are some other historic Canadian brands here, some of which have been exited. Two stellar global examples are Bank of Ireland and Eurobank in Greece, the latter testing the company's patience before emerging as a gem and major contributor to the third stream of earnings.

Commodity plays. Alongside Wilbur Ross, Fairfax had great success with International Coal. Others were turnarounds like Resolute and Tembec. Exco entered bankruptcy but turned into a big cash flow generator. The biggest recent success story is Stelco, the Canadian steelmaker that turned heads with astute investments in furnace technology, cost containment, and strong stock returns before being taken out by Cleveland-Cliffs for $2.5 billion, landing Fairfax a gain of about $440 million on a $205-million investment. Fairfax also has public stock exposure to gold (Orla Mining), copper (Foran), resource royalties (Altius), and various stakes in oil and gas companies.

Asset management and infrastructure. Fairfax had a bad investment banking experience with Walwyn in its early days. But Fairfax India has built up an impressive collection of brokerage assets, in addition to the hotly watched Anchorage holding that controls the airport in Bengaluru. Fairfax Africa, publicly traded, fell far short of its goal of becoming another Fairfax India; the company is rebuilding its asset mix now with new partners as Helios Fairfax Partners.

Real estate. Fairfax has had great success partnering with, and investing directly in, Kennedy Wilson. It also expanded then rolled up Grivalia Properties into Eurobank in Greece.

Private equity. Funds have been invested with external managers at a variety of global firms including ShawKwei and BDT & Company.

The cannibal "buy-up." One of the closely watched strategies in recent years is Fairfax's move to boost exposure to assets it controls but doesn't fully own. Fairfax calls them "bolt-ons"; some commentators call it a "self-cannibalization" strategy. It's really a case of Fairfax buying what it couldn't fully absorb the first time around. Buying more adds to cash flow, dividend income, and float to invest. When you already know an asset from the inside, like its prospects, and you have the cash, this strategy is the kind of smart allocation that the legendary Peter "Buy More of What You Know" Lynch would endorse enthusiastically. For Fairfax, these buy-ups or bolt-ons might be piecemeal or full buyouts/privatizations, and they have the added appeal of avoiding the kinds of integration costs that come with brand new investments.

Fairfax has been steadily buying up pieces of Allied World, Eurolife, and Singapore Re. Recipe and Atlas/Poseidon (owner of container shipper Seaspan, one of the top drivers of earnings from noninsurers) have been privatized with partners. A large stake in Gulf Insurance was recently more than doubled. Meanwhile, stakes in Odyssey and Brit were monetized to raise capital. In 2024, all that Brit stake was bought back. Indirectly through Fairfax India, it has been steadily increasing its stake in Bangalore International Airport Limited.

THE POWER OF PARTNERS

There are names that keep popping up as partners in Fairfax's forty years. Some of them are off the radar a bit, such as ShawKwei in Asia and BDT & Company in the U.S. Fairfax invests in their funds and sometimes these partners bring deals to co-invest on. There was Wilbur Ross, a repeat partner on commodity and banking investments. Kennedy Wilson has become a big investment for Fairfax; the Beverly Hills–based real estate investor has brought deals to Fairfax overseas as well as a major piece of the real estate loan book of Pacific Western after the regional bank was caught in the crossfire of the major bond bear market in 2022.

One of the most successful partners that Fairfax invested with was Ramaswamy Athappan, based in Singapore. Fairfax backed Athappan with an initial $35 million to help set up First Capital, an insurer, in 2002. Athappan was hugely successful at it and took on additional roles, including leading Fairfax Asia and helping to bring Singapore Re into the fold as well. Fairfax was always adamant that its companies should never be sold, but Athappan convinced Watsa that First Capital needed a bigger regional partner. When it was sold to Mitsui Sumitomo in 2017, it was the largest P & C insurer in Singapore. The price tag was $1.7 billion, handing Fairfax a $1-billion gain.

Athappan passed away in 2024 and he holds a special place in Watsa's heart as a legendary builder of the Fairfax empire and as "one of the world's best underwriters." Fairfax has created a prize in Athappan's honour to be awarded annually to a Fairfax company that achieves underwriting excellence. Shortly after Athappan's death, Watsa announced his son Gobinath would carry on the family's name as chairman and CEO at Fairfax Asia as well as chairman of Singapore Re, which has become a new vehicle of regional expansion.

LET'S GET OMERS ON THE LINE

Watsa has looked to one partner in particular over the past decade. Much as he loved the idea of sitting back patiently waiting for the phone to ring, he was doing a lot of the calling with OMERS, and it has been a unique, active, and lucrative relationship for both parties.

Initially, the guy at the other end of the line was Satish Rai. A smart value guy, Rai had built a portfolio for retail and institutional clients at TD Bank from zero to C$250 billion before moving to Ontario Municipal Employees' Retirement System (OMERS), where he managed C$125 billion in pension assets. "Satish had been building out partnerships across the world and it dawned on him that he had Fairfax right across the street with feet on the ground in those countries," explains Watsa. "So that's how we formed a relationship. When he moved out of the role, I started dealing with the CEO, Blake Hutcheson."

OMERS offered Fairfax a like-minded, deep-pocketed partner, with a flexible interest in taking a piece of insurer or infrastructure assets, for the medium or longer term. With the Allied purchase, Fairfax didn't have the full $5 billion in its back pocket; it financed the deal by issuing shares and partnering with OMERS and a few other partners to help. Initially, Fairfax secured just over two-thirds of its target, with a third going to OMERS and the Alberta Investment Management Corporation (AIMCo).

All in, OMERS financed a full billion dollars of the deal and AIMCo contributed $500 million. In return, those partners received preferential treatment on dividends from Allied while Fairfax secured the right to buy out its partners in a few years. In 2022, Fairfax paid OMERS and other partners almost $750 million to increase its stake in Allied to 83 percent by the end of 2023.

OMERS had some history investing in Fairfax going back to 1994, when the pension fund participated in a C$76 million private placement. It must have made a good impression when OMERS didn't balk at paying $76 a share, at a time when the stock was $62. The money was put toward the tab for Continental (Lombard), one of the deals that lifted Fairfax shares to the C$600 level later that decade.

Two decades later, in the $1.8-billion acquisition of Brit in 2015, Fairfax arranged to buy 100 percent of the insurer up front, funding it through stock and bond issues totalling $1.1 billion. On the deal's mid-year close, Fairfax sold 30 percent of Brit to OMERS for just over half a billion dollars, to assist in the financing. Fairfax bought back an 11.2 percent stake for $252 million three years later. Fairfax ended up with full ownership of Brit.

Brit and its insurtech subsidiary Ki, which has brought digital innovation to the Lloyd's follow-on market (a way to sell add-on coverage based on existing partner firm insurance contracts), have had a major impact at Fairfax. Brit wrote $3.8 billion in premiums in 2024—12 percent of Fairfax's total business—at a combined ratio of 93 percent. It also contributes 10 percent of the total Fairfax investment portfolio, which stands at $70.2 billion. It is a star holding.

Fairfax decided to bring OMERS in on another asset transaction to raise money for a stock buyback in 2021—the Odyssey manoeuvre, part of the Big Long. This time, Fairfax leveraged a stake in Odyssey to fund a buyback of its own cheap stock.

One of the most closely watched OMERS partnerships is Anchorage Infrastructure Investments. Anchorage's core asset is the highly successful Bangalore International Airport Limited (BIAL). Fairfax India has been building up its holding (74 percent as of 2025) in BIAL and has shifted 43.6 percent ownership to Anchorage to capitalize it for further infrastructure acquisitions. OMERS came into the picture when it paid about $130 million to acquire 11 percent of Anchorage, giving it an indirect stake in the airport and a front-row seat on potential privatization opportunities in India. OMERS also owns 15 percent of Fairfax India itself, so that gives them further exposure to Anchorage.

Chapter Thirteen

VALUE INVESTORS VERSUS THE RATING AGENCIES

"In the past, they thought we were riskier than most companies." —Andy Barnard

Reputation is everything in the insurance business. Unfortunately, the gatekeepers on reputation and risk have not always seen eye to eye with Fairfax. The problem stems largely from the fact that as a value investor and operator, Fairfax is often contrarian and the credit rating agencies prefer companies to follow the herd. Sometimes a traditional approach can get a company into danger.

When Fairfax got a bit stretched, Bradstreet says the agency approach caused knock-on stresses for the business in a number of ways: "We had some legitimate problems, to be sure. We had large insurance losses. Like everyone in the insurance business, we were under tremendous pressure. When our stock got hammered, the conventional thinkers went along with the herd. They worried because they never really understood us all that well to begin with."

Rating agencies assign debt ratings to corporate bonds and financial strength ratings to insurance companies. Low ratings not only make it more expensive to tap debt markets, they can put a company offside with industry rating standards. It can be a fine line with fat consequences. Watsa remembers the scramble when Crum was downgraded to A- from A. "A-minus means you're on the edge of the cliff, one touch and you're gone." Sometimes, credit rating agencies did not like, or even understand, Fairfax's way of handling its finances. On the other side of the fence, Fairfax had a strong mind on risk assessment that often conflicted with what the agencies were seeing or how they felt companies should respond.

FAIRFAX VERSUS THE RATING AGENCIES: ROUND ONE

"I am not sure we are actually a lot more complicated, but it is very true that Fairfax operates under different principles than the conventional industry," explains Peter Clarke. "For one thing, we've never been overly focused on matching our assets and liabilities."

Matching involves investing the amount of float for the same duration as the length of the insurance term—i.e., a ten-year bond for claims expected to be paid in ten years. It's regarded as a conservative way to cover your liabilities. Fairfax, on the other hand, believed that kind of passive strategy was actually riskier than not matching. The priority at HWIC was principled: to get the highest returns while steering clear of the highest risks and maintaining enough liquidity to pay claims.

So, while the debt raters rewarded insurers with good ratings if they had loaded up on thirty-year bonds in the recent past, Fairfax was steering clear of the long end entirely because those bonds carried added risk of price losses, explains Clarke. "We have been prepared to accept less yield, with more safety, with shorter durations. That allowed us to be in a better position to redeploy our assets at much higher interest rates without taking a hit from selling long bonds."

There has been a lot of head-scratching at Fairfax when they watched competitors. In Europe, where matching liabilities is popular, insurers loaded up in the 2010s on long-term government bonds with little to no, or even negative, yields. Fairfax steered clear, figuring those firms would take a bath when rates went up again, which is exactly what happened.

It's part of a bigger problem, according to Fairfax, where the herd adopts unsound practices. It's not only about matching; it's also the "reach for yield" game. Insurers figure their prime objective is to maximize operating income so they buy riskier corporate debt or, in the run-up to the Global Financial Crisis, fixed-income product backed by subprime mortgages. "Many in the industry just gobbled these up, and they relied on the security rating," says Clarke.

As fixed-income value investors, the job is to be smarter about the balance between risk and returns, says Brian Bradstreet. "That involves being value thinkers and being contrarian. The rating agencies will punish you if you don't have your durations match. But they don't take into account the direction of interest rates. They just want to have you prepared to meet your obligations if you went bankrupt tomorrow and had to pay all your claims out. That's not a great way to run your business. We match when matching makes sense."

FAIRFAX VERSUS THE RATING AGENCIES: ROUND TWO

Fairfax feels frustrated when the agencies are encouraging poor investments and when they penalize Fairfax for what they think are risky strategies. The company has been able to attract higher ratings in recent years with its dramatic rise in earnings, but most agencies still use the term "aggressive" to describe Fairfax's investment strategy, while noting it has higher exposure to "risky assets" than its peers.

"The agencies had us at the same rating for decades. No matter what we did, they just didn't like our decentralized model. They thought we were riskier than most companies and more complicated in our structure; it didn't matter what our performance was or how our return on equity was or the book value growth we demonstrated. They wanted to see a longer track record. They didn't like our investment strategy. They didn't like our governance."

Looking back at 2006 to 2009, when Fairfax made billions while others were losing their shirts, Clarke recalls that Fairfax did well because it not only avoided asset-backed securities in its portfolios, but also it was hedging against the systemic risks those securities posed. The debt raters punished Fairfax because it wasn't buying the same garbage it was protecting itself against.

The credit downgrades in 2000 did a lot to encourage the hedge funds to explore Fairfax as a short opportunity. Odyssey lost its S&P A- rating in 2000, which was one of several reasons Fairfax moved to IPO the company, a tactic that regained the rating as well as brought in cash. The holding company lost its last investment grade rating in 2002 over the lack of turnaround progress on Crum and TIG.

"We do not know of another publicly traded financial institution, of any size, that has survived after being downgraded to non–investment grade status," says Watsa. They beat the odds and as the lean years played out, things began to improve. The cash windfall from the Big Short bet put the house of Fairfax back in great financial shape. The subsidiaries regained their investment grade status, as did the holding company. The improved performance of Fairfax's insurers in recent years has not gone unnoticed, leading to further increases. In June 2025, S&P lifted the insurers to AA- and the holding company to A+.

FAIRFAX VERSUS THE RATING AGENCIES: ROUND THREE

The company had particular trouble with Fitch Ratings during the long war with the shorts. It was one thing to have the media repeating false accusations, but Fairfax was concerned the agency was disseminating a lot of disinformation as well.

In mid-2004, Fairfax took the extraordinary move of issuing a news release clarifying its relationship with Fitch—specifically explaining that Fitch did not have access to Fairfax's financials like other agencies and therefore was in no position to issue ratings or commentary. "Fairfax has not met with Fitch or provided information to Fitch since the spring of 2003," the release said, "and since that time has requested Fitch to withdraw its ratings on Fairfax."

Relationships are generally on the mend these days, says Roger Lace. "It was frustrating of course, but we know we need the agencies. We can't bear a grudge. We just need to work harder to win them over to the real story that is going on." A good example of that, and what was absent in the years of the war with the shorts, is Fairfax's record of conservative reserving at its insurers. The company's streak of years with reserve redundancies is eighteen and counting, which has translated into a lot of surplus cash later flowing back into earnings.

Chapter Fourteen

THE RENAISSANCE OF VALUE INVESTING

"Just as seasons repeat, we expect our style of value investing will again come to the fore and will again become very profitable for our shareholders." —Prem Watsa

Fairfax's CEO and chairman has a great record of calling out dangerous bubbles. It's classic Graham to reassure shareholders that bubbles will burst, logic will reassert itself, the high flyers will descend, and rational value will again have its day. But most market commentators will tell you that value has not really had its day for a long time. Welcome to the value investing debate. Why isn't value investing more prevalent? Is it a perennial loser? Is it dying out? Already dead? Despite the fact that the past decade saw epic underperformance for value versus growth, it still has its believers and you can count Fairfax in that camp.

Watsa is actually convinced the renaissance of value has already arrived. He does not mean that value is going to trounce growth stocks quarter to quarter or year to year. What he sees are several factors that are supportive for stock pickers, and they came into place by 2019. The post-2022 interest rate backdrop has helped even more. Throughout the early 2020s, he told shareholders it looked like "the long drought in value investing" was coming to an end. That hasn't stopped new bubbles from forming in the Magnificent 7, artificial intelligence, cryptocurrencies, and meme stocks—but he has expressed confidence that value stock pickers can come out ahead.

For anyone managing a value fund, the recent drought was painful, as Watsa explained: "For the decade ended December 2019, value-oriented stocks had the worst ever relative decline versus growth stocks (particularly tech stocks) over the last 100 years. And then Covid-19 hit, and the Nasdaq went up 44% in 2020. The divergence in 2020 was the worst ever in a single year as the spread between growth and value indices averaged between 20 and 30 percentage points."

Graham, it turns out, had identified a similar cycle shift back in 1974. Two years before his death at age eighty-two, in a seminar for the Financial Analysts Research Foundation, Graham presented his assessment, which he entitled "The Renaissance of Value." Forty-seven years later, Watsa declared history was repeating itself. "I mentioned last year that 2021 may see the renaissance of value that Ben Graham referred to in 1974," Watsa wrote. "The rotation to value stocks began in 2021—with lots more to go."

What was Graham seeing in 1974 that Watsa wanted to talk about again? Let's peek back at 1974, the age of Nixon and Watergate when *The Rockford Files* finally proved good writing was compatible with network TV serials. The S&P 500 was coming off a sharp 50 percent slide from the previous year. Inflation was surging and it brought an end to a decade led by the frothy large-cap stocks known as the Nifty 50.

Graham's intent was to offer hope of redemption to his audience of money managers by convincing them value was sleeping, not dead. He preferred to call it a temporary "eclipse" of value—or, in classic Graham-speak, "the virtual disappearance of the once well-established distinction between investment and speculation."

The fifty in Nifty 50 refers to the number of rocketing blue-chip companies driving the index, but it was also the level most of them surpassed when it came to P/E ratios. (Historically, the S&P 500 had traded at 15 to 20 times earnings.) The market had collectively lost its mind, and the mania drew in a massive surge of new investors who were soon schooled that easy money teaches hard lessons. Graham, the high priest of value, sermonized the way to light through darkness for anyone managing money:

> Do those things as an analyst that you know you can do well, and only those things. If you can really beat the market by charts, by astrology, or by some rare and valuable gift of your own, then that's the row you should hoe. If you are really good at picking stocks most likely to succeed in the next twelve months, base your

> work on the endeavour. If you can foretell the next important development in the economy, or in technology, or in consumers' preferences, and gauge its consequences for various equity values, then concentrate on that particular activity. If you believe—as I believe—that the value approach is inherently sound, workable and profitable, then devote yourself to that principle. Stick to it and don't be led astray by Wall Street's fashions, its illusions and its constant chase after the last dollar.

Stocks would trade largely flat in the 1970s. But even against the threat of stagflation, the market managed to collectively triple earnings and value investors found logic indeed reasserted itself. The parallels are there for Watsa: In recent years, a handful of tech stocks have accounted for almost all the gains of the indexes. "Just as seasons repeat," he told shareholders in 2022, "we expect our style of value investing will again come to the fore and will again become very profitable for our shareholders."

TEACH IT AND THEY WILL COME?

At the time Watsa went to business school in the 1970s, professors spent little or no time teaching value investing. "I might never have read Benjamin Graham if not for my mentor, John Watson, at Confederation Life," says Watsa. "No one I worked with in the early days actually learned about Graham and value at university."

Watsa, like Buffett, is unable to figure out why value never really caught on in a bigger way. Ten years after Graham's renaissance seminar, Warren Buffett stepped up to that podium on the fiftieth anniversary of the publication of *Security Analysis*. To Buffett in 1984, it seemed like business schools had already relegated both the fifty-year-old book and value thinking to the archives.

"I can only tell you that the secret has been out for fifty years . . . yet I have seen no trend toward value investing in the thirty-five years that I've practised it," he told a Columbia University audience. "There seems to be some perverse human characteristic that likes to make easy things difficult. The academic world has actually backed away from the teaching of value investing over the last thirty years. It's likely to continue that way.

Ships will sail around the world but the Flat Earth Society will flourish." Buffett's faith was clearly intact. "There will continue to be wide discrepancies between price and value in the marketplace, and those who read their Graham and Dodd will continue to prosper."

The 2010s tested the faith of a lot of value investors, however. A random scan through value investing coverage at the end of the decade in *The Economist* revealed a morbid popular sentiment, although the final one may just signal that popular sentiment is back on the fence:

- "The agony of the value investor" (October 2018)
- "Value investing is long on virtue but has been short on reward" (February 2019)
- "Value investing is struggling to remain relevant" (November 2020)
- "A value stock comeback, maybe" (January 2024)

If students want to go deep on value investing in security analysis, there are few rounded programs. North America is led by Columbia University in New York (where Graham and Dodd taught Warren Buffett) and Canada's Ivey School of Business in London, Ontario (part of Western University). Fairfax is a sponsor of the latter, which is Watsa's alma mater; it runs a popular value conference in Toronto each April timed to the annual meetings of Fairfax and its publicly traded subsidiaries. (Five years ago, a second annual conference was added in Europe as well.)

At Ivey, the founder and director of the Ben Graham Centre for Value Investing lamented the lack of a proper modern textbook on value to use in his class. So he wrote his own in 2022. With *Value Investing: From Theory to Practice—A Guide to the Value Investing Process*, Professor George Athanassakos is out to groom the next generation to carry the value torch deeper into the twenty-first century.

Athanassakos, a contrarian, believes value is already the clear winner. Mind, there are a lot of ways to calculate who's winning the race, and like any good analyst, professor, or institutional investor, you need to figure out how you try to measure it. What does it even mean anymore when we have firms branding themselves as deep value or quality value or value growth? Does Fairfax's own stock sit in value indexes when it's languishing and switch to team growth stocks when it breaks out? Here are five ways to play with the numbers and figure out for yourself who's winning.

PERFORMANCE ONE: OF COURSE, VALUE OUTPERFORMS

Hearing increased chatter about a possible return of value investing, Athanassakos quickly counters that "value never really went away." He says value averaged an outperformance over growth in Canada by an average of 3 percent and a median of 4 percent between 1983 and 2018. In the U.S., he says value averaged a premium of more than 5 percent over growth between 1966 and 2019. Separately, he notes the premium globally for large value over large growth was 7 percent between 1985 and 2014, according to Brandes Institute data.

The secret behind value's outperformance, according to Athanassakos, is all about expectations over the long term. Growth stocks are based on high expectations, and when they stumble, which they often do, they fall hard, and that adjusts their multiples. Expectations for value stocks for various reasons are pessimistic, and while some of those firms may fail, the ones that stick around are more likely to outperform given how far they fell in the first place. "In other words," says Athanassakos, "value beats growth not necessarily because value does so well, but rather in the long run because growth does so poorly."

And where do we go from here? If the cycle in interest rates and inflation has indeed shifted, equities will generally underperform but the value premium of outperformance will rise, he predicts. That's because more than half of equity returns for developed countries over the last thirty years can be attributed to rising corporate margins, according to Bridgewater Associates estimates. Many of the trends that buoyed margins and stock prices are now reversing, he argues.

"In my opinion, the secular trend toward globalization has ended with predictable adverse—and long term—effects on inflation and interest rates, as well as on bonds, real estate and stocks," reasons Athanassakos. "It is the long-run, not the short-run, effect on inflation, interest rates and financial markets that concerns me."

Under this scenario, it's a changing of the guard in a new cycle and rigorous value stock pickers can benefit. "The outlook appears particularly unfavourable for growth stocks, which will be hurt the most by deglobalization and higher inflation [and] interest rates. For example, during the Cold War years between 1966 and 1991—with U.S. inflation averaging 4.3 percent annually—value stocks outperformed growth stocks by 10.8 percent per annum, whereas between 2008 and 2020—when inflation averaged only 1.7 percent—growth outperformed value by 4.2 percent."

One last point here from the professor in value's favour—and it's a biggie: Value cannot actually die. People and the investment industry will always be irrational, he insists, which means the value premium will always exist. To illustrate that point, Athanassakos is fond of pointing to Blackstone research that shows equity mutual fund gains of 8.2 percent between 1992 and 2011, but actual investor returns of just 2.3 percent. How did that happen? Athanassakos has a two-part answer.

First, the investors thought they could move in and out and end up ahead: "Individual investors are the worst market timers. They were panic stricken at the bottom of the market and exuberant at the top." The culprit here is emotion, a no-no for value investors, as Graham taught. Second, he blames the investment industry. The investment industry has a constant stream of studies showing that most money managers underperform the indexes, but few appreciate one of the reasons they are so bad at their jobs. Emotion is not to blame, Athanassakos says. It's that they are punished if they deviate from the herd. "If they go out on a limb and invest in value stocks and underperform even for a few quarters, what do you think will happen to them? They are going to get fired. The safest thing for them to do is to gravitate towards an index."

What the obsession with short-term results and mimicking the indexes does is lead managers to buy way too many stocks and end up becoming closet indexers. Performance tends to be much stronger among managers who pick a small number of stocks, says Athanassakos. "In other words, portfolio managers underperform not because they lack stock-picking abilities, but rather because institutional factors force them to overdiversify."

Those factors will never change unless humans follow the lead of their value sisters and brothers and learn to rewire the most basic motivations in their brains. "No matter what," the professor offers, "value investors would rather minimize risk than maximize returns. They adhere to Aristotle, in that 'the aim of the wise is not to secure pleasure but to avoid pain.'"

He suggests value would come across even better if researchers defined their subjects better: "Value investing is more than choosing stocks with a low P/E. Unfortunately, academic research has tended to focus only on stocks with low P/Es, which is only the first step of the value investing process, and this has created confusion in the public sphere about what value investing is and whether the strategy is dead."

PERFORMANCE TWO: OF COURSE, GROWTH HAS TROUNCED VALUE

It is a lot easier to find statistics showing value has trailed miserably, especially in the last decade but also for much longer than that. Jefferies Group calculates a whopping two-to-one outperformance by growth over value since 1991. This is consistent with a lot of thinking on the Street and Jefferies analysts insist the growth premium has never been wider than across the thirty-three years they studied. In its calculation, Jefferies used the reliable growth and value subindexes of the Russell 1000 index for U.S. stocks. It's hard to argue against that calculation. Value managers will tell you, by any measure, the last decade has been one of the worst and investors in value funds would probably agree after reviewing their brokerage statements.

PERFORMANCE THREE: STILL OUTPERFORMING—BUT BY MUCH LESS

Ken French and Eugene Fama from the University of Chicago Booth School of Business are credited with authoritatively measuring the value premium back in the early 1990s. The original study, which covered twenty-eight years ending June 30, 1991, defined a 0.36 percent monthly premium for larger value stocks and a 0.58 percent premium for smaller value stocks. The study caused a stir in the financial world and spawned a proliferation of value funds. For fun, the researchers went back after another twenty-eight years (ending June 2019) and found the premium had tailed off considerably to 0.05 percent and 0.33 percent, respectively.

Having written one of the most cited papers in their field, the authors were acutely aware of the industry interest in their findings. Would they revise their conclusions? Is it basically a tie? Unfortunately, it was more of an anticlimactic shoulder shrug. In response, they asked for yet another twenty-eight years and said they would get back to us. Maybe eighty-four years of data might be more conclusive.

It makes you wonder if we got the question wrong in the first place; maybe what really matters is the stock picker, not the asset class. "There are a lot of questions one would like to know the answer to, but you just can't tell," quipped French. "If I get to ask God a question, I'm probably not going to ask this one."

PERFORMANCE FOUR: FROM CLEARLY WINNING TO CLEARLY LOSING

Okay, more academics. Baruch Lev (New York University Stern School of Business) and Anup Srivastava (University of Calgary) set out with their paper "Explaining the Recent Failure of Value Investing" to clear up the whole discussion of value's relative success in the past and its future prospects. They wrote, "The reasons for this putative failure of value investing elude investors and academics, making it a challenge to assess the likelihood of the return of value investing to its days of glory."

They were able to mimic French and Fama's conclusion that value used to hold an advantage—but they concluded there was a drop-off in the 1980s and that value has been a dog since 2007. However, they worked with different data than French and Fama. Instead of only using indexes, they defined value performance by tracking the returns of a long bet on the cheapest 30 percent of value stocks and a short on the most expensive 30 percent for growth.

The first half of the French and Fama study and the fresh research by Lev and Srivastava cast value in a great light. "These were obviously attractive returns," Lev and Srivastava concluded. "However," they added, "this seems to have been the 'swan song' of value investing." As a strategy, value "had already lost its potency in the late 1980s, and yielded negative returns in the 1990s."

What are we to make of it? The authors figure value strategy permanently lost its way in 2007 and they assigned much of the blame to accounting deficiencies in overweighting book value in an age of tech-driven intangible values. Even when they tried to alter the variables to minimize the effect of those changes, the authors ended up with the same or larger underperformance.

PERFORMANCE FIVE: ETFS AND THE DEATH OR REBIRTH OF VALUE?

The investment industry has pointed a finger at the ongoing dominance of exchange-traded funds and indexing as another factor weighing on value investing. That kind of pressure is just adding to the dread surrounding value, offers David Einhorn, founder of Greenlight Capital. Curiously enough, however, Einhorn sees a Darwinian silver lining in it for the hard-core value crowd.

His thesis is that passive investing through ETFs has created an environment where fundamentals are much less important than chasing the overvalued stocks that move the indexes. Throw in the fact that quant traders are also chasing short-term moves in the overpriced index movers and what happens? "Instead of stocks reverting toward value, they actually diverge from value," he asserts. "It's a structure that means that almost the best way to get your stock to go up is to start by being overvalued." The outcome? "The value industry has gotten completely annihilated."

Where does the opportunity come in? Einhorn got a lot of press for that comment, made in an investor presentation. He later clarified that value investing and the value investing industry, where analysts and stock pickers have been laid off in large numbers, are two different things. "With all these unemployed people and their [assets under management] gone, it's actually a great time for value. For the few of us who are left, it's a great time to be a value investor. There is so little competition that the opportunities to buy fine companies with double digit cash-on-cash returns are more abundant than at any time in my career, other than at the bottom of a bear market."

What is Watsa seeing? "This is the environment in which value stocks will thrive. We feel our best investing days are ahead of us," Watsa told shareholders in the spring of 2021, even before the Big Turn. He is still saying it now and believes some of Fairfax's rough spots in the past came from losing focus.

"I think discipline can be one of the hardest things about value investing," he explains.

> Even if you don't go back on your principles, sometimes you can slide away from them. I know we got away from our value roots in the 2010s. It wasn't just with the equity hedges, as we genuinely felt they were good insurance for a while. But they weren't good value investing. Value isn't just a calculation or a short-term strategy. There were smarter ways to achieve long-term goals. We probably should have sold the hedges in 2011 and 2012 and just focused on what we were really good at, which was value investing. Finding good companies at good prices. We got back to that with a vengeance.

PART FOUR

CULTURE AS COMPETITIVE MOAT

Management Strategy

"The actual business of insurance is not that differentiated. What differentiates us is culture." —Prem Watsa

What is the value of corporate culture and people? Good luck measuring them with any accuracy in dollars, ratios, or returns. What kind of calculation could weigh the value of sustaining a culture that embraces entrepreneurialism and treating people right? The golden rule is more an act of faith than a business plan.

There are, however, telltale signs when a company is getting it right. The most obvious clue that a company's culture is paying dividends is when economic performance is high and employee turnover is low—especially at the leadership level. If a company like Fairfax is outperforming while measuring leadership retention in decades instead of years, that is a pretty clear outward sign that the culture is driving performance, asserts Watsa. That's why he sees the company's culture as a competitive moat that gives Fairfax an edge on performance for the long term.

When Salsberg and Watsa charted the Fairfax Way with its Guiding Principles, they made sure to draw a red line at sacrificing values and principles for performance. Elementally, they believed the result would be a stronger culture and an all-round "good" company. They also believed that a good company would perform at a higher level over time. It was the way they wanted to win.

"Doing the right thing is just the way we agreed we wanted to live," offers Watsa. "Rick and I talked for a long time about how we wanted to define our culture. We put those ideas down in words and have tried to live by them. So doing the right thing, being fair and honest, isn't a business strategy per se, but we also happen to believe it has proven to be good for business."

In a 2019 speech, Watsa painted his version of the contrarian magic that happens when you can inspire employees and win trust by acting outside the dog-eat-dog norms of the business world:

> We have found it odd, but business tends to be considered a jungle and a war zone. And many people do not treat people well but just treat them as bodies. We have found just the opposite. Treating people well has been a major plus for us. When we say treating people well, we mean every single person you come across. This just happens to be the way we want to live, but the advantage in a business sense over time is that inside your company, you see ordinary people do extraordinary things. And outside your company, people trust you.

Obviously, Fairfax is not the first company with a strong values orientation. You would be hard pressed to find a company that did *not* have an enlightened mission statement or inspiring set of guidelines on employee conduct. Many firms have purpose-driven missions built into their DNA, whether it is planting a tree for every sale or donating to a cause. Making values part of your marketing is good for business. It can make employees happier about working for your company. Fairfax's corporate culture, however, comes in a different flavour from most. It's a company that asks you, as a ground rule, to be kind. Its guidelines on conduct actively discourage a "confrontational style" and "egos." Instead, it promotes the golden rule, which elevates respect and trust.

"Anyone who's rude, arrogant, proud, foul-mouthed or not team-oriented has never managed to last long here," Watsa once explained. "We are very open about our culture being one where you treat others well, so that should discourage anyone who thinks otherwise. We want people who are smart, hard-working, humble and honest. That means no put-downs, no personal agendas and the best ideas win, no matter who they come from."

In the early days, it was easy for the culture to root and grow in Toronto. Fairfax had come together as a small, tight-knit group of like-minded people. From the outside, Bay Streeters immediately saw the team as a type. An executive who did business with the company in the early days described how Fairfax employees were regarded as black sheep, compared to the swagger of high finance: "Fairfax guys don't go to lunches. They don't go to dinners. They just work really hard." They observed a different way of doing business: "There is no guile. There is no pretense in anything."

The rare time the company added talent, it was through their network. Fairfax even maintained an online warning that if anyone were ever approached by a recruiter about an opportunity there, they should know it was a scam. Fairfax did not use recruiters. It did not even have a human resources department at the holding company. The HR strategy was simple: Don't find us, we will find you—and if you have any doubts about coming aboard, they will be assuaged if you get a chance to meet our persuasive CEO.

The bigger challenge of building and nurturing Fairfax's culture came with acquisitions. Today, there are 57,000 employees working at the company's operating subsidiaries, 22,000 of them at the insurers specifically. That is a lot of people to have under the big tent with relatively high expectations on attitude and behaviour.

Integration has proven to be much easier when Fairfax buys companies with strong management who are fans of the culture. In theory, the trick is to hold them close on culture and alignment, while giving them a long decentralized leash to run their own show. It did not always work out that way, at least at first.

The first challenges Fairfax faced in fostering a winning culture was getting people to actually believe they were serious: All the golden rule and being nice stuff could sound corny. And with so many companies and employees to win over, the culture was only as strong as its weakest links.

"You cannot flip a switch and expect people to get it," reasoned Salsberg. "And the toughest part is continuing to do it—it's more than just words. A lot of companies have kind principles, but if those are the words and the culture still comes down to beating each other around, what is the point? Where is the trust? If you say, 'We are always going to try to treat people well, and we are always going to try to do the best for you,' then you make an exception or come up short, people are not going to believe you anymore."

With expansion, Fairfax has always insisted that this culture needed to be pervasive throughout all of its operating companies, explains Barnard. The company made a priority of elevating leaders it believed were long on empathy and nurturing fellow employees. Management through fear, with public beratings and humiliation, was off limits, and excessive micromanagement that betrayed a lack of confidence in the judgment of subordinates would act as a red flag.

That trust issue extends to the company's external reputation as well as its employees. Forty years later, Roger Lace says he has people in his own network who, up close, in Toronto, have seen the company grow and still find it too unorthodox. Dealmakers, of course, are supposed to be sharks, and as such, they figure anyone talking about doing the right thing and being friendly must be playing you. "I have a friend who just doesn't trust the fair and friendly thing," says Lace. "He doesn't get it. He figures Prem must be a huckster."

Running your values up the flagpole can work for a company like Fairfax in complementary ways: One, as a beacon to attract people who want to work that way, and two, as a warning sign to discourage the inconsiderate and uncouth. There are more than a few people on Bay Street who wouldn't last long at a firm where long tenure is incompatible with big egos or the dropping of F-bombs. "Prem likes people to behave themselves and to be kind," says Wade Burton. "If you are a big swear jockey, it's probably not for you."

Chapter Fifteen

FAIRFAX DEFINES ITSELF

"You want to get to the point where you think culture first. That's how you build it. That's what Prem does." —*Kari Van Gundy*

Watsa's personal value system was mostly baked by the time he left for Canada at twenty-two, but he'd never had a reason to put it down in words. Launching a company changed all that. With a business, he was building a house where those words could guide how all people inside would be treated. From the outside, they could provide the appropriate curb appeal to attract the right customers and partners.

Another prompt to put pen to paper was finding his co-author and translator. By the time he had wrested Salsberg from Torys and drawn him into his orbit at Fairfax, Watsa knew he had someone who shared his values and could read, complement, and translate him. Salsberg was Watsa's right-hand man, advisor, confidante, *consigliere,* shareholder letter editor, and jack-of-all-trades, in addition to being the in-house legal whiz on mergers and acquisitions. He was whip smart, kind, and, like Watsa, driven to build a good company.

The two men started with the basic values they both shared and then adapted them to the broader corporate mission of a modest but ambitious Bay Street investment company with a growing investment in insurance. They ended up with a road map for a company that they hoped would make a lot of money and be inspirational for everyone involved and for long after the two of them left this world.

The Guiding Principles they drafted are a list of seventeen items over three different subheadings, breaking down like this (see full list of principles in Notes, pages 359–360):

- four objectives for corporate performance, in targets and in conduct;
- four principles for structure, outlining how the subsidiary companies and the holding entity itself would operate; and
- nine principles on the values that would apply to every single employee.

"We had the principles finalized by 1990," said Salsberg. "There are a lot of things that Prem just instinctively knew. They may have been informed by his faith as well, but mostly they were just sitting there inside him. He acted like a spark to make the culture come together. We knew at the time that we had to make these principles and values explicit—you have to capture it and write it down. They were meant to be observed. And they were meant to be permanent."

Adds Watsa, "Rick and I wanted to build a 'good' company, and we were definitely soulmates when it came to defining what that actually meant. We wanted to set high performance expectations but at the same time set the kind of parameters for success, including the way we wanted to act and be recognized. Because those are the things we never wanted to sacrifice for the sake of performance."

The only addition to the principles came in 2024. The new entry—"We follow the Golden Rule"—was hardly a new idea at Fairfax, but it needed to be codified and the company found a way to express it in a way that would resonate with all religions, as well as pantheists and atheists alike. It made its debut as value number four, bumping the section's total from eight to nine. Most of the principles would probably find themselves at home at other companies while others stand apart with a folksy, fair-and-friendly flavour to them, such as:

- "We are team players—no 'egos'";
- "A confrontational style is not appropriate";
- "We are hard-working but not at the expense of our families"; and
- "We believe in having fun—at work!"

Prior to the 2024 addition, Fairfax had only tinkered with its Guiding Principles over the years. The main changes were adjustments to the key performance objective: first, to drop the target return on equity from an annual 20 percent to 15 percent, and second, to switch that metric from ROE to book value per share growth over time.

WALKING THE TALK ON TRUST

"We made sure the principles stayed top of mind," said Salsberg. "We'd mention them off the top of senior leadership meetings. You have to elevate this stuff. People might even roll their eyes a little, like kids at a school assembly, but it's important."

Ideally, Fairfax wanted trust to become its calling card and a core cultural trait. "People learn how you operate and they learn you are not going to pull any tricks and a deal will be done in a fair way," he said. "If you act that way consistently, then that becomes your story and people get to know it. Some people will say this isn't a smart way to do business—that you should just make as much money as you can. We think that in the long run this kind of behaviour is what will help us be the best company."

One idea is elevated in the Guiding Principles—trust. Trust drives reputation in the marketplace. Trust is the targeted behavioural outcome of living in a culture that follows the golden rule. You can tell it is working when people do not want to leave, explains Barnard, but it needs constant nurturing because everything depends on it.

"When I meet with our leaders," says Barnard, "I always emphasize a cycle of three things we need to feed the culture: mutual respect, trust, and communication. The absence of good communication erodes trust and if you erode trust, you will erode respect. Getting all three qualities working on a virtuous cycle reinforces the value system and becomes stronger." Micromanagement is more than just a no-no, he says. "That kind of style does not work at Fairfax because it implies a lack of respect and trust if you cannot be comfortable delegating. If you don't have trust, you don't have anything. It can take a long time to build and can disappear in a flash."

Fairfax leaders talk about how a strong culture builds good habits to the point that it becomes harder to mess up. People start naturally applying the filter of doing the right thing before they make decisions, offers Van Gundy. "You want to get to the point where you think culture first. That's how you build it. That's what Prem does."

Watsa points to Mike Abrashoff for some important lessons on delegating authority at Fairfax and has shared those thoughts with his leadership teams at offsites. Abrashoff, a former U.S. Navy captain turned corporate performance executive, says leaders do huge damage to their organizations when they assume their direct reports are primarily concerned about salary and job titles. Abrashoff studied the reasons people leave an organization and found that trust was paramount.

"I assumed that low pay would be the first reason, but in fact it was the fifth," he says. "The top reason was not being treated with respect or dignity; the second was being prevented from making an impact on the organization; third, not being listened to; and fourth, not being rewarded with more responsibility." Abrashoff's formula for success through culture? "Show me an organization in which employees take ownership, and I will show you one that beats its competitors."

Salsberg and Watsa made a habit of bringing up certain dealmaking anecdotes that highlight the fair and friendly credo in action. For Watsa, it is always the time the two of them hammered out an acquisition into the early hours and included a clause that would mistakenly pay Fairfax regardless of the outcome. A year later, expecting a fight, the CFO of the other party rang up to raise it and Fairfax amended it on the spot and apologized, much to the caller's surprise. It was a done deal, so they did not have to, but Fairfax realized it was unfair. A decade later, the CFO was CEO of another company and they did business again—quickly and smoothly, with trust and at favourable terms. (This was the crucial $1 billion deal for the Swiss Re cover.) "It was a good reminder that doing the right thing is good for business," says Watsa.

Salsberg pointed to times companies would be flummoxed when Fairfax failed to adhere to norms. The biggest part of the effort behind dealmaking is upfront. Standard practice, however, dictates that whoever has the upper hand will come back and squeeze for improvements at the end. "Prem and I found ourselves ready to close a deal one time," recounted Salsberg, "and the other CEO rings up and says, 'OK, let's have it.' We had no idea what he was talking about. He tells us, 'I know you are going to take the price down. Let's get this out of the way.' We told him, 'No, we're good.' But he just kept asking the same question. He didn't believe us. If we say 'That's the deal' to another party, we stick to it." Winning over that skeptical CEO meant winning a possible future partner on another deal. What goes around comes around; fair and friendly pays its own kind of karmic dividend.

THE VALUE CROWD AND THE VALUES CROWD

As odd as Fairfax might come off to private equity bankers, it is not so unconventional when we view the company against the value crowd. To some extent, it's tempting to believe the value crowd seems to have a predisposition to the kind of temperament and self-discipline that finds itself at home with good character generally. Prof. Athanassakos captures that sentiment like this: "Patience, discipline, and long-term perspective are traits that define one's character and can help investors achieve not only investing success but also a balanced and full life."

The denizens of Graham-and-Doddsville inspire one another. Ask them who their heroes are and many will name other value builders who happen to stand out as good humans as much as good investors. Watsa points to people like Buffett and Singleton as good humans and business leader heroes and to a few particular individuals whose rare combination of estimable character and professional acumen deeply influenced him personally: Ben Graham, Sir John Templeton, and John Watson, Watsa's former boss. The two Philips—Carret and Fisher—also come up as influential thinkers on investing as well as culture and management. For Buffett, Graham inspired him personally as much as professionally: "To me, Ben Graham was far more than an author or a teacher. More than any other man except my father, he influenced my life."

In business, outside investing, Buffett points to Tom Murphy of Capital Cities/ABC. After Murphy died in 2024, Buffett said he "taught me more about running a business than any other person" and inspired "very imperfect humans, myself certainly included" to be better parents, more generous, and to lead in a kinder way. Murphy also influenced Buffett's thinking on decentralization, which, in turn, influenced Watsa considerably.

Sam Walton's story at Walmart made a huge impression on Watsa, especially how the company kept a human touch even while enjoying explosive growth. The retail jobs may not be high paying, but Watsa loved the customer service culture and that Walton espoused treating the cashier and front-line employees as well as the people at the top. "You should share profits with everyone," he says. "That's what Sam Walton did. It always struck me that that's a good way to live your life."

Watsa bubbled like a teenager one time he drove his family to a particular outlet in the U.S. His kids, however, did not really get it. Watsa asked all the staff if Sam ever came in and things like that, recalls Christine McLean, his daughter: "He had said we were going to visit some place that was so exciting. And we're kids, we're under ten, so we think we are going to an amusement park or something. He had read everything about Sam Walton and his approach to culture. He was excited to see the greeters."

Watsa offers kudos in his letter to other CEOs who have inspired him. For both professional and personal reasons, Sir John Templeton sits at the top. In 1997, Watsa also singled out the late Coca-Cola CEO Roberto Goizueta for writing "the best article I have come across on why every company in the private sector should have a focus on increasing long-term shareholder value." The words had appeared in Coke's 1996 annual report. "The gist of Roberto's article is that increasing shareholder value in the long term benefits not only shareholders but customers, employees and also the community," Watsa told shareholders. "Trying to increase shareholder value in the short term ultimately benefits no one." In other words, it was a shareholder value game, not a market share game.

Another company Watsa and the HWIC team find inspirational, for its performance as well as how it treats its people, is J&J. "Johnson & Johnson has perhaps the best long-term track record we have come across," he wrote in 2007. "They have compounded sales and earnings for the last 100 years in excess of 10% per year. The growth prospects for their products on a worldwide basis are unlimited." Fairfax was delighted to be able to add Bill Weldon, former J&J CEO, to serve on its board and has modelled some of its healthy workplace policies on J&J's. Watsa finds the company's longevity inspirational.

It's uncanny how value builders often run their businesses in a similar fashion and even have a common way of valuing corporate culture. In *The Outsiders*, William Thorndike describes his brilliant allocator CEOs and the characteristics of culture for their companies like this:

"As a group, they shared old-fashioned, premodern values including frugality, humility, independence, and an unusual combination of conservatism and boldness. They typically worked out of bare-bones offices (of which they were inordinately proud), generally eschewed perks such as corporate planes, avoided the spotlight wherever possible, and rarely communicated with Wall Street or the business press. They also actively avoided bankers and other advisers, preferring their own counsel and that of a select group around them. Ben Franklin would have liked these guys."

Sounds like Watsa, even though the company does actually have a corporate jet. Interesting, too, is the Ben Franklin reference, given it was the American founding father's words that inspired Watsa's much-beloved expression "Doing good by doing well"—which informs Fairfax's charitable impulse.

Chapter Sixteen

FAIRFAX LEARNS TO PUT INSURANCE FIRST

"There are a lot of ways to misunderstand risk." —Andy Barnard

"We started off as investing people and investors sometimes still like to talk about Fairfax as an investment company that invests in insurance and other things," says Watsa. "But everything we do as a company rests on the strength of our insurance assets. Without them, there is no Fairfax." That is obvious today, but for years the investments not only did a lot of the heavy lifting performance but also occupied a disproportionate share of management discussions and investor attention.

Insurance was a really difficult business when Watsa stepped into it. It still is. The company was served a gift in its first full year of operations when its only competition imploded, but it still narrowly escaped going under a few years later. Part of the problem was they were cocky enough to think they could turn around broken insurers on their own. Another contributing factor was their reluctance to hire head office insurance expertise like a future Andy Barnard, because Fairfax worried an added layer of management would be incompatible with decentralization.

What resulted was a record of hits and misses. Sometimes, the decentralization strategy worked great. The Federated and Continental/Lombard deals were examples where great assets were snapped up on the cheap because their U.S. parents didn't want to play in the Canadian market anymore. Those firms came with great management attached, and the transition under the Fairfax umbrella was smooth. But Ranger was a nightmare. TIG was half solid and half disaster. At first, Crum & Forster was a complete mess. Fairfax learned insurance the hard way.

They could strategize all they wanted about buying companies with strong management, keeping the acquisitions intact, and going the decentralized route. But when you are buying broken assets, you are often going to find broken management. That is not a situation where you want to hand over the keys to the car and ask leadership to keep on driving. Ranger was finally cut up for parts, something Fairfax hated to do. Crum finally came together because Fairfax, after years of trying with several strong leaders, tapped Marc Adee and left him in place to execute long term. With Odyssey, the deal was improvised in real time. Fairfax secured two key leaders from another firm to run Odyssey only after it had already bought it. And the business plan was redrawn on the fly in a three-way merger when the salvageable assets of CTR and TIG were rolled up into it, with others to follow.

Looking back on these wild years, Watsa is forever grateful that the two leaders brought in to run Odyssey were Andy Barnard and his long-time protege Brian Young. A string of other leaders have been developed in that talent factory, feeding the pipeline of succession. No one has been as important to Fairfax as Andy Barnard. Barnard's experience was unmatched, and his leadership was gold. Young was adeptly soaking up his mentor's expertise.

When they initially met, Barnard knew Watsa lacked the experience of running an insurer, but the two men found a common ambition in building up a great insurer, launching a reinsurance business line, and lifting all the insurance operations into blue-chip leaders. What cemented their vision was their common thinking on value, decentralized management, and discipline.

"Prem was very aware of how important it was to not follow the herd," says Barnard. "It was an application of his value investing principles and how you manage your portfolio in the insurance or reinsurance business. You manage for the long term in each case. If everyone is withdrawing from the market you get less intense competition and prices go up and the opportunities to make a lot of money become much more compelling. Prem realized that when cycles changed, the past became irrelevant and it became a new ball game. His philosophy was very much in sync with mine."

The difference was Watsa had long been relying on his insurer leads to explain their strategies; Barnard, on the other hand, could tell if what those executives were describing was actually well reasoned. Having that experience as a filter on communications made a world of difference in managing risk. "I know my way around and how to ask key questions," says Barnard. "No one prior to me had that knowledge."

THE PREMIUM MIND

Choose your lines carefully. Barnard encouraged Fairfax to stay focused on reinsurance and commercial lines, which are harder to manage, more profitable, and jointly account for more than 90 percent of the company's book of business. Personal lines, like home and auto, are run by the law of large numbers, which means they are easier to predict. Fairfax instead steered itself into the more lucrative lines of business, which also happened to be the easiest ones to get yourself in trouble. Lucky for Fairfax, Barnard was one of the few true industry leaders on commercial insurance and, particularly, reinsurance.

"Commercial insurance has much bigger premiums but far fewer transactions, which makes it a pretty dangerous business," he explains. "You collect all these premiums as your revenue, but you don't know what the costs of those sales are going to be for at least a year when the policies expire. With liability insurance, you issue a policy for one year and collect the premium. But you are covering any liability that the insured party might incur in the future. To know the true value of the liability can take ten or fifteen years or much longer."

Barnard says this business is vulnerable to human follies that make it especially treacherous when it mixes short-term strategy with long-term risks. "In our own business, especially in commercial lines and reinsurance, we are very much aware that our results are really just estimates. Human folly comes into play because there is always a tendency to think optimistically about what those losses might be. Your assumption is only going to be validated over many years and you have to square that against the market tendency to reward sales and efforts to bring in more business in the near term." As they say in insurance, there is no such thing as bad risk, just bad premiums.

The inherent high levels of uncertainty and complexity of risk are additional reasons Fairfax prizes humility in the leadership of its insurance subsidiary companies, says Barnard. "One trait we look for in our leaders is a willingness to say, 'I don't know.' Insecurity is one of the greatest obstacles to learning and you should not fear admitting ignorance. Often, what you should fear is someone who professes to have all the answers. Of course, saying 'I don't know' too often presents a new kind of problem."

Young says a different kind of folly plays out in managing people in an insurance business, where you have employees bouncing around for experience or when their jobs change after a merger: "They work somewhere for four to five years and miss the period where the claims finally come in. They do not learn from what they did to see how to do it better." If you gain the necessary experience, by this thinking, you can learn to be friends with both fear and greed.

Buffett likes to talk about a "money mind" as a rare trait that is independent of IQ and enables a person to be effective at investing and allocation. Most CEOs lack it, no matter how good they are at other things, he figures. For Barnard, it might be a "premium mind" that sets his type apart. Many insurance CEOs who happen to be great operators have driven their companies off a cliff by making bad calls that misread risk.

"It's a very abstract business," Barnard says. "People can get mesmerized by PowerPoints, plans, and budgets that seem to make sense. But an awful lot of people in the business do not really understand what they are dealing with, even more so with reinsurance. A reinsurance underwriter is quite far removed from the original premium. It's very abstract to be that far removed." It helps to be a contrarian if you want to manage the cycles, which run on human nature's predilection to consistently do the wrong thing at the right time. "There is a law of nature in the insurance business," offers Barnard. "You need to have that contrarian mindset and be disciplined to pull back during periods of oversupply. Otherwise, you can become overwhelmed with your own problems later when you should be expanding. Ultimately, it all boils down to managing a cycle of fear and greed."

You could see Barnard's risk appetite when he took on the huge Odyssey challenge. That same appetite was what brought him into the business in the first place: "My father had been in insurance. I had no plan to follow in his steps but I went to Skandia for an interview and the CEO made a point that really stuck with me: He said in finance, insurance was the most abstract and intellectual business because you are always dealing with things that have not happened yet. It's competitive, and there are a lot of ways to misunderstand risk. I found that all very tempting."

Fairfax owes a large debt to Barnard's ability not just to be a great manager and drive profitable expansion but also to excel at the hardest aspects of outperforming in this abstract business. As Watsa stresses, "Reinsurance is a business that magnifies the abilities of management."

MANAGING CLIMATE RISK AND SOCIAL INFLATION

Being the insurance person at a cocktail party can be tough. Some people will assume you are dull; others will think you are dull and then corner you and vent about the rising cost of their policy premiums. Broader topics to steer to might be social inflation, climate change, and private equity.

This is a problem in the U.S., and Florida in particular, where the weather is as volatile as the courtrooms are busy. A *Newsweek* report noted a 206 percent rise in Florida insurance premium costs since 2018. Citizens of the Sunshine State account for 6 percent of national claims but 79 percent of the litigation, which includes things like roof-replacement schemes. You can't blame it all on the weather—some of it should go to lawyers or fraudulent claims.

"Social inflation," explains Young, "is one of the key challenges facing the industry." That's what the industry calls runaway jury verdicts and escalating body injuries and frivolous claims. "There is a cottage industry in U.S. class action lawsuits, and private equity is accelerating it. Juries are younger today and there is a misunderstanding about how the cases should be an opportunity to punish businesses because business is bad. But what would they think if they knew a big chunk of the money was going to private equity in these claims? It tends not to be disclosed to the jury if the litigation costs are covered by PE."

Climate risk is clearly accelerating and there are other factors making the work more challenging for actuaries, according to Lou Iglesias, CEO of Allied World. "The world is more dangerous than it has been in a long time," he says. "It's war, it's climate, it's typhoons, and it's Covid. Many of these emerging risks are not built into the actuarial tables. For climate factors, for example, you have to use the old methods of prediction, but then you have to layer a judgment factor on top of it. It's a new way of looking at it. Meanwhile, the costs of everything are up."

The added dangers mean more risk for customers and insurers, though it also serves to make the industry more relevant, he reasons. "We just need to ensure that we, as the risk takers for the global economy, can take in enough money to carry that function out." The key safeguards, other than writing smart premiums? Keep a fortress balance sheet and enough reserves and capital to ride out disasters.

Fairfax firms are also navigating a lot of new emerging lines of insurance where risks are not as clearly understood. The danger there lies in chasing market share. "Companies need to be patient," says Iglesias. "There are a lot of things that we are still learning about AI, cyber, or facial recognition, and weather patterns. You don't win a prize by being the first one to market. With AI, for example, there will be a lot of legal wrangling as we learn how to define coverage. The market chasers, I think, are making a big mistake, and it's going to come back and bite them pretty good."

Chapter Seventeen

MANAGING THE MOAT

"Outside hires have to learn a new way to get things done under our roof. If you recruit and promote from within, you can avoid that kind of disruption." —Rick Salsberg

Being a value guy, Watsa has always been acutely aware that culture can be a secret weapon—especially for a company united around high performance and doing the right thing. Engaged employees who share a store of knowledge, strategy, and tactics can be an enormous advantage in driving future earnings growth. Put another way, in all senses of the word, this human element represents intrinsic value and can act as a competitive moat if you manage it right. Looking back over four decades, with so many acquisitions, Watsa insists the biggest factor in widening the company's moat has been the focus on bringing Fairfax subsidiary management into tighter alignment with the founding culture.

Warren Buffett, not surprisingly, had something wise to say about culture and moat. In his 2005 letter to shareholders, he describes how culture is a long-term commitment and consistency is an ingredient you cannot substitute. "Every day, in countless ways, the competitive position of each of our businesses grows either weaker or stronger," he wrote. "If we are delighting customers, eliminating unnecessary costs and improving our products and services, we gain strength. But if we treat customers with indifference or tolerate bloat, our businesses will wither. On a daily basis, the effects of our actions are imperceptible; cumulatively, though, their consequences are enormous. When our long-term competitive position improves as a result of these almost unnoticeable actions, we describe the phenomenon as 'widening the moat.'"

Almost twenty years after Buffett's comment, Watsa reminded Fairfax shareholders of its similar effort. "The huge strength of our company—and impossible to copy—is the fair and friendly culture we have built in each of our companies over the past 38 years," he said in his 2023 letter. "On average, our officers have been with us for 19 years. The bedrock of our company is trust with a long-term focus."

Fairfax has a great investment record and a stable of leading insurers, but the biggest factor setting Fairfax apart is cultural, Watsa insists. "The actual business of insurance is not that differentiated. What differentiates us is culture."

In a 2017 speech on receipt of an honorary doctorate of laws at University of Waterloo, where he had already served a term as chancellor, Watsa noted the negative effects of ego-driven culture at companies: "We have found ego or pride to be a major problem in business. As Warren Buffett has said, there is no question, as the Bible says, the meek shall inherit the earth. The question is: Will they remain meek after they inherit the earth?"

A reference to one particular quote often makes its way into Watsa's speeches. It's one attributed to many people and rendered in different wording. U.S. president Ronald Reagan was one to repeat it and he kept a version on his desk. Watsa has handed out desk versions to his team as a tribute and a message to remember: "There is no limit to what a person can do or where they can go if they don't mind who gets the credit."

THE MAGIC OF DECENTRALIZATION

The best way to get the best out of your best people is to get out of their way. That adage was especially appealing to Watsa and the HWIC team when they started buying insurers. They knew very well what they did not know, which was how to run an insurance company. Even if they had known insurance, they knew it was better to leave management alone. That strategy would be tested and have its challenges, but it has never been abandoned.

At the outset, Fairfax, as Markel Financial, retained Steven Markel in an oversight and advisory role to assist the newly recruited Keith Ingoe, who was tasked with running things day-to-day. Steven knew the company inside out and with an additional Markel presence on the board, Fairfax's investment guys felt they were covered. After making his first two deals, Watsa thought Fairfax should explain to shareholders how things were supposed to work. After all, they had not written their Guiding Principles yet, so he offered up a four-point summary of the acquisition strategy, which gave an indication of how he saw the evolving relationship between head office and the subsidiary operating companies.

1. We will acquire companies with good management already in place.
2. We will not acquire companies unless we believe they can achieve a 20% return on capital.
3. Each company will be run independently and be measured against the targeted return of 20% on capital invested.
4. We consider our stock as good as cash. We will not issue stock indiscriminately.

Fairfax was buying a lot of companies but always had the plan, when they had reached adequate size, to stop growing by M & A and let the local management grow their assets organically. Behind that thinking was the understanding that empowered decentralized firms with smart leaders drive growth better themselves, not by running decisions up through bureaucratic layers of vice-presidents at head office.

At the holding company, Watsa always wanted operations to remain lean. Bloat would mean more than higher costs; the bigger danger was a chaotic structure of bureaucracy with overlapping responsibilities and matrixed reporting lines. To express to shareholders and any company thinking about what life would be like under the Fairfax tent, Watsa spelled out the priority responsibilities head office would retain while otherwise leaving local leaders alone:

1. Leaders run their own companies, but we evaluate the performance.
2. We need to be comfortable with their successors.
3. We handle acquisitions and major shifts in corporate strategy.
4. We tackle financings and capital decisions.

Answering a shareholder question at Berkshire's 2004 annual meeting, Buffett explained how his company operated. Word for word, it could have been Watsa up on the stage talking about the inherent distractions of overpopulated head offices: "We don't have a human relations department, we don't have a legal department, we don't have an investor relations department, we don't have a public relations department. We don't have those things because they make everything more complicated and everyone gets a vested interest in going to conferences and calling in other consultants and it takes on a life of its own."

As we have seen elsewhere, Fairfax's practice of maintaining a lean head office and surrendering control to the individual insurers isn't quirky at all when compared to the management style of the other leaders of Graham-and-Doddsville or Singletonville. Henry Singleton was a proponent of extreme decentralization to drive responsibilities and accountability down to the people closest to the front lines of their particular operations. His companies staffed more than forty thousand, but head office had fewer than fifty .

At Capital Cities, Tom Murphy included a blunt message on the inside cover of each annual report that made his view on decentralization 100 percent clear to employees and outsiders alike: "Decentralization is the cornerstone of our philosophy. Our goal is to hire the best people we can and give them the responsibility and authority they need to perform their jobs." Leaving people alone to manage meant Murphy could get out of the way and concentrate on allocating capital.

Frank Smith, who ran Capital Cities with Murphy, explained a magic wrinkle of decentralized management. It wasn't only about freeing up the CEO; it was about making the jobs of the senior leaders so amazing that they would never want to leave. What he called "corruption by autonomy" is in sync with Watsa's thinking on retention and decentralization. "Some of you fellows may think I tie you to Capital Cities by corrupting you with compensation and stock options," Smith said once. "But I've decided the reason you are afraid to leave this company is more because our system naturally corrupts you with autonomy and authority. And I suspect that after living that way for a time, you're fearful that someplace else might not operate in the same manner."

Ben Watsa, appointed chairman at Fairfax India in 2024 and, eventually, slated to serve the same role at Fairfax Financial as well, stresses that once a company starts calling the shots from the top down, the culture's momentum erodes: "If everyone is running their own baby, the entrepreneurial people stay in the company. If you start telling people what to do, the entrepreneurial people don't want to stay."

As an allocator, Singleton took a lot of tactics to extremes, and this extended to what he did with his time day to day as CEO. Great people running the decentralized companies under him with a long-term focus gave him the personal freedom to use his rational mind to guide him, whether it was to find companies to buy or sell, stock to buy back, or debt to retire.

"I don't reserve any day-to-day responsibilities for myself, so I don't get into any particular rut," he explained. "I do not define my job in any rigid terms but in terms of having the freedom to do whatever seems to be in the best interest of the company at any time."

John Varnell, who has served in a number of capacities on the senior Fairfax team, looked back at three things that made the division of duties work so well between head office and the operating companies:

1. **Financial risks:** "Many of the things Prem went ahead on struck most people as too risky. After a lot of discussion, Prem makes the call. He knows that it's his financial health that will be affected as well, and he's an eternal optimist."

2. **Complexity:** "When we bought a lot of things, we got kind of complicated but then would simplify. Instead of making everything more complicated, as many of our competitors did, we retrenched. It made us better."

3. **Control and ego:** "Prem always says it doesn't matter who gets the credit at Fairfax. It underlies everything the company does. If you have people who believe in that, you can keep ego out and get things done. Too many companies want the head office to control everything but the local boss is the one who is out in the field

> every day seeing the customers. They should be the ones controlling operations. Then you just have to get the right people at head office who are happy with the idea that it's an information transfer rather than a power transfer."

There are ample examples of times the investment guys at Fairfax left the wrong insurance people alone to run the insurers and paid the price. The company had to scratch plans to leave management in place at firms like Markel Financial, some of the claims businesses, plus Ranger, CTR, TIG, and Crum. The true test of the Fairfax way always comes back to attracting and retaining quality management, and that means having leaders who have a strong balance of humility, talent, and confidence.

"Overconfidence leads to arrogance," Watsa offers, "and arrogance leads to disrespect and the erosion of trust and communication. On the other hand, humility encourages respect, both internally in the operating company and with the holding company. When Rick and I highlighted 'no egos' in the Guiding Principles, that was our shorthand for the idea of humility."

Over time, Barnard led teams to put more oversight and coordination into Fairfax leadership. They introduced profit centres for better channels of communication and monitoring. That trend accelerated under the leadership of Andy Barnard, through regular calls with a group of the major insurers as well as the full group, which was now spread out across Asia, the Americas, Europe, and the Middle East. Soon, he had entrenched a deep culture of doing things the Fairfax Way. And newer acquisitions (such as Brit and Allied) were in much better shape with stronger management that made them easier to integrate.

"When Peter and I built up the meeting structure and added the profit centres, we got a lot more visibility into the different lines of business," says Barnard. Later, with president Peter Clarke, he added quarterly financial reviews and a Leadership Council for training and deeper collaboration between the companies on things like IT, tax, and industry research. "We find out quickly where things are on track, where they might be going off track, and what strategies we are trying out to get them back on track."

There is a strong culture at Fairfax to share as much learning across the companies as possible while strictly avoiding groupthink or cost synergies. The companies are diversified across business lines and geographies, and some could be expanding aggressively into a hard market, while others are pulling back when prices are soft. Fairfax leaders insist each piece has its own rationality and the worst thing would be to have everyone trying to move in sync.

At Fairfax, you would never form an idea at the holding company level and kick it down to the subsidiaries to implement. Crum & Forster's Marc Adee likes to describe Fairfax's decentralized collaboration in supply-demand terms: "In a centralized world, you get a lot of 'supply push.' What we want is 'demand pull.'" If a parent company pushes people to play together, it gets difficult operationally. "Demand pull is more organic."

Watsa is a constant advocate of never pushing Fairfax companies to seek synergies between them, says Lou Iglesias, CEO at Allied. "Prem is a real champion of not going there. He says those potential savings would not be worth the price because they would erode the model." The people running the subsidiaries need to feel that the arrangement of working under a holding company actually gives them a role no less attractive than running a fully independent company outside. "It is the kind of structure where we can attract the best and brightest people in every single country and region where Fairfax operates," says Watsa.

One thing Fairfax never wants to see anywhere in management are followers. With leaders who try to fit in with what the rest of the industry is doing, you risk suffering from inertia or copycat strategies. And that is just one way to get it wrong, according to academics and Fairfax leaders. Buffett termed this lazy behaviour an "institutional imperative" when leaders blindly follow the crowd. It's the CEO's job to ensure this unseen enemy does not creep in.

The institutional imperative presents itself in other ways, such as when companies build flashy head offices to stand out. Thorndike had another term for the "edifice complex" of overspending on elaborate headquarters. The CEOs he identified as brilliant avoided the edifice complex: They were drawn to modest structures that didn't try to elevate the importance of central management. "There is a fundamental humility to decentralization, an admission that headquarters does not have all the answers and that much of the real value is created by local managers in the field."

British economist Dan Davies studied growing companies that shoot themselves in the foot when they try to manage too much from the top down. The casualty ends up being accountability, as everyone surrenders decisions to others. Bad decisions result, things go wrong, and everyone blames the system instead of being accountable, argues Davies in his book *The Unaccountability Machine: Why Big Systems Make Terrible Decisions—and How the World Lost Its Mind*. Davies, a former regulatory economist with the Bank of England, observes, "As the network builds out, it gets more complicated and the ability of the head office to manage it doesn't grow faster." The solution? The only way to match the bandwidth of management to the task is to give autonomy to the subsidiaries.

"What we always see in any big organization is that it grows, it gets more complicated, it tries to deal with that by adding more resources at head office, it ends up not being able to keep up and then it reorganizes. And the reorganizations almost always either involve pushing responsibility down to the branches or they involve spinning off parts of the business into a separate organization and giving up the task of controlling it at all." Decentralization guards against that series of actions.

One area that can easily fall to an institutional imperative is human resources, particularly in recruitment and compensation. Once you hand over HR to people who work with outside consultants, you can find your culture weakened, Watsa cautions. He is personally involved in finding and promoting leadership for his companies and ensuring they have a deep pool developed for succession. When he meets talent, he is Fairfax's most persuasive recruiter. That power of persuasion was on display when he recruited Rick Salsberg, Francis Chou, Andy Barnard, as well as Wade Burton and Lawrence Chin from Cundill. Only a few leaders have left before retirement or death in almost forty years.

"We like to avoid going with search firms," said Salsberg. "It is often really awful. You just can't tell what you are getting and outside hires have to learn a new way to get things done under our roof. It's just a bad idea. If you recruit and promote from within, you can avoid that kind of disruption."

In the Q & A at the 2004 annual meeting, Buffett described how corporate compensation committees end up not with Dobermans standing guard for your culture and finances but rather with "chihuahuas that have been sedated." Munger cheerfully chimed in with the rejoinder: "I would rather throw a viper down my shirt front than hire a compensation consultant."

What Brian Bradstreet fears most from an institutional imperative is bureaucracy: "One thing that has never changed is we hate it. You can't let bureaucracy creep into an organization. If that happens, you can't be nimble and you can't move quickly. You need to maintain the culture to keep people motivated to do the right thing."

LEADERSHIP AND THE ROLE OF THE CEO

What does Watsa think Fisher-style scuttlebutt analysis (as explored in chapter 9) would say about management at Fairfax?

"I think the scuttlebutt on us would say that we believe deeply in decentralization and that it helps drive organic growth," says Watsa. "If you look closely, you would see that the culture that drives that growth acts as a moat that gives us an edge. The intrinsic power of talent working for the long term drives earnings power. The fact that we are deep in talent, and many of our leaders have been with us for decades, is proof it's working. As CEO, I see myself mostly as a coordinator of great leaders and employees."

One of the attributes that others say truly defines Watsa is his optimism. He is an enthusiastic and relentless cheerleader. A good portion of his letters is given over to praise for Fairfax company leaders, with special attention to those who are headed for retirement and managing a smooth succession by promoting from within.

"Prem is an incredible cheerleader of his teams," offers Jake Taylor, a value investor and commentator. "He speaks so highly of everybody. You can see why everyone shows up to work wanting to impress him.

I mean, Warren is good about that but the energy that Prem conveys is even stronger."

Leading by example is always good, of course. Looking back after the first twenty-five years, working side by side with him, HWIC's original head trader Frances Burke said Watsa was always right there beside you and made it obvious through his own hard work what was needed for the company. "Prem is a very generous person—financially, emotionally of himself and of his time," she said. "He's really right there with you, which isn't something you see in a lot of other companies where the CEOs are ten floors up having a cigar or brandy or whatever they do up there. I'm not saying Prem doesn't demand a lot of you. He moves fast, so when he wants something, he wants it now. But it's easy to take because he works so hard himself."

At Northbridge, CEO Silvy Wright credits Watsa's inspiration as a major reason behind the successful culture at Fairfax: "Prem is one of the most optimistic people I know. He's also very quick to acknowledge his mistakes. His drive and optimism are inspirational. On the insurer side and the investment side, look at the deep layers of people Fairfax has developed. Prem is our biggest cheerleader but as a group we are so strong."

Watsa's definitiveness of purpose infectiously spreads trust and confidence, offers Kari Van Gundy at Zenith: "He is the most interesting person I have worked for. He seems to have the unique skill of focusing on the person and building relationships based on trust. He has a unique ability to judge people. And then to influence them. It's just who he is. And he is the most optimistic person I know—and not just blindly optimistic. It's confidence. He brings his optimism as a capability to drive toward an outcome and make it successful."

That confidence and optimism allow a leader to tune out the noise—and Fairfax experienced a lot of noise over its four decades. "To get Fairfax to where it is today, Prem needed a vision and resiliency, Van Gundy says. "He didn't get distracted by the obstacles that came up or criticisms from the market that were directed at him. He stuck with it. Successful people in business or generally in life are those who learn how to work through challenges and problems."

In all interviews with Fairfax leaders, the discussion of the CEO role keeps coming back to decentralization and trust. Building that trust could be Watsa's most important legacy. "The model is built on two-way trust between the holding company and the operating companies," says Lou Iglesias at Allied. "I saw that coming in, just how much trust there is. Prem is very steady, very committed and doesn't blow in the wind. Which is good for me. This tremendous trust factor is the cornerstone of what works so well with everyone here and it just gets reinforced over time, over and over again. That culture is going to attract strong people. And the people who stay are the ones who see that. The people who endorse those values are going to be quality people."

There are lots of ways a CEO can cheerlead, and recognition is a big one. In the letters to shareholders, at length in every issue, Watsa prominently singles out the people behind the success of dozens of operating companies and investments; he also marks anniversaries, illnesses, and deaths. If Watsa is going to beat up on anyone, it is typically himself, with a dose of humour-flavoured humility. In one example, he had a running joke when shareholders were riding the roller coaster down. Each year in his letter, he would close out by making light of the genuine awkwardness of having to meet face to face on the day of the annual meeting:

- "Given the fluctuations in the price of Fairfax stock, I may come incognito." (1997)
- "While we cannot answer your questions on the telephone, we look forward to answering them all at our Annual Meeting—and our Presidents, Fairfax officers and HWIC principles will also all be there, to shield me from the tomatoes, I hope!!" (1999)
- "In spite of much trying, we were not able to postpone our annual meeting to 2003! . . . I hope to attend!" (2001)

Watsa and Salsberg made sure they included in the Guiding Principles the message that it's okay to fail, as long as we learn from our mistakes. Watsa has made sure he publicly owns his own blunders and keeps his patience when leaders trip up. The one thing that Fairfax culture demands never be compromised is trust.

At Northbridge, Silvy Wright says she will never forget the trepidation of having to loop Watsa in on how a tech project had gone completely off track. Forced to pull the plug and take a $25-million hit, she went to head office to brief him and take the heat. There were no fireworks, just a CEO who listened and then asked her what she learned from it. "He asked me not to repeat it. Did I think I would lose my job? No. But I really feared I would lose a lot of trust equity. I left with the trust intact and I still had my confidence to take risks. We are in the business of taking calculated risks. You own the consequences, but you cannot stop taking risks."

Marc Adee, CEO at Crum & Forster, had a similar experience when he came to Watsa with bad news of further reserve shortfalls at the hard-to-fix insurer: "My first meeting with Prem was when I was up in Toronto and needed to share a big number—a $300-million reserve hole that needed to be plugged. I braced for the screaming you might get from the typical explosive CEO type. It did not come and that's one of the reasons I have never left."

What makes Watsa such a strong leader, explains Adee, is his infectious optimism and commitment to do whatever it takes and make the rest of the employees believe they will come out on top, as Adee did soon thereafter with Crum: "He believed that over the long term we could work our way through any rough patch, no matter how bad. He makes you want to walk through walls to prove him right."

It helps to have the kind of personality that makes the CEO a talent beacon. Wade Burton got to know Watsa and Fairfax as an investor, not an employee. It was a curious dynamic: His interactions with Watsa evolved into sessions of generous mentorship about value investing, leadership, and life in general. When his firm, Cundill, was sold, Burton had a windfall and the time to take a break and reflect on future challenges—until Watsa leaned in with his trademark passionate persuasiveness: "Prem told me I was too young to step away. He said, 'No, you can't do that. Manage some money for us.' So I did. It was a great introduction to Fairfax, right in the middle of the financial crisis. I am still here."

All that time with Watsa before signing on with Fairfax gave Burton a pretty good idea of what to expect working there, especially as he had seen the CEO under fire: "I have met so many CEOs and so many companies. But Prem was different—he was a joyful dude. Analysts are such a skeptical and grumpy group, right? I could instantly tell that this was a guy that a lot of people would not appreciate. They wouldn't trust him; after all, who can be so joyful when the company is in the middle of all that mess? Obviously, they would think to themselves, 'There must be something wrong with him.'"

As a mentor, Watsa taught Burton how to do the interpersonal part of his job better, how to deal with impatient clients, and how to stay disciplined to weather the grind while waiting for underperforming value picks to rally off the floor. For value guys, it's one thing to have conviction about your long-term view; it's another to take the heat from clients who doubt your conviction. "He told me, 'Wear your bottom quartile with pride. You're doing the right thing.' And he was right. Most of the time, the advice wasn't about money at all. He was the most helpful to me as a human being, as opposed to being an investment guy."

That kind of avuncular role as a coach continues to evolve for a great CEO. Munger almost hit one hundred at Berkshire. Buffett is creeping into his mid-nineties and trying to pull back. Watsa, meanwhile, is a relative youngster in his mid-seventies and he has no intention of stepping away any time soon. The value club is full of CEOs who don't want to quit until they have to. But the years ahead could see him trying to off-load more direct responsibilities and adopting a "chief grandparent officer" role.

That idea has come up on leadership retreats. The CGO thinking is inspired by Peter Kaufman, CEO of Glenair and a popular speaker on finding success in both business and life in general. Kaufman attracts a crowd that is less interested in Glenair's business in industrial connectors and more drawn to his way of thinking about getting the most out of everything by treating people well. He believes genuine respect is always reciprocated and that it helps people be amazing.

Kaufman—who is also well-known with the value crowd, having edited *Poor Charlie's Almanack: The Essential Wit and Wisdom of Charles T. Munger*—shared his thinking with Fairfax leaders a few years ago at a management retreat. Watsa says his way of talking about the grandparent role in a corporate role resonated with him. "We see our organization at Glenair as a family, not a 'team,'" explains Kaufman. "At Glenair, as the CEO, I choose to play the role of a 'grandparent.' Why? Because the 'nuclear family' model has been honed over tens of thousands of years of human experience—it is the optimal model for unity and sustainability. And the role of 'grandparent' is an integral, essential part of that model. Grandparents, in a functional family, are on call for advice but don't intrude into day-to-day 'parenting,' knowing it often results in arrested development and poor morale in the actual 'parents' responsible for managing daily operations."

The ultimate goal is to leverage the value of experience in driving practical goals such as stronger retention and succession. "It took me many years to develop this unique arrangement," explains Kaufman. "Standard CEO roles, as traditionally viewed internally by teams and owners, and externally by customers, do not foster grandparent roles." An inspired Watsa let it be known to Fairfax employees, "I will try to be a good grandparent!!"

ALLOCATION AND THE ART OF THE INVESTOR CEO

Cheerleading is great, but what about results? Does the classic value approach of decentralization lead to better returns? Ivey Business School's George Athanassakos thinks so, and he devised a way to go out and prove it.

"One misunderstanding perpetuated by academics is the idea that value investing is only about a particular style of investing," explains Athanassakos. "But it is not. Value investing is also about corporate finance. In fact, value investing incorporates two points of view, one is that of an investor (the value seeker) and the other that of a CEO (the value creator)." The great allocator CEOs, he believes, are both value seekers and value creators.

Athanassakos argues that CEOs perform two roles and most are only good at one of them: "Most CEOs focus on managing operations and tend to be good at that. They acquired the skill of managing operations through years of working in various functions within their organizations. Capital allocation, however, is a skill that most executives do not learn on their way up."

Buffett has made the similar observation that many CEOs have no clue what they are doing on the investment and allocation side and end up hiring consultants to help who, in turn, tend to make things a lot worse. The Oracle of Omaha has observed: "Their inadequacy is not surprising. Most bosses rise to the top because they have excelled in an area such as marketing, production, engineering, administration or, sometimes, institutional politics." As CEO, however, a boss "now must make capital allocation decisions, a critical job that they may have never tackled and that is not easily mastered. To stretch the point, it's as if the final step for a highly-talented musician was not to perform at Carnegie Hall but, instead, to be named Chairman of the Federal Reserve."

Allied's Iglesias offers: "Allocation is what the Fairfax team is so great at. They figure out buybacks and when to increase ownership stakes, the best way to do financings, and the whole investment side. They don't spend their time managing insurance companies and pretty much leave us to run those assets."

Athanassakos studied successful CEOs who were strong allocators and he determined that the stronger ones are good investors, and the absolute strongest among them are value investors. His research's key determinant to gauge strong allocation performance was the ratio of goodwill to assets, together with operating margins, between 2001 and 2020. He then measured performance returns for the good and bad allocators: "I found that companies managed by CEOs who allocate company cash flows according to a value-investing style seem to outperform . . . For example, between 2001 and 2020, on average, the portfolio of good asset allocator companies outperforms the portfolio of bad asset allocator companies by 33 percent in terms of cumulative three-year returns." True to value orthodoxy, a big part of the heavy lifting in that asset outperformance was done by low purchase prices.

Chapter Eighteen

THE COMPANY CASE STUDIES

"We have found some people need some time to come around to our way of thinking." —*Rick Salsberg*

There's no greater test for Fairfax's corporate culture than bringing in a new company under its holding company tent. The plan sounds simple enough: Buy good companies with great management at a fair price, avoid layoffs, and re-energize the new company with a culture of treating everyone right. It's not always that simple in the short term, especially with companies that have been struggling for good reason. And if leadership doesn't buy in, it becomes nearly impossible.

If you read the letters of Watsa the cheerleader, these acquisitions often sounded easy, but a look behind the scenes reveals some very challenging transitions. Sometimes, there were a lot of problems to fix before decentralization was possible. In other cases, leaders did not adapt to the Fairfax culture. And yet, each challenge gave the overarching culture a chance to grow stronger. Here are nine compelling organizational transitions, how they came together or fell apart in the case of Walwyn, along with the key learnings they offer.

CASE ONE: THE EARLY LESSONS AT MARKEL FINANCIAL HOLDINGS

Markel Financial Holdings was an early test of Fairfax's decentralization strategy. It failed in the short term but taught the young company valuable lessons. Still a little green, Watsa and his team took a hands-off approach—and paid a severe price for it.

The newly minted chairman and CEO had marvelled at how smoothly things were coming together. He knew the main competitor in trucking insurance was on the ropes, but no one expected it to simply self-implode and allow Watsa's recapitalized company to dominate right out of the gate. Then he and the team got schooled on the insurance industry's cruel turns.

It remains unclear whether the insurance team at Markel Financial was incompetent or reckless, thinking they suddenly had the market to themselves. Either way, Fairfax found itself facing a culture problem writ large. Management seriously misread the risks on one line of business—surety coverage on commercial construction—and then lacked the sense to pull back when market pricing turned against them in an ill-conceived expansion into insurance for busses, taxis, and rental cars. Fairfax was lucky enough to put out the first fire, but bad underwriting on the latter almost burned the house down.

One fundamental problem here was that all reporting lines led straight to the corner office. What were the lessons? "Why did this happen at Markel?" wrote Watsa in the 1989 letter. "Could Fairfax have responded sooner? Do we need to be more centralized, more hands-on in our operations?"

The fallout

- *Tighter reporting lines and better communication.* Watsa had too many leaders reporting to him. He delegated oversight of Markel Financial Holdings plus two new companies—Shand, Morahan, and Evanston Services as well as Morden & Helwig Ltd.—to Rick Salsberg and other executives. The company needed to find its own kind of middle ground between bureaucracy and managing by way of impromptu hallway chats and kitchen conversations.
- *Markel was not an easy or quick fix.* First, Bill Grant, formerly of SphereRe, was given the nod to tighten premiums with a focus on trucking, while also overseeing an amalgamation of Markel with other Canadian assets—Otter Dorchester and another early acquisition called Chequers Transport. However, the market was tough. Mark Ram, then in his mid-twenties with four years at Fairfax, landed in the role and made major progress by 1995. It was still a

grind, but Watsa lauded the efforts to rebuild the company "brick by brick," and Ram succeeded in getting it back to solid profitability in 2001 and 2002, before it was rolled into Northbridge.

Major learning: Keep the strategy, fix the execution

Fairfax learned from mistakes, added accountability, was transparent about it, and never gave up on its approach. "We continue to believe strongly in decentralized operations with Fairfax responsible for performance measurement, succession planning, acquisitions and financing," Watsa wrote to his shareholders. "For performance measurement, each of our companies submits annual business plans, which are reviewed and signed off by the person responsible for the individual company. This method of operation we feel will make it unlikely that our experience at Markel will be repeated and if it were necessary, we would be able to react much sooner. We continue however to run on a decentralized basis and let the presidents manage their companies."

Last word to Rick Salsberg: "That rescue effort really helped us. It gave some sense that although we will always be decentralized, as we promised, we would have to keep a close tab on what our holdings were doing."

CASE TWO: IN THE SPOTLIGHT'S GLARE WITH MIDLAND WALWYN

Fairfax's short and uncomfortable experiment expanding into investment banking did not fail specifically because of loose decentralization—but decentralization didn't help. It was more of a cultural issue, which made the decentralized approach a hurdle they could not clear. The Hamblin Watsa Investment Counsel (HWIC) gang knew Bay Street. They acquired Walwyn for less than book value and, as controlling shareholders, lined up Tony Arrell to run it. A value investor and fan of both Berkshire Hathaway and Fairfax, Arrell was the same guy who originally recruited Watsa to Gardiner Watson. Watsa was working his network; Fairfax even brought in Confederation Life as a partner.

Perhaps naively, the hope was to make over the Bay Street company with a lower profile and a focus on long-term value investors. At the time,

Fairfax was keen to get other banking investments going and eventually roll them into a separate, publicly traded company. The timing was good for the price tag, but that price also reflected the market's mood: Many investors were still reeling form the 1987 crash and had sworn off stocks entirely.

A bigger challenge was the culture. Bay Street's swagger and egos made it hard for Fairfax to quietly go about building a different kind of investment shop. Fairfax found it difficult to gain traction in hiring the kind of people who could help set the firm apart. As the noise and rancour of Bay Street grew louder, the mission was thrown into doubt.

"The stock brokerage business is very people intensive," Watsa explains. "While this could be a negative, we believed that Walwyn could truly be a very different company in a short period of time if it could attract capable people, as we felt it could."

Things only got messier when Walwyn quickly merged with Midland, which prompted the exit of Tony Arrell—Fairfax's great hope as a talent beacon. Media attention, already unbearable to Fairfax, ratcheted up a few notches.

The fallout

- *Get me out of here.* Showing uncharacteristic impatience—and distaste for Bay Street's ways "where short-term thinking prevailed"—Fairfax was relieved to dump its 37 percent stake in Midland Walwyn at a loss, selling it to Watsa's former employer, Confederation Life.
- *Get me out of IB completely.* This dally into the brokerage business was part of a contemporaneous push into investment banking with turnaround venture capital. The plan was to roll everything up with Midland Walwyn, but the strategy failed.

Major learning: Beware—culture can be oil and water

Fairfax had the leader it wanted in place at Midland Walwyn and a plan to recruit talent that aligned with its culture—all part of the decentralized strategy. But too many gunslinger egos and too many mergers made it impossible to build a value-driven operation on Bay Street. Arrell had trouble getting the team aligned with Fairfax's vision, and personality clashes were frequent.

If you step into this kind of situation, make sure you own more than 37 percent—enough to exert control, think long-term, and retain your key talent. As Watsa said, "The major assets of the firm go down in the elevator every day: They may not come back up—for whatever reason!" Case in point: Tony Arrell.

"It is fair to say we will not do any more venture capital deals and will be extremely cautious of 'turnaround' opportunities." At the end of the day, Bay Street was simply a bad cultural fit for Fairfax to plant its fair and friendly flag of expansion. It's worth repeating that Watsa didn't blame his generals—he pointed to the industry and bad timing instead: "The investment banking losses were mainly due to your Chairman's bright ideas!"

CASE THREE: THE CURIOUS CENTRALIZATION OF NORTHBRIDGE

In need of greater flexibility and access to capital, Fairfax rolled up its Canadian assets and launched a C$22 1-million IPO for 29 percent of the company in 2003. Later, CEO Mark Ram provided strong oversight of the group, but decentralization remained the mantra: Fairfax kept the subsidiaries independent even though they reported their financials together.

In 2009, Northbridge was reprivatized, giving Fairfax full access to cash flow and reigniting discussions about the structure of an insurance group that was still essentially four small, decentralized parts: Markel Financial Holdings (trucking), Lombard Insurance (commercial), Commonwealth Insurance (property and energy), and Federated Insurance Holdings of Canada (direct commercial sales). Each had its own market segment, history, and culture. Moves were made to push the subsidiaries closer together, but these didn't go smoothly. "The changes made it harder for the individual company heads to lead and to sort out accountabilities," says Barnard. The search for direction created uncertainty, and Fairfax found itself in real danger of going in two directions at the same time.

Enter Sylvia Wright, who was promoted to CEO in 2011 and tasked by Watsa to recommend the best way forward. She landed in a quandary: "My opportunity was to either continue combining the talent and the scale by bringing the companies together or stop the plan cold and leave the subsidiaries separate."

Wright was torn. Watsa's inclinations were obvious, and she had personally experienced the upsides of decentralization: "I grew up with Markel and I was really loyal to that one unit." The consideration that became paramount was the small size of the Canadian companies—not just compared to Fairfax's growing U.S. operations, but even within an increasingly consolidated domestic market. "If we didn't leverage the talent across the companies, as well as the competitive scale, we may have become weaker. That was my overriding concern, so I recommended we combine the four companies."

The fallout

- *Convincing Prem.* "I told Prem we would foster the culture but also bring the group together and make it stronger," says Wright. "It wasn't easy—he was hard to convince—but it worked because we made the transition with Fairfax culture and the Guiding Principles front and centre." In the end, Watsa trusted his leaders in the field, and he says Wright got it right.
- *Convincing everyone else.* "You have to work with empowerment all the way through your organization," explains Wright. "I can be empowered, but if I don't empower others, it stops at me. You end up with an autocratic leader. So your choice in people who believe in the culture is crucial. We used that and the focus on culture was a big part of why we succeeded and didn't lose employees."
- *Avoiding layoffs.* "As the plan developed, Prem would keep asking how many people I was going to let go," says Wright. "In the end, there would only be about twenty, and they were strategic, not just cost decisions. He took a very personal interest."

Major learning: We can also centralize first, then decentralize the right way

"The lesson we learned is we can say we are decentralized and we want to leave companies to run themselves, but we have to do it the right way with the right people," says Barnard. "And then we have to get out of the way. It does not work if you try to go in two directions at the same time—you are going to end up with two cultures."

Clarke adds, "The Northbridge experience taught us how important it is to ensure that we let our principles guide us throughout the Fairfax group. The decentralized system we operate does not mean CEOs are free to behave in disregard of those important cultural values. But we also need to give them the freedom to execute."

You could argue that rolling up the companies was contrary to decentralized thinking. On the other hand, delegating the ultimate decision to the person who would run it all was classic decentralization. "There were times in the transition where Prem was still tempted to unwind the combination because he feared the individual companies would lose their distinctive identities," Barnard adds. "It's a testament to Silvy, who was brought on to make that combination work. The culture and performance are really strong, so all that talk about whether we made a mistake just died away because of what she was able to deliver."

CASE FOUR: ODYSSEY'S JOURNEY FROM FRANKENSTEIN'S MONSTER TO CROWN JEWEL

The acquisition of Skandia America—and the other assets that became Odyssey—was a classic Fairfax value pickup. It very quickly became a roll-up of broken or nearly dead-on-arrival businesses that were stripped for parts and stitched together on a conference room table under the midnight lights on the eighth floor of 95 Wellington West.

The flurry of acquisitions that fed into the creation of Odyssey arrived in classic Watsa fashion. The phone rang, impaired assets were purchased, and the prices were dirt cheap; Fairfax stock was at an acquisition-friendly high, and the pieces offered a rapid entry into new lines of business and geographies. The fact that they all came at once just made things more intense. Welcomed to the family were Skandia America, Compagnie Transcontinentale de Réassurance (CTR), Hudson Insurance Group, Newline Group, TIG Holding, Bermuda, and Sphere Drake.

Only Sphere Drake turned out to be irredeemable, while pieces of the other parts all squished nicely together with Odyssey. With TIG Holding, Fairfax got burned on half the deal (the insurance business had been delegated to undisciplined outside salespeople), but the remaining reinsurance assets were valuable.

Of course, none of this followed Fairfax's playbook of buying good companies with strong management and leaving them alone. (Buying whole businesses to just retain some parts and shut down the rest is more of a raider's playbook, which has always been anathema to Watsa.)

Brian Young, Andy Barnard's successor—first as Odyssey CEO and later as senior leader of global insurance at Fairfax under Barnard—describes Odyssey's tumultuous birth as something rare, weird, and wonderful: "Odyssey is in many ways a unicorn."

The fallout

- *Thinking big paid off.* Adding half a billion in net premiums through the Skandia America and CTR assets boosted the Fairfax total almost 60 percent to $1.4 billion. A few years after the market turned in 2001, Odyssey alone was doing $2.5 billion in premiums. Dreaming big also helped convince Andy Barnard to come on board and build Fairfax a global reinsurance business. Strong leaders like big challenges—and Barnard became the key architect of Fairfax's insurance empire. He was tested quickly with the next wave of big moves coming barely a week after he'd clocked in.
- *Patience paid off.* Odyssey started slow. The market was soft, and the company had some bad practices to fix. "At first, Odyssey was a second- or third-tier insurer," explains Barnard. "Its book of business was made up of a lot of leftovers that competitors didn't want to touch." Writing a lot of business would have been a losing strategy in this kind of market, so instead Odyssey concentrated

on fixing its strategy and culture. It was all a warm-up—so when the market hardened post-9/11, the company took off.

- *Synergies sometimes make sense.* At first, the company had been more optimistic that rationalization could be avoided. Half of TIG Holding (the reinsurance assets) was integrated into Odyssey, but the rest of it (the insurance business) was deemed unsalvageable. Many analysts dismissed TIG as a disaster of a deal, but Watsa insists it was a win because the reinsurance assets alone gave Odyssey a huge entry into that line of business—and a major boost in float.

Major learning: When pressed, drop the playbook and improvise

"It's all very well to say let's avoid change, decentralize, and retain management," reflects Young, Odyssey's former CEO who now oversees insurance under Barnard. "That makes sense when the business is running well. But when you're buying an underperforming business, you have to make changes too. We had no choice. But the lesson was learned. We operate differently today than we did back then."

As much of an upheaval as Odyssey's formation was, there was absolute clarity on management. It would not become a revolving door like Ranger Insurance Company or, in the near future, Crum & Forster. It was Barnard's show and having been inside the Skandia America machine, he knew exactly why the company had been unsuccessful—and which pieces would fit together. Looking back, he says the overwhelming evidence of this decision's success lies in Odyssey's lifetime underwriting profit: the highest at Fairfax.

A big plus for Barnard was the fact he had a designated successor and right-hand man from day one: Brian Young. On culture, both leaders were totally in sync with what Watsa was preaching and set themselves to replicate it from the top down and bottom up at Odyssey. Young—in his thirtieth year with Fairfax in 2025, including fourteen years as CEO at Odyssey before transitioning into the number two top insurance role at Fairfax's head office—puts it simple: "We are all about culture," he says. "It starts right at the top. And what better way to serve your culture than to promote from within? It sends a wonderful message to people who work in the organization. It also means employees are not going to be subject to an outsider boss every few years with a new strategy, goals and way of doing things."

CASE FIVE: HOW CRUM WAS THE TOUGHEST DEAL THAT EVER WENT RIGHT

Fairfax had its unequivocal disasters, such as Ranger Insurance Company. But Crum & Forster was one success story that tested management's faith to the brink for years before it finally succeeded. The Crum & Forster that Fairfax purchased came with a diminished market profile. It was a lower-tier, undifferentiated player in the agency middle-market commercial sector. It also had a bloated home office, left over from its flagship years. Hopes were raised when Bruce Esselborn made good on a three-year promise in 1999 to shrink the bad business. The number of policies written plummeted from 32,790 in 1999 to 6,226 in 2002, while the value of the premiums grew from $19.8 million to $108.5 million. On paper, it was fixed. But the reality was different. The company survived a debt downgrade to A- in 2002 but continued to fall short on profitability due to major reserving shortfalls and a mixed record on new business and growth.

Renovating Crum & Forster proved an exhausting challenge for Fairfax. From 1998 to 2013, the company produced underwriting losses in all but two years. Over that time, Crum & Forster went through four different CEOs. Watsa insists they had the talent, but suffered from a lack of continuity.

"We hired some exceptional leaders and managed to get the problems fixed. But it was harder to establish growth. We had Esselborn and Nick Antonopolous, who did a fantastic job installing underwriting discipline. Doug Libby, who had a great track record with Seneca, and Mary Jane Robertson, both had an impact stepping in before they retired. It was tough. We did all the right things: We increased the reserves, we created a disciplined underwriting machine, but for a couple of years the current insurance market was terrible and we had to pay for all the careless business that had been written by the former owners. That put pressure on our investment portfolio, because we needed cash to pay the claims."

Somehow, the problems just kept coming, recalled Salsberg. Even after shrinking itself into better financial shape, the firm had trouble learning how to grow again. "Crum & Forster was probably the most challenging deal for us," he said. "We knew it was being sold by Xerox for a good reason but we were still too over-optimistic. We understood that they were desperate to sell and we could get it at a really good price and it would work out well. But the problems were extremely deep."

The good news is that new assets were being polished up and rolled into the mix. A few of those were run by Marc Adee. Now in his twenty-sixth year with Fairfax, Adee came aboard as Crum & Forster's CFO and Chief Actuary, while also creating a business out of pieces of TIG Holding and Ranger Insurance Company, as well as tending to Seneca Insurance and First Mercury. In 2014, it was his turn to take the wheel as CEO.

At first, the culture actually got worse for a few more years, says Adee: "When I got there, we were able to seed a cultural transformation. We needed to make it a workplace where people wanted to go. It was sad to see a company that used to be so great just get beaten up so bad. Insurance is tricky: There are incredibly many ways to do it wrong. And there aren't that many ways to do it right."

The fallout

- *Fixed from the inside, with a better book of business.* When Adee finally stepped into the CEO role, Crum & Forster was doing \$1 billion in premiums—and still shrinking. But Adee had his finger on the company's strengths and weaknesses. The firm now generates more than \$5 billion and well over half of that is from the side projects that Adee had been tasked with shepherding into Crum & Forster's barn. "You don't ever really shrink to greatness," he quips. In the end, it wasn't a turnaround so much as a reinvention of the company. Crum even managed to build a pet insurance business that grew dramatically and was sold off for \$1.4 billion in 2022. "Marc transformed it into much more of a boutique speciality insurer," says Barnard.

- *The upside of doing the right thing.* "TIG and Crum would have been cheaper to throw in the bin," says Adee. But that's not the way Watsa rolls, he adds. "The more responsible way to approach it is to say, 'Hey, we bought this thing. We are going to take care of the business, and we'll keep at it until we get it right for the long term.' Treat people right and that goes for your customer and your employees. A lesser person might not have been as supportive."

Major learning: Continuity and patience win in the long term

The Crum & Forster experience was hard on Watsa. He loves continuity and is no fan of revolving c-suite doors. He has said in the past that Fairfax would never do another acquisition of a company with the kinds of problems Crum & Forster had. But in hindsight, his lasting learning isn't that Fairfax made a mistake in doing the deal—it's that the turnaround project cycled through too many CEOs. Until Adee, no one, he explains, stayed long enough to see the job through. "We tried a number of different CEOs to right the ship. We had some very smart people, who were able to improve the company's focus and standing. If anyone of them had been able to stay the course, the results may have been different. Even if it took fifteen years!"

Adee says winning his team over to the Fairfax way was crucial in finally turning it all around. In the early days, Crum & Forster was still a "centralized monster" without accountability, he explains. People felt isolated, under-resourced, and abandoned: "We did a lot of work on people—attracting and keeping the right ones. A lot of that came from what worked at Fairfax. It wasn't easy and probably went sideways for six months but we never looked back. We said no excuses, which took a lot of air out of the complaining."

The transformation really only felt done about five years ago, said Adee in 2023. "Today, nobody really remembers what it was like before we had decentralization. No one talks about the bad old days. You have to remember—it's about culture, but your culture has to lead to being a winning team. You want to make money. We wanted it to work like it works at Fairfax head office."

Final word to Barnard: "Crum is Exhibit A for demonstrating the importance of management continuity. Marc had a running start when he took over in 2014, having deep familiarity with many of the diverse businesses at Crum. Once in charge, he was able to focus on building, rather than dismantling. The results over his tenure speak for themselves."

CASE SIX: ZENITH HERALDS A SHIFT TO BUYING QUALITY

After years of acquiring troubled assets, and learning from those ventures, Fairfax finally decided to kick the bargain-bin habit. "Zenith will be the highest quality company we ever bought," Watsa said shortly after the deal closed in early 2010.

Fairfax already had a fruitful history with California-based Zenith National Insurance, dating back to 2000, when it acquired about forty precent of the company's common shares from Reliance Group, which was soon to be bankrupt. This purchase brought diversification to the Fairfax portfolio with its focus on workers' compensation and employee insurance.

When CEO Stanley Zax decided to retire and take Zenith National Insurance private, Watsa knew there were many other insurance groups that would have loved to own the company. After all, it had a top-drawer reputation as a workers' compensation specialist. So, he pounced, paying a handsome premium over book and market value to quickly secure the deal. The timing was not ideal: Zenith was in the middle of a 50 percent retrenchment in premium writing, due to market conditions in the aftermath of the financial crisis. As a result, the company's initial earnings were terrible, with combined ratios of 136 percent, 128 percent, and 116 percent in the first three years. Cumulatively, Fairfax took a $300 million hit in underwriting losses during that stretch.

But Zax was upfront with Watsa and Fairfax about the tough road ahead. He rightly knew Fairfax was comfortable taking a long-term view, and would make the ideal patient parent to see his company through to better times without damaging the unique franchise he had spent decades building.

"All of that together led to one of the roughest patches we had been through in twenty years—just after we had some really great profitable years," says Kari Van Gundy, who took on the CEO role in 2014. "That was a really tough time for Fairfax, given that they paid a premium." By the time Van Gundy stepped fully into the role, the combined ratio was below 90 percent and Zenith was humming again.

"The culture alignment was really strong," says Van Gundy. "If you look at Prem's Guiding Principles, they were very similar to what we had at Zenith. I think the combination just reinforced them and made them stronger. Both companies believed in treating people well, doing the right thing, no egos. I think the one thing that we lacked as an explicit principle was having fun! We were so impressed with their patience and understanding during this time. It made us more motivated than ever to do well for them once the market moved in our direction."

The fallout

- *Management shows its intrinsic value.* Fairfax bought Zenith National Insurance when the company was driving into a three-year pothole, but management handled the challenge with the discipline and long-term thinking of a well-run insurer. That meant the company could sprint when it came out the other side. Not only did it soon become Fairfax's most profitable unit, but the growth was also the best kind: all organic. Workers' compensation runs on its own cycle, and it takes smart management to navigate, which was starkly evident in how the company handled the workplace upheaval brought on by the Covid-19 crisis.
- *Fair and friendly means avoiding layoffs.* There were a few layoffs on the investing side—where Fairfax remains centralized and lean (i.e., HWIC was not hiring on the investment team). Zenith National Insurance was proud of its record on retention and avoiding churn. Van Gundy says, "It's so hard to find really good people who make good decisions, treat others well, and want to stick around to build long term. In tech and other companies, you see cycles of mass hiring and mass layoffs. We don't operate that way. If any Fairfax company got in the news headlines because of layoffs, Prem would be very unhappy. It's a starting point that he expects us to run our companies so that we don't do that."

Major learning: No more shopping from the bargain bin

In completing its cleanest, highest quality acquisition to date, Fairfax had officially kicked its habit of buying insurer assets on the cheap—and it worked.

As market conditions improved, Zenith National Insurance's fortunes improved dramatically. It became one of Fairfax's most profitable companies, repaying the $300 million underwriting deficit and remaining one of the top players in the U.S. workers' compensation market.

Weathering that slump together brought the two companies closer. So, instead of spending a few years rebuilding senior management or fixing the underwriting strategy, Zenith National Insurance could keep its head down and make money. Some changes are inevitable after being bought, but it is a perfect way to prove your culture works, says Van Gundy.

"Culture is a word that gets thrown around a lot and there is a lot of hype about it. It starts with values and with the behaviours you want to nurture to keep those values in place. It's crucial to think about the long term—for the company as well as people's careers. You have to think about how people are treated in a downturn or when your company is bought." Van Gundy was CEO of Zenith until 2024 before moving into an executive chairman role and elevating Davidson Pattiz, former COO and now in his sixteenth year with Fairfax, into the corner office. She is in her sixteenth year with Fairfax and twenty-eighth with Zenith.

CASE SEVEN: MAKING A CLEAN SPLASH IN THE U.K. WITH BRIT PLC

Fairfax's acquisition of Brit PLC in 2015 brought a solid British footprint and diversification into the Lloyd's marketplace, where Fairfax previously had limited reach. It confirmed Fairfax's promise to buy only quality assets, and, unlike with Zenith National Insurance, there was no need to clean up underwriting problems or manage a retrenchment. The initial deal was rather straightforward. But the acquisition soon developed some unexpected corner office challenges: The Brit deal required a rethink when a small internal start-up exploded out of the gate.

Brit PLC CEO Mark Cloutier had known Watsa and Fairfax for decades, having worked with them on past deals before this one came together. The acquisition moved quickly with Fairfax making the purchase, and then selling a 30 percent chunk to OMERS to lighten the tab. (It bought back that minority stake in late 2024.) Cloutier moved into a chairman's role in 2017 before leaving the company. Leadership fell to Matthew Wilson, Brit PLC's chief underwriting officer, who had to navigate through a rough stretch of catastrophes.

Wilson was getting the house in order when he fell ill in 2021 to blood cancer. Watsa, who was instrumental in getting Wilson diagnosed and treated, asked Wilson who he thought would be ideal to step in, and Wilson picked Martin Thompson.

Martin who? The Martin Thompson story is classic Watsa. Earlier that year, Thompson had reached out to Peter Clarke at Fairfax when a merger at his firm in Canada left him exploring new options. Watsa found him to be ideal Fairfax leadership material, and Thompson quickly found himself in a strange negotiation that didn't seem to involve an actual job.

"Culture was all he wanted to talk about," Thompson says. "He spent some time explaining decentralization, long-term thinking and how to treat people right. In listening to it—I have to be honest—I thought this can't be for real. That's not the business world I came up in. His perspective was [the] polar opposite." So was the recruitment, which ran a lot like this over the course of a few Sunday video calls during peak Covid-19 lockdowns:

Watsa: "You gotta join us, Martin. You'd be a great fit for our culture."

Thompson: "I would love to join you, but what's the job?"

Watsa: "We don't have one, but we think you'd be a great fit for the culture."

Thompson: "I am flattered but don't feel comfortable joining a business where I don't have a role. Maybe you could give me a ring when something comes up?"

(One week later.)

Watsa: "Okay, how's this? Come aboard. I think we are going to buy you a company, probably in western Europe."

A few days later, formal job offer in hand, Thompson still wondered if it was just a weird recruitment strategy: "I understood the words he was saying, I just didn't know what it would look like to work at a company like that. But I was curious. So, after a little due diligence, I said yes. Then, after a few meetings, I realized it was real."

The fallout

- *Bottomline impact.* In 2015, when Brit PLC's results were included in Fairfax's reporting, the company reported a solid combined ratio of 94.9 percent—right in line with its ten-year average—that made it an instant contributor to earnings. Its $1.63 billion in net premiums put it almost equal to Crum & Forster, with only Odyssey above them. Strategically, a few underwriting strategies needed some tinkering: decisions such as figuring out how deeply Brit PLC wanted to get into delegated selling of premiums and, more importantly, how the company could reduce its exposure to disaster risk. Thompson and team dramatically scaled back Brit PLC's exposure to the underperforming segments, while ramping up where prices had hardened.
- *Cultural shift.* Management says the transition into the Fairfax tent was aided by a major culture reset. The company had previously been operating under private equity ownership (Apollo Management and CVC Capital Partners), a dynamic that tends to encourage sweating to meet short-term goals. Under Fairfax, "fair and friendly" thinking took hold.

Major learning: Hire talent for a rainy day

This was a new tactic for Watsa. With Odyssey, he had once bought a company—and then a few more to combine with it—without even having a leader in mind to run the new monster. Only afterward did he find a genius by the name of Andy Barnard, along with his talented colleague, Brian Young. This time around, however, Watsa was trying out the reverse tactic of hiring key talent and then trying to figure out what to do with them. He hadn't expected cancer to be the wild-card catalyst in terms of what Thompson would ultimately do at Fairfax.

Thompson clearly was not interviewing for the CEO role at Brit PLC, but Wilson had seen enough to gauge his talent before he fell ill. Now in his fifth year with Fairfax in 2025, Thompson still finds himself shaking his head from time to time at the whole experience: "Prem is a very unconventional figure, unlike any I've ever experienced in the market."

Brit PLC is clearly a standout blue-chip for Fairfax, and Mark Cloutier and Matthew Wilson deserve a lot of credit for rebuilding its brand under the Fairfax umbrella, says Clarke. "It was amazing to have talent at the calibre of Martin to be able to step in and carry the ball. And he showed his experience in management and as an underwriter to raise Brit's game even higher."

Thompson's arrival coincided with yet another big learning moment on decentralization and digital innovation, with the rapid, successful rollout of Ki Syndicate 1618. Led by Mark Allan and Wilson, Ki was incubated as a digital platform that could leverage technology to juice up the so-called "follow-on market," where insurance could be sold as an supplement to existing policies instead of originating it from scratch. It launched in 2021 and is enjoying explosive growth. "No one really knew if it would be a success, never mind become a billion-dollar company in three years," says Thompson. The company quickly realized Ki had become too big to live within Brit PLC. By January 2025, it began a decentralized life as a standalone reporting firm within Fairfax.

CASE EIGHT: ALLIED WORLD TICKS ALL THE BOXES

Allied World was a game changer, pushing Fairfax into the global big leagues. Some of the abovementioned case studies stand out because of how Fairfax made strategic exceptions to its decentralized approach, like Northbridge and Odyssey. However, the Allied World acquisition stands out for how decentralization won the day on every count.

Barnard points out that Allied World's mix of business lines already overlapped with a lot of other Fairfax companies. The assumption was that Fairfax would break it up. "Allied was a mirror image to Odyssey, in that each was exposed to both insurance and reinsurance, Allied more so to the former and Odyssey to the latter. And with Crum, Allied overlapped again by participating in some of the same market segments in the U.S."

Allied World had come up for sale because management felt it had peaked, and there was disagreement on which way to go next. In numerous merger discussions, the most common analysis was how Allied would be carved up to fit into its prospective acquirer's assets. When Fairfax introduced itself, Barnard recalls, then-CEO Scott Carmilani just assumed the reinsurance assets were destined to be immediately hived off to Odyssey. But Watsa made it clear he had no intention of deviating from his M & A playbook this time.

Watsa's unconventional thinking got the attention of Lou Iglesias, the current CEO of Allied. Iglesias and his team wanted to build the company with Allied's teams intact. They listened intently as Prem opened up about the Fairfax approach, and the commitment to have its companies run separately. It was a different way of thinking and, while they at first had their doubts about whether Watsa and Fairfax would follow through, Iglesias and his team were ultimately won over by the strategy.

"Generally, a large driver of doing a takeover is to keep the business and save money. It might make sense on the surface, but seldom works out," Iglesias asserts. "The buyer winds up losing key people and the business. Whatever expense savings are made come at the larger cost of dissipating the business. At Fairfax, expense management is left entirely to the company CEOs rather than directed from Toronto. While we were able to streamline our own company, and reduce all the extra costs that come with being public, we were not required to chase additional savings from acquisition synergies."

The fallout

- *The numbers tell the whole story.* Five years in, Allied had already doubled its premiums—organically—and accounted for more than a third of Fairfax-wide underwriting profits. Allied joined Odyssey as another crown jewel.
- *Very few goodbyes.* The changeover included the departure of only half a dozen senior executives. "There was some of that that had to happen," offers Iglesias. "But it was very limited."
- *Culture was a big fit.* The culture was not a hard sell on those who remained. "Honestly, it seems obvious," says Iglesias. "Who doesn't want to live by the values of a company that declares people should live by strong values in their work lives and personal lives?"

Major learning: The definitive case in favour of decentralization

The history of Allied at Fairfax has been a persuasive win for decentralization. The company has since more than doubled in size. It is delivering underwriting profits at record levels. This acquisition stands out for being the biggest, most successful, and most impactful deal Fairfax has completed. The bargain bin was nowhere in sight and Fairfax chased off every competing rationale for a breakup or combination of assets. In the end, they got the people and the culture they wanted to protect.

They still had to win the new Allied team over to the Fairfax Way. Allied's experience was that rationalized synergies were an inevitable part of dealmaking. There were lingering doubts about whether Fairfax would be willing and able to keep its promise.

"During my annual visit to Allied World several years after we closed, I got the shock of my life when employees were asking me questions about merging pieces of the company with one or another Fairfax company. We never had any intention of doing so, but, I suppose, the company had been so conditioned to expect that outcome, it took a while to dislodge." They believe him now.

The reality is, conventional thinking is lodged in so deep that even someone like Barnard was slow to fully convert. "I was not always as passionate a defender of the approach as I am today," he says. "I used to think it was more important to concentrate each of our businesses behind our leading edge. For example, all workers' compensation should be written at Zenith National Insurance. Over the years, and continually counseled by Prem, I have come to appreciate the benefits of our empowered decentralized structure far outweigh the alternative."

Those actions will also send a fair and friendly message to the market: Fairfax is worth calling if any company were ever considering selling, offers Iglesias. "The way Prem does it, he can attract companies that are strong and don't need fixing and then grow them organically. It's a great model. It's also going to attract strong people. And the people who stay are the ones who see that. The people who endorse those values are going to be quality people."

CASE NINE: A NEW GLOBAL GIANT IN GIG

Gulf Insurance (GIG) was a classic patience-followed-by-pounce deal made possible by Fairfax's efforts to build out its network—and assets—globally. In 2008, it started small by picking up stakes in Arab Orient in Jordan and Alliance Insurance in Dubai.

Earlier, in Japan, Chandran Ratnaswami had connected with Fuji Fire and Marine Insurance CEO Bijan Khosrowshahi. Ratnaswami was impressed with him and let Watsa and Salsberg know back in Toronto. The following year, Khosrowshahi was exploring a new role, and it was Watsa's turn to be impressed, so much so that he seized the opportunity to bring him on to run what would eventually become Fairfax International, something which had yet to be invented. As with Thompson, Watsa was hiring for quality and culture, rather than for a job opening.

Watsa had his man, and it was up to fate to help him find the opportunity to put that man to work. In 2010, the two attended an industry event in Jordan, had tea with an ex–prime minister, and were introduced to Faisal Al Ayyar, who was vice-chair of KIPCO, a holding company that, in addition to having ties with the Saudi royal family, had an 82 percent stake in Gulf Insurance. Khosrowshahi and Jean Cloutier, the two-man team slated to run Fairfax International, quickly initiated due diligence on Gulf Insurance. "Before we could really get started, Prem said he and Faisal had already shaken hands on a deal," says Khosrowshahi. The deal gave just over 40 percent each to Fairfax and KIPCO.

The fallout

- *Patience and the first pounce.* Arab Orient was sold to GIG, where gross premiums reached $417 million. Fairfax sat back, made Khosrowshahi its point man, and watched the holding grow. That was the patient part. A decade later, in its first pounce, GIG bought AXA's regional assets, and the combined firm had premiums of about $2.6 billion with operations in thirteen countries in the Middle East and North Africa.
- *Time for the big pounce.* Sheikha Dana Naser Al Sabah, who had replaced Al Ayyar at KIPCO, decided to sell GIG and shift to other investments. For just under $900 million, Fairfax acquired KIPCO's 46 percent, added it to its own 44 percent, and then increased its ownership to 97 percent by buying out most of the minority shareholder base. "Our strategy of waiting for the phone to ring continues!" quipped Watsa in his letter.
- *A new heavyweight.* GIG is now Fairfax's fifth largest insurer by gross premiums, after Allied World, Odyssey, Crum & Forster, and Brit PLC. Gross premiums reached $2.74 billion, 8 percent of the company-wide total, and it contributes $2.34 billion toward Fairfax's investment portfolio. When Khosrowshahi joined in 2009, Fairfax's total premiums stood at $5.1 billion.

Major learnings: A portable culture works best for decentralized global expansion

Now in his sixteenth year with Fairfax, Khosrowshahi emphasizes just how portable Fairfax culture is: "We have seen the culture get embraced at companies around the world, and that is no small feat because there are added sensitivities between national cultures and languages. What amazes me, actually, is that Fairfax Guiding Principles and fair-and-friendly thinking is totally at home in all cultures around the world. That has been a real strength for us."

The core relationship between subsidiary and head office is much the same as with other insurers in the Fairfax group—with a few notable wrinkles. Cultural differences between the Middle East and the West are a factor to consider, and independent management at GIG runs its own show under CEO Khaled Saoud Al Hasan, now in his sixteenth year with Fairfax and forty-eighth with Gulf. The GIG team had more than a decade to see how Fairfax liked to operate, felt about succession, and worked the Guiding Principles in real life. GIG flourished.

GIG Gulf (the former AXA assets) represents yet another layer of decentralization. That company, whose financials are reported together with Gulf, has totally separate ex-pat management, led by Paul Adamson as CEO, now in his fifth year with Fairfax and twenty-fifth with GIG Gulf and its predecessor. "They definitely still had their doubts about how they would be integrated into not just the parent company in the Middle East but Fairfax itself," says Khosrowshahi. "They had the nice surprise to see that Fairfax walks its talk."

Khosrowshahi was tempted by past experience to seek synergies but Fairfax resisted. "It was tempting to combine some operations. But we didn't because, with Prem's urging, messing around like that undermines the culture that made those operations a success in the first place."

Chapter Nineteen

DOING GOOD BY DOING WELL

"We think capitalism is great, but it can be even better with compassion." —Prem Watsa

When Watsa and Salsberg talked in the early days about building a "good" company, they had a simple idea about how that good would cycle through in what they did. You start with making money by providing a valuable service, while ensuring you treat people right. Then you share the wealth where you make it.

"Very simply, we truly think of business as a good thing," explains Watsa. "By providing outstanding service to our customers, looking after employees, providing a return for shareholders, and then redirecting a portion of the profits into the communities we serve, we think business can be a calling."

In the early days, the two kicked around a few alternatives on the best approach for the company on giving. They wanted it to be enshrined like the Guiding Principles and to continue for the life of the company. They came up with the basic plan that set a target of 1 percent on pre-tax income and directed contributions in a decentralized way to the communities in which Fairfax did business. The logic to the formula was that charitable giving would be tied to profits. The formula was deliberate—you need to make money in order to have something to share, and the more Fairfax made, the more it would share. A few decades later, Watsa doubled the target to 2 percent, as part of the commitment to, as he likes to say, do good by doing well.

"I think those words really capture how we wanted to achieve success as a company," he offers. "This is why we consider business a force for good and why countries that are business-friendly succeed mightily. We are a small microcosm of what business does worldwide."

Each year, Watsa likes to update a running tally on what Fairfax's efforts have yielded. As revenue and profit growth kicks into a higher gear, those numbers are compounding considerably. To date, it has written $290 billion in premiums. Annual salaries total $2.6 billion and the company has paid $7.1 billion in taxes.

The annual donations program, which kicked off in 1991 with $200,000, has cumulatively reached nearly half a billion dollars and compounding is working its magic: The 2 percent target was $80 million for 2024 and Fairfax kicked in some extra to reach $95 million. "Over the 34 years since we began our donations program, our annual donations have gone up approximately 550 times at a compound rate of 20 percent per year," Watsa notes in his 2024 letter.

Whatever the recent political strains in the U.S., Watsa believes that conservatism has a strong history around making sure capitalism shares the wealth, as he told me in a 2021 interview: "I love how George Bush talked about a 'compassionate conservatism,' which is the idea that if you do well, you have a responsibility to give back," he said. "Because if you think you did it all by yourself, you didn't. I see our opportunities and advantages as blessings and you have to give back. As the Good Book says, 'To whom much is given, much is expected.'"

GIVING, THE DECENTRALIZED AND TRANSPARENT WAY

Two years ago, Fairfax debuted a separate annual charitable report to showcase its activities, which are broken down by geographic region. At the parent holding company itself, the bulk of its donations are made to Fairfax foundations, which the company expects to become self-funding at some point. It also matches on employee charity contributions. In offering more transparency into how the company gives, Watsa reasons, Fairfax wants employees to see the impact of their giving and be inspired to give more.

Companies are encouraged to hit their 2 percent target individually, which is no problem in the mature North American assets but harder elsewhere. The general policy is for the insurers to split their 2 percent evenly between charities in the communities where they operate and Fairfax foundations. If companies cannot hit the target, the holding company makes up the difference. "As these companies mature, we expect they will all eventually fund their full 2 percent directly," says Watsa.

The corporate donation policy is only one formal piece of the giving at Fairfax and for Watsa and others at the company individually, in India as well as Canada. Watsa has been a big supporter for SickKids hospital where he sat on the board and worked wonders with the performance of the hospital's foundation fund. He served as chancellor at the University of Waterloo and at Huron University, where Fairfax recently donated C$10 million to create the Fairfax Centre for Free Enterprise. Watsa leveraged the SickKids connection in creating a connection between the Toronto hospital and a new $40-million children's hospital Fairfax is funding in Vellore, India.

One of the organizations he is particularly passionate about is the Horatio Alger Association, which recognizes those who have pushed themselves to entrepreneurial and other achievements, as well as to provide needs-based scholarships to students who are pulling themselves up. He is sitting president of the Canadian chapter. The idea of an extra boost to those future leaders who need a leg up holds special appeal to Watsa: "It means they will be in the position to achieve business success and be able to lift others as well, as a compounding effect of giving back. Some of us, whether by birth or parenting or geography, don't get the opportunity. And all of us who are doing well should have compassion for them."

As the money grows, so does the job of managing the foundations, which includes the family foundation as well. Stephanie Watsa, Prem's youngest child, is sitting in the middle of those efforts with a seat on both the Fairfax and Watsa charity boards. When one generation makes this much money, it takes a lot of people to step up and nurture the legacy to make it as impactful as possible. That's giving as a calling.

Chapter Twenty

SUCCESSION AND LONG-TERM CONTROL

"As you know, we are building Fairfax for the next 100 years (long after I am gone, I think!!)." —*Prem Watsa*

It's hard enough to build a company to last a generation. How about a century? How about two? Or, a more pressing issue, how do you manage the corporate handover involving a founder whose vision is behind Fairfax's remarkable story? The issue of succession has been on Watsa's mind for as long as Fairfax has been around. But in recent years, the seventy-five-year-old entrepreneur has elevated its priority. These days, he spends a lot of time digging into best practices for corporate longevity to see what has worked for others.

The statistics on survival appear to be against him. When it comes to large public firms globally, corporate lifespan is often rendered as tenure on the Fortune 500 or S&P 500 composite. When Watsa was born, the average tenure of a firm on the major U.S. index was over sixty years. Today, it's less than twenty. Of course, companies grow and shrink their way on or off the index, and they also get taken over or split themselves into pieces. In his search for insights, Watsa's preferred strategy is to find admirable companies that are still alive past the century mark and then see how closely their strategies line up.

Books that have turned up on his bedside table for research include *The Living Company: Habits for Survival in a Turbulent Business Environment* by Arie de Geus and *Lessons from Century Club Companies: Managing for Long-Term Success* by Vicki TenHaken. In his 2020 letter, he shared a four-point summary of major takeaways from the two books. Uncannily, the characteristics of successful companies he distilled read like they could have been lifted from Fairfax's own Guiding Principles:

1. They are sensitive to the business environment, so that they always provide outstanding customer service.
2. They have a strong culture—a strong sense of identity that encompasses not only the employees but also the community and everyone they deal with. Managers are chosen from the inside and considered stewards of the enterprise.
3. They are decentralized, refraining from centralized control.
4. They are conservatively financed, recognizing the advantage of having spare cash in the kitty.

"These messages really resonated with me," Watsa says. "There is a lot written on the subject, but I think the basic guidelines are simple ones. And I would say retaining trust is at the centre of long-term success. Maintaining that for any length of time takes discipline, hard work, and maybe a little luck."

Survival is an ultimate measure of performance success. One point TenHaken makes is companies that pass one hundred years in age tend to survive because they never lose sight of the fact that an organization is a community of humans with institutional memory and not just one of economic activity. Companies that focus only on economic activity, she argues, are likely to die prematurely.

One of the most popular books on corporate longevity is *Built to Last: Successful Habits of Visionary Companies,* written in 1994 by Jim Collins and Jerry Porras. It has since borne the brunt of criticism as many of its celebrated subject companies subsequently went into decline. Many of its insights, however, are in sync with the Fairfax Way when it comes to singling out "cult-like cultures" and promoting management from within as markers for longevity.

Success stories involving the longest-living companies fascinate Watsa. The German Merck family, for example, founded its industrial, pharmaceutical, and banking empire back in 1668 and is still at it. At this point, Watsa is just trying to set up a role for the second generation and is about thirteen generations behind Merck, which has a family university to train siblings and cousins to be future executives. Any thoughts about a Watsa University will be for future generations to ponder.

"Prem has always had the idea that Fairfax should endure and the team has done what they can to build it to last. We watch him spend a lot of time studying companies to see what works over a long, long time," says Brian Bradstreet. "For all of us, one of the advantages of working on the investment side is you get to see a lot of corporate models of what works and what doesn't. Culture is crucial to success, but it is a challenging thing to keep it intact. It is always a work-in-progress. We have grown a lot, but we are capable of growing a lot more. We have to keep working on it."

THE HOLDING COMPANY CONUNDRUM

In Fairfax's unwritten contract with shareholders, management control of the company is non-negotiable. It is also permanent and therefore a key part of Fairfax continuing its life long after Watsa's passing.

Dual-class structures were traditionally common with holding companies, where a parent holdco held multiple independently run subsidiaries, often in entirely different sectors. A key reason people used to love holdcos was the diversification they brought. In recent decades, however, there has been pressure on companies to drop dual-class control. Critics figure the structure is prone to entrenching weak management and underperformance. And although conglomerates once commanded a higher multiple on share price, these days they tend to trade at a shareholder-unfriendly discount to the value of the assets they hold.

The market likes pure plays. So, who likes holding company structures then? Well, value-minded contrarian CEOs with unconventional, long-term asset allocation strategies like Watsa. Buffett, for one, argues that holdcos are cheaper to run and therefore good for shareholders. In his case, he says shareholders save on the money that would be spent on "money shufflers"—the cross-departmental teams who drive strategy simply to justify their jobs and pay themselves bonuses. "If the conglomerate form is used judiciously, it is an ideal structure for maximizing long-term capital," he has said. "Even tax-free institutional investors face major costs as they move capital because they usually need intermediaries to do this job. A lot of mouths with expensive tastes then clamor to be fed—among them investment bankers, accountants, consultants, lawyers and such capital-reallocators as leveraged buyout operators. Money-shufflers don't come cheap."

Watsa, whose M & A team always consisted of just him and Salsberg, stands with Buffett. Watsa especially likes to tout the advantages of Fairfax having capital allocation done at the central holding company for all subsidiaries, rather than having each of those companies do it themselves. It is the one area he would never want to see decentralized.

THE ART OF BEQUEATHING CONTROL

In the early days, Watsa put a provision in his will that his holding would be maintained by his family and in the unlikely event that the family needed to sell, that transaction would require Salsberg's consent. Later, Watsa explored the idea that he could pass on his wealth through a charity trust structure. But the more he thought about it and learned from people like the Waltons at Walmart, he decided that was not attractive because it would fail to safeguard control.

"You can leave the asset in the control of a charity," says Watsa, "but it's really only a matter of time before it gets divested. For that reason, I decided control has to be with the family." Once that decision was made, Watsa focused on hammering out details with legal advisors on the best way to structure the family trust. There need to be added advisors working with the family, and all that had to be written up in detail. And there needed to be restrictions on the role of the family, with none of them acting in an executive management role. Watsa sees inevitable pressures coming at Fairfax. "I think our family-control strategy will easily shoot down any breakup proposals," he says. "But you know there will be other kinds of incremental pressure at some point in the future. Someone, not just some private equity outsider but even someone on our board, is going to look at Allied, Odyssey, and Crum and see separate departments for legal, for underwriting and finance, and they are going to do the math and make a case to just put the companies all together. It may be in ten years, twenty years, or thirty when I am not there. And self-interested people are going to make the case for selling companies outright."

Barnard says the scenario of a takeover and breakup of Fairfax by corporate raiders with dollar signs in their eyes is the nightmare the company has to do everything in its power to guard against: "I joke with Prem that if it ever came to pass that private equity took over Fairfax, they would just be licking their chops at all the costs they could see taking out. It would look massive and probably look great in PowerPoint presentations. What would be missing are all the intangible benefits of people that would disappear."

What else could stop those ideas before they get started? One reason Watsa was open to co-operating on this book was to allow the full history to be told of what made Fairfax so successful over time: "I would hope the Guiding Principles will short-circuit that kind of thinking. And the book can help. If some smart person comes in and tries to break up the company, there will be a clear case for why they should not."

Many family-controlled companies have been torn apart by greed and grievance as control shifts between generations, but Ben Watsa figures that kind of internecine warfare stoked by outside activists has zero chance of getting traction with his sisters or him. It's happened with all kinds of prominent family-controlled companies like the Murdochs at News Corp., but it won't happen at Fairfax, he says. "We have seen it when different family members have different ideas about stepping in and taking the company in a different direction. It's a tough game out there. But that is off the table for us."

Christine McLean, the middle Watsa child, has served on the Fairfax board since 2018, while her brother was nominated in 2014. She sees the family presence acting as stewards of the culture in a future without her father at Fairfax. Together with the rest of the board, the relationship with whoever is in the CEO role is going to be crucial. "It's a very close-knit relationship for alignment while also standing back," she says. "You have to trust each other. Your interests are aligned, but you should be supportive versus controlling. The family doesn't work there." Of course, Fairfax should never be afraid of risk or change, she stresses, but never at the expense of decentralization and internal succession. "As stewards, not owners, we would trust the CEO if there was a scenario where there is a different way of doing something. We can't make the decisions that a CEO should be making."

Ben, forty-six, has been managing money under his own firm, Marval Capital Ltd., since 2017, taking a value approach and now focusing on Indian assets. After following in his father's footsteps as an institutional value manager—and sporting the top returns among institutional funds in Canada in the five years to June of 2025 for his Marval Guru Fund—Ben has been groomed for years to take on a bigger role at Fairfax. After a decade's experience on the board, Ben took a major step up in responsibilities in 2024 by taking over for his father as chairman at Fairfax India Holdings. The elder Watsa kept his seat as a director, as part of a broader shuffle that saw CEO Chandran Ratnaswami shift into an executive vice-chairman role where he would groom the younger Watsa while also overseeing Gopal Soundarajan, who moved from COO to CEO, and Sumit Maheshwari, who manages the company's assets directly as CEO of Fairbridge Capital.

Watsa says the plan is set to have Ben replace him as chairman at Fairfax Holdings but the timing is open: "I have absolutely no plans to step away from the company, but it's important that shareholders and the company know there is a plan for continuity and to promote the culture of the Fairfax Way. It's not like I will be ruling from the grave, but I will die knowing the culture will continue to flourish and Fairfax and its main companies will never be sold."

Watsa continues to work with lawyers to make sure he leaves the company's affairs in the best shape for the next generation. That means passing control to his family and avoiding a hefty tax bill in the process, which is where the trusts come in. Today, Watsa personally controls 43.3 percent of the votes through 1,548,000 multiple-voting shares and 519,919 subordinate voting shares of Fairfax.

SUCCESSION, CONTINUITY, AND PETER CLARKE

What is particularly satisfying for Watsa, especially as he loses some close colleagues, friends, and partners to illness and advancing years, is that a younger management team has really gelled in the past five years to one day run the show without him.

As the old guard gets older, the pace of succession has picked up dramatically. Andy Barnard has moved up to allow Brian Young to move into the senior executive role for the insurance group. Roger Lace and Brian Bradstreet are still active but passing the knowledge to Wade Burton, age fifty-four, and Lawrence Chin, forty-nine. While Watsa is learning how to step back more and play more of a "grandfather" role, he remains front and centre, alongside Peter Clarke, on allocation strategy such as investments, buybacks, and bolt-ons.

Clarke is the one executive that Fairfax's closest watchers have been getting to know slowly—and who is perhaps the lowest-profile president of any major company in Canada. Clarke, fifty-four, is happy with that. A product of the Fairfax Way, he has grown up at the company.

"I have a bit of a unique role in that I am on both sides of the balance sheet. Investing and insurance operations," explains Clarke. "I started as an actuary, working with the insurance companies on reserving and on acquisitions. As I progressed, I took on responsibility for the rating agencies, then for the overall operations, investments, and risk management. I look at how the investment side ties back to the insurance side. I am not that involved in identifying the investments themselves. We have Hamblin Watsa to handle that. That's Roger, Brian, and Prem, now with Wade and Lawrence."

As CEO-in-waiting, Clarke knows it could be a long wait for someone like Watsa to step aside. He is in no hurry and continues to confidently run the matrix of moving parts of a major global company as it approaches C$60 billion in value. Everyone inside Fairfax knows who he is, and now that Fairfax is attracting attention again, Clarke and Burton are getting more public visibility. The two double-team it as hosts on the quarterly conference calls, taking over from Watsa.

As a product of the culture, Clarke is a perfect ambassador for decentralization. In his role, he is the only person, other than Watsa, who leads on both the operational side with the insurers and the investment side with HWIC. Mild-mannered, thoughtful, and wickedly smart, he is a Clark Kent type without the complicated baggage of having a superhero alter ego. "I would say Rock of Gibraltar," says Bill McFarland, the company's lead director. "He is strong as hell, knows the whole business, and has the right style to fit the culture of the company." It is now only a few years that the company has had that person in place, he adds.

When Rivett exited the president's role, Watsa woke up to the fact that Fairfax's true future leader was the guy next to him: "We took awhile to realize it but Peter had already been doing the job as president. I can't think of anyone who is stronger at representing the culture at Fairfax. He is super smart and has no ego whatsoever."

Clarke's rise is perhaps Fairfax's best-imaginable case study of grooming internal talent. Salsberg said he and Clarke were regularly tasked by Watsa over the years to tackle projects and oversight of the insurance subsidiaries together. Their combined talents were formidable but Watsa had an ulterior motive. He had always relied on Salsberg's opinion in everything, including the assessment of character, judgment, and management ability. As he and Clarke dug into things and came up with improvements, Salsberg said he quickly noticed a pattern: Issues were solved quickly and everyone walked away feeling like they'd played a key role. He discovered Clarke had grasped the deeper challenge quickly and then helped ferry others across the river to come to the same conclusion through their own thinking and contributions.

"Peter understood everything better than I did," said Salsberg. "But he modestly never acted like it, and he makes people feel like they did it themselves. He never needs to take the credit. He grew up in this culture. He breathes it. If Prem were somehow out of the picture, I have no doubt Peter would do a fantastic job. He understands insurance and how to allocate capital across all our companies. Of course, he is not the founder. No one else can be the founder."

So how does a guy who never worked anywhere else even know how lucky he is? It helps to work at a firm that is constantly investigating other companies. "I started in 1997," says Clarke, "so Fairfax is actually the only company I have worked for in my professional career. And yet I have looked at so many companies over the years in the role of investor or acquirer, I've seen first-hand how different it is. The key difference—and one of our biggest strengths—is the culture and the decentralized structure."

That major edge and how it builds depth of talent should never be underestimated, Clarke asserts. "Each of the operating companies at Fairfax has its own CEO/president, CFO, chief risk officer plus leads for the underwriting and actuary teams. This set-up allows each firm to attract very talented senior people. They love running their own companies. These are leaders who would be running their own companies even out from under the Fairfax umbrella. Being part of Fairfax gives them long-term certainty as far as the strategic plan and the commitment to back it. They can build for the long term. So it really is the best of both worlds."

The era of messy bargain buying of assets is over and that suggests less drama ahead. "That is the period where we really had to work through," he offers on the troublesome turnarounds. "Looking back today, I am not sure we would have done it differently. But our focus today is on buying quality assets, not just value on a book value basis. Today, we can grow premium organically and there is a lot less uncertainty with that approach than with doing acquisitions. If we consider acquisitions on the insurance side, they are more likely to be smaller bolt-ons, and they are going to be high-quality assets rather than turnarounds." (If the company's shares continue to trade below whatever intrinsic value Watsa has in his head, a lot of money will also keep going to buybacks.)

Clarke says he learned first-hand the advantage of having a creative founder-CEO in absolute control over the vision: "There would have been many times where if we weren't so focused on the long term, other people in Prem's position would have felt pushed to sell off some core assets to fix things more quickly for short-term results."

The fact that Fairfax was tested in many ways and disciplined enough to meet the challenge is a major part of the legacy Watsa will leave on culture, says Clarke. Those tests defined a clear Fairfax Way to manage for everyone. It is hard to imagine a Fairfax without Prem Watsa, but Clarke insists the group has had thirty-nine years with a consistent strategy for all the lessons to sink in.

"You have never had a change in strategy. You don't have a company with a new CEO every five years and a new vision to do things differently. Our companies don't have to worry about the top line and meeting quarterly targets to keep the Street happy. Other organizations can really struggle with direction when there is a change at the top. We all know the direction here."

ACKNOWLEDGMENTS

The Fairfax Way is an appropriately unconventional book for an unconventional company. What made most sense was to begin with a corporate and personal history that laid out the foundations for this incredible story. Then, in the second half, to take the reader deeper into Fairfax's value philosophy, explaining how the company invests, as well as the management strategy the company has nurtured to foster a unique corporate culture built on trust and in doing the right thing. It's almost two books in one, which I hope makes it a good start in playing catch-up on a story that has remained inaccessible for far too long.

The way this book came into being was also unconventional. Warren Buffett often speaks about an inner scorecard where you can track how you live up to your own principles. Prem Watsa's scorecard includes loyalty to one's principles, doing his absolute best, controlling what he can, and letting his actions speak for themselves. Wholly absent is self-promotion; he was circumspect about the idea of a public book. I invested the time to understand the Fairfax story, then I started writing *The Fairfax Way* with his cooperation but no guarantee there would be a public book. He certainly didn't want it for the publicity. He wanted it if I could understand the future they have been trying to build for the past four decades.

In the end, the company gave me the freedom to decide how to tackle this book. They were generously open and candid in sharing their ups and downs. So, a big thank you to Prem Watsa and his team. Also, a big thank you to Rick Broadhead, my invaluable agent, and the editors at Penguin Canada, who helped polish this undertaking within tight deadlines—once its publishing fate was secured.

Endless appreciation and love to Maggie. Thank you for your patience during our discussions on long-tail liability, yield curves, and retrenching strategy in a soft market. I am also indebted to the grace of 'Lord and Lady of Otterburn,' who created the opportunity for me to break the back of this venture in a bucolic setting with ginger biscuits, burgundy, a goat with its own Instagram account, and a quiet place to write and rest my temporarily homeless head.

There was an earlier, shorter, privately published book written on Fairfax's first twenty-five years, written by Ron Graham. I want to acknowledge that undertaking—it offers insight into the early days, and I made sure to weave some of its quotes into this book to bring them into public record.

NOTES

Direct quotes and attributions from extensive interviews with primary Fairfax executives and Watsa family sources are not included here, except when they provide additional context. Most of these interviews were conducted in 2023 and 2024.

Quotes and attributions from Watsa's letters to shareholders are also not included here, unless the year of the letter was not mentioned in the text.

PART ONE: THE FORMATIVE YEARS: FROM INDIA TO CANADA

CHAPTER ONE: Watsa's Road to Value Investing

12 **"We've worked very hard purposely to avoid speaking to the media . . ."** From Watsa's speech accepting the 1999 Ivey Business Leader Award in Toronto.

The little kid from Hyderabad

13 **The Watsa family history in India** is based on interviews, augmented by Ryan Touhey's book on Watsa family history: *Faith, Fortitude and Family: The Watsas* (Toronto: Navo Chinoy, 2019). Touhey is associate professor and chair of the department of history, St. Jerome's, at the University of Waterloo, Ontario.

14 **"Attracting a Brahmin in 1857 . . ."** Touhey, 31.

16 **"Immigrating to new countries requires fortitude, curiosity . . ."** Ibid., 86–7.

The immigrant's experience

20 **Details on Watsa's brief experience in appliance sales** are from interviews and from Peter Kuitenbrouwer, "Fairfax Financial Ltd. Chief Prem Watsa Tells His 'Horatio Alger' Story," *Financial Post*, May 22, 2015.

The road to Damascus—via King and Bay

27 Ben Graham classics including:

Benjamin Graham and David Dodd, *Security Analysis*, McGraw Hill, 2023. First published in 1934; the latest (7th) edition is edited by Seth Klarman with new outside contributions.

Benjamin Graham, *The Intelligent Investor*, HarperCollins, 2006. Revised edition, with 1973 edition text by Graham. First edition published in 1949. Includes chapter-by-chapter commentary by Jason Zweig from the Wall Street Journal. A revised edition was released in 2024.

"It either grabs you immediately, or it never grabs you at all"

Several quotes about the early days at Fairfax first appeared in the company's private book written by Ron Graham, *The First 25 Years of Fairfax*, Fairfax Financial, 2010. They include quotes by:

Roger Lace: "Prem was very outspoken, very enthusiastic . . . ," 17.

Paul Fink: "He's like a pit bull . . . ," 28.

Lace: "He took some pretty big positions . . . ," 18.

"Come on out into the real world and play"

More from Graham, *The First 25 Years of Fairfax*:

31 Tony Arrell: "You're not an institutional kind of guy . . . ," 19.

32 Tony Hamblin: "There is a big difference between a good analyst . . . ," 21.

32 Hamblin: "We both wanted . . . ," 21.

Now what?

33 Napoleon Hill, *Think and Grow Rich*, Random House, 1960. First published in 1937.

33 "This is a capitalistic country . . . ," 115.

34 "Definitiveness of purpose," 136.

35 "For what shall it profit a man . . ." The Bible, Mark 8:36.

"I think this is going to be a really bad investment"

43 **Fink's quote: "What you have to realize about Prem front and centre is that . . ."** Graham, *The First 25 Years of Fairfax*, 28.

PART TWO: THE DEALMAKING MACHINE: PUTTING THE PIECES TOGETHER

CHAPTER TWO: Let's Buy Some Float (1985–1988)

A dramatic win on trucking

50 **"There is no question that the insurance cycle is on the downswing," Watsa told shareholders . . .** Watsa, Letter to Shareholders, 1986.

Markel becomes Fairfax Financial

54 **"You may be surprised to know that [the new name] did not come . . ."** Watsa, Letter to Shareholders, 1986.

CHAPTER THREE: Growing Pains and Mea Culpas (1989–1992)

The saga of Morden & Helwig

63 **"To really rub salt into the wound . . ."** Watsa, Letter to Shareholders, 2007.

The gory details from FCA

64 **"I would rather not comment on one of my major mistakes in the past decade . . ."** Watsa, Letter to Shareholders, 1998.

Love and hate—and Walwyn

64 **"To our surprise," Watsa would quip, "this purchase really took the press's fancy . . ."** Watsa, Letter to Shareholders, 1989.

65 **"We believe that over the long term Walwyn will . . ."** Watsa, Letter to Shareholders, 1989.

65 **"We are no longer in the high-profile stock brokerage business . . ."** and quotes on the aftermath and exit of the investment. Watsa, Letter to Shareholders, 1990.

Learning to manage volatility

71 **"A word about our press and/or investor relations department . . ."** Watsa, Letter to Shareholders, 1991.

71 **"The inevitable happened. For the first time since we began in 1985, we did not earn a return . . ."** Watsa, Letter to Shareholders, 1992.

72 **"We expect to encounter as many problems . . ."** and the quotes that immediately follow. Watsa, Letter to Shareholders, 1990.

72 **"Looking back, these investors must have been special . . ."** Watsa, Letter to Shareholders, 1992.

CHAPTER FOUR: The Go-Go Years (1993–1998)

Wave One

75 **"We had barely heard of Ranger prior to October 1993 . . ."** Watsa, Letter to Shareholders, 1993.

75 **"In insurance there is always the possibility that something . . ."** Ibid.

76 **"We think we have licked the reserving problem and perhaps gone too far."** Watsa, Letter to Shareholders, 1995.

"I hope I don't have to eat humble pie again!"

76 **"I hope I don't have to eat humble pie again!"** Watsa, Letter to Shareholders, 1996.

76 **"We feel comfortable that Ranger's combined ratio . . ."** Watsa, Letter to Shareholders, 1997.

76 **"Ranger has been a problem child for us for five years now . . ."** Ibid.

77 **"We thought the soft market wouldn't go down further."** Graham, *The First 25 Years of Fairfax*, 70.

Bigger deals, bigger impact

79 **"We should note here . . ."** Watsa, Letter to Shareholders, 1994.

80 **"We thank them for an excellent job . . ."** Watsa, Letter to Shareholders, 1996.

80 **"[We] request them not to extrapolate . . ."** Ibid.

80 **"should be an excellent fit . . ."** Rossa O'Reilly, "CIBC WM Research Report," December 21, 1993.

Wave Two

Watsa's powers of persuasion

84 **"the final foster home for companies no one else would take."** Richard Sauer, *Selling America Short: The SEC and Market Contrarians in the Age of Absurdity*, Wiley, 2010, 251.

Backstory: How Skandia became the next whale

87 **"Reinsurance is now a very significant activity for Fairfax and our future will . . ."** Watsa, Letter to Shareholders, 1996.

88 **"Don't be surprised if we make no acquisitions in the next five years . . ."** Ibid.

Wave Three

89 **"one of the reasons we entered the business many years ago."** and **"We come to the insurance business with an investment mindset . . ."** Watsa, Letter to Shareholders, 1998.

Meanwhile in Asia . . .

93 **"In case you think we must have been suffering a sudden case of the Asian Flu . . ."** Watsa, Letter to Shareholders, 1997.

Topping out: The end of an era

94 **"While this growth is mind-boggling even for us . . ."** and **"This growth cannot be extrapolated in the future (we will own the world if it is!)"** Watsa, Letter to Shareholders, 1998.

94 **"You have to wonder if Watsa's bargain-basement purchases are going to get him in trouble."** Jonathan Harris, "Invisible Man," *Canadian Business*, 1999.

Bubble watching with Prem

95 **"The investor with a portfolio of sound stocks should expect their prices to fluctuate . . ."** Watsa, Letter to Shareholders, 1995.

96 **"So I really don't know what the stock price will do in the short term . . ."** Ibid.

96 **"Have we been successful in attracting this type of investor?"** Ibid.

96 **"This is perhaps a good time to discuss stock price fluctuations . . ."** Watsa, Letter to Shareholders, 1997.

97 **"If you cannot handle the short-term fluctuations, then perhaps we are not the stock for you."** Ibid.

The street goes ga-ga for Fairfax

99 **"While this appreciation has been phenomenal, we do not expect this to be repeated . . ."** Melanie Ward, "RBC Capital Markets Research Report," April 18, 1996.

99 **"We believe Fairfax's acquisition expertise . . ."** Melanie Ward, "RBC Capital Markets Research Report," July 26, 1996.

99 **"Anybody who expected this stock to reach $260 is a magician."** Mark Maxwell, "CIBC World Markets," via Susan Yellin, "Fairfax outpaces expectations," *Financial Post*, September 28, 1996.

You can fix all this in eighteen months, right?

100 **"While we remain cautious over the rapidity of . . ."** Quentin Broad, "First Marathon Securities Inc. Research Report: Got a TIGer by the Tail," December 24, 1998.

CHAPTER FIVE: The Long Attack of the Shorts (1999–2005)

"We feel satisfied that we have adequately warned you"

105 **"While I have refrained from discussing fluctuations in our stock price . . ."** Special edition of Watsa, Letter to Shareholders, November 3, 1999, available as an appendix in the 1999 Annual Report.

105 **"So do annual stock price fluctuations connote high risk? Was the price decline in 1990 or in 1999 . . ."** Ibid.

The seven lean years

106 **"[The year] was a disaster for almost all our underwriting operations. There is no other word for it."** Watsa, Letter to Shareholders, 1999.

106 **"Almost makes you nervous watching the weather channel . . ."** Ibid.

107 **"atrocious three years"** Watsa, Letter to Shareholders, 2001.

108 **"We would expect these initiatives to start making themselves visible in mid to late 2000."** Quentin Broad, "National Bank Financial Research Report," November 30, 1999.

"Nobody—and I mean nobody—truly knows what you are buying when you buy an old book of insurance"

108 **"Nobody—and I mean nobody—truly knows what . . ."** Jeffrey Bronchick, *Fairfax Is Back*, Grant's Interest Rate Observer Online, June 22, 2021.

109 **"It is quite astounding how wrong one can be in this industry."** Watsa, Letter to Shareholders, 2001.

109 **"What's wrong with Fairfax? Can it survive?"** Watsa, Letter to Shareholders, 2000.

110 **"The last seven years have been very disappointing to me personally . . ."** Watsa, Letter to Shareholders, 2005.

Blame Canada? The "ultimate long-memory stock"

111 **"If you have been burned on a stock in the past, it can take years . . ."** Andrew Pastor, "New Growth" (Fourth quarter, 2022) and "Trust the Process" (Fourth quarter, 2021), equity commentaries, EdgePoint Wealth Management.

Fairfax earns its stripes for bearish bets

112 **"Predicting rain doesn't count . . ."** Warren Buffett, Berkshire Hathaway Letter to Shareholders, 2001.

113 **"If history is any guide, when the music stops, these stocks will be down 90% . . ."** Watsa, Letter to Shareholders, 1999.

113 **"We have been very wrong over the past three years . . ."** Ibid.

When doomsday becomes boomsday

115 **"We hope we can do as well when we are positive . . ."** Watsa, Letter to Shareholders, 2003.

The hedge funds: Welcome to the Big Apple

116 **"Does Anyone Understand . . ."** Scott Adams, "Does Anyone Understand This Stock?" *National Post,* January 31, 2003.

117 Mock Memo: **To Wall Street. From: Canada.** Derek DeCloet, "Make No Mistake: Watsa Isn't Warren," *National Post,* December 18, 2002.

117 **"We Are Back!"** Special edition of Watsa, Letter to Shareholders, November 8, 2022. Available as an appendix in the 2022 Annual Report.

117 **"Has Fairfax fallen into a deep hole it can't climb out of?"** Peter Eavis, "Unsure Times for Insurer Fairfax Financial (Opinion)," *TheStreet,* January 15, 2003.

The formidable Mr. Chanos: "We think this is a zero"

119 **"We think this is a zero."** John Daly, "Prem Watsa Revealed: Short Shrift," The Globe and Mail *Report on Business Magazine,* cover story, February 2006.

"It took us some time to figure out that . . . these hedge funds were trying to destroy us"

120 **"The Fairfax fiasco is a tale of harassment on a grand scale . . ."** Matt Taibbi, *The Divide: American Injustice in the Age of the Wealth Gap,* Spiegel & Grau, 2014, 248.

121 **"The record suggests that their collective belief . . ."** Ibid., 271.

Bad timing for antelopes

123 **"Eyes have been opened to Fairfax's accomplishments over the past 15 years."** Bronchick, "Fairfax Is Back."

"A full colonoscopy"

125 **"Quarter after quarter, both sides wait for someone to blink."** Ian McDonald, "Fair Facts," *Wall Street Journal,* October 27, 2005.

125 **"There is just a bunch of rabid fans . . ."** Derek DeCloet, "Mixed Signals a Fact of Life with Fairfax," *Globe and Mail,* November 3, 2004.

125 **"It took us some time to figure out that this group of shorts, these hedge funds, were trying to destroy us."** Anthony Effinger, "The Case of the Hedge Fund Hitman," *Bloomberg Markets,* October 2007.

Fairfax fights back: Enter Paul Rivett

126 **"They saw us as an easy target."** Bethany McLean, "The Inside Story of a Battle Royal," *Fortune,* March 6, 2007.

126 **"Paul was instrumental in making me realize that as you get big . . ."** *The First 25 Years of Fairfax,* 80.

"The Case of the Hedge Fund Hitman"

127 Anthony Effinger, "Hedge Fund Hit Man Hired by Cohen, Loeb, Sender, Says Insurer," *Bloomberg News,* August 24, 2007.

127 **"We do work based on speculation—and last I checked, it wasn't illegal."** From a Contogouris report cited in McLean, "The Inside Story of a Battle Royal." Ibid.

A rogue's guide to intimidation

131 **"Die Prem die."** Dan Loeb email. Taibbi, Ibid., 248.

131 **"I want his head in a box."** Adam Sender. Taibbi, Ibid., 247.

131 **"Brain is Fairfax fried."** Taibbi, *The Divide,* 295.

131 **"Noooooo. . . ."** Sender email. Taibbi, Ibid., 295.

If you can fool the debt raters, the whole house can fall down

132 **"It's one thing if the shorts attack a company with a certain kind . . ."** Staley Cates Q&A with editor, *Outstanding Investor Digest,* Year-end 2001 Edition.

132 **"the way to get this thing down is to get them where they eat, like the credit analysts and holders."** and **"We're taking this baby down for the count."** Taibbi, *The Divide,* 273.

132 **"He had to fill reserve potholes . . ."** and **"Lots of people are nervous about this one . . ."** and **"One of the best indicators . . ."** Cates Q&A, *Outstanding Investor Digest.*

"Shorting Fairfax might be very hazardous to your wealth"

133 **"It's not that the shorts aren't reading the footnotes."** Cates Q&A, *Outstanding Investor Digest.*

133 **"Fairfax had an enormously expensive borrow."** Taibbi, *The Divide,* 273.

Showdown: Five days in July

136 Roddy Boyd stories from July 2006:

Roddy Boyd, "Island Hopping: Insurer's Offshore Deals Eyed by Feds," *New York Post,* July 22, 2006.

Roddy Boyd, "Inside Calls Probed: Feds Eye Odyssey," *New York Post,* July 25, 2006.

Roddy Boyd, "Lender Bender—B of A Never Owned Stock It 'Sold' to Fairfax," *New York Post,* July 31, 2006.

Epilogue

142 **". . . the distinct possibility that Watsa and his company are not, in fact, victims . . ."** McLean in *Fortune.*

142 **"As had happened at least twice before, Prem Watsa confounded . . ."** Sauer, *Selling America Short: The SEC and Market Contrarians in the Age of Absurdity,* 270.

142 **"As soon as we found that out, we fired him"** and **"Our batting average is about 65 to 70 percent. So a third of the time we're wrong."** Michelle Celarier, "How Jim Chanos Uses Cynicism, Chutzpah—and a Secret Twitter Account—to Take on Markets (and Elon Musk)," *Institutional Investor,* September 17, 2018.

CHAPTER SIX: Betting on Disaster (2006–2009)

"What happens if we hit an air pocket?"

149 **"The best shareholder letters are those that treat readers as business partners, by offering deep insights."** Lawrence Cunningham, *Dear Shareholder: The Best Executive Letters from Warren Buffett, Prem Watsa and Other Great CEOs,* Harriman House, 2000, xii.

"What do we do with all the money?"

155 **"Perhaps we missed some things we should have bought . . ."** Graham, *The First 25 Years of Fairfax*, 87.

CEO celebrity: Thanks, but no thanks

156 **"He called it. And he has $2 billion to prove it."** Derek DeCloet, "(The Reluctant) CEO of the Year," The Globe and Mail *Report on Business Magazine*, December 2008.

157 **"the richest, savviest guy you've never heard of."** Alec Scott, "The $2-billion Man," *Toronto Life*, October 2009.

157 **"Once in 20 years. Hey, you just got lucky."** Daly, "Prem Watsa Revealed."

Global expansion takes hold

160 **"From humble beginnings in Canada . . ."** Watsa, Letter to Shareholders, 2007.

CHAPTER SEVEN: Driving with the Brake On (2010–2016)

162 **"Our view was twofold . . ."** Watsa, Letter to Shareholders, 2010.

Waiting on disaster: Assessing the threat

165 **"Unfortunately," Watsa told shareholders . . .** Watsa, Letter to Shareholders, 2016.

No more shorting! "Your chairman continues to learn—slowly!"

167 **"The hardest ones to spot are where the industry or management hasn't changed."** Pastor, "Trust the Process," equity commentary.

167 **"We believe that the impact of historical investment decisions has cast a long shadow . . ."** Nik Priebe, "CIBC World Markets Research Report," December 22, 2021.

167 **"a little bit equivalent to driving around with the parking brake on."** Jake Taylor, an episode in the podcast *We Study Billionaires*, October 4, 2020.

Shopping again—away from the bargain bin

168 **"No story has been as remarkable over the last half dozen years as that of Zenith . . ."** Watsa, Letter to Shareholders, 2019.

India, here we come!

171 **"For the first time in 67 years, India has an unabashedly business-friendly government."** Watsa, Letter to Shareholders, 2014.

171 **"A lot of people looked at Paul [Fink], Prem, and me and said, 'What's wrong with you guys?'"** Graham, *The First 25 Years of Fairfax*, 61.

The rise and rise of Andy Barnard

173 **"During this time period we asked Andy Barnard to oversee all of our insurance operations . . ."** Watsa, Letter to Shareholders, 2019.

173 **"Much like a large ship turning at sea, it takes time to change investor opinions . . ."** Trevor Scott, "Fairfax Shares Merit Consideration for Investors Willing to Look Beyond Past Headlines," *Globe and Mail*, October 4, 2022.

Passing the torch

175 **"You bought Fairfax for the insurance business?"** Pastor, "Trust the Process," equity commentary.

CHAPTER EIGHT: Coming into View (2017–2024)

Passing the Covid tests

182 **"The world stopped in 2020. Literally!"** Watsa, Letter to Shareholders, 2020.

183 **"As the Covid-19 pandemic hit in March/April 2020 . . ."** Ibid.

184 **"Because of cash and marketable securities in our holding company of almost $2 billion . . ."** Ibid.

Getting creative with swaps

188 **"We think this will be a great investment for Fairfax, perhaps our best yet!"** Watsa, Letter to Shareholders, 2020.

Timing the Big Turn: Getting the investment portfolio back on track

190 **Watsa called it "another cost of hedging" and "a costly mistake we will try not to repeat."** Watsa, Letter to Shareholders, 2017.

PART THREE: THE VALUE MASTERS: INVESTING STRATEGY

CHAPTER NINE: Value Thinking in Watsaville

203 **"Why Value Investors Are Different."** Seth Klarman, *Barron's*, February 15, 1999.

204 **"Graham-and-Doddsville" speech by Warren Buffett.** Warren Buffett, "The Superinvestors of Graham-and-Doddsville," *Columbia Business School/Chazen Global Insights*, May 17, 1984.

204 **"Intellectual mavericks."** William Green, *Richer, Wiser, Happier: How the World's Greatest Investors Win in Markets and Life*, Scribner, 2021.

205 William Thorndike Jr. *The Outsiders: Eight Unconventional CEOs and Their Radically Rational Blueprint for Success*, Boston, Harvard Business Review Press, 2012, xvi–xvii.

The margin of safety

207 **"This is not a 'how to make a million' book."** Graham, *The Intelligent Investor*, 1.

The Reformation of Graham

208 **"wonderful businesses at fair prices . . ."** Buffett has served up variations on this quote over the years. The first likely appeared in his 1989 Letter to Shareholders.

Heard it through the grapevine: Valuing management

210 Philip Fisher, *Common Stocks and Uncommon Profits and Other Writings*, Wiley, 1996. First edition published in 1958.

210 **"[Fisher] saw as a good sign any management . . ."** and **"The management should also have an ability to develop . . ."** Robert G. Hagstrom, *The Warren Buffett Way*, John Wiley & Sons, 2014.

210 **Buffett . . . being 85 percent Graham and 15 percent Fisher.** "How Omaha Beats Wall Street," interview with Warren Buffett, The Money Men feature, *Forbes*, November 1, 1969.

210 Carret's full quote is reproduced in the 2021 Letter to Shareholders.

Short-term thinking is bad for your wealth

212 Munger quote on the first $100,000 being "a bitch" is likely a comment from the 1998 Berkshire annual meeting.

Where did the term come from?

213 **"If the market value of a stock is substantially less than its intrinsic value . . ."** The Columbia Business School credit and the quote from the "Lessons for Investors" pamphlet are cited in *The Warren Buffet Way*, 5.

CHAPTER TEN: The Shareholder Contract

Setting goals and targets

223 **"Our focus right from day one . . ."** From Watsa's speech accepting the 1999 Ivey Business Leader Award in Toronto.

To our shareholders: The Letter

225 **"There is simply no more authoritative source . . ."** and **"Outstanding shareholder letters are well-written, honest . . ."** and **"Above all, these executives hold fast to a long-term horizon . . ."** Cunningham, *Dear Shareholder: The Best Executive Letters from Warren Buffett, Prem Watsa and Other Great CEOs*, xii–xiii.

Control is essential

227 **"There is much discussion in the media about corporate governance . . ."** Watsa, Letter to Shareholders, 1996.

227 **"We are one of the very few companies in the P&C industry . . ."** Watsa, Letter to Shareholders, 1998.

228 **"Prem Watsa's beneficial dictatorship."** Andrew Bell, "Fairfax Stock Shoots Up to $487," *Globe and Mail*, March 18, 1998.

CHAPTER ELEVEN: Where Fairfax Puts All Its Money

A Long Wait at the Short End

237 **"We were one of the few insurance companies in the world . . ."** and **"Years of refusing to reach for yield . . ."** Watsa, Letter to Shareholders, 2022.

Henry Singleton: The Michael Jordan of buybacks

238 **". . . one of the better investments we have made!"** Watsa, Letter to Shareholders, 1999.

240 **"To say Singleton was a pioneer in the field of share repurchases . . ."** Thorndike, *The Outsiders*, 46.

Buybacks, taxes, and "economic illiterates"

242 **"It's gotten quite common to buy back stock at very high prices . . ."** Buffett, Letter to Shareholders, 2016.

242 **"Generally speaking, in America, when companies go out hell-bent . . ."** Charlie Munger quoted in "Warren Buffett Explains the Enduring Power of Stock Buybacks for Long-term Investors," CNBC.com, September 1, 2018.

Why the Value Crowd Avoids Stock Splits

244 **"In fact, if our stock was split 100:1 (don't worry, it won't happen), many of you . . ."** Watsa, Letter to Shareholders, 1997.

CHAPTER TWELVE: A Fair & Friendly Guide to M & A

247 **"Private equity has to be careful on their time frame and getting in and out."** Watsa interview with Staley Cates, an episode in *The Price-to-Value Podcast with Southeastern Asset Management*, March 6, 2019.

248 **"This is a major advantage for Fairfax in today's world of corporate activism . . ."** Watsa, Letter to Shareholders, 2015.

249 **"While we disclose these positions, we should emphasize . . ."** Watsa, Letter to Shareholders, 2007.

CHAPTER FOURTEEN: The Renaissance of Value Investing

260 **"For the decade ended December 2019, value-oriented stocks . . ."** Watsa, Letter to Shareholders, 2020.

261 **"I mentioned last year that 2021 may see the renaissance of value . . ."** Watsa, Letter to Shareholders, 2021.

261 **"Do those things as an analyst that you know you can do well . . ."** From Benjamin Graham speech, *The Renaissance of Value: The Proceedings of a Seminar on the Economy, Interest Rates, Portfolio Management, and Bonds vs Common Stocks*, Financial Analysts Research Foundation, September 18, 1974.

Teach it and they will come?

262 **"I can only tell you that the secret has been out for fifty years . . ."** Buffett, "The Superinvestors of Graham and Doddsville."

Performance one: Of course, value outperforms

George Athanassakos and value investing discussion:

264 **value never really went away and related performance statistics** from "The Secret Behind the Outperformance of Value Stocks," *Globe and Mail,* January 5, 2023.

264 **"In my opinion, the secular trend toward globalization has ended with predictable adverse . . ."** and quotes that follow on margins and historical cycles from "Stock Market Returns over the Next 30 Years Will Be Nothing to Write Home About," *Globe and Mail,* January 24, 2023.

265 **"Individual investors are the worst market timers . . ."** and subsequent comments on index investing and investor behaviour excerpted from his book in: "Why Value Investors Can Still Outperform the Market," *Globe and Mail,* January 12, 2022.

Performance three: Still outperforming—but by much less

266 **French and Fama study summarized by Amy Whyte** in Ken French, "'There Is No Way to Tell' If Value Premium Is Disappearing," *Institutional Investor,* January 29, 2020. Quotes by French appear in the same article.

Performance four: From clearly winning to clearly losing

267 **Baruch Lev** (Philip Bardes Professor Accounting and Finance, Stern School of Business at New York University) and Anup Srivastava (Canada Research Chair, Haskayne School of Business at University of Calgary), "Explaining the Demise of Value Investing," *SSRN Electronic Journal,* October 25, 2019.

Performance five: ETFs and the death or rebirth of value?

268 **"It's a structure that means that almost the best way to get your stock to go up . . ."** David Einhorn, "Solve-AI", Presentation, Sohn Investment Conference, New York, April 3, 2024.

268 **"With all these unemployed people and their [assets under management] gone, it's actually a great time for value."** Barry Ritholtz, "David Einhorn: Market Structures Are Broken," an episode in the podcast *Masters in Business*, from Bloomberg News and iHeartMedia, February 8, 2024.

PART FOUR: CULTURE AS COMPETITIVE MOAT: MANAGEMENT STRATEGY

274 **"We have found it odd, but business tends to be considered a jungle . . ."** From Watsa's speech accepting the 1999 Ivey Business Leader Award in Toronto.

274 **"Anyone who's rude, arrogant, proud, foul-mouthed or not team-oriented . . ."** Graham, *The First 25 Years of Fairfax*, 43.

275 **"Fairfax guys don't go to lunches. They don't go to dinners . . ."** Jonathan Harris, "Invisible Man: Financial Wizard Prem Watsa's Aversion to Publicity Is Earning a Reputation as the Howard Hughes of Bay Street," *Canadian Business*, October 9, 2001.

CHAPTER FIFTEEN: Fairfax Defines Itself

The full Fairfax General Principles

Objectives:

1. We expect to compound our mark-to-market book value per share over the long term by 15% annually by running Fairfax and its subsidiaries for the long term benefit of customers, employees, shareholders and the communities where we operate—at the expense of short term profits if necessary.
2. Our focus is long term growth in book value per share and not quarterly earnings. We plan to grow through internal means as well as through friendly acquisitions.
3. We always want to be soundly financed.
4. We provide complete disclosure annually to our shareholders.

Structure:

1. Our companies are decentralized and run by the presidents except for performance evaluation, succession planning, acquisitions, financing and investments, which are done by or with Fairfax. Investing will

always be conducted based on a long term value-oriented philosophy. Cooperation among companies is encouraged to the benefit of Fairfax in total.

2. Complete and open communication between Fairfax and subsidiaries is an essential requirement at Fairfax.
3. Share ownership and large incentives are encouraged across the group.
4. Fairfax will always be a very small holding company and not an operating company.

Values:

1. Honesty and integrity are essential in all our relationships and will never be compromised.
2. We are results oriented—not political.
3. We are team players—no "egos." A confrontational style is not appropriate. We value loyalty—to Fairfax and our colleagues.
4. We follow the Golden Rule: we treat others as we would want to be treated.
5. We are hard working but not at the expense of our families.
6. We always look at opportunities but emphasize downside protection and look for ways to minimize loss of capital.
7. We are entrepreneurial. We encourage calculated risk taking. It is all right to fail but we should learn from our mistakes.
8. We will never bet the company on any project or acquisition.
9. We believe in having fun—at work!

Walking the talk on trust

280 **"I assumed that low pay would be the first reason, but in fact it was the fifth . . ."** Michael Abrashoff, *It's Your Ship: Management Techniques from the Best Damn Ship in the Navy*, Grand Central Publishing, 2012, 13.

The value crowd and the values crowd

281 **"Patience, discipline, and long-term perspective are traits . . ."** George Athanassakos, "The Parallels Between Success in Value Investing and a Well-balanced Life," *Globe and Mail*, September 13, 2022.

281 **"To me, Ben Graham was far more than an author . . ."** Warren Buffett, Introduction, in Graham, *The Intelligent Investor*.

281 **"taught me more about running a business . . ."** Buffett's comments about Tom Murphy were included in a news release from Berkshire Hathaway on February 14, 2022, when Murphy left Berkshire's board, just months before he passed away at ninety-six.

283 **"As a group, they shared old-fashioned, premodern values . . ."** Thorndike, *The Outsiders*, 3.

CHAPTER SIXTEEN: Fairfax Learns to Put Insurance First

Managing Climate Risk and Social Inflation

288 Giulia Carbonaro, "Florida Insurance Premiums Have Soared 206% Since DeSantis Became Governor," *Newsweek*, July 13, 2023.

CHAPTER SEVENTEEN: Managing the Moat

The magic of decentralization

292 The four points beginning with "1. We will acquire companies with good management already in place" are from Watsa, Letter to Shareholders, 1986.

292 The four points beginning with "1. Leaders run their own companies, but we evaluate the performance" are from Watsa, Letter to Shareholders, 1987.

293 **"Some of you fellows may think I tie you to Capital Cities by corrupting you with . . ."** Walt Hawver, *Capital Cities/ABC, the early years, 1954-1986: How the Minnow Came to Swallow the Whale*, Chilton Book Co., 1994, 89.

294 **"I don't reserve any day-to-day responsibilities for myself . . ."** James P. Roscoe, "The Many Lives of Teledyne," *Financial World*, November 1, 1978.

294 **Varnell's three points on division of duties.** Graham, *The First 25 Years of Fairfax*, 51.

296 **Buffett's "institutional imperative . . ."** Buffett, Letter to Shareholders, 1989.

296 Thorndike's "edifice complex." Thorndike, *The Outsiders*, 88. **"There is a fundamental humility to decentralization, an admission that headquarters does not . . ."** is from his section on Capital Cities. Ibid., 23.

297 **"As the network builds out, it gets more complicated . . ."** Dan Davies, *The Unaccountability Machine: Why Big Systems Make Terrible Decisions—and How the World Lost Its Mind*, Profile Books, 2024. Davies's comments come from the June 28, 2024 episode of the "Odd Lots" podcast by *Bloomberg*.

Leadership and the role of the CEO

298 **"Prem is an incredible cheerleader of his teams . . ."** Taylor, in the podcast *We Study Billionaires*, October 4, 2020.

299 **"Prem is a very generous person—financially, emotionally . . ."** Graham, *The First 25 Years of Fairfax*, 90.

302 **"'Chief grandparent officer' role."** Peter Kaufman's comments come from materials supplied by Kaufman to Watsa.

Allocation and the art of the investor CEO

303 **"One misunderstanding perpetuated by academics is the idea that value investing . . ."** Athanassakos's commentary on the CEO as value seeker and creator are sourced from his "A Message from the Director" notes accompanying the Ben Graham Centre Value Investing Conference, April 19, 2023.

304 **"Their inadequacy is not surprising. Most bosses rise to the top . . ."** Buffett, Letter to Shareholders, 1987.

CHAPTER NINETEEN: Doing Good by Doing Well

329 **"I love how George Bush talked about a 'compassionate conservatism,' which is the idea that . . ."** Interview with the author. David Thomas, "Capitalist Manifesto: How Capitalism and Canada Made Prem Watsa," *Financial Post*, December 20, 2021.

330 **"It means they will be in the position to achieve business success . . ."** Ibid.

CHAPTER TWENTY: Succession and Long-Term Control

The holding company conundrum

333 **"If the conglomerate form is used judiciously, it is an ideal structure for maximizing long-term capital . . ."** Buffett, Letter to Shareholders, 2014.